Understanding Deviance

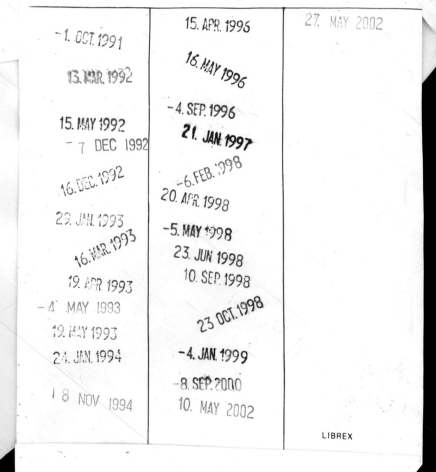

**This book is to be returned on or before
the last date stamped below.**

-1. OCT. 1991	15. APR. 1996	27. MAY 2002
13. MAR. 1992	16. MAY 1996	
15. MAY 1992	-4. SEP. 1996	
-7 DEC 1992	21. JAN. 1997	
16. DEC. 1992	-6. FEB. 1998	
29. JAN. 1993	20. APR. 1998	
16. MAR. 1993	-5. MAY 1998	
19. APR. 1993	23. JUN 1998	
-4 MAY 1993	10. SEP. 1998	
19. MAY 1993	23. OCT. 1998	
24. JAN. 1994	-4. JAN. 1999	
18 NOV 1994	-8. SEP. 2000	
	10. MAY 2002	

LIBREX

Understanding Deviance

*A Guide to the Sociology of
Crime and Rule-Breaking*

DAVID DOWNES
and
PAUL ROCK

Second Edition

CLARENDON PRESS · OXFORD
1988

Oxford University Press, Walton Street, Oxford OX2 6DP
Oxford New York Toronto
Delhi Bombay Calcutta Madras Karachi
Petaling Jaya Singapore Hong Kong Tokyo
Nairobi Dar es Salaam Cape Town
Melbourne Auckland
and associated companies in
Berlin Ibadan

Oxford is a trade mark of Oxford University Press

Published in the United States
by Oxford University Press, New York
First edition, 1982
Second edition, 1988

British Library Cataloguing in Publication Data
Downes, David, 1938–
Understanding deviance: a guide to the
sociology of crime and rule breaking. —
2nd. ed.
1. Deviance—Sociological perspectives
I. Title   II. Rock, Paul
302.5'42
ISBN 0–19–876214–3
0–19–876213–5 (Pbk)

Library of Congress Cataloging in Publication Data
(Data Available)

Set by Joshua Associates Ltd., Oxford
Printed in Great Britain
at the University Printing House, Oxford
by David Stanford
Printer to the University

For our children

Preface

The sociology of deviance has been in a state of excitement for some twenty years. It has exploded with ideas and theories. It has passed through intellectual revolution after intellectual revolution. Its tumultuous history has been based on a great procession of books and articles. And the outcome has been a confusing, argumentative, and fluid discipline practised by sociologists who are themselves factious and partisan. It is sometimes difficult for the student to move through such a bewildering and extensive maze of quarrels and claims. Books pretending to be guides are themselves frequently quite partisan, acting as press-gangs for different theories. What appears to be disinterested commentary may well have commitments and purposes which cannot be competently judged by the novice.

We have individually and jointly taught the sociology of deviance in England, Canada, and America. It had seemed to us that our discipline lacked a sober, calm, and relatively dispassionate introduction to its ideas that drew at all fully on both American and European sources. The formidable array of American texts is characteristically parochial. Immense as the parish is, it no longer exhausted the full range of theoretically significant work. Much British work of considerable interest has emerged over the past two decades or so but it has been largely ignored by American authors. By contrast, British texts, few in number, have had to attend to the major contributions of American theorists. Their stance, however, has tended to be innovative and partisan, with ambitions that go well beyond our own. Criminology is still so indeterminate that its authors can always hope to make a mark on it. Textbooks should often be seen as bids for immortality and influence, bids which may well be quite successful for a while.

We would not list *Understanding Deviance* with these other works: it is intended to steer the new student through the major themes of the major theories which have come to form the sociology of deviance. We have tried to present those themes as fairly as possible, sympathetically reproducing their more important arguments, offering criticisms and constructing defences.

Our selection of theories aims to cover the underlying thought of sociological criminology. We have not discussed all the specific problems and propositions currently preoccupying the criminologist. Our own parochialism is evident in our greater acquaintance with British and North American sources than with those from other parts of the world. And it would be *faux naif* to claim that we have attained the impartiality that we sought. As may become apparent, our own preferences lie with Weber rather than Marx, and with interactionists rather than functionalists: but we have tried to subdue such preferences in the interests of presenting all approaches as fairly as possible. Within these limitations, we have examined the significant frameworks of the discipline, preparing the reader for the more detailed and focused arguments which may be found elsewhere.

This second edition was written some six years after the first. Inevitably, portions of the sociology of deviance have moved in interesting and significant directions during that period, and we have tried to register what has happened. We have taken account of comments made about the first edition. Importantly, too, we have added a new chapter on feminist criminology and the deviance of women. Feminist sociology is beginning to make a mark and no introductory book can ignore it.

David Downes and Paul Rock
London School of Economics

1987

Contents

1

Confusion and Diversity

Introduction

The very title of the discipline which we shall describe, the sociology of deviance, is a little misleading. A singular noun and a hint of science seem to promise a unified body of knowledge and an agreed set of procedures for resolving analytic difficulties. It suggests that the curious and troubled may secure sure answers to practical, political, moral, and intellectual problems. And, of all branches of applied sociology, the demands placed on the sociology of deviance are probably the most urgent. Deviance is upsetting and perplexing and it confronts people in many settings. Turning to sociology, enquirers are rarely given certain advice. They are more likely to encounter something akin to the Tower of Babel. They will not be offered one answer but a series of competing and contradictory visions of the nature of man, deviation, and the social order. Very typically, they will be informed that their questions cannot even be discussed because they are not correctly phrased: they must first reconstruct their problem so that it can be placed with others in one of the master theories of deviance.

The sociology of deviance is not one coherent discipline at all but a collection of relatively independent versions of sociology. It is a common subject, not a common approach, which has given a tenuous unity to the enterprise. At different times, people with different backgrounds and different purposes have argued about rule-breaking. The outcome has been an accumulation of theories which only occasionally mesh. Since deviance is strategic to all ideas of morality and politics, its explanation has been championed with great fervour. Writings tend to be factious, partisan, and combative. After all, substantial consequences can flow from the acceptance of a particular argument. The reader will be bombarded by magisterial claims and criticisms, propelled towards final solutions and new approaches. Few authors have attempted to reveal all the uncertainties and complexities of their discipline. They serve as poor guides. After a while, the reader is prone to become giddy, defeated, or prematurely committed.

Novices are evidently vulnerable. It is only through prolonged exposure to a mass of conflicting ideas that they can stand back and understand what has been omitted, what evidence has not been examined, and which assertions have been challenged. Having been exposed, however, they are no longer novices. In the beginning, they are ill equipped to judge the merits of an apparently persuasive work.

Understanding Deviance is intended to answer some of these difficulties. We have prepared it as an intellectual framework in which the various theories of deviance can be set and assessed. It cannot be regarded as an entirely satisfactory substitute for the reader's own analysis. Yet it may provide a rough map for someone who enters the labyrinth of deviance for the first time.

We shall not pretend that the very diverse perspectives on deviance can be reduced to a fundamental harmony. There *are* common preoccupations and methods which lend the sociology of deviance a loose working consensus. Despite their disagreements, one sociologist can still recognize and talk to another. But the consensus is rudimentary and it is sensible to acknowledge disunity by reviewing the divergences which mark the discipline. Accordingly, we shall undertake a survey of each of the major schools of thought, not trying to pretend that they can be easily reconciled. We shall state those schools' assumptions in a fairly bald and pure form, marshal the doubts which others have voiced, and repeat or invent the replies of the schools' champions. Instead of protecting one or other fragment of the discipline, we shall simply parade different alternatives so that the whole may be appreciated and organized by the reader. The reader, in turn, would do well to suspend final judgement about the worth of particular ideas until the whole conflicting array has been examined.

The Character and Sources of Ambiguity

We have observed that the sociology of deviance contains not one vision but many. It is a collection of different and rather

independent theories. Each theory has its own history; it tends
to be supported by a long train of arguments which reach into
philosophy and metaphysics; it discloses a number of distinct
opportunities for explaining and manipulating deviant behaviour; and, in the main, its assertions will be put in such a
discrete language that they resist immediate comparison with
rival arguments. The pivotal conceptions of deviance are self-
contained and self-maintained. Thus one intellectual faction,
radical criminology, may speak of the oppression and alienation wrought by the institutions of capitalist society. It will call
deviance liberation and conformity collusion. It will prophesy
the coming of a society rid of all crime.[1] Another faction,
control theory, will depict institutional restraints as indispensable to a properly conducted society. Deviance becomes a
regression to a wilder state of man. Conformity is a laudable
achievement.[2] Yet another faction, functionalist criminology,
portrays deviance as an unrecognized and unintended buttress
of social order. The claim is made that seemingly harmful
conduct really underpins convention. The work of prostitutes,
for instance, is held to preserve marriage.[3] Organized crime
lances rebelliousness and undermines social inequality.[4]
Heresy may be used to defend religious orthodoxy.[5] It is not
certain that those theories could be reconciled or matched. On
the contrary, they are embedded in opposing metaphysical
beliefs which can be neither 'proved' nor 'disproved'. One
embraces an image of man as once perfect, corrupted by the
organization of a particular phase of society. Another retains
the doctrine of original sin. The third makes the sum of individual transgressions a collective virtue.

Such a lack of unison should not necessarily be regarded as a
failing which ought to be remedied. Indeed, it is not entirely
obvious what profit would flow from an attempt to marry or
rank such disparate ideas. For the exploitation of the utter
diversity of intellectual postures *can* be instructive. Confusion is
an important phenomenon in itself and its very existence can
emphasize special properties of deviance. One might conjecture

---

[1] See I. Taylor *et al.*, *The New Criminology*; I. Taylor *et al.* (eds.), *Critical Criminology*.
[2] See T. Hirschi, *The Causes of Delinquency*; G. Nettler, *Explaining Crime*.
[3] See K. Davis, 'Prostitution'.
[4] See R. Merton, *Social Theory and Social Structure*.
[5] See K. Erikson, *Wayward Puritans*.

that deviance would actually be a rather different process if people *did* agree on its constitution and significance. But people do not agree, and deviation might not be susceptible to a single definition and a single explanation.

On one level, it is quite possible that ambiguity and uncertainty are 'integral' characteristics of deviance itself. Some of the phenomena of everyday life are neatly arranged and classified. Others are not. Sociologists do not always accept common-sense classifications as binding: they may wish to impose their own schemes and categories. But the sociological task is complicated if problems and processes are murky and elusive before the intervention of any sociologist.

Ambiguity does seem to be a crucial facet of rule-breaking. People are frequently undecided whether a particular episode *is* truly deviant or what true deviance is: their judgement depends on context, biography, and purpose. Behaviour can provoke discomfort in those who witness it, but not such a transparent response that people display no hesitation in defining it as wrong, sinful, or harmful. Many are prepared to tolerate *some* pilfering (but from institutions and not an excessive amount),[6] *some* sexual misconduct (if it is discreet and does not impinge on others),[7] or *some* impertinence and frivolity (if it takes place on a licensed occasion or in a proper setting).[8] Very often, there is a reluctance to identify activity as deviant until alternative explanations are exhausted. Thus, in one study, wives preferred to attribute their husbands' misbehaviour to tiredness or strain. There was an initial unwillingness to accept a diagnosis of mental illness.[9] Similarly, there may be reticence about passing judgement on groups which are rather dissimilar to one's own.

If 'pluralism' and 'shifting standards'[10] work on deviant behaviour to render it ambiguous and fluid, no coherent and definitive argument can ever completely capture it. The sociologist may have to reconcile himself to the fact that logical and systematic schemes are not invariably mirrored in the 'structure' of the social world. That structure contains a measure of

---

[6] See J. Ditton, *Part-Time Crime*.
[7] See C. Sundholm, 'The Pornographic Arcade'.
[8] See S. Cavan, *Liquor License*.
[9] See M. Yarrow *et al.*, 'The Psychological Meaning of Mental Illness in the Family'.
[10] D. Matza, *Becoming Deviant*, 12.

contradiction, paradox, and absurdity. Some have tried to accommodate logicality and illogicality together in a 'sociology of the absurd',[11] but social life often defies precise description. Something will always have to be left out. Phenomena will frequently be caricatured. In turn, it can be argued that the analytic possibilities of sociology can be realized only when there is an abundance of discrepant theories which stress the ideas which no one theory can contain. The contrasting features of deviance might find adequate expression only in contrasting theories. Even so, difficulties will remain because deviance probably eludes final definition. As Bittner argues, it is impossible to predict and control all the implications of moral rules:

If we consider that we must so order our practical affairs as not to run afoul of a very considerable variety of standards of judgment that are not fully compatible with each other, do not have a clear-cut hierarchy of primacy and are regarded as binding and enforceable only in the light of additional vaguely denied information; if we consider that for every maxim of conduct we can think of a situation to which it does not apply or in which it can be overruled by a superior maxim; if we consider that unmitigated adherence to principle is regarded as vice or at least folly; . . . then it is clear that all efforts to live by an internally consistent scheme of interpretation are necessarily doomed to fail.[12]

Superficially, then, it would seem that the application of rules cannot always be orderly and categorical. Deviance is a little messier than science. Sociologists may argue that the appearances of everyday life are deceptive. Scientific reason might illuminate deeper principles of organization which hide beneath the muddle of ordinary thinking about deviance. Yet, as we have observed, there appears to be little concord amongst the sociologists themselves. Each may be decisive. Collectively there is great indecision. Academic disputes suggest that the sociological profession is just as confused as common-sense thought. Of course, it is conceivable that the claims of one school *are* valid and that deviance is actually unambiguous

[11] See J. Douglas, 'The Experience of the Absurd and the Problem of Social Order'.
[12] E. Bittner, 'Radicalism and the Organization of Radical Movements', 934.

when it is properly interpreted. It is also conceivable that there is no single truth.

Just as an addict, a judge, a psychiatrist, and a policeman share no one perspective on the use of opiates, so different sociologists face deviation in numerous guises and situations. Psychiatric knowledge may be adequate enough, but it may not solve all the practical problems of policing and justice.[13] It would become the sole truth only if psychiatric issues were alone important. Similarly, functionalists' problems may not be the same as radical criminologists'. Radicals might state that the problems *should* be the same, but functionalists are unlikely to be instantly persuaded. They could retort that the radicals are themselves misguided. A settlement of the argument would have to take the form of a conversion that would be more metaphysical than rational. More prosaically, sociologists interested in the effects of shop design on theft or of policing patterns on vandalism might find radical criminology less helpful than other approaches. It might be improper for them to investigate those effects but, again, that question of propriety removes one from a consideration of the immediate effects of control and into the metaphysics of control policies. Importantly, too, theories and theorists shape their own materials. It is not as if difficulties arose simply because radical and functionalist move about the same world with different problems. In some significant measure, they seem to act as if they do not inhabit one world at all. The social world can of course answer back and there are limits to the diversity of its appearances, but believing is often seeing.

In short, there may be no still, perfect, and absolute centre from which deviance may be surveyed *as it really is*. Neither need there be a simple test to discover the superiority of one approach. (To be sure, the members of each intellectual faction hold that they occupy that still centre, concluding that they alone can see what is true. But not all those claims can be valid and there are many centres. It is not our intention to ally ourselves with any one position for very long.)

Deviance cannot constitute a single problem with a single solution. It is so significant that it has been forced to serve a

---

[13] See A. von Hirsch, *Doing Justice*.

multitude of purposes. Indeed, it seems as if all the contrasting styles of argument which abound in the larger world have been turned on deviance at some point, and each has imposed its own distinctive gloss. Each represents a separate way of seeing such conduct and, as Kenneth Burke would argue,[14] each is a separate way of *not* seeing such conduct. Together, they compose a great kaleidoscope of theorems. An examination of even one small part of that kaleidoscope can be enlightening. It should demonstrate how deviance reflects the ambitions and visions of those who probe it, laying itself open to an extraordinary range of interpretations.

Some sociologists (and certainly not all) would assert that deviance is a political phenomenon. After all, it is intimately connected with the exercise of power and the application of rules. But they would not agree on the consequences of that assertion. To a number, deviance poses a series of questions about the practical management of social pathology. Useful knowledge would then be generated by the need to formulate policy. Thus, James Wilson dismissed all those theories that made no manifest contribution to the business of controlling crime. He took much deviance to be patently distressing and disruptive, inflicting pain and subverting trust and community. Theorizing which offers no assistance to the legislator and administrator is cast as fanciful and irrelevant, mere speculation without apparent purpose, utility or responsibility.[15] Others have joined Wilson to transform the writings on deviance into a repository of practical information and advice. One such instance is Morris and Hawkins's *The Honest Politician's Guide to Crime Control*, a compendium of useful political recipes that urges policy-makers to appreciate the unintended and undesired consequences of action. It advocates caution and modesty in the construction of schemes for the suppression of law-breaking. More minutely, there have been those who have focused on specific problems and their solution: the design of public vehicles and its effects on vandalism;[16] the design of public space and its effects on opportunities for monitoring

---

[14] K. Burke, *A Grammar of Motives*, pt. 1, ch. 2, 'Antinomies of Definition'.
[15] J. Wilson, *Thinking About Crime*.
[16] See P. Mayhew *et al.*, *Crime as Opportunity*.

deviance;[17] the organization of social life and its effects on the superintending of the young.[18]

Some have held that the unrecognized consequences of control are so grave and diffuse that they have moved towards a flirtation with anarchism, libertarianism, or extreme conservatism. Arguing that rule-enforcement tends only to exacerbate social problems, they preach the politics of *laissez-faire*, *laissez-aller*. An echo of libertarianism may thus be discovered in Schur's contention that interference with juvenile delinquency typically amplifies deviance: formal regulation acts merely to confirm the deviant in an outcast status.[19] Again, Becker and Horowitz extol the virtues of San Francisco, describing it as a civilized compact between peaceable deviant groups.[20] Szasz, too, castigates the intervention of the State, arguing that it has no business managing the private and moral problems of its citizens.[21]

More sceptically still, it has been concluded that the 'unintended' consequences of control are actually intended. Politicians are taken to require the presence of a criminal population. The visible petty law-breaker is manufactured in large quantities to perform the role of scapegoat for the ills of society. The minor criminal is given great prominence, deflecting outrage away from the evils performed by the lawless powerful.[22] It is held that there is a symbiotic relationship between the State and a specially designated pool of deviants who are exploited for dramatic purposes.[23] Foucault, for example, observes that it has long been apparent that prisons generate criminality. It is not neglect or ignorance which prevents the abolition of imprisonment. On the contrary, the penal system is deliberately tended as a deviant preserve.[24]

Pursuing that vision of oppression, deviants may be put to work in the service of revolution. For instance, Thomas Mathiesen took a leading part in the Scandinavian prisoners' unions, seeking to induce changes that could not be accepted without an unspecified but profound upheaval in penal policy.

[17] See O. Newman, *Defensible Space*.   [18] See P. Morgan, *Delinquent Fantasies*.
[19] E. Schur, *Radical Non-Intervention*.
[20] H. Becker and I. Horowitz, 'The Culture of Civility'.
[21] T. Szasz, *The Manufacture of Madness*.
[22] See F. Pearce, *Crimes of the Powerful*.
[23] See D. Matza, *Becoming Deviant*.   [24] M. Foucault, *Discipline and Punish*.

Maintaining that participation in rational negotiations would only strengthen the grip of officials and domesticate the unions, he wittingly adopted an irrational posture. Formal discipline being unsupportable in an unjust society, Mathiesen countered with an apocalyptic dream of deviants belabouring their masters with their crutches.[25] The political domination of analysis can thereby turn criminology into a combatant in the class war, its ideas being judged by their impact on conflict. It may even be inferred that criminology cannot revolve around scholarly objectivity and a civilized interchange with unsympathetic theorists. Quinney[26] and Platt[27] proclaim that it must be surrendered to the demands of ideological struggle, promoting only those truths which fuel insurrection.

Marxist historians, too, have pored over crime. They claim that crime and deviance may be rescued from obscurity to provide an unofficial commentary on the past. Rule-breaking can reveal the suppressed under-life of society. It documents the stirrings of the illiterate and dominated, demonstrating patterns of communal opposition to the State and its masters. Thus poachers and smugglers can be used to illustrate the hostility which attended the emergence of class society in England.[28] Attempts to enclose land were met by traditional demands based on the rights of people to use pastures, commons, and forests.[29] Efforts to mechanize agriculture or assert the supremacy of the market were stalled by resort to 'collective bargaining by riot'.[30] The very attempt to reduce poachers, smugglers, rioters, and rick-burners to 'criminals' may be read as an aspect of the politics of naming.[31] Crime becomes politics, and the criminal is a prologue to conscious and articulate resistance by the dispossessed.[32]

Yet the politics of deviance does not have to be analysed with passion or partisanship. Some have adopted a relatively neutral perspective, preferring to describe the forms of rule-breaking

---

[25] T. Mathiesen, *The Politics of Abolition*.
[26] R. Quinney, 'Crime Control in Capitalist Society'.
[27] A. Platt, review of *The New Criminology*.
[28] See D. Hay *et al.*, *Albion's Fatal Tree*.
[29] See E. Thompson, *Whigs and Hunters*.
[30] See E. Thompson, 'The Moral Economy of the English Crowd in the Eighteenth Century'.
[31] See G. Rudé, *The Crowd in History*.   [32] See E. Hobsbawm, *Primitive Rebels*.

without condemnation or applause. It is evident that those forms are diffuse and complex. On occasion, deviance can take expressly political directions: thus certain homosexuals grouped to become the Gay Liberation Front[33] and prisoners adopted the tactics of student demonstrators.[34] On occasion, politics can take a deviant path: thus the early Bolsheviks, the Irish Republican Army, and the Baader–Meinhof gang[35] robbed banks, and Eldridge Cleaver raped to chastise the white world.[36] On occasion, however, the deviant and the political can merge into a definitional fog. Argument can turn on whether people are 'really' freedom fighters, criminals, guerrillas, or terrorists. There may be debate about whether a riot is 'really' a political event or 'mere' lawlessness. Description becomes even more difficult because political consequences can sometimes flow from the acts of criminals who are not overtly committed to a political stance. Conversely, political motives can be claimed by those who seek an acceptable front for predatory activity.[37] All these shifts, pronouncements, and conflicts require delicate analysis. They prepare opportunities for abundant work. Sociologists may choose to follow Gusfield,[38] describing the history of public designations of deviance and professing an interest only in the forms and effects of change. They can dwell on the development and use of publicly legitimate motives, examining how people attempt to explain their conduct.[39] They may focus on the influence of varied styles of behaviour, analysing the repercussions of presenting deviance as political, expressive, or entrepreneurial activity.[40] They can produce a commentary on culture and authority,[41] or a thesis about the beliefs which affect the actions of the powerful.[42] They might recognize the fluidity of allegiances and motives as evidence of collapsing public symbolism, suggesting that identities have lost firm anchorage and are instead traded and explored in an effort to build

[33] See L. Humphreys, *Out of the Closets*.
[34] See M. FitzGerald, *Prisoners in Revolt*.
[35] See J. Becker, *Hitler's Children*.   [36] See E. Cleaver, *Soul on Ice*.
[37] See T. Wolfe, *Radical Chic and Mau-Mauing the Flak-Catchers*.
[38] J. Gusfield, 'Moral Passage'.
[39] See M. Scott and S. Lyman, 'Accounts, Deviance and Social Order.
[40] See P. Rock, *Deviant Behaviour*.
[41] See I. Horowitz and M. Liebowitz, 'Social Deviance and Political Marginality'.
[42] See G. Pearson, *The Deviant Imagination*.

'authenticity' in an 'inauthentic' world.[43] The sociologists who pursue these questions need feel no duty to take sides. Indeed, the espousing of political causes may be thought dangerous. It can be argued that involvement in practical concerns deforms judgement and thwarts curiosity. Analysis can proceed only when sociologists have gained an adequate distance from their object.[44]

It is apparent that just one segment of the sociology of deviance can encompass sundry ideologies and ambitions. Part of our task will be to recount how such diversity arose and how the separate explanations attained plausibility.

In some measure, intellectual variety is a simple product of exposure. Sociology is not enclosed or sealed against arguments which exist in the wider world. It is heir to a long tradition of brooding about crime and sin. Politics is but one strand of that tradition. Lawyers, psychiatrists, theologians, moralists, anthropologists, philosophers, statisticians, social reformers, historians, and psychologists have severally laid claim to the problems of crime and deviance. Each group has tried to impose its own stamp on thinking. Each has had some significant stake in the outcome. Not only will the acceptance of a particular view confirm a system of morals, law, or politics. It will also have implications for the rise and fall of policies and occupations.[45] Thus the right to manage the mad was contested by clergymen, magistrates, and doctors. The prize was the administration of asylums.[46] Similarly, juvenile delinquents were fought over by social workers, psychiatrists, and lawyers. The prize was power over juvenile courts and reformatories.[47]

Sociology has its own disciplines, language, and techniques. But it has also fed on ideas which have been prepared by others. In this sense, it lends a special form and focus to familiar arguments. It would be remarkable if this were not so. No thinking about social problems can be insulated against what has gone before. The reworking of old conceptions need not be conscious or deliberate. After all, few sociologists are fully

---

[43] See O. Klapp, *Collective Search for Identity*.
[44] See M. Phillipson, *Sociological Aspects of Crime and Delinquency*.
[45] See M. Foucault, *I, Pierre Rivière*.
[46] See A. Scull, 'Mad-Doctors and Magistrates'.
[47] See E. Lemert, *Social Action and Legal Change*.

versed in the history of ideas. Yet earlier thought shapes the
environment in which all speculation takes place. The disputes
of the medieval schoolmen and eighteenth-century pamphlet-
eers have been handed on to acquire new shapes in the university of the twentieth century. For example, radical criminology
can trace its lineage back to such dispersed thinkers as Plato,
Kant, Hegel, Rousseau, and Marx. Control theory incorpor-
ates the political philosophy of Hobbes, the psychiatry of
Eysenck and Freud, and the sociology of Durkheim. Functionalists may be clustered with the biologist Cannon, the political
economist Petty, the philosopher Plato, and the anthropologists Malinowski and Radcliffe-Brown. It may be said that the
sociology of deviance is simply another opportunity to organize
all that has passed for intellectual work in the West. It gives
another life to the principal ideas of the principal schools. Just
as those schools were varied in their thinking, so the sociology
of deviance is varied. Just as those schools' disputes have never
been conclusively settled, so the internal debates of the sociology of deviance remain unresolved.

The those diffuse themes can set very different goals for the study
of deviance. Sociologists may elect or be required to control
crime; increase or exploit deviance; undertake dispassionate
analysis; provide moral commentaries; design, criticize, or close
prisons; study the past or predict the future. They may, indeed,
have no great interest in deviance but search for answers to
analytic puzzles which have their roots elsewhere: thus
Cicourel explored probation and police practices in order to
illuminate some general properties of social interaction;[48]
Durkheim treated crime and law as indices of social solidarity;[49] and Merton took crime to be a demonstration of the
processes by which a society maintains itself.[50]

The interplay of projects and thoughts becomes more complicated as the minds of different sociologists work on the
materials which are offered them. There is an ever increasing
body of arguments, criticisms, and studies, and no sociologist is
capable of mastering or even reading all that is produced. Every
scholar will acquire a most selective experience of the sociology

[48] A. Cicourel, *The Social Organization of Juvenile Justice*.
[49] É. Durkheim, *The Division of Labor in Society*.
[50] R. Merton, *Social Theory and Social Structure*.

of deviance, an experience shaped by contingency, knowledge, choice, fashion, and practical objectives. He or she may consider a work important, although few of his or her colleagues may have read it. He or she may combine its arguments with those of other writings, generating a new personal synthesis. Ideas therefore reflect the biographies and preoccupations of particular people at particular points of time. What is held to be fascinating and provocative now can be defined as extremely dull later on. The intellectual significance of a book or theory is consequently unstable: it will depend on the circumstances of those who encounter it and on its place in a sequence of thoughts. People can have very different memories of the same book and their own memories can change over time.

The sociology of deviance has thereby accumulated a vast number of nuances. They are nuances which typically become exaggerated and publicized as sociologists try to make a mark on the world. Often working in a university, sociologists are encouraged to pursue the new and the original. After all, the university is supposed to be more than a vehicle for transmitting received truths. Its staff are urged to submit doctoral theses before or during their period of appointment. One of the chief criteria for the acceptance of a thesis is its originality. Promotions and tenure may hinge on successful publication, and publishers are not anxious to print the simple parrottings of others' ideas. There is thus a clear imperative to be distinctive. Sometimes, of course, sociological works are recognizably and importantly novel. Often they are not. Sociologists frequently strain after the identifiably new, the special emphasis that will set him or her apart as one who deserves honour and reward. That stress can foster a proliferation of petty attempts at intellectual revolution. Almost every published work will carry the assertion that it constitutes a major revision, synthesis, or formulation of ideas.[51] The market economy of academic thought and persons has resulted in a confusing array of efforts to achieve product differentiation. Publicly, at least, there is little merit or profit in the humble examination of second-hand thought. There may be an explosion of knowledge in the West,

---

[51] See M. Davis, 'That's Interesting!'

but the sociology of deviance suffers from the hyperinflation of a debased currency.

Product differentiation has been accompanied by the making of proprietorial claims. People tend to acquire very real stakes in their ideas. They 'possess' them, being reluctant to share authorship or ownership. Personal theories are conserved in a relatively pure state, guarded against adulteration. Thus Douglas complains of a drift towards the artificial segregation of arguments. Employing the somewhat unlovely term 'simplificationism', he observes:

. . . simplificationism has grown largely out of the modern scientists' self-imposed professional myopia, the insistence of each specialist on seeing everything as caused by the few particular variables he happens to 'own' professionally. . . . Most . . . theories are right to some degree about some part of the things they are studying, but they almost all deal with small parts—as if the parts were the whole thing—and the theories wind up being distortions of the vastly complex realm of human life.[52]

There is considerable attraction in resolutely pursuing the logic of an argument. A few axioms and a few assumptions may be all the materials that a sociologist requires. They may be all that he or she can handle. Excessive complexity and a surfeit of reservations can render analysis unmanageable. Slight initial divergences can therefore culminate in radically different conclusions.

The academy both spurs and limits the growth of intellectual variety. It does enforce its own special controls, and they can be most taxing. Ideas are scanned in reviews, lectures, and seminars. Our own book is devoted to such a survey. It is an occupational duty of sociologists to dissect their colleagues' work: theses are examined for their logic, methodology, and coherence. The routine activities of university work accordingly sustain a process of natural selection which condemns some arguments and upholds others. Reputations have been lost irrevocably. But what passes for damning criteria is itself variable, enjoying a history of fashion and the popularity of schools. The ideas of the 1950s were subjected to criticisms

[52] J. Douglas *et al.*, *The Nude Beach*, 51.

which seem to have lost some of their force in the 1970s. Similarly, interesting developments in the mid-nineteenth century were suppressed by the end of the century, only to be revived in the 1930s.[53] Ideas can fail and so can principles of selection.

The matter is yet further complicated by the very different traditions that are borne by university departments and schools. Institutions of learning are so numerous and the sociological profession is so large that antagonists need never confront one another. The advocates of a particular theory can surround themselves with their own circle of followers and their own network of journals and publishers. It is quite possible for one intellectual faction to create, examine, and extend its ideas without much interference from outsiders. Challenges can be ignored. Indeed, they may never be issued. For example, radical criminology has not dominated the sociology of deviance. Many, probably most, sociologists do not entertain its assumptions. Yet radical criminology has received almost no critical commentary. It has simply been neglected by those who are not its adherents. In this fashion, phenomenology, interactionism, structuralism, functionalism, and the other major schools can flourish independently and unmolested. They constitute a number of parallel intellectual universes which need never intersect. Their isolation is supported by a university system which does not really make scholars accountable, which is supported by many publications, and which imposes a division of labour *within* departments. Students require schooling in a collection of specialist areas, universities recruit appropriate staff to service them, and there is a consequent weakening of ability to monitor and judge the works of one's colleagues in the same institution. Sociologists of religion or development may not believe themselves equipped to assess the competence and range of a criminologist's writing. There is an attendant reduction of discipline: sociologists of deviance (like any other sociologist) have acquired a charter to issue almost any argument provided a publisher will broadcast it and some colleagues somewhere will endorse it.

[53] See A. Lindesmith and Y. Levin, 'English Ecology and Criminology of the Past Century'.

The Social Contexts of Differentiation

One of the chief constraints on intellectual production is the setting in which it takes place. The sociology of deviance is practised in different contexts which frame what may be said and the manner of its expression. We can do no more than provide a few scattered instances of those contexts, but our illustrations should emphasize the part played by environment.

Perhaps the largest single setting is the State, and the State can dramatically affect creativity. We have claimed that the sociology of deviance may be pregnant with implications for moral and political reasoning. Particular conceptions of deviance can fold back on ideas of legitimacy, power, and pathology. They are capable of subverting the absolute authority of the State and may be thought to require censorship. One important example is offered by the position of criminology within the Soviet Union. Soviet government is ostensibly centred on Marxism, and Marxism makes quite specific assertions about the character and significance of crime. Crime is held to be a defect which stems from the larger defects of capitalism itself. It is an outcrop of the moral disorganization and possessive individualism of a society based on social classes. A truly Marxist society cannot engender crime. As the director of the Moscow Institute of Criminology pronounced, 'socialism does not give birth to crime, . . . the regularities immanent in socialism do not give birth to crime.'[54] A sociology of crime would locate some of the sources of criminality in social organization. It would upset Soviet Marxism and the claims of Russia to be a Marxist society. It has not been allowed to develop. On the contrary, criminology is preoccupied with the quest for explanations which do not touch on the social order: crime is presented as a consequence of foreign influence, capitalist survivals, or organic and psychological disturbance. Criminology has become a refined technical instrument which abstains from unlicensed questioning.[55]

Control can be quite informal. Social organization can give rise to particular images of society which advance or retard the

---

[54] I. Karpets, Director of the Moscow Institute of Criminology, quoted in W. Connor, *Deviance in Soviet Society*, 168.

[55] P. Solomon, *Soviet Criminologists and Criminal Policy*.

evolution of an intellectual doctrine. Not all sociological schools are equally plausible in all societies. Some seem to mirror common-sense truths, others appear incredible, and others again are apparently irrelevant. The inner organization of a theory may be less important than its seeming correspondence with the world familiar to a particular people. The affinities between theory and common-sense assumptions are nicely revealed by a comparison between Norway and California. Norway houses a rather small population of just under four millions. It may have relatively fewer internal divisions than some other societies. Its intellectual and political life is regulated by a somewhat cohesive middle class which is concentrated in Oslo. Norwegian sociologists of deviance are quite celebrated but they are unprepared to work with the phenomenology which has beguiled many of their British and American colleagues.[56] We shall discuss the detailed composition of phenomenology in a later chapter. However, it is important to know that phenomenology postulates that meanings be treated as arbitrary and negotiable. It claims that people construct their actions on a foundation of practical knowledge, that their responses embody particular interpretations of their situation, and that a different interpretation would lead to a different course of action. Acts are taken to be an aspect or reflection of meaning. It is only by understanding how meaning is constructed that actions can themselves become intelligible. In turn, phenomenology maintains that the sociologist would do well to refrain from imposing his or her own sense of significance on a situation. After all, not many people put sociological definitions to work, and the sociologist would also do well to suspend his or her belief in conventional descriptions of phenomena. It is those descriptions which he or she would explore and explain, and a too ready acceptance would merely blur interesting questions. Phenomenology accordingly demands a kind of disinterested incredulity: a naïve refusal to trust objective appearance. It invites one to gaze upon one's own society as if it were unfamiliar and problematic. It would seem that Norwegian sociologists are reluctant to accept that invitation. Their society does *not* seem

[56] See T. Mathiesen, *The Politics of Abolition*.

arbitrary, negotiable, or subjectively uncertain. It is not ambiguous or fluid. Its intellectuals concede a measure of conflict, but that conflict is thought to be rooted in clear divisions which are not at all subjective. Phenomenology, the hesitating sociology, has no place in Oslo. By contrast, it *does* loom large in California. California is a large state with a mobile population, a substantial tradition of social experimentation, and a seeming absence of gross constraint on personal and collective choice. Ernest Gellner may have been a little unfair when he stated that phenomenology breeds in an environment experienced as free and that there is less reality in California than anywhere else.[57] Phenomenology cannot be so readily slighted. But the West Coast of America may provide a greater array of existential opportunities, a sense of openness, which advances the plausibility of phenomenology. It has produced a copious ethnomethodology and phenomenology of deviance.[58]

Within societies, too, there are quite disparate contexts for the pursuit of criminology. The discipline is so salient that it can be put to very different uses. Its practitioners may be discovered in a host of unlike organizations. Those organizations will shape goals and dictate intellectual style. Institutionally, the demands of government research agencies like the Home Office Research Unit in London and the Law Enforcement Assistance Administration in Washington are most dissimilar to those imposed by universities and polytechnics. There is a clear stipulation that ideas be presented in a form useful to policy and action, that arguments be put in a fashion intelligible to the administrator, and that there should be little flirtation with the metaphysics of crime. Research tends towards a model of natural science, employing statistical methods in small, utilitarian projects. Its reasoning is designed to be universal, based on a general rationality. It can contribute much that is valuable, mapping events and relationships which escape others. It is not calculated to feed a revolutionary consciousness or redefine the universe. It is constrained by rules of order which need to restrain no university lecturer. People

---

[57] E. Gellner, 'Ethnomethodology: The Re-Enchantment Industry or The Californian Way of Subjectivity'.

[58] See J. Douglas, *American Social Order*; A. Cicourel, *Method and Measurement in Sociology*.

working in official agencies are not expected to be original. They are required to be reliable. To be sure, agencies constantly hanker after new programmes and policies. There is a perennial hunt for the obviously efficient reform. But organization is imposed by the disciplines of political rationality and practicability. One who worked in a British criminal justice policy planning unit declared: 'it is perhaps not a particularly difficult task to formulate the objectives of policy oriented research. They might be stated as being to assist and contribute to the formulation and development of policy and to evaluate the effects of its implementation.'[59]

By contrast, the lecturer is relatively unconfined. There is a licence to father a great litter of theories. Many academics *do* busy themselves with moral and political concerns, but they are not obliged to do so, and they are as often devoted to a kind of boundless speculation. Consider the scale and character of the task described in the preface to one book on the sociology of deviance:

This book is the product of my own search for a coherent view of the relationship between persons and institutions, conducted in a context of conflicting ideas about human character and social reality. Seeking theoretical continuity, I discovered that discontinuity characterized explanations of social order and change. Reviewing these historical perspectives and issues, I found that, rather than clarifying ambiguities, deviance theories illustrate how scholarly controversies over styles of reasoning and world views produce radically different versions of social reality.[60]

Those rather different definitions of the criminological task extend outwards to affect the network of supporting and feeding institutions that train and house sociologists of deviance. There is an undoubted overlap and interference between institutions. They are not completely insulated from one another. But there are divergent emphases which explain some of the variation in theorizing.

On the one hand, the work of the academic sociologist of deviance is subordinate to rather particular demands. Quite frequently, he or she is but one sociologist amongst many,

---

[59] T. Rawsthorne, 'The Objectives and Content of Policy-Oriented Research', 5.
[60] N. Davis, *Sociological Constructions of Deviance*, xi–xii.

contributing to the general education of students. Such socio-logists will certainly be required to know more than the teach-ings of criminology alone. Their interests may be subservient to the wider development of sociology itself, and their criminology can become little more than yet another perspective on broad social problems. In this sense, their attachment to crime is somewhat arbitrary. They could ask much the same questions of innumerable other areas.

On the other hand, criminologists may be discovered in special institutes or schools whose goal is not the promotion of a general theoretical competence. Throughout the world, Institutes of Criminology and Criminal Justice have been established with rather precise charters. Their chief aim is the production of professionals in one discipline. They are dedic-ated to the exploration of the substance of crime instead of the more metaphysical and metatheoretical problems of socio-logical explanation. And they are often designed to meet the requirements of employing organizations in government and applied research. In the pursuit of these ends, they often achieve vastly more than the preparation of technicians. Many institutes have attracted sociologists of distinction. Yet their organization has been shaped by practical career contin-gencies. For example, the Centre of Criminology, University of Toronto, was established with this mandate:

The objectives of the Centre of Criminology, as formulated from the recommendations of the President's Special Advisory Committee, are as follows:

1. The development of the most effective approach to the study of crime in Canadian society, its causes and its prevention, and the treatment of offenders, by way of collaborative efforts involving people trained in the disciplines of, *inter alia*, law, psychiatry, psychology, economics, philosophy, sociology, and social work.

2. The study and investigation of problems directly concerned with the administration of criminal justice, the operation of the Criminal Code and of provisional legislation in the field of criminal law, the efficacy of existing sentencing practices and penal sanctions and of old and new methods of dealing with offenders in federal and provin-cial penal institutions.

3. The provision of graduate teaching courses and the supervision of

research studies by graduate students in the general field of crime and corrections.

4. The organization of teaching courses in some aspects of criminology at the undergraduate level for students who may have in mind a career in the penitentiary, probation, parole or aftercare services, in the police forces or in the pertinent departments of government concerned with crime and corrections.[61]

Similarly, the University of Maryland Institute of Criminal Justice and Criminology offers a 'graduate program in criminal justice and criminology' which is intended 'to prepare students for research, teaching and professional employment in the operational agencies in the field of criminal justice'.[62]

The appointments secured by criminologists depend on vagaries of the market and personal history. One who teaches in an Institute of Criminology may have as great a dedication to abstract theorizing as his colleagues in a sociology department. The criminologist in a sociology department might have preferred a post in an Institute. Moreover, the formal charters of institutions rarely describe the exact activities that take place: there may be many departures from official goals. None the less, the difference between 'pure' and 'applied' sociology is real enough.

There is perhaps one further source of differentiation. Universities and university departments have undergone histories which are shaped by national, local, and intellectual influences. The study of deviance has only recently become a professional pursuit and its adherents have had to find a place for themselves in long-established organizations. Criminology has been grafted onto institutions whose structure defines its character and evolution. In South America, for example, many criminologists have had to associate themselves with physical anthropology: their quest has been the detection of organic sources of deviance. In Germany, criminology has typically been adopted by law departments. In the United States, it is largely identified with sociology. In Britain, criminologists are scattered amongst departments of sociology, psychology, and

---

[61] Centre of Criminology, University of Toronto, *Handbook and Annual Report 1976*, 1–2.

[62] Institute of Criminal Justice and Criminology, University of Maryland, Maryland, undated, 3.

social administration. The outcome has been the introduction of complexity and greater diversity. Whilst a department or university may be regarded as intellectually alien, a strange environment which one enters without full commitment, it does force certain teaching and academic duties on its members. Thus, sociologists in a law department must attend to a distinct syllabus and a distinct set of aims. Their students will not be versed in sociology. Whatever their interests may be, sociologists so placed will inevitably find that their thoughts are focused on special problems and a special body of writing. In turn, their thinking may come to develop in a distinctive manner. Theirs will still be the sociology of deviance, but it will have acquired a particular complexion.

Implications

It is clear that the sociology of deviance is likely to remain a disunited enterprise and, to a great extent, such diversity cannot but be useful. However hard they may try, particular sociologists cannot impose a single orthodoxy upon their readers. Their arguments can always be set in the context of their competitors and critics, revealing not only their strengths but their limitations. And the limitations may be very real, greater indeed than the arguments' champions might care to admit. Sociology has a self-relativizing strain which can chasten people who seek immediate and unambiguous answers to moral and intellectual problems.

In the beginning, then, readers would do well to assume a warily disinterested approach to the study of deviance, being simultaneously open, sceptical and charitable. It would be quite imprudent to form premature attachments. Eventually, to be sure, there will be a need to organize one's thought and discard certain ideas but it would be unwise to do so without having first considered their rivals. If only because they persuaded some people, at some time, rival theories are unlikely to be lacking in all merit. And no theory can be assessed intelligently until it has been regarded with sympathy. Ideas can be appreciated only if there is some willingness to take their authors' assumptions and preoccupations seriously. We would argue that the early stages of understanding deviance are most fruitful when one tries to grasp the opportunities presented by very different systems of thought, the problems which con- fronted their authors, and the doubts which they may cast on favoured arguments.

Wary disinterest is also to be commended because it is very easy to condemn and lose what may actually be quite valuable. We shall enlarge on the problems of criminological methods in the next chapter. Nevertheless, it is apparent that those methods are peculiarly fraught. They revolve around the diffi- culties of knowing and describing groups which have little to gain from becoming known. The world of deviance and social control is riddled with discredited information and guilty knowledge. Although research is often more flawed and slight than its authors and audience might wish, it is sometimes no mean feat to bring it to a conclusion at all. It would not do to dwell disproportionately on the flaws and to neglect what has been accomplished, and critics are all too prone to dismiss the whole because of the deficiencies of a few of its parts. When ideas and information can be extracted only with great effort, it is sensible to examine work for what it may offer instead of stalking it for its failings.

Only rarely will a single study exhaust all the interesting pos- sibilities of a problem. When observation is hindered, per- spectives will be partial and inferences incomplete. Few instances of deviance are paraded before a sociologist in their entirety, and a consequence is the inevitable relativism of argu- ment. With great good fortune, a sociologist like Ianni might obtain access to a family of organized criminals.[63] It would have been impossible to examine all such families or even every aspect of one single family. It would be correspondingly absurd to fault Ianni for the limitations of his sampling. Such methodological considerations invite one to treat the sociology of deviance as a series of what may be little more than tenuously connected glimpses of the world. Much would be sacrificed by the assumption that each work must be approached as if it were defensible and complete in itself, an entity that can survive or fail only so long as it remains intact. It is not attractive to be intellectually promiscuous, but neither should one forget that it is perfectly possible to treat sociology

[63] F. Ianni, *A Family Business*.

as a reservoir of different, sometimes contradictory arguments that can be dismantled and reassembled with some freedom.

Work on juvenile delinquency provides an admirable example. Delinquency has worried criminologists for decades: there has been a continuous stream of writings flowing from different sources, times and contexts. Thrasher observed Chicago gangs in the 1920s,[64] William Foot Whyte discussed Boston delinquency in the 1930s,[65] Cloward and Ohlin analysed East Coast delinquency in the 1950s,[66] Matza argued about New Yorkers in the 1960s,[67] and Parker the Liverpool of the 1970s.[68] There has been a curious and quite indefensible tendency in criminology to proceed as if all these random sightings should be treated as attempts to confront an identical problem with identical data. One study has been played off against another as if only one explanation should be allowed to survive. There is no good reason to suppose that delinquency in the 1920s was the 'same' as delinquency in the 1970s.[69] Neither is there warrant to assume that the events of Chicago must be reproduced in Liverpool. It is not necessary to try to resolve all differences between studies into simple questions of error and rectitude.

Finally, it may be argued that even bad sociology has its uses. Readers will discover that they will have to resort to second-rate reporting and theorizing because there is often no adequate alternative. Sociology may not always do its job well, but there is usually no competent competition.

On the one hand, sociological theories of deviance tend to represent the most articulate versions of arguments that have currency in everyday life. Almost every major common-sense explanation of deviance has a modified sociological expression. In this sense, sociology may not always be novel and surprising but it does expose ideas that are only dimly reviewed elsewhere. The conventions of ordinary conversation do not really allow one to inspect the weaknesses and opportunities of argument in any detail. Commonplace theorizing about deviance touches on delicate moral and social matters: it is difficult, often sub-

---

[64] F. Thrasher, *The Gang*.   [65] W. Whyte, *Street Corner Society*.
[66] R. Cloward and L. Ohlin, *Delinquency and Opportunity*.
[67] D. Matza, *Delinquency and Drift*.   [68] H. Parker, *The View From the Boys*.
[69] See H. Finestone, *Victims of Change*.

versive, to challenge it. Thus it would be a fundamental breach of taste and courtesy to offer certain arguments although they can receive prolonged and sober attention in the university. It would also be considered tedious and ill-mannered to demand a proper defence of every statement. Yet, many statements do require that kind of exposition if their qualities are to be assessed. Sociology rests on canons of proof, presentation and evidence that are foreign to everyday talk. It permits one to be banal, boring, naïve, or outrageous at will, suspending some of the inhibitions which restrict discussion outside the university. If the sociology of deviance is sometimes accused of merely repeating common-sense observations, it may be countered that it works on those observations in an unusual, taxing, and rather exhaustive fashion. It probably represents the only important means of dismantling commonplace explanation and gauging its worth. What emerges may not always be especially momentous, but it is usually a significant advance on the thinking that is conducted elsewhere. Even the most ordinary examples of the sociology of deviance will continue to be justified so long as they are more methodical and reflective than alternative structures of argument. They are buttressed by the conscious deployment of techniques and critical procedures which are not in common use. They subject their ideas to an organized scrutiny. And they are supported by a substantial body of fieldwork and research. Whatever its faults may be, the sociology of deviance is a relatively orderly, disciplined, and cumulative process of enquiry. Even when it is flawed, and it *is* often flawed, a confrontation with its obvious defects can force the reader to think usefully and perhaps for the first time about criticisms and alternatives.

On the other hand, sociologists can move beyond the mere analysis and recitation of arguments. They often display a willingness to become closely involved with matters that most people shun. In this, they are unusual and perhaps a little deviant themselves. Not only is it eccentric and wayward to defend certain arguments about deviance, it is quite improper to associate with deviants without good purpose. Rape, homosexuality, theft, drug-taking, and violence are some of the dangerous and contaminated areas of social life. People typically avoid or disclaim intimacy, and they may be suspicious of those who do not heed taboos. There are very few who have an occupational mandate to be publicly curious and adventurous in deviant regions. Yet sociologists have come to know poolroom hustlers,[70] drug-users,[71] homosexuals,[72] receivers,[73] armed robbers,[74] and child molesters.[75] Not infrequently, the result has been a breaking down of barriers and an extraordinary knowledge. Almost all lay, political, and journalistic theorizing about deviance is second-hand and speculative, based upon imagination, others' reports and hostile encounters. On occasion, sociological understanding is not speculative argument about dimly glimpsed strangers. However ineptly it may be reported and interpreted, it is still frequently valuable. It is often worth wading through poor theory in order to encounter, unwrap and retrieve that knowledge.

The judgement of theory and research should not therefore be precipitate. It is a delicate process and theory is rarely as useless and theorists as foolish as their critics would pretend. It is very easy to construct theoretical counterparts of an Aunt Sally which possesses no vitality, conviction or endurance. More worthwhile is an intellectual approach which puts arguments in their most solid form. Only in this way will the reader actually face the possibility of learning and synthesizing ideas. Few systems are so barren that something cannot be retained. By crediting other sociologists with intelligence and sensibility, the parochialism of one's own understanding might be overcome. Thus, Functionalism and Marxism can disclose previously unknown terrain. One might not care to treat their maps as definitive. One might prefer other maps. But an introduction could be made to once unconsidered phenomena and processes.

Accordingly, we shall invite readers to consider a succession of interlocking and competing ideas. By the end of this book, readers should be reasonably familiar with the basic theories, preoccupations, debates and authors of the sociology of deviance. Our discussion will be ordered historically, beginning with the 'Chicago School' of the 1920s. Such a chronological

[70] See N. Polsky, *Hustlers, Beats and Others*.
[71] See A. Lindesmith, *Opiate Addiction*.
[72] See K. Plummer, *Sexual Stigma*.   [73] See C. Klockars, *The Professional Fence*.
[74] See. W. Einstadter, 'The Social Organization of Armed Robbery'.
[75] See C. McCaghy, 'Drinking and Deviance Disavowal'.

organization seems satisfactory enough: ideas do follow one another in time and sociologists often respond to the work of their predecessors. But it should not be presumed that the sociology of deviance has evolved smoothly, logically, or incrementally. Neither should it be presumed that later ideas necessarily displace those that went before. On the contrary, the temporary eclipse of a theory may have little to do with its merit. More important are the effects of fashion, the desire to innovate, an impatience with the old, changing political and intellectual environments, and the turnover of generations of sociologists. Older ideas have clearly suffered a longer period of criticism and they may seem more wanting. Often, that is all. Those ideas also deserve serious attention and it will not do to take the judgement of later sociologists on trust.

2

Sources of Knowledge about Deviance

Introduction

Sociologists of deviance attempt to explain a world of laws, rules, courts, criminals, rule-breakers, police, and prisons. That world is vast and changing and little of it has been charted. Much of it is unusually difficult to observe, and its very obscurity has complicated problems of exploration. Venturing into it, the sociologist will continually confront dilemmas about the selection of questions and methods. Every decision to examine one possibility rather than another entails some risk and some profit and loss. The framing of such decisions is central to explanation and theory, and debate can turn endlessly around the wisdom and yield of particular choices. It is inevitable that the uses and character of evidence have been brought into dispute. Certain facts invite the acceptance of certain theories, and certain theories propel one to search for certain facts. Any exploration of the sociology of deviance must then consider the ways in which deviation may be seen and how those ways affect argument.

The Elusive Quality of Deviance

We have not yet provided a formal definition of deviance. Our omission has been deliberate and it stems from our reluctance to commit ourselves prematurely to any one position. Major theories cast deviance somewhat differently and subsequent chapters will examine various possibilities in their turn. It is, however, clear that there is some basic, if unwritten, agreement that deviance may be considered as banned or controlled behaviour which is likely to attract punishment or disapproval. It little matters who issues the ban or how many people support it. Those who deviate tend to make their lives rather more hazardous and problematic. Of course, there is abundant deviation which is never recognized, censored, or sanctioned: adulterers may be undetected, burglars may not be apprehended, and drug use may flourish. But deviant pursuits do multiply the perils of ordinary existence. Only occasionally will they be publicly exhibited. Whilst homosexuals sometimes 'come out' and proclaim their homosexuality, or women announce that they had had an illegal abortion, most deviants would not choose to advertise themselves. Instead, there is a real strain towards concealment. As Matza observed, deviation often becomes devious.

Sociologists working on visible and undisguised processes have problems enough. Their work becomes vastly complex when subjects and events are deliberately hidden. Not only is deviance generally covert and secretive, but deviants themselves are unlikely to be immediately co-operative when they are detected. After all, they have little to gain from exposure. Much rule-breaking is consequently represented as something else, denied when suspected, and shielded behind walls or locked doors. Sociologists must be exceptionally alert to its presence, defining otherwise conventional appearances as façades or deceits. They must be sceptical, assuming that all is not as it seems. Thus Jason Ditton[1] and Stuart Henry[2] have uncovered widespread deviance in apparently normal settings. Ditton disclosed the existence of systematic 'fiddles' at most levels of the bread industry. Henry revealed how very ordinary sites like public houses and clubs were the centres of extensive amateur receiving. They have become market-places in which stolen goods are commissioned and distributed. Farberman, too, has described how the American automobile industry is riddled with organized illicit practices.[3] The distribution of alcohol has been similarly documented as an enterprise which has substantial illegalities.[4] Most occupations, it seems, provide opportunities for illegal but unrecorded activity.[5] Deviance abounds but it is methodically veiled. It is only by taking a jaundiced perspective on the world that its disreputable life

---

[1] J. Ditton, *Part-Time Crime*.   [2] S. Henry, *The Hidden Economy*.
[3] H. Farberman, 'A Criminogenic Market Structure'.
[4] See N. Denzin, 'Crime and the American Liquor Industry'.
[5] See S. Henry and G. Mars, 'Crime at Work'.

becomes apparent. Surfaces reveal little. They certainly do not point one at deviant populations.

Secrecy can have varied social ramifications. It can fold back on deviance itself, making research doubly complex. When rule-breaking is guarded, and when it is surrounded by devious explanations, it is quite possible that deviants themselves are not fully aware of the extent and nature of their own activity. Many deviants are segregated from one another, not knowing who their fellows are and what they are doing. Homosexuals, for instance, may believe that unassuming and inconspicuous men are probably heterosexual. The identification of homosexuality may then be profoundly shaped by the conduct of those who are relatively flagrant and extravagant. Child molesters, too, need take no part in organized activity. Their principal knowledge of sexual deviance may flow from the mass media, gossip, and everyday conversation. Their conceptions of misconduct can embody that knowledge, moulding description and motivation.[6] Deviants rarely engage in collective efforts to interpret their own behaviour. A few homosexuals have done so,[7] and a number of drug-takers did so in the 1960s, but many rule-breakers possess no more than a fragmented and second-hand knowledge of deviance. In one important sense, that knowledge is quite adequate and authentic. It infuses and changes the world of deviance, explaining how projects are formed and responses are made. In another sense, it should not be confused with a developed sociological description. Having successfully penetrated the defences which surround rule-breaking, sociologists cannot be entirely uncritical in their response to what they encounter. As Manning observed, they should not assume 'the "underdog's" narrow, often very simplistic view of large complex social segments which directly affect changes in the underdog's behaviour'.[8] Penetration is not enough. Analysis must feed on further materials which may be beyond the subject's grasp, and the discovery of those materials is quite onerous.

Secret practices and organized ignorance result in most

---

[6] See L. Taylor, 'The Significance and Interpretation of Replies to Motivational Questions'.

[7] See L. Humphreys, *Out of the Closets*.

[8] P. Manning, 'Deviance and Dogma', unpublished paper, 1975.

research being limited and parochial. A considerable expenditure of time and effort may give the sociologist access to a deviant world. Additional expenditure might allow useful learning to take place. Months or years may have to pass before intimacy develops, a reasonable range of acts are observed, and processes are seen in their completeness. What will emerge is almost inevitably a partial sighting. One might acquire some knowledge about a receiver,[9] a delinquent gang, or a hotel for geriatric hustlers.[10] It would be quite absurd to expect to become familiar with many instances of such deviance. It would be even more absurd to pretend that one had achieved an understanding of its 'essential' or 'universal' characteristics.

Even one intensively studied subject will resist full surveillance. After all, how can and why should a sociologist be given unfettered access to every intimate moment and thought? There will always be a number of discreditable, forgotten and private processes which are practically censored and cannot be reported. Those who study delinquent adolescents are very rarely admitted to their homes, schools, or more secluded settings. Those who study legislators and administrators will not be privy to every conversation and document. On the contrary, research tends to be confined to public and controlled occasions, occasions which permit a careful preparation of appearances. Yet even those occasions can be so densely textured that sociologists are still plagued by problems of what to record and how to organize their observations. It is not at all remarkable that theories and theorists will tend to describe phenomena quite differently. Not only do phenomena change from time to time and from setting to setting, but there are other sources of divergence that reflect the sheer variety of choices facing an observer. The 'same' process can be reduced to quite conflicting analyses, all of which have been produced in good faith.

For instance, early criminology seemed to neglect policing. It was as if police work was thought to be analytically inconsequential, an uneventful backcloth to criminal processes. Then came the first wave of research on the police in the 1950s and it stressed the dramatic and the spectacular. The police were represented as a besieged and hostile group involved in

[9] See C. Klockars, *The Professional Fence*.
[10] See J. Stephens, *Loners, Losers and Lovers*.

ceaseless activity and a long succession of violent incidents.[11] There was to be a second phase of research in the 1960s and 1970s, and the police were no longer frenetic. Instead, policing was reactive, banal, boring, and commonplace, an occupation like any other, affected by anxieties about promotion, overtime, monotony, and tired feet.[12] More recently again, there has been a move to depict the police as besieged *and* bored. Police officers define themselves as agents of order in the midst of disorder, performing dull work which is punctuated by spurts of hedonistic and frenzied activity.[13]

It is rather improbable that such shifts in emphasis can be explained solely by changes in the social structure and behaviour of the police: the police of the 1950s also cared about avoiding unpleasant weather and getting cups of coffee; and the police of the 1960s and early 1970s had their violent moments (indeed, in 1970, Bittner defined the police role as 'a mechanism for the distribution of non-negotiably coercive force'[14]). It was not changes in policing alone but changes in their conception of the interesting that led sociologists to turn their gaze towards different facets of policing over time. There is a dialectic which moves a focus backwards and forwards. The first sociologists of the police considered the petty, everyday features of policing analytically unimportant. There was a more absorbing story to be told. That story having become accepted and having grown familiar, a contrasting description could be given that re-emphasized the typical and mundane. And once the police had become uneventful again, there could be a third phase, with a renewed interest in violence. The sociology of the police has undergone a series of transformations but it is not always evident that each has been more truthful than the last.[15]

[11] See W. Westley, 'Violence and the Police'; J. Skolnick, *Justice Without Trial*.

[12] See M. Punch, *Policing the Inner City*; S. Holdaway, *Inside the British Police*; D. Smith and J. Gray, *Police and People in London*.

[13] See M. Cain, *Society and the Policeman's Role*; P. Manning, *Police Work*; J. Rubinstein, *City Police*.

[14] E. Bittner, *The Functions of the Police in Modern Society*, 46.

[15] Punch would argue that the transformation is anything but complete; studies 'have neglected boredom and routine. However hard ethnographers try to tell us what it is really like out there, they invariably end up with rich, gripping material. . . . Researchers concentrate ineluctably on the dramatic (either in terms of hectic action or interpersonal relations) and even conspire to make tedium of interest because they describe the "easing" practices which make inactivity tolerable.' M. Punch, 'Officers and Men', 9.

Rather, each has performed a different service and each has tended to obscure something in the process.

Sociological research consists of a long train of constraining relationships. Every movement about the social world is obstructed and eased in a number of ways, and it would be unwise to presume that all groups are equally accessible. There *are* those who claim that obstacles are slight and that a little application will overcome them.[16] Most would acknowledge that sociologists are not capable of passing effortlessly into every alien situation. One will not be at ease everywhere. There are always likely to be certain social groups who defy research by certain sociologists. James Carey, for example, found that his work on amphetamine users was dangerous and disturbing because his subjects were prone to erratic violence.[17] Few Whites could now undertake research on sections of American Black society.[18] Blacks might find it awkward to study some white groups. Men are not welcomed by radical feminists. The old might be rebuffed by the young. Many of the barriers which divide people from one another in everyday life also keep the sociologist at bay. They are actually rather more formidable because the sociologist is more demanding, asking questions and exploring secrets which are not part of commonplace exchanges between strangers.

To be sure, most sociologists do know deviants outside the formal domain of research. Their life is not wholly absorbed by their university duties. They may well be deviants themselves. As one commented about his early and influential writings, 'after all, we were only talking about ourselves'. But criminologists are generally familiar with only a few forms of rule-breaking. Their biographies are unlikely to encompass friendships with arsonists, rapists, and murderers. More common is an acquaintance with a restricted group of sexual deviants, drug-users, and political radicals. There has been a massive preoccupation with the people who may be found in a university environment. Others have been neglected.[19] Unusual subjects must often have to stumble or force themselves into

[16] See N. Polsky, *Hustlers, Beats and Others*.
[17] J. Carey, 'Problems of Access and Risk in Observing Drug Scenes'.
[18] See J. Spiegel, 'Problems of Access to Target Populations'.
[19] There *are* exceptions. For instance, see W. Einstadter, 'The Social Organization'.

the sociologist's life before they receive attention. Contingency plays a part. Thus some criminologists have been prisoners,[20] some have been mental patients, and some have been jazz musicians.[21] Some have even been hobos.[22] But they have not known many other deviants. British criminologists, in particular, are a somewhat protected and insulated profession. Unlike their American colleagues, they have not had to 'work their way' through university by undertaking a variety of part-time and vacation jobs. They have not been exposed to the experiences and milieux which can be subsequently exploited for research purposes.[23]

Another, often unacknowledged problem is the sheer volatility of much deviance. Research frequently entails a careful preparation of finance and time: leave may have to be requested, funds sought, and plans made. In turn, there must be some reasonable guarantee that one's research subjects will be stable and immobile enough to be there when one wants them. It is much easier to study the 'gay world' of homosexuals than the solitary homosexual. The 'gay world' is based on a network of bars, public settings, and groups. It does not disappear or move unexpectedly. The lone individual may simply leave the sociologist's orbit or decide not to be studied after all. Organized and settled congregations of deviants are the most readily and intensively observed. Especially accessible are groups which need to maintain contact with strangers. The 'gay world' required a constant flow of unknown people for its anonymous sexual couplings. The sociologist became one more benign visitor. By contrast, he or she would be spurned by those who keep themselves apart. Still more work is required of one who is curious about professional crime, because the professional criminal is suspicious of the stranger.[24] The most work is demanded of sociologists who seek the isolated and unpredictable bomber or blackmailer.

There are also barriers *within* social worlds. Concentration on one area may bar access to others. A group may not trust a person who has ingratiated himself with a rival faction. The

[20] See J. Irwin, *The Felon*.
[21] See H. Becker, 'The Culture of a Deviant Group'.
[22] See N. Anderson, *The Hobo*.
[23] See F. Davis, 'The Cab-Driver and his Fare'.
[24] See T. Parker and R. Allerton, *The Courage of His Convictions*.

police might not encourage a sociologist who has been with a delinquent group for some time. It is usually impossible to predict the inner politics of a group: only when contacts have been established will the limits and hazards of research become apparent. But contracts bring allegiances and alleged commitments in their wake. They cannot readily be undone.

Some Methodological Strategies

We have implied that effective analysis requires the cultivation of intimate associations. Close acquaintance is often clearly necessary, especially when knowledge is somewhat tentative. It would be foolish to venture explanations before the character of deviance has been properly charted. None the less, there are many questions which cannot be settled by such anthropological methods. Historical research, for instance, obviously demands very different strategies. Even when anthropology might be thought appropriate, there are many sociologists who are quite content with formal interviewing or the use of indirect evidence. Yet, whatever strategy is employed, there are inherent uncertainties which all criminology must confront. Criminologists have advanced a number of methods to dispel those uncertainties, and we shall review them in turn.

We have observed that there are many deviants who are distinguished by their visibility. Particular styles of rule-breaking rely on public assembly. Indeed, the 'hippy' or 'punk' identity would become void without mass display. Rather unkindly, Klapp has defined expressive deviance which requires an audience as 'ego-screaming'. Street gangs, demonstrations, the 'street people' of North America, prostitutes, homosexuals, and drug 'scenes' are reasonably conspicuous, and the sociologist can attach himself to a suitable congregation. It is often possible to join the fringes of deviant activity, witnessing exchanges and exploiting opportunities. The fringes are generally ill-defined. Few groups have strict and enforceable criteria of membership. The mere decision to stand in the road or on the pavement will usually proclaim one's part in a demonstration. Sheer physical proximity can signify that one is either sympathetic or uninterested. In the absence of self-policing, such deviance is largely bared to scrutiny.

Sociologists have accordingly moved in on deviant assemblies. Some have reported the conduct of demonstrations.[25] Stan Cohen followed the migrations of the 'Mods' and 'Rockers' in the 1960s, monitoring what they did.[26] David Downes frequented a café used by local delinquents. In time, he became accepted as a companion.[27] Cavan, too, simply visited the bars of an American city, recording their deviant underlife.[28] There was little questioning of the presence of outsiders in a situation which could not neatly discriminate between insiders and outsiders. When deviance rests on exhibition in public places, access is assured. Even the partially secluded can be laid open to observation. The more involved participants may tolerate or prepare particular identities which can be donned by observers. Voyeurism is not wholly resented by some sexual deviants. Laud Humphreys insinuated himself as a 'look-out' or 'watch queen' in American lavatories, which allowed him to survey casual sexual encounters between homosexuals.[29]

Despite the wealth of behaviour which is publicly flaunted, it must be recalled that much important activity will remain concealed. Public behaviour is but a part of life. It is complemented by other conduct which may be equally significant in the understanding of deviance. Public interchanges have their own character which may be quite coercive. Not only will people behave rather differently apart from the crowd, but they may also have private reservations about the apparent commitments of public occasions.[30] Thus Matza has described the 'multiple shared misunderstandings' which mould deviant projects.[31] He argues that there may be personal, unvoiced misgivings about public beliefs: it would be misleading to assume that all delinquents are as zealous in their support for criminal enterprises as they appear to be. On the contrary, group activity engenders a rhetoric which is at odds with personal sentiment. Even a small group is capable of producing an alien reality. For instance, McCorkle and Korn have provided a

[25] See J. Halloran *et al.*, *Demonstrations and Communications*.
[26] S. Cohen, *Folk Devils and Moral Panics*.
[27] D. Downes, *The Delinquent Solution*.
[28] S. Cavan, *Liquor License*.
[29] L. Humphreys, *Tearoom Trade*.
[30] See J. Dollard, *Caste and Class in a Southern Town*.
[31] D. Matza, *Delinquency and Drift*.

history of a delinquent episode in which none of the participants was willing but each assumed that the others wanted a
robbery to take place.[32] Only three people were involved, but
there *was* a robbery.

The language and conduct of public gatherings are not only
coercive; they are also too standardized and anonymous to
permit the expression of individual interests. It is those interests
which often influence how general understandings are translated into practical action. It would be mistaken to imagine that
the slogans of a public march distil all its members' political
perspectives. It would be equally mistaken to imagine that all
homosexuals embrace the 'gay world' with enthusiasm: participation may be an unwelcome penalty inflicted on those who
seek a partner.

Analysis therefore requires a mapping of private qualifications. Without such a map, public language would be regarded
as an accurate guide to conduct and belief. It is not an accurate
guide, and many who speak it recognize that it serves something of a rhetorical or ritual role. Thus the behaviour and
statements of football crowds must frequently be read as a
series of feints and mock battles, not as aggression which will
inevitably culminate in physical assault.[33] Private qualifications
are also organized and circulated. Sykes and Matza have
discussed the 'techniques of neutralization' which delinquents
employ in the explanation of conduct.[34] Claiming that would-
be delinquents confront the problem of guilt, they catalogued
the public formulas of mitigation and extenuation which ease
the commission of delinquency. It might be argued that the
victim 'deserved' his fate or that he suffered no real loss. It might
be argued that higher loyalties were at stake or that those who
condemn action are in no moral position to judge. Reiss, too,
has analysed the accounts which some adolescent gang
members gave of their homosexual prostitution.[35] Not permitting themselves to take an 'active' role, and affirming their 'real'
heterosexuality, the prostitutes recognized no worrying loss of
integrity or masculinity.

[32] R. Korn and L. McCorkle, 'Social Roles'.
[33] See P. Marsh *et al.*, *The Rules of Disorder*.
[34] G. Sykes and D. Matza, 'Techniques of Neutralization'.
[35] A. Reiss, 'The Social Integration of Queers and Peers'.

Secluded deviation cannot be so effortlessly discovered. It may be furtive or disguised. Its practitioners may be distrustful and wary, unwilling to have dealings with a strange sociologist. The role and functions of a sociologist are not well understood in the wider world. If they were understood, there is no reason to assume that trust would be any greater. There being no assemblies to observe and no home territories to frequent, the sociologist is obliged to adopt alternative strategies. One device has been called 'snowballing', the collection of a sample by incremental contacts. If a sociologist is able to gain the confidence of one deviant, he or she may then seek a series of introductions to others in the deviant's world. Those introductions will serve as a limited reassurance to those who are suspicious. In time, a sizeable population may be met. A prime example has been provided by Nancy Lee's hunt for women who had undergone abortion.[36] Very typically, such women neither declare themselves nor court attention from research sociologists. They may well have concealed their abortions from their own families. Despite their great reluctance, Lee managed to unearth a considerable number of women, being passed from one to the next in a long chain. She produced a sample of otherwise inaccessible subjects.

There are manifest limitations to snowballing. Chief amongst them are the restrictions imposed by any social network. A sociologist will encounter a sample thrown up by the relationships and knowledge of a particular group. The boundaries around that group will be the boundaries of a sample. That constraint may not be especially important. The difficulties of research are often so impressive that every interview and meeting is an accomplishment. What remains uncertain is the peculiar character of the group that has revealed itself. In one sense, all groups are unique and none can claim typicality. In another sense, distinctiveness *can* become a problem. Initial acquaintance is likely to be with someone in or near the sociologist's circle. One may become exposed to a group whose politics, stance, or milieux are rather similar to one's own. The homosexuals, drug-users, or thieves unearthed by snowballing may then compose a rather special network.

[36] N. Lee, *The Search for an Abortionist*.

Drug-users may be unusually articulate: there has been disproportionately voluminous research on the self-conscious and middle-class addict. Working-class addicts are relatively neglected.[37] Similarly, snowballing can give salience to politically active homosexuals, or homosexuals of the professional classes. It will almost certainly generate an impression of social structure and collective behaviour. It is not and can never be designed to reach the isolated. By extension, it invariably suggests that deviance is a group achievement.

Sometimes snowballing does not lead very far. Introductions are not forthcoming or else prove fruitless. Sometimes, too, the sociologist expresses no great desire to construct a sample. On the contrary, knowledge may be meagre enough to warrant an intensive exploration of just one subject. That exploration might be justified by the search for a developmental analysis of deviance or by the exploitation of an extraordinary opportunity. Criminologists have quite frequently collaborated in the writing of deviant life-histories,[38] attempting to understand the part played by rule-breaking in the life of a single person. It would be an exceptional individual who consented to such documentation. Co-operation is sometimes secured when sociologist and deviant establish intimacy after a period of prison visiting or as a result of intense interviewing. More exceptionally, volunteers are recruited by advertisement in general or special newspapers. Sometimes simple friendship can be turned into a research relationship.

The case history can never be described as a basis for substantial generalization, but the criminologist may not want to produce sociological laws, or may believe that such laws are premature. In the place of generality, the deviant biography offers depth and detail. At one level, it undoubtedly yields more than brief interviews or short spates of observation. It can be conducted in a leisurely manner: questions can be asked or postponed at will; minute knowledge can be acquired; the evolution of deviant careers can be plotted, and disclosures can be made which might otherwise have been withheld. Sociologists of deviance have accordingly returned repeatedly to the

---

[37] See P. Rock, Preface to *Drugs and Politics*.
[38] See E. Sutherland, *The Professional Thief*; cf. Shaw, *The Jackroller*, W. Probyn, *Angel Face*; W. Chambliss, *Box Man*.

stock of criminal biographies in order to tap a source of unusually informed knowledge.[39] Biographies tend to under-score the perils of superficial classification and argument: they often appear more complex, intricate, and open to diverse interpretations than much criminology supposes.[40]

Observation, snowballing, and the case study are somewhat distant methods. They preserve the sociologist in his or her professional role, keeping the subjects apart. Occasionally, distance is impossible: the sociologist is a deviant anyway and research consists simply of observing oneself and others.[41] Occasionally, participation is foisted on the sociologist, flowing from the inescapable entanglements that surround research. After all, it is often difficult to remain aloof and disengaged. One's mere presence may be read as collusion or complicity. Little by little, relations can draw the sociologist in so that detachment becomes insupportable.[42] Indeed, a refusal to collaborate may be construed as unfriendliness, threatening to undermine research.

Again, some forms of deviance make no provision for spectators. Intimacy, danger, or discretion militate against the presence of possibly incompetent bystanders. Homosexual couples may consent to be interviewed, they may provide autobiographies, but the detail of their everyday affairs cannot be monitored from without. A third person would be wholly intrusive, transforming a relationship into a qualitatively new mode of life.

Research that entails the active collaboration of the sociologist has been called 'participant-observation' and it has been employed with especial frequency in the study of deviance. Sometimes it is contingencies of biography or situation that throw a sociologist into such an anthropological role. Sometimes it is more than contingency but a theoretical commitment which asserts that social behaviour cannot be understood until it has been personally experienced. The argument is

[39] See H. Becker, 'The Life History and the Scientific Mosaic'.

[40] Thus Plummer is working on the life-histories of a number of sexual deviants. He argues that no conventional sexual categorization adequately describes their conduct or self-definition. Instead of 'homosexuality', for example, he would now prefer to talk of 'homosexualities'.

[41] See T. Shibutani, *The Derelicts of Company K*.

[42] For a fictional description of such a process, see A. Lurie, *Imaginary Friends*.

made that sociologists who lean on external accounts and objective evidence can have no appreciation of how people act. Neither can they grasp environments and history as their subjects do. They are imposing an alien explanation whose links with a problem may be a little tendentious. What is represented as causal might well have had no influence on a person or a group.

Participant observation is supposed to allow the sociologist to know what it is like to be cause and effect in a particular social setting. It is with that knowledge that explanation can be built. Those who employ participation as a strategy[43] are the bearers of a long tradition that may be linked in part with the University of Chicago in the 1920s. One early student of that university recalled how, in general, academic knowledge was thought to be an unreliable basis for speculation. It gave no sure understanding. A sometime head of the sociology department at the university, Robert Park, 'made a great point of the difference between knowledge about something and acquaintance with the phenomena. That was one of the great thrusts in Chicago, because people had to get out and if they wanted to study opium addicts they went to the opium dens and even smoked a little opium maybe. They went out and lived with the gangs and the . . . hobos and so on.'[44]

The subject of deviance seems to provide an unusually attractive solution to those confronting the problems of participant-observation. Participant-observers try to perform a most intricate feat. They are required to reach the probably unattainable state of one who is both insider and outsider, a person who sees a social world from within in the manner of a member yet who also stands apart and analyses it in the manner of a stranger. As insider, the sociologist will move as his or her subjects move, learning responses, definitions and actions as they do. Their gestures will be the sociologist's own, becoming so familiar that they can be unfalteringly reproduced and described to a larger audience. As outsider, the sociologist will treat those gestures as problematic and uncertain, requiring close examination and questioning. Ideas and practices must be

---

[43] See P. Rock, *The Making of Symbolic Interactionism*, ch. 6.

[44] Interview with Leonard Cottrell, quoted in J. Carey, *Sociology and Public Affairs*, 156.

regarded as simultaneously natural and unnatural. It is the case that deviance frequently represents a satisfactory meld of the familiar and the unfamiliar, allowing one to imagine that he or she is inside and outside the worlds it creates. For instance, drug-taking or sexual misbehaviour in one's own society combines the strange and the known in a composition which excites curiosity but does not defeat understanding. There is an important affinity between the sociology of deviance and participant-observation, and a substantial number of studies have adopted an ethnographic style in consequence.

None the less, there are often good reasons why participant-observation should not be conducted. The method may not necessarily furnish the kind of information demanded by a particular problem. There have been allegations that anthropological techniques pose specially intricate ethical problems.[45] Many sociologists are indifferent to the role of meaning and experience in explanation, looking for more objective and solid variables. And others find observation difficult in certain settings. Not everyone would pass uneventfully into the world of punk rockers or Hell's Angels.[46] Older sociologists might find it awkward to merge with the young, men with women, Whites with Blacks, Arabs with Jews. Some have pulled it off. Liebow, a White sociologist, conducted a masterly anthropological study of Washington Black street-corner society. But he was exceptional. Safer and less taxing methods *can* be productive, and much of the sociology of deviance has turned to them instead.

There is one very common strategy for reaching deviants without engaging in participant-observation. Sociologists can proceed directly to a prison or mental hospital and the advantages of doing so are obvious. One who is confined and controlled is likely to be a little more amenable to interview. A meeting with a sociologist might actually help to overcome the boredom of a monotonous regime. And, for the sociologist, captives are neatly assembled samples requiring little pursuit. There may be problems encountered in trying to gain access to the institution itself,[47] but prisons and hospitals are convenient 'warehouses'.

[45] See K. Erikson, 'Disguised Observation in Sociology'.
[46] See H. Thompson, *Hell's Angels*.
[47] See S. Cohen and L. Taylor, *Prison Secrets*.

Interviews and studies of captive populations can be put to two major uses, and one raises rather fewer difficulties of interpretation and application than the other. The first transforms an enclosed community into a sociological subject in its own right. There has been a long history of sophisticated work on the social structures of prisons and asylums. Thus, Ward and Kassebaum explored a women's prison,[48] Cohen and Taylor discussed the effects of long-term imprisonment,[49] and Goffman analysed the mental hospital as a 'total institution'.[50] Their intention was to explain the social organization of very special institutions, and there was no pretence at an exhaustive discussion of deviance outside the walls. Neither was there a very detailed analysis of what inmates did and thought before their confinement. In this first instance, institutions themselves were the focus.

Institutions are not objects of particular curiosity in the second use. They are instead repositories of people who are of interest to the sociologist. Captives may well be the only available representatives of a certain group. There are many individuals who are not easily to be found in the world at large. They lack the fixed social positions and physical locations which aid discovery. Thus, only the most unusual circumstances would bring about a profitable encounter between a sociologist and a murderer or rapist. Sometimes offending is very rare and haphazard, not easily monitored: an observer might have to spend unproductive months waiting for something to turn up. Deviants are sometimes too well guarded, threatening or secretive to be comfortable subjects. Sociologists could well feel trepidation about spending long periods of time in the unprotected company of those who are often violent or disturbed. If certain people are to be seen at all, it will probably be in prison or mental hospital. In effect, the sociologist will entrust the business of collecting samples to the police and official agencies.

There is some risk that organizations will then become sources of distortion. An institutional setting limits enquiry about past conduct. There can be little appreciation of matters

[48] D. Ward and G. Kassebaum, *Women's Prison*.
[49] S. Cohen and L. Taylor, *Psychological Survival*.
[50] E. Goffman, *Asylums*.

which originally escaped the subject's interest and attention. Events before incarceration cannot be observed as they unfold: they must be pieced together retrospectively. The earlier responses of others cannot be witnessed. There are few external checks on what is said. Institutions tend to deform communication, inhibiting the delivery of unguarded replies and gestures. They are certainly very different from the older milieux that prompted the behaviour which the sociologist would describe. They impose their own history on conduct, making it difficult to detach the effects of treatment, punishment and control from experiences undergone before.[51] There is always the possibility that a sociologist will be identified with the staff of an organization. Responses may be tailored appropriately, becoming ingratiating, cautious or hostile. Moreover, there are gross problems flowing from the special recruitment of inmates and patients. For example, clinical reports about homosexuals, prostitutes or drug addicts can deal only with those who presented themselves as people in need of treatment. They cannot be extended to the unexplored world of untreated deviants. Basing their knowledge on a selected population, it is generally impossible for sociologists to claim typicality. Few deviants at large are apprehended, and only a few apprehended deviants enter custody. Indeed, Mack has suggested that prisoners are often no more than inept criminals and that research on inmates centres on the particularly incompetent.[52]

There are less focused and discriminating methods of rendering deviant and other populations visible. They are versions of what might be described as sociological saturation coverage. Pursuing certain problems and assuming that deviance is ubiquitous, sociologists will launch a mass attack on a substantially undifferentiated population of people. There will be no attempt carefully to single out groups in advance. On the contrary, those groups will surface as the work progresses. Early instances are the self-report studies conducted by Kinsey, Porterfield,[53] Wallerstein and Wyle,[54] Nye and Short,[55] and

[51] See A. Lindesmith, *Opiate Addiction*; E. Hooker, 'Male Homosexuality'.
[52] J. Mack, '"Professional Crime" and Criminal Organization'.
[53] A. Porterfield, *Youth in Trouble*.
[54] J. Wallerstein and C. Wyle, 'Our Law-abiding Law-breakers'.
[55] F. Nye and J. Short, 'Scaling Delinquent Behavior'.

Nettler.[56] A population most often consisting of schoolchildren will be subjected to a battery of questions about criminal incidents. Its members will be required to indicate which acts, if any, they committed. The most sophisticated and recent example has been Belson's massive study of London boys, a study which revealed, like many of its predecessors, that every boy interviewed had committed some act of theft.[57] The specific concern is usually with the incidence of unrecorded delinquencies in an effort to establish the 'true' rate and distribution of criminality.

Another form of saturation coverage is the victim survey, pioneered in the United States[58] and applied in Holland, Britain, and elsewhere.[59] Mass surveys have been conducted of households, probing the extent of their members' experience of victimization during a particular period of time, usually a year. Again, the primary intention has been to discover 'real' crime rates. Thus, the first British Crime Survey of 1981 showed that only 8 per cent of offences of vandalism known to victims were reported to the police. The rates for theft from a motor vehicle were 29 per cent, for burglary 48 per cent, for theft from the person 8 per cent, and for robbery 11 per cent.[60] Victim surveys have introduced quite dramatic changes in thinking about crime and deviance. In turn, almost inevitably, their original goals have been supplemented and displaced. They are rich sources of information that not only revealed new research possibilities as interests and priorities changed, but also affected the very agenda of the sociology of deviance. Such surveys could not long continue as mere exercises in counting crimes. They have given a new analytic prominence to the victim of crime;[61] they have raised questions about the distress of victimization and the ways in which it may be relieved;[62] they have directed research at the problem of the fear of crime and the measures which people take to avoid victimization;[63] and

[56] G. Nettler, 'Antisocial Sentiment and Criminality'.

[57] W. Belson, *Juvenile Theft*.

[58] President's Commission on Law Enforcement and the Administration of Justice, *Crime and its Impact: An Assessment*.

[59] See R. Sparks *et al.*, *Surveying Victims*.

[60] See M. Hough and P. Mayhew, *The British Crime Survey: First Report*.

[61] See P. Rock, *A View from the Shadows*.

[62] See M. Hough and P. Mayhew, *Taking Account of Crime*.

[63] See M. Maxfield, *Fear of Crime in England and Wales*.

they have encouraged a re-emergence of the social geography of criminal events.[64] Perhaps equally interesting has been the revolutionary impact on radical criminology. As we shall argue, a revelation of the extent and intensity of working-class victimization has led some radical criminologists to reappraise their stance towards the social meanings and consequences of crime. They no longer discuss everyday crimes committed by and against the working class as if they were a petty and irritating diversion from more substantial political issues or as a kind of ruling-class myth.[65] They have instead begun to take very seriously issues which were once the exclusive domain of their ideological opponents, issues focusing on the problems of police effectiveness and community controls.[66]

Victim and self-report studies may be combined in a blanket onslaught on a locality or social stratum. The Sheffield project,[67] for example, represented a major sociological invasion of a city, merging ethnography, official records, self-reports, claims to victimization and a variety of secondary sources.

Indirect Sources

Deviance is everywhere and it leaves traces everywhere. It marks those who report it, those who attempt to control it, those who gain from it, those who suffer from it, those who imaginatively describe it, and the contexts in which it is accomplished. Properly read, almost every man-made environment can be interpreted as a record of the effects and responses which deviance produces. Locks, doors, walls, graffiti, guards, police, prisons, newspapers, films, insurance companies, ticket-collectors, and bank vaults all embody the influence of rule-breaking. But they represent much more than simple reactions. They provide sets of opportunities and constraints for the commission of further deviance. They are not fixed or static. Indeed, Mary McIntosh has described the historical evolution of crime as a competitive struggle between preventative and illegal technologies.[68] Those

---

[64] See S. Smith, *Crime, Space and Society*.
[65] See S. Box, *Crime, Power and Mystification*.
[66] See J. Lea and J. Young, *What is to be Done about Law and Order?*
[67] See J. Baldwin and A. Bottoms, *The Urban Criminal*.
[68] M. McIntosh, *The Organization of Crime*.

signs also compose the emerging situation in which deviance is defined and transacted. They work back on deviant and conforming populations to shape the manner in which events can be described and managed.

It therefore becomes urgent to turn to indirect evidence. Only then will there be an adequate appreciation of the settings and processes which manufacture deviation. The practical limits set by policing, common-sense assumptions, and physical structures[69] explain the channelling of conduct. They explain how people acquire motives and attitudes. They explain how deviants must contend with organized assumptions and policies. The world of deviance consists of a web of relationships which must be fully explored before its separate parts are understood.

Sociologists have accordingly worked on layer upon different layer of evidence. Their objectives may not always have been congruent, but the outcome has been the development of overlapping perspectives on similar problems. For example, there has been some interest in examining literary descriptions of crime,[70] building on the tacit thesis that literature can be treated as a special history of ideas and ideologies of crime and control. There has been a particularly intense fascination with the part played by the mass media. It is actually very difficult to disentangle and inspect the effects of crime reporting on its audiences, and debate about the matter has been acrimonious and seemingly barren.

In response, many sociologists decided to move away from the observation of effects and have instead turned their attention to the social construction and composition of crime news.[71] It has been argued that news agencies are vital disseminators of second-hand knowledge about deviance, furnishing a landscape of evil-doers and villains which appears to be as real as anything known to limited immediate experience.[72] People are taken to live in a universe which has been prefabricated by news reports.[73]

[69] Cf. J. Jacobs, *The Death and Life of Great American Cities*.
[70] See D. Davis, *Homicide in American Fiction*; J. Palmer, 'Thrillers: The Deviant Behind the Consensus'.
[71] See M. Fishman, *Manufacturing the News*.
[72] See J. Tunstall, *Media Sociology*; S. Cohen and J. Young (eds.), *The Manufacture of News*.   [73] See L. Wilkins, *Social Deviance*.

Other groups and institutions have been mapped in an effort to analyse how they mould conduct. Deviance is shaped in its transactions with events and people around it. Indeed, it is often practically and conceptually difficult to distinguish between deviation and its settings. Sociologists, and 'labelling theorists'—phenomenologists and interactionists in particular—have consequently occupied themselves with the character and workings of the social reaction to deviance. An exploration of courts,[74] prisons,[75] and police forces will produce oblique but powerful information about deviation itself.

Such 'secondary' evidence has a major part to play in explanation, and it tends to be easier to compile than anthropological data: newspapers are more tractable than burglars. Further, secondary evidence is abundant and it may be studied safely in congenial surroundings. Its producers are typically more civil than deviants themselves. Journalism, the police force, the prison service, and the civil service are occupations with stable and accessible memberships. They are part of the everyday middle-class world of the sociologist. In all these senses, they constitute a most amenable research population.

There are sociologists who seek indices and measures which are even more remote from the sites of deviant activity. Arguing that the business of science is the exploration of 'deep' social structures, they turn to indicators which reflect the changes and states of an underlying order. Those indicators may be a little different from the evidence considered in a more immediate appreciation of deviance. They may be movements of the business cycle,[76] trends in architecture or in educational practice,[77] or signs of political crisis.[78] The organizing assumption is that deviance is but a part of society and that society itself is a moving whole. Transformations of that whole will reveal themselves in many areas: they are present in shifting ideologies or in the political and economic system. Connections

[74] See P. Carlen, *Magistrates' Justice*; M. Atkinson and P. Drew, *Order in Court*; W. Bennett and M. Feldman, *Reconstructing Reality in the Courtroom*.

[75] See M. Foucault, *Discipline and Punish*; T. and P. Morris, *Pentonville*; D. Clemmer, *The Prison Community*; G. Sykes, *The Society of Captives*.

[76] See H. Mannheim, *Social Aspects of Crime Between the Wars*; G. Rusche and O. Kirchheimer, *Punishment and Social Structure*.

[77] See M. Foucault, *Discipline and Punish*.

[78] See S. Hall *et al.*, *Policing the Crisis*.

and developments can be traced at almost any point. Thus Foucault argues that there was a wholesale revolution in the management of people at the beginning of the nineteenth century: new disciplines were introduced into factories, work-houses, prisons, schools, and armies. Changing postures towards criminals were echoed elsewhere. They can be properly appreciated only by comprehending the entire revolu-tion: new styles of handwriting and child-rearing are as instruc-tive to the criminologist as the more obvious data of penal practice. Indeed, they are more instructive because they are *not* obvious. Similarly, Stuart Hall and his colleagues take the regulation of deviance to be one of a number of repressive strategies adopted by the capitalist state. All strategies are inter-connected, and it is their articulation and relations which provide illumination about the functions of crime.

What gives plausibility to such evidence is the theory that links its varied manifestations. Those who are unpersuaded by the theory will dismiss the evidence as irrelevant. By extension, they will find little substance in conventional demonstrations of the theory. Without its supporting evidence, theory wilts. Con-versely, a theory's advocates tend to maintain that their ideas have a forcefulness and scale which are lamentably absent in other systems of explanation. The issue hinges on whether there *is* a concealed order which shapes human affairs, whether that order projects a few visible outcrops, and how those outcrops should be interpreted. The issue is especially complicated because it typically centres on submerged patterns and the activities of the powerful. Ruling élites are often held to be the prime manipulators of the real social order. They are difficult to approach and their motives are sometimes thought to be inaccessible even to themselves. Motivation and conduct have frequently to be imputed by the analyst, taking their credibility from beliefs about plausible courses of action. They cannot be effectively proved. Thus Chambliss produced arguments about the engineering of law and its real effects on society.[79] He did not, and could not, document the conversa-tions and intentions of legislators. He was forced to proceed by making attributions on the basis of disclosed evidence. That

[79] W. Chambliss, 'The State and Criminal Law'.

evidence was equivocal unless Chambliss's theoretical framework is accepted.

The most common and orthodox form of indirect evidence is that contained in official statistics. There has been a long tradition of bureaucratic record-keeping in the West. For example, censuses have been conducted in Britain since 1801. In turn, there has been a heavy reliance upon Government-sponsored statistics as a barometer of social change. In the beginning, particularly, a new science of 'social physics' arose to respond to the opportunities presented by the new evidence.[80] It was believed that it had become possible to produce laws of social motion akin to those furnished by the natural sciences. Statistical rates were taken to be independent sources of commentary. They revealed truths which were quite superior to impressionistic and subjective evidence. That stance still persists: for instance, Chevalier's history of nineteenth-century Paris contrasted the unreliable and partial accounts of novelists and journalists with the sound checks offered by crime rates.[81] Historians are particularly prone to defer to police and court records as indisputably sound.

Official statistics would seem to provide an unparalleled foundation for speculation. They are the fruits of an expenditure which no ordinary research criminologists could afford. They are neatly tabulated for immediate analysis. They are compiled without any effort on the part of the sociologist. In some cases, they have no rivals. Historical work must lean on published rates.[82]

Over time, however, there has been a growing accumulation of reservations about the utility of official records of crime.[83] The arguments are complex and incompletely settled, but they take two major tacks. Apart from a brief and probably unproductive debate about whether criminologists should accept classifications which have been devised for unscientific purposes,[84] uncertainties hover around the problem of the 'dark figure' and around the negotiated character of rates.

[80] See A. Quetelet, *Essai de Physique Sociale*.
[81] L. Chevalier, *Labouring Classes and Dangerous Classes*.
[82] See T. Gurr *et al.*, *The Politics of Crime and Conflict*.
[83] See S. Box, *Deviance, Reality and Society*; R. Hood and R. Sparks, *Key Issues in Criminology*.
[84] See T. Sellin, 'The Significance of Records of Crime'.

The dark figure is that universe of incidents which is *not* recorded by the police and the courts. Official statistics are not, and do not pretend to be, a report of the total volume of illegal activity. They are simply a record of crimes known to officials. Criminologists concerned with the 'real' or 'true' rates may then become preoccupied with the events that escaped police attention. Only when those events have been enumerated, it is argued, will there be a reliable index. Criminologists have accordingly devoted themselves to a cataloguing of the processes which enhance or undermine the validity of official figures. Listed in that catalogue are the ability and willingness of people to recognize crimes, their willingness to report crimes, and the character of the police response to public reports. It is acknowledged that many crimes are furtive, hidden, or technically sophisticated. Burglaries, frauds, and embezzlement may never be identified. Even if crime *is* known to have occurred, there may be a reluctance to notify the police: it may be thought that the amounts involved do not warrant intervention; the police may be defined as uninterested or ineffective; the victim may be implicated (as a collaborator, or as the client of a prostitute, perhaps); the victim may be vulnerable (as a homosexual or an adulterer); there may be sympathy for the offender; there may be little sympathy for the victim; there may be hostility towards the police; or the crime may itself be condoned. The police themselves can declare that no crime has taken place, they may take no official action, or they may prefer changed charges.[85] There is a long chain of problematic decisions between the commission of a possible crime and its registration, and records have come to be treated with some suspicion.

There are indeed certain crimes that seem to be accurately reflected in statistics. For example, the first British Crime Survey recorded that victims notified 100 per cent of thefts of motor vehicles to the police.[86] There is a real enough incentive to approach the police after the loss of a motor car because a report must be made if an insurance claim is to be met. But there are gaps in other records of deviance. Only 8 per cent of thefts from the person were reported. Some amounts will be

[85] See D. McBarnet, 'Pre-trial Procedures and Construction of Conviction'.
[86] See *The British Crime Survey*, 1983.

considered too petty to merit action. Some thefts will be inappropriately interpreted as the mere mislaying of property. Some thefts will be of things that were never gained lawfully. Some possessions may not be missed or may not have been insured.

The emergence of victim surveys as competing sources of information has reinforced a drift towards analysing official criminal statistics as records, not of criminal acts, but of the number and distribution of police acts. Those figures convey little about the 'actual' volume of rule-breaking, but they are an excellent guide to the deployment and behaviour of police forces.[87]

More recently, it appears that the official statistics may have been rather slighted. There is evidence that they are more useful than their criminological critics have imagined. For instance, crime surveys of Sheffield suggest that variations between different areas' officially recorded rates of offending are matched by variations in their victimization rates.[88] Although Sheffield's police statistics may not capture the city's 'true' volume of crime, they may at least reveal the pattern of dispersal of crimes.[89] If such a finding could be generalized, official statistics would provide helpful information about the geographical and social spread of crime.

A more interesting description of crime records has emerged from phenomenology and ethnomethodology. Instead of portraying official statistics as more or less 'wrong', sociologists have defined them as compressed summaries of complicated interchanges between people.[90] A statistic then ceases to be a poor measure of the worrying dark figure. It is no longer simply a self-evident trace of police action. It becomes a condensed, shorthand expression of all the work that is undertaken when a 'suspect' is named, apprehended, charged, and prosecuted. It is a product of copious activity, and it will be literally meaningless until that activity is first understood. Unless one has a grasp of typical processes of plea-bargaining, for example, no sig-

[87] See K. Bottomley and K. Pease, *Crime and Punishment* for a useful summary of the official statistics of crime.
[88] See A. Bottoms, R. Mawby, and M. Walker, 'A Localised Crime Survey in Contrasting Areas of a City'.
[89] See R. Mawby, 'Crime and Law'.
[90] See J. Kitsuse and A. Cicourel, 'A Note on the Uses of Official Statistics'.

nificance can be attached to the classification of an offence.[91] Unless one has an understanding of interrogation procedures,[92] police strategies,[93] and courtroom practices, it will remain unclear what the statistics represent. They are not impersonal products of mechanical registration. They incorporate operating assumptions and predictions which are intelligible chiefly to their producers.

A supreme example of the phenomenological stance is provided by Douglas's[94] (and, latterly, Atkinson's[95]) criticism of Durkheim's *Le Suicide*. Durkheim depicted suicide rates as preeminently objective phenomena: they were analysed as entirely accurate measures of different states of social integration. It was the alleged independence of such rates that Douglas challenged. Rates are not autonomous, they are *constructed* by officials who confront the onerous task of deciding how deaths might have occurred. Officials operate with lay theories about the nature and meaning of death. 'Suicide' is itself the outcome of theorizing: it is a categorization which embodies assumptions about the significance of loneliness, loss, grief, and social integration. In doubtful cases, the detached and dislocated are the most eligible candidates for placement as suicides. In short, suicide rates are compiled by officials, they encase particular hypotheses about the nature of the world, Durkheim came to the study of those rates with identical hypotheses, and his book demonstrated their cogency. *Le Suicide* is based on tautological reasoning. Suicide rates, and all other rates, must be decoded before they can be put to any analytic use.

To be sure, crime rates may be examined as influential phenomena in their own right. Instead of exploring their validity or construction, it is possible to discuss them as part of the environment in which deviance is displayed. Journalists, politicians, the police, and laymen ascribe importance to rates, responding to them as vital moral facts. Control policies will be devised to alter known trends in criminal activity. The police may define rates as indicators of productivity which must be

[91] See J. Baldwin and M. McConville, *Negotiated Justice*.
[92] See A. Cicourel, *The Social Organization of Juvenile Justice*.
[93] See E. Bittner, 'The Police on Skid Row'.
[94] J. Douglas, *The Social Meanings of Suicide*.
[95] M. Atkinson, 'Societal Reactions to Suicide'.

defended, applauded, or carefully built up. Resources may be solicited, staff recruited, and technologies changed in answer to shifts in rates. Political debate often revolves around the impressions of success or failure conveyed by rates. Lay reactions sometimes manifest concern about the rates. Crime statistics are palpably important.

Sociologists now probably treat victim surveys as the more substantial and useful reserves of Government information about the distribution and character of crime. Not only are the surveys interesting descriptions of patterns of victimization, but they also touch on such ancillary matters as the fear of crime, connections between types of housing and crime, and the relations between styles of life and victimization. In Britain, the raw materials of the surveys have been deposited in the ESRC data archive in Essex University where they are accessible to research criminologists who can perform their own additional analysis upon them. Victim surveys are a significant corrective to rates of officially notified crimes, but they are not without flaw. Reverse record checks, for instance, have established that some 10 per cent of crimes reported to the police would not be disclosed to an interviewer working on a victim survey. Victim surveys map crimes against people not the victimization of bureaucracies and institutions, although there are many thefts and acts of criminal damage committed against organizations.[96] There seems to be a severe undercounting of crimes committed against women[97] and ethnic minorities.[98] In time, to be sure, some of these flaws may be corrected and, indeed, recent work has concentrated quite heavily on under-represented populations of victims.[99]

Implications

The quest for criminological evidence is burdensome: it entails an outlay of money, time, and energy. Except for a few instances of indirect evidence, data are rarely *given*. They should more appropriately be called *capta*, items which are

---

[96] See E. Smigel and H. Ross, *Crimes Against Bureaucracy*.
[97] See the Review Symposium in the *British Journal of Criminology*, Apr. 1984.
[98] See T. Jones *et al.*, *The Islington Crime Survey*.
[99] The 1988 *British Crime Survey* is intended to rectify some of these deficiencies.

seized with difficulty. The defects and biases of particular traces cannot therefore be automatically remedied by accumulating a great range of evidence. Commitments must usually be made to a rather restricted group of data. Each group will preclude certain kinds of knowledge and deliver certain truths. For example, a leaning upon the official statistics cannot produce textured deviant histories. It cannot offer much information about deviant interpretations or the private handling of social control. Instead, the criminologist is thrown towards epidemiology, the study of the distribution of events in time and space. By contrast, the participant-observer is not empowered to proclaim the typicality of his group. He has only the most limited foundation for inferences about the population of deviants at large.

A decision to adopt particular methods and particular evidence reflects need, vision, and intention. *Need* is anything but uniform. The requirements of an official in the Home Office or a Ministry of Justice tend to hover around policy and planning issues. They are concerned less with the subtle and intricate facets of deviation, more with the projected size of a prison or criminal population. They turn on demonstrable connections between official action and officially-recorded response. The official statistics lend themselves to the satisfaction of those needs. It was for that very reason that they were compiled. Formal records are rather tangential to the purposes of other criminologists. As we have argued, they do not capture the realities which some sociologists would study. Those who dwell on deviance as an evolving process tend then to ignore the statistics, generating their own alternative methodologies.

By extension, it becomes apparent that need often intersects with vision. It is not easy to extricate one from the other: theories prompt questions and conceptions of what is urgent. The officially-sponsored criminologist would not always feel at home in the academic department. Neither would he define observational methods as useful or appropriate to the real issues of criminology. The intersection can be reinforced by the problems that are typically thrown up in the course of research. Prolonged exposure to the world made visible by statistics will suggest gaps and projects for the future, each being defined and answered by statistical means. It will increase statistical competence, put one in the company of fellow-statisticians, and encourage one to become a reader of statistical journals. All those choices will be at the expense of other pursuits. The cultivation of statistical capacities demands the use of time which might have been otherwise employed. Only the Herculean can now remain in mastery of very disparate skills. The participant-observer will probably become more innumerate as his observational aptitude increases. The statistician will find phenomenological arguments ever more alien and unintelligible.

Forms of evidence, then, tend to be accompanied by forms of theory. Their deployment cannot really be neutral: they lead one to perceive deviance as a property of groups or of individuals, as rooted in profound causes or lodged in the understandings of people immediately involved, as evolving or static, as predicted by theory or unknown before active enquiry. The exponents of various sociological schools drift towards the collection and inspection of appropriate knowledge, disdaining information which others believe significant. The relevant fact of one school is described as trivial or ambiguous by another school. Theories tend to be neatly self-confirming, devaluing all that might upset their reasoning.

3
The University of Chicago Sociology Department

Introduction

We have chosen to present the sociology of deviance chronologically, describing a succession of significant intellectual
episodes. Each episode may be said to have contributed a
distinctive idea or set of ideas, and each is independent enough
to merit separate examination. Some difficult assumptions
underlie such an approach. Theoretical developments are not
neatly insulated from one another. Neither are they arranged
in neat phases. On the contrary, there is much borrowing,
overlapping and ambiguity at the boundaries. Thoughts
emerge from common sources and they frequently flow into
one another. Sometimes, indeed, the principal difference
between theories is their use of language, similar schemes
being expressed in dissimilar vocabularies.[1] And there is
another, minor problem: a history of thought about rule-
breaking is offered no obvious beginning.

The sociology of deviance did not appear full-grown. It was
heralded by abundant work. If sociology is taken to be the
orderly analysis of social life, it is as antique as any other kind of
thinking. It is certainly the case that crime, sin, and sheer difference have been persistent and prominent moral problems.
Thoughtful people have responded in their turn, producing a
body of writings which could properly be called a proto-
criminology. Thus, theology may be understood as a prolonged attempt to make sense of the existence of wickedness.
Legal commentaries invariably dwell on deviance. Plays,
poems, and sagas have repeatedly revolved around the conflict
between good and evil. More particularly, there has been an

[1] See S. Cohen, Preface to *Folk Devils*, 2nd edn.

enduring series of literary and intellectual essays devoted to the subject of crime. This 'shadow criminology' is older than the work of the universities and it is probably more prolific. It is composed of accounts of notorious people, sinister happenings, and awful institutions.[2] In the sixteenth century, particularly, there emerged a kind of 'low-life reporting' which purported to offer detailed information about the underworld.[3] There was a fond description of thieves, thief-takers, prostitutes, and pickpockets, their social organization and careers, their techniques, and their relations with victims. That reporting has continued to flourish. It contains much that is repetitive, conjectural, and fanciful. It also contains a great deal of valuable material and sensible observation. Properly read, it may be recognized as an anticipation of the theorizing that now passes for the sociology of deviance. After all, the stock of plausible analysis is actually rather limited and many ideas are unremarkable. Rudimentary conceptions of anomie,[4] labelling theory,[5] functionalism,[6] and ecology[7] are to be discovered in writings of the seventeenth, eighteenth, and nineteenth centuries. In this sense, the bulk of contemporary criminology is really little more than a reinvention of past explanations. On occasion, too, those shadow criminologists produced work which is still unsurpassed. The ethnography of Henry Mayhew and John Binney, for instance, is quite outstanding. It represents an excellent documentation of the crime of Victorian London.[8] Its scale and attentiveness have not been reproduced again in England.

Shadow criminologists are generally forgotten by academic writers. Some, like Henry Mayhew, Herbert Asbury, and Lucas Pike,[9] deserve much fuller incorporation into sociology. They have suffered a neglect which is unmerited but quite explicable. Sometimes their writing is superficially naïve,

---

[2] For general examples, see A. Hayward (ed.), *Lives of the Most Remarkable Criminals*; A. Griffiths, *The Chronicles of Newgate*; C. Gordon, *The Old Bailey and Newgate*; D. Defoe, *The True and Genuine Account of the Life and Actions of the Late Jonathan Wild*.

[3] See A. Judges, *The Elizabethan Underworld*; J. McMullan, 'Aspects of Professional Crime'.

[4] See T. Nourse, *Campania Foelix*.

[5] See P. Colquhoun, *A Treatise on the Police of the Metropolis*.

[6] See B. Mandeville, *The Fable of the Bees*.

[7] See T. Beames, *The Rookeries of London*.

[8] H. Mayhew, *London Labour and the London Poor*, Vol. 4.

[9] See H. Asbury, *The Gangs of New York*; L. Pike, *A History of Crime in England*.

developed without the conventional forms of scholarship. Indeed, much of it was published before those forms were established. They worked outside universities and did not address a university audience. Their ideas display discontinuities, lacking an incremental or evolutionary character. More importantly, their authors were recruited from very diverse backgrounds and they acquired little organizational support. They were variously journalists, playwrights, prison chaplains, magistrates, novelists, policemen, and lawyers. Because they were rarely retained as professional experts on crime, their interest in criminological problems could not but be sporadic, and their skills could not be transmitted to a body of students who would succeed them. After all, it is only very recently that the university syllabus has expanded to cover the projects which they initiated.

The University of Chicago sociology department was distinctive because it accomplished a decisive break with the haphazard, solitary, and ill-maintained studies which we have identified as proto-sociology. Speculation about crime and allied processes became orderly. The department's first chairman, Albion Small, transformed sociology into a permanent and co-operative enterprise. He employed people to become professional social investigators, teaching what they had learned and how they had learned it to others. Modelled on the research seminar of the German university,[10] their work was a continuous, busy, and integrated attack on academic problems. James Carey observed: 'the first systematic group-related efforts to apply sociological knowledge were made in Chicago during the second and third decades of this century.'[11] Everett Hughes observed that 'in Europe various philosophically minded persons had written books about something called "sociology"' but 'the Department of Sociology at Chicago . . . was really the first big and lasting one in the country; thus, also the world'.[12] Leonard Broom observed: 'in Chicago, sociology was implanted in American academic life and after that nothing was the same.'[13] Albion Small himself stated that,

---

[10] See E. Shils, 'Tradition, Ecology and Institution in the History of Sociology'.
[11] J. Carey, *Sociology and Public Affairs*, 9.
[12] E. Hughes, Preface to W. Raushenbush, *Robert Park*, vii.
[13] L. Broom, Preface to R. Faris, *Chicago Sociology 1920–1932*, xi.

before the founding of his department, sociology was 'more of a yearning than a substantial body of knowledge, a fixed point of view, or a rigorous method of research'.[14] If these claims are even partially warranted, it would seem that the creation of the University of Chicago provides an appropriate opening for the history of the sociology of deviance. Marxism flourished in Europe, the *Annales* group was active in France, the Manchester and London statistical societies performed significant work, but it was at Chicago that sociology was industrialized. Thereafter, there appeared a more or less coherent criminology.

The University, the Department and the City

It is a veritable Babel, in which some thirty or more tongues are spoken. . . . Gunmen haunt its streets, and a murder is committed in them nearly every day in the year.[15]

The University of Chicago was an extraordinary invention. It was designed to be a nonpareil. It was taken to be the only instance of a major university being established anew.[16] Rockefeller donated thirty-five million dollars to found a university; William Harper, its first president, proceeded to rape other institutions by offering their staff salaries which were virtually double those normally paid; and a number of departments were established almost simultaneously. The sociology department was itself constituted in 1892. Those processes were of great consequence for the shaping of criminological work: sociology was not a late-comer to be resisted or dominated by better-entrenched disciplines; there was a freedom to appoint those who were commonly regarded as uncommonly able; and there was ample funding for research. Moreover, innovation was defined as the distinguishing feature of the university. Thus Leonard Cottrell recalled that '[we were] rejecting all the traditional answers and institutions that were allegedly the stabilizers of society'.[17] Such rejection could not but be propitious for the development of sociology. After all,

[14] A. Small, 'Fifty Years of Sociology in the United States', 802.
[15] Chatfield-Taylor, quoted in H. Zorbaugh, *The Gold Coast and the Slum*, 1.
[16] See R. Faris, *Chicago Sociology*, 22.
[17] Quoted in J. Carey, *Sociology and Public Affairs*, 154.

the academic legitimacy of the discipline was slight. There was no earlier generation of professional sociologists; the very respectability and tenability of the approach were disputed; and the qualifications of the Chicago department were meagre enough. Few of the department's members had been able to study sociology in any formal setting. They stemmed, instead, from philosophy, biology, religion, journalism, and linguistics. One of the most distinguished Chicago sociologists, Robert Park, claimed never to have heard the word 'sociology' whilst he was a student at the University of Michigan between 1883 and 1887. Indeed, no university course was offered in sociology during that period.[18]

The tentative and unformed nature of American sociology revealed itself in the rather lengthy period of time that lapsed before the Chicago department came into its own. Some of the early appointments were to display little interest in the creation and dissemination of an academic sociology. It was only later that a special working organization and array of styles emerged, an array that could be identified as distinctive of Chicago. Those who fashioned that style were principally of the second generation.[19] As we discuss their works, it must be remembered that we are telling a history within a context set by the sociology of deviance. Others, like Bulmer[20] and Faris,[21] would tell a different story. So manifest were the achievements of the Chicago department that it is possible to trace their influence on functionalism, epidemiology, attitude research, survey methods, and much else. Our own focus will be on the social anthropological and ecological study of deviance, and its chief author was Robert Park, who was to become head of the Chicago department. In 1915, Park published an article that was to become a manifesto for urban ethnography. 'The City' described a problem, a programme, and a procedure:

Anthropology, the science of man, has been mainly concerned up to the present with the study of primitive peoples. But civilized man is quite as interesting an object of investigation, and at the same time his life is more open to observation and study. Urban life and culture

[18] See W. Raushenbush, *Robert Park*, 78.
[19] See J. Short (ed.), *The Social Fabric of the Metropolis*, xiv.
[20] See M. Bulmer, *The Chicago School*.
[21] R. Faris, op. cit.

are more varied, subtle and complicated, but the fundamental motives are in both instances the same. The same patient methods of observation which anthropologists like Boas and Lowie have expended on the study of the life and manners of the North American Indians might be even more fruitfully employed in the investigation of the customs, beliefs, social practices, and general conceptions of life prevalent in Little Italy on the Lower Side in Chicago, or in recording the more sophisticated folkways of the inhabitants of Greenwich Village and the neighborhood of Washington Square, New York.[22]

Most sociology departments are inattentive to the physical and social contexts in which they exist. The 'Frankfurt School' left no record of Frankfurt. Perhaps there is no 'necessary' reason why sociologists should concentrate on the environment which is immediately about them. Most prefer to dwell on relatively abstract or global matters. But Chicago sociology was to become the sociology of Chicago itself, a detailed anthropological mapping of the social territories that made the city. Its particular thrust must be explained by the interplay between some peculiar phenomena and a peculiar responsiveness.

The city of Chicago was an exploding mosaic of contrasting social worlds. Its growth was extraordinary, advancing as it did from a small log fort in 1833 to a substantial city in 1900: 'the newspapers show the city of Chicago amazed at itself from its very beginnings . . . The population expansion was spectacular.'[23] The bulk of that expansion was fed by immigrants from a succession of exporting countries: Ireland, Sweden, Germany, Poland, and Italy. Each group had to make a place for itself in the city. Each had to confront a series of recurring problems. Urban life resembled a phantasmagoria, a welter of shifting scenes and identities. As Park observed, 'everything is in a state of agitation—everything seems to be undergoing a change. Society is, apparently, not much more than a congeries and constellation of social atoms.'[24]

It is not unusual for burgeoning cities to attract a fascinated gaze. In its time, London was itself thought to be an extraordinary object, revealing a vast kaleidoscope of new social

[22] R. Park and E. Burgess (eds.), The City, 3.
[23] R. Faris, Chicago Sociology.
[24] R. Park, 'Community Organization and Juvenile Delinquency', 107.

combinations and possibilities. Victorian journalists and novelists devoted themselves to reporting the strange and remarkable events that unfolded in the city. But their fascination could not prepare the foundation of an enduring scholarship. It passed away. It was the Chicago sociology department that allowed curiosity to become a stable tradition. Itself influenced by the work of journalists like Lincoln Steffens and by the newspaper experience of Park, the department sought to document interesting worlds before they altered and disappeared.[25] The city was to be grasped as a laboratory in which all the nuances and interconnections of social life could be observed.[26]

The Roots of Responsiveness

As long as one continues *talking*, intellectualism remains in undisturbed possession of the field. The return to life can't come about by talking. It is an *act*; to make you return to life, I must set an example for your imitation, I must deafen you to talk, by showing you, as Bergson does, that the concepts we talk with are made for purposes of *practice* and not for purposes of insight.[27]

We do not propose to offer a lengthy commentary on the intellectual development of sociology at Chicago. That development is intricate and complicated and its analysis cannot be easily compressed.[28] However, it is imperative to stress that the responsiveness of the Chicago School did not arise out of a mere journalistic impulse. Neither was it an 'obvious' reaction to the beguiling qualities of a city undergoing rapid transformation. It was the fruit of a carefully resolved philosophy of thought and action, a philosophy which emphasized the primacy of practice. Many, although not all, Chicago sociologists were wedded to two principal schools, pragmatism and formalism. It was the fusing of those schools that produced the strain towards focused, grounded studies of observable social scenes.

The pragmatism of Charles Peirce, William James, and

[25] See E. Hughes, 'Robert E. Park'.
[26] See R. Park, 'The City as a Social Laboratory'.
[27] W. James, *A Pluralistic Universe*, 290.
[28] For a fuller account of that development see P. Rock, *The Making of Symbolic Interactionism*.

John Dewey extracted themes from German philosophy and translated them into a radical phrasing of the nature of knowledge. In brief, they maintained that knowledge resided neither in properties of the world alone nor in properties of the observer alone. Facts, it was held, are not self-evident. They are selected and interpreted by the mind that surveys them. People with different perspectives and different problems will not see exactly the same phenomena. On the contrary, they will respond to those facets of phenomena which answer particular purposes.[29] Thus the meaning of food will not be identical for the chef, the chemist, the waiter, and the guest at a meal. It will shift in response to the peculiar dealings which one has with the object. But that shift is not wholly dependent on the whim of the contemplating intelligence. The imagination is not free to create anything which it may choose to devise. It is constrained by the capacity of the world to answer back and impose itself upon thought.[30] Hence it came about that pragmatism placed effective knowledge in a transaction between the observer and the environment which he observed: knowledge was no longer defined as a state or as a condition but as a *process*, as action, and it was alleged that 'the problems of perception and science are straightened out when looked at from the standpoint of action, while they remain obscure and obscuring when we regard them from the standpoint of a knowledge defined in antithesis to action'.[31] Useful understanding proceeded from the activities of an engaged intellect which explored practical problems. It proceeded from experiences anchored in the world. Experience was to become elevated to a pre-eminent position: it was the guarantee of valid knowledge. Formal speculation was a pallid and misleading substitute for personal acquaintance with phenomena: 'It is the personal experience of those best qualified in our circle of knowledge to *have* experience, to tell us *what is*. Now what does *thinking about* the experience of those persons come to, compared to directly and personally feeling it as they feel it? The philosophers are dealing in shades, while those who live and feel know truth.'[32]

[29] See J. Dewey, 'The Reflex Arc Concept in Social Psychology'.
[30] See C. Peirce quoted in C. Mills, *Sociology and Pragmatism*, 158.
[31] J. Dewey, 'Perception and Organic Action', 648.
[32] W. James, *Pragmatism*, 30.

Such an extolling of experience brings copious problems in its train. It leads to a systematic distrust of systematic reasoning, of the writings of others, and of analysis. As George Herbert Mead remarked, 'our own experience in so far as it is not reflective does not involve knowledge. . . . Experiences simply are . . .'[33] Any attempt to distance oneself from experience and to describe it is a betrayal of the raw process of immediate involvement in action. It is a qualitatively different form of understanding, different from experience itself and not readily transformed back into it. Pragmatism evidently tends towards becoming self-silencing, denying the possibility of prolonged exposition and explanation. It threatens to end itself.

Robert Park was one of the major architects of the rescue of pragmatism and its transformation into a practicable sociology. He had studied under William James, and he recalled that James had taught him 'the real world was the experience of actual men and women and not abbreviated and shorthand descriptions of it that we call knowledge'.[34] Park had also studied under Georg Simmel in Germany,[35] and Simmel's formal sociology provided a limited resolution to the difficulties posed by pragmatism. Formalism held that it was the task of sociology to explore the structures of social activity and that those structures could be regarded as independent of the settings in which they appeared. In one sense, every social occasion is unique. It will never return with an identical history, context, and membership. In another sense, it is but part of a wider display of formal processes. For example, the Inland Revenue has a number of offices which are utterly distinct. No office is quite the same as any other: it houses different people with different pasts, problems, and ambitions. Yet it is also an instance of the operation of hierarchy, which is a general feature, of bureaucracy, which is also general, and of a limited conflict with taxpayers, which is general too. Simmel would argue that it is possible to examine hierarchy, bureaucracy, and conflict as more or less autonomous forms which manifest themselves in very diverse contents. It is those forms which are

[33] G. Mead, 'The Philosophy of John Dewey', 74.
[34] R. Park, quoted in W. Raushenbush, *Robert Park*, 29.
[35] See 'The Life Histories of W. I. Thomas and Robert E. Park'; L. Brauda, ' "Park and Burgess": An Appreciation'; and the Preface to R. Park, *The Crowd and the Public*.

analysable, not the contents themselves. Grafted onto pragmatism, formalism permitted a restricted description of an otherwise indescribable experience. It became feasible to abstract, discuss, and compare examples of social action.

Together, pragmatism and formalism brought about a special phrasing of sociological work. It was argued that the business of research is to understand the social world, and the social world is itself manufactured by the practical experience of those who live in it. It is on that experience that sociology must concentrate, not on some alternative order which theory predicts. Theory deals with a realm of 'facts' and processes which is less solid than the concrete personal knowledge of those who actually produce the behaviour that is to be explained. Thus Park argued that 'sociology is not interested in facts, not even in social facts as they are commonly understood ... Sociology wants to know how people re-act to so-called facts, to what is happening to them'.[36] And Louis Wirth argued: 'the important features of each cultural situation are not immediately evident to the observer and do not constitute objectively determinable data. They must be seen in terms of the subjective experiences and attitudes of ... individuals.'[37]

Practical experiences themselves are responses to situations and problems, and they change as those problems change. Indeed, the very task of working on a problem transforms it with characteristic repercussions on one's knowledge of it. In turn, sociology is not devoted to the study of states but of *processes*, of things and people in change. It must be so organized that it can observe and report processes over time. It must also be so organized that it can reach those processes practically and not by surmise and logic alone. The most effective research strategy requires sociologists to participate personally in the world which they would analyse. Without such participation, knowledge is not experience but an uncertain commentary on experience. So Park urged a student embarking on an exploration of a religious sect in Los Angeles[38] to 'think and feel Molokan'.[39]

[36] Quoted in W. Raushenbush, *Robert Park*, 112.
[37] L. Wirth, 'Culture Conflict and Misconduct', 240.
[38] P. Young, *The Pilgrims of Russian Town*.
[39] Quoted in R. Faris, *Chicago Sociology*, 71.

Largely unimpressed by truths and essences which could not be delivered by experience and observation, the Chicago sociologists tended to proceed to the small social scenes which lent themselves to anthropological research. In particular, they moved out to the territories which adjoined the university. Organized class visits were made to the ethnic communities which littered Chicago, 'term papers and dissertations naturally followed, and in time, research volumes'.[40] Research training itself typically consisted of a number of seminars which culminated in an instruction to leave the university for the streets. There were studies of gangs,[41] organized crime,[42] prostitution,[43] taxi-dance halls,[44] real estate offices,[45] local newspapers,[46] the rooming house district,[47] hobohemia,[48] the central business district,[49] and the Poles,[50] Blacks,[51] and Jews[52] of Chicago. Collectively, 'they seem to have emerged as the most durable and widely used bases for describing the community life of the city.'[53]

Ecology

We have argued that the description of experience using experience was tempered by Simmel's formalism. Social forms were held to be relatively abstract structures creating a kind of architecture of experience. Any situation could be described simultaneously in terms of its unique and its general properties. Those general properties were features that seemed to cut across particular events and give them a common history and a common character. Conflict, assimilation, succession, symbiosis, co-operation, and invasion are processes which appear to transform events in predictable ways. For certain

---

[40] R. Faris, *Chicago Society*, 70.   [41] See F. Thrasher, *The Gang*.
[42] See J. Landesco, *Organized Crime in Chicago*.
[43] See W. Reckless, 'The Distribution of Commercialized Vice in the City'.
[44] See P. Cressey, *The Taxi-Dance Hall*.
[45] See E. Hughes, *The Growth of an Institution: The Chicago Real Estate Board*.
[46] See R. Park, *The Immigrant Press and its Control*.
[47] See H. Zorbaugh, *The Gold Coast*.   [48] See N. Anderson, *The Hobo*.
[49] See E. Johnson, 'The Function of the Central Business District in the Metropolitan Community'.
[50] See W. Thomas and F. Znaniecki, *The Polish Peasant in Europe and America*.
[51] See S. Drake and H. Cayton, *Black Metropolis*.   [52] See L. Wirth, *The Ghetto*.
[53] G. Suttles, *The Social Construction of Communities*, 5.

purposes, it is practically irrelevant whether conflict is waged between the partners of a marriage, street gangs, or nations. It is still conflict and manifests a number of those special qualities which are peculiar to conflict.

City life and urbanization were analysed by one collection of master forms which had been borrowed from biology. They were represented as the workings of an ecological order. Ecology is an emphasis on the patterns and organized changes which are produced by different species living together in the same physical territory. The development of a biological ecology was attractive to sociologists who were searching for metaphors and principles to advance their own rather incoherent discipline. It proved especially attractive to those who were seeking to explain the evolution of different human groups in the geographical context of the city. Just as plants, insects, and animals translate a physical terrain into a mosaic of distinct communities so people become separated into a network of unlike communities which form an intelligible whole. As Wirth remarked, 'whatever else men are, they are also animals, and as such they exhibit the effects of physical aggregation and of their habitat.'[54]

Biological ecology was rarely taken to be more than a convenient working description of an otherwise excessively complex process. It was acknowledged from the first that human communities are constructed on quite unique principles. People are capable of detaching themselves from their 'own' territories; they display rational behaviour; they can organize themselves into institutions which impose a distinct order; their works are modified by an elaborate technology; their activities are shaped by conscious planning; and they are governed by a symbolism which interprets and changes what they do.[55] Moreover, ecology was not regarded as a total explanation. It was but a 'segmental view'[56] which neglected much. With perhaps two exceptions, the Chicago sociologists tended to refer to ecology as a useful metaphor which ought not to be applied with full seriousness. Many, indeed, appear to have made a mere token bow before a theory which they largely

[54] L. Wirth, 'Human Ecology', 178.
[55] See R. Park, 'The City', 4. L. Wirth, 'Human Ecology', 180.
[56] L. Wirth, 'Human Ecology', 188.

ignored. Nevertheless, ecology offered a systematic framework for analysing the flowering of interrelated social worlds:

The city is not merely an artefact, but an organism. Its growth is, fundamentally and as a whole, natural, i.e. uncontrolled and un-designed. The forms it tends to assume are those which represent and correspond to the functions it is called upon to perform. What have been called the 'natural areas of the city' are simply those regions whose locations, character, and functions have been deter-mined by the same forces which have determined the character and function of the city as a whole.[57]

Of principal interest to the Chicago sociologists was the manner in which cities expand and become internally differen-tiated. The emergence of Chicago itself was explained by what came to be known as the zonal hypothesis, the contention that cities evolve in a series of concentric zones of activity and life. At the very centre is the business district which is typified by a small residential population and high property values. About it is the zone in transition whose population is fluid and poor, whose housing is deteriorating and whose stability is threat-ened by the encroaching business district. About that zone, in turn, are areas of working-class housing, middle-class housing, and, on the fringes, suburbia. Each zone is itself composed of diverse 'natural areas' which abut on one another. They are natural because they are not entirely intended, because they represent unplanned groupings of like people, and because they manifest a rough correspondence to the territorial division of species in nature:

In the course of time every section and quarter of the city takes on something of the character and qualities of its inhabitants. Each separate part of the city is inevitably stained with the peculiar sentiments of its population. The effect of this is to convert what was at first a mere geographical expression into a neighborhood, that is to say, a locality with sentiments, traditions, and a history of its own.[58]

Deviance, Crime, and Pathology

It was not the express ambition of the Chicago sociologists to focus on deviance. Deviant populations formed but one

---

[57] R. Park, foreword to L. Wirth, *The Ghetto*, viii–ix.　　　[58] R. Park, 'The City', 6.

segment of the city and they were no more engaging than any other. But they were discernible strains which encouraged the development of criminology. One was the funding and sponsorship provided by a variety of voluntary organizations which sought solutions to social problems. Another was a leaning towards practical intervention which had originated with Small and was retained by many of his staff. A third was the sheer availability of deviance: graduate students, in particular, were ill-equipped to study any but the relatively undefended and exposed neighbourhoods in the zone in transition. Other areas demanded of students an assurance, patronage, and support which were difficult to secure.

What was impressive and obvious to the urban anthropologist was the massive concentration of 'pathological behaviour' in the zone in transition. Partly because of its great visibility, such behaviour appeared to be confined to a limited territorial belt. Within that belt there was a piling-up of all those phenomena that are conventionally identified as social problems: mental disorder, prostitution, suicide, alcoholism, infant mortality, juvenile delinquency, crime, disease, and poverty.[59] The incidence of pathology could be plotted with data collected from court records, census reports, and special surveys. Deviance may have been present elsewhere but it was hugely conspicuous in the transitional zone and, as Lemert remarked, the early criminologists imitated Custer's men by riding to the sound of the guns.[60]

Analytically, the significance of the zone in transition was that it seemed to possess a distinctive social organization which could not be explained simply by the characteristics of the populations who lived there.[61] An area with the cheapest rents, an appreciable circulation of inhabitants, and few settled institutions, it tended to be the home of the most recent generation of immigrants. National group after national group lived there. Each in its turn reproduced the same patterns of behaviour. Above all, it produced crime. Part of the Chicago project then turned on the explanation of how deviance arose in a particular quarter of the city.

[59] See R. Faris and H. Dunham, *Mental Disorders in Urban Areas*.
[60] E. Lemert, *Social Pathology*.
[61] See C. Shaw and H. McKay, *Juvenile Delinquency and Urban Areas*.

The zone in transition was taken to be unruly. It housed people who were unaccustomed to one another, to city life, and to America. Lacking substantial resources and deserting much that had been familiar, they were required to establish a way of life in a difficult and shifting environment. One of the prime problems which they faced was the sheer array of different worlds around them. When the inner composition and external relations of those worlds appeared unstable, the whole invited the description of social disorganization. Disorganization was a face of moral dissensus: 'the degree to which the members of a society lose their common understandings, i.e. the degree to which consensus is undermined, is the measure of a society's state of disorganization.'[62] Disorganization also characterized the fragmented, the fluid, and the anonymous elements of urban life: 'contacts are extended, heterogeneous groups mingle, neighborhoods disappear, and people, deprived of local and family ties, are forced to live under . . . loose, transient and impersonal relations.'[63]

Disorganization is a most awkward conception which deserves some reflection. At one level many sociologists shun it because they are ill-prepared to entertain the idea of social disorder. Their own orderly systems of explanation are calculated to confer a measure of coherence on what they discuss. The very idea of disorder suggests that coherent analysis may be unattainable and the sociologist is correspondingly belittled. Thus Matza claimed that the Chicago School wrote of disorganization when they actually described diversity.[64] Diversity lends itself to schematic theory. Disorganization does not.

Ultimately, it would seem that there can be no sociology of disorder. But the theoretical stance of the Chicago School did tolerate the presence of *some* disorganization. After all, it was not designed to produce a body of interconnected laws which made everything harmonious.

None the less, an allusion to disorganization tends to inject other problems into analysis. Almost any prolonged period of observation seems capable of revealing intelligible patterns in even the most chaotic situations. Indeed, Whyte asserted that

---

[62] L. Wirth, 'Ideological Aspects of Social Disorganization', 46.

[63] L. Wirth, 'Culture Conflict', 236.

[64] See D. Matza, *Becoming Deviant*.

reference to social disorganization merely signifies that the observer has not understood what has been seen.[65] There will always remain the insoluble problem of whether the observer has recognized or imposed the patterns which have been discerned, yet the Chicago sociologists who talked of disorganization went to the jungles of Hobohemia and the streets of the slums and unearthed what they described as very real social structures. Their discovery of structure and order makes the term 'disorganization' appear inappropriate and in need of redefinition. At the very least, it is clear that the word was used in an unfamiliar manner. It was not actually intended to refer to an utter collapse of order. As we have argued, the Chicago sociologists displayed an unusual ability to find organization in hitherto uncharted areas. In their work, 'disorganization' points to two distinct but occasionally linked properties of social life. One such property is the reduction of social relations to a rather rudimentary condition in which mistrust, heterogeneity, and change abound. In that condition, new opportunities and combinations arise and disappear with some rapidity. Old habits are broken.[66] Life becomes unpredictable. Cohesiveness is threatened. The dependable group shrinks in size. A world so disorganized possesses a palpable order, but it is an uncomfortable order which is sensed as *comparatively* vestigial and unreliable.[67] Such a world is both more and less complicated than one conventionally defined as organized. It has its own complexities and intricacies which demand a particularly delicate analysis.[68] For its inhabitants, the negotiation of relations in uncertainty is fraught, fragile, and problematic.[69] Thus defined, disorganization is mainly a facet of *experience* and, curiously, the experience of disorganization can itself be highly organized.

On a more elevated analytic plane, disorganization could be described as a property of the wider social structure. It would then refer to the relations *between* and not within worlds. Social differentiation, a period of excited social change, or uneven

[65] W. Whyte, *Street Corner Society*.
[66] See R. Park, 'Community Organization', 107.
[67] See K. Erikson, *In the Wake of the Flood*.
[68] See G. Suttles, *The Social Order of the Slum*.
[69] See L. Rainwater, *Behind Ghetto Walls*; G. Suttles, 'The Defended Neighborhood', in *The Social Construction of Communities*.

development can exaggerate the instability of those relations, leading to strain and a breakdown of local order. In turn, particular worlds can become dislocated, thrown up out of their context and exposed. They can achieve a social and moral independence which some sociologists have chosen to emphasize. In one sense, the zone in transition was wholly dependent on the city which surrounded it. In another, it could be cast as an isolated and deregulated area, an area uncontrolled by the 'master institutions' of society. Church, law, school, and commonplace morality were thought to have no sway there. Thus a criminal area may be organized, and its wider environments may be organized, but there is little or no articulation between them. Whyte described one instance, the Boston North End of the 1930s: 'Cornerville's problem is not lack of organization but failure of its own social organization to mesh with the structure of the society around it. This accounts for the development of the local political and racket organization and also for the loyalty which people bear toward their race and toward Italy.'[70]

'Disorganization' may be an unfortunate word for such a lack of integration. The idea is better conveyed by the metaphor of the geological fault. But it is evident what was meant. Cornerville and areas like it are akin to the old thieves' quarters of the European cities. They possessed a peculiar character, at once attached and detached. Neatly delimited, they seemed to justify an ethnographic response.

Integral to the conception of disorganization was the companion idea of indiscipline. Those who stressed internal disorder could cite numerous obstructions to social control. Moral habits could not be properly implanted.[71] People were neither effectively curbed, nor could they curb one another. They did not know each other well, formed few commitments to the area or to its population, were confused by moral diversity, and were loath to intervene in the affairs of their fellows.[72] Morality could no longer be taken for granted. It became relativistic and circumstantial, readily adapted for selfish purposes, permitting the evolution of extenuating accounts. More particularly, its influence

[70] W. Whyte, *Street Corner Society*, 273.
[71] See R. Park, 'Community Organization'.
[72] See L. Wirth, 'Culture Conflict'.

could not extend very far. Those entitled to exercise moral claims were confined to their family and immediate neighbours, all others becoming moral strangers. Such 'amoral familialism' transformed the zone in transition into an unsettled and unsafe region which abounded in potential victims. Fighting gangs might have been represented as a rudimentary effort to defend territory and impose security on the neighbourhood.[73] But they committed violent acts of law-breaking which exacerbated insecurity.

All these conspicuous moral and structural infirmities could become amplified. The inhabitants of the zone in transition had often been immigrants from Europe or the country. Their lives had been punctuated by cultural discontinuities which became especially taxing for the second generation.[74] Language, custom, and religion could fall into disuse or change significance. The children of immigrants sometimes declared themselves marginal to the new world of the native American and the discarded world of their parents. Morally displaced, economically and politically peripheral, they might innovate. Most typically they created a social order which corresponded to neither world but was a shifting amalgam of both.[75] They also improvised new styles, styles which could well embrace delinquency.[76] A resort to crime was defined as a possible solution to the dilemmas of exclusion and impotence. The racketeer and hustler consequently attained a special local importance: 'what needs to be appreciated is the element of genuine popularity of the gangster, home-grown in the neighborhood gang, idealized in the morality of the neighborhood.'[77]

The experience of social disorganization could thus redefine deviance. Those who did not subscribe to the novel definition were usually without effective power. Local politics and local crime were intertwined, supporting one another and recruiting the same people.[78] Police forces in the United States are radically decentralized, placed under the authority of local

[73] See G. Suttles, *The Social Construction of Communities*.
[74] See W. Thomas and F. Znaniecki, *The Polish Peasant*.
[75] See H. Lopota, 'The Function of Voluntary Associations'.
[76] See C. Shaw, *The Natural History of a Delinquent Career*.
[77] J. Landesco, *Organized Crime in Chicago*, 169.
[78] Ibid.

politicians, and vulnerable to 'community control'.[79] There were few voluntary associations to press for the expulsion or disciplining of the disreputable.[80] Even if they *were* pressed, the police might not comply: corruption and administrative strategy conspired to contain deviance in segregated territories where it could be monitored. There was a corresponding growth of prostitution, gambling, and illegal markets in the zone in transition. Deviant life-styles were encouraged commercially and administratively. Territorial reputations were established. People were sifted: 'each urban area . . . has its own moral code. A population seeks an area in which its members can be gratified with the least amount of interference.'[81] In turn:

What lends special importance to the segregation of the poor, the vicious, the criminal, and exceptional persons generally, which is so characteristic a feature of city life, is the fact that social contagion tends to stimulate in divergent types the common temperamental differences, and to suppress characters which unite them with the normal types about them. Associations with others of their own ilk provides also not merely a stimulus, but a moral support for the traits they have in common which they would not find in a less select society.[82]

The Normal and the Pathological

It should be observed that not all the sociologists practising at the University of Chicago were in accord with one another. Moreover, their ideas evolved over time and reflected social changes in the city itself. The crimes that were described ranged from petty delinquency to organized crime. Different features were emphasized as analysis moved from argument to argument. The explanation of criminality thus contained a number of apparent contradictions. Inconsistency would not have exercised the Chicago sociologists: they were not engaged in a quest for a single scheme which laid all bare. Indeed, Wirth claimed 'in the face of the imposing series of exploded theories

[79] See W. Miller, *Cops and Bobbies*.
[80] See W. Reckless, 'The Distribution of Commercialized Vice'.
[81] L.Wirth, *The Ghetto*, 285–6.
[82] R. Park, 'The City', 45.

of criminality, prudence dictates that a new theory avoid the persistent error of claiming universal applicability.'[83] But inconsistency *is* there. There is much that refers to the instability and pathology of the disorganized zone in transition. There is also the theme that crime is an unremarkable consequence of normal conditions. In this latter sense, deviance is allowed to escape what has been identified as the 'like-causes-like fallacy'. Few sociologists would baldly champion the assertion that displeasing phenomena *must* have their origins in displeasing conditions. However, many do quietly advance that argument by concentrating the search for the roots of crime in certain areas: the slum, poverty, low intelligence, exploitative capitalism, or family breakdown. The Chicago sociologists had no binding commitment to the discovery of any particular kind of explanation. On the contrary, they sacrificed theorizing to a version of anthropology which required a confrontation with the unexpected and the unpalatable. Deviance was encountered in a host of confusing and detailed settings. It was difficult to reduce its explanation to a single cause. It was as difficult to explain it by pathological causes alone.

The ethnographic strain in Chicago sociology emphasized moral diversity rather than discord or disorganization. It mirrored John Dewey's pluralistic realism, a philosophy which urged the existence of numerous and equally authentic truths.[84] Dewey had defined truth as situated and local, a matter of the practical experience of people managing particular problems. So too some sociologists analysed morality as parochial and contingent. Society became a great mosaic of social worlds which celebrated diverse forms of conduct. Deviance was a possible attribute of a world, another form of conduct, and it had to be explored as an embedded feature of social organization. It was not merely an absence of order or an assault upon order.

Crime and delinquency were principally attributed to the effects of the isolation of certain natural areas. Deviance became a surrogate social order, an alternative pattern, which replaced the workings of conventional institutions.[85] Its forms

---

[83] L. Wirth, 'Culture Conflict', 229.
[84] See J. Dewey, 'Realism without Monism or Dualism—II'.
[85] See F. Thrasher, *The Gang*.

were themselves explained as a functional response to deprivation, to the structure imported by immigrants, and to the
experience of growing up in the city. Deprived of political
control and economic resources, the earliest immigrants generated their own shadow politics and shadow economy. They
produced rackets and illegal markets in which men of practical
influence distributed protection and patronage. It was a
scheme shaped by older conceptions of order. In Cornerville,
for instance, the Italian Catholics recognized an affinity
between the practical organization of their community and the
wider order of the Church and Heaven. The world was held to
be hierarchical, divided into big people and little people. Just
as saints intercede with God on behalf of sinners, so police
captains might intercede on behalf of those given a traffic ticket.
Social conduct hinged on networks of obligation which bound
one to local people and substituted personal morality for a
more impersonal subordination to law.[86] It was those networks
and the reputations which were secured in them that confined
the person living in the zone in transition. People *did* move
away, sometimes in groups, but such movement often represented a betrayal:

To get ahead, the Cornerville man must move either in the world of
business and Republican politics or in the world of Democratic
politics and the rackets. He cannot move in both worlds at once; they
are so far apart that there is hardly any connection between them. If
he advances in the first world, he is recognized in Cornerville only as
an alien to the district. If he advances in the second world, he
achieves recognition in Cornerville, but becomes a social outcast to
respectable people elsewhere. The entire course of the corner boy's
training in the social life of his district prepares him for a career in the
rackets or in Democratic politics.[87]

Children raised in the crowded zone in transition led an
intensely public life, playing with others on the street, forming
into small groups which could eventually crystallize into gangs.
Such exposure placed the child under constant surveillance
from others. From an early age, he was awarded a communal
identity and reputation. In an insecure environment, the

---

[86] Cf. H. Gans, *The Urban Villagers*.
[87] W. Whyte, *Street Corner Society*, 273–4.

preservation of reputation acquired strategic importance. Responsibilities and claims revolved around one's public character. Teasing play repeatedly tested the validity and credibility of character. It became vital to retain face by supporting and initiating joint projects in which reputations could be established or lost. Much of the early delinquency described by Thrasher consisted of a playfulness and a daring: stealing fruit from stalls and stores, impertinence to authority, and playing truant. Ignored, it might progress in no discernible direction, although adult criminality was possible. Identified as law-breaking, the group could achieve a new imagery in an environment which had lost some of its opportunities. Managed as boyishness, the beginnings of delinquency could be channelled into organized sports and neutralized. What *is* significant is the persistence of tradition in the zone in transition. Ideas of conduct are passed on from generation to generation of boys living the public lives of the street: 'to a very great extent . . . traditions of delinquency are preserved and transmitted through the medium of social contact with the unsupervised play group and the more highly organized delinquent and criminal gangs.'[88]

In some measure, it became normal for young people to flirt with delinquency. Those who did not do so were unusually cloistered, marginal, or ostracized.[89] Delinquency was no longer portrayed by the Chicago sociologists as an undertaking which only pathological people could contemplate. It became commonplace, petty, and open in its implications for future experience and conduct. More particularly, it became the basis of a career which people might abandon or change unless they were under unusual constraint. Autobiographies and extended interviews were employed to grasp the development of deviance over time, an emphasis being given to the delinquent's own comprehension of his life.[90] That development was placed in the context of peculiar meanings and distinct subworlds: 'if we fail to see that a gang has a moral code of its own—however immoral it may appear to the rest of us—we will not be able to understand the solidarity, the courage and the self-sacrifice of

---

[88] C. Shaw and H. McKay, 'Male Juvenile Delinquency and Group Behavior', 260.
[89] Cf. W. Reckless *et al.*, 'The Good Boy in a High Delinquency Area'.
[90] See C. Shaw, *The Jack-Roller*; E. Sutherland, *The Professional Thief*.

which gangsters are capable.'[91] Thus, criminology became an exercise in practical social anthropology, a disinterested analysis of strange peoples and customs.

The social anthropology of deviance has survived. As we shall argue, it is at the core of symbolic interactionism. In part, survival was made possible in a dark time by the enthusiasm of Edwin Sutherland, once a student at the University of Chicago and eventually a professor at the University of Indiana. During the 1930s and 1940s, and in a period when the University of Chicago sociology department was in partial eclipse, Sutherland and his students (and Donald Cressey in particular) became the tenacious champions of the argument that deviance is a way of life passed from generation to generation. First advanced in 1934, his theory of differential association attempted to make systematic the thesis that crime and deviation are culturally transmitted in social groups. It was laid out as a series of numbered propositions, taking on the appearance of formal theory and intended to be a general explanation of crime. Differential association theory holds that criminal behaviour is learned in interaction with other people, especially in intimate personal settings, in a process of communication. Learning is held to embrace techniques of committing the crime and the direction of drives, motives, attitudes, and definitions of the law. It is argued that a person will become criminal if he or she is exposed to an excess of definitions favourable to the violation of the law over definitions unfavourable to violation of the law, the process itself being described as differential association. Such differential association will be affected by variations in frequency, duration, priority, and intensity. Learning criminal behaviour is supposed to involve all the social and psychological mechanisms at work in other learning. Finally, it is claimed that, although criminal behaviour is an expression of general needs and values, it is not explained by those general needs and values because non-criminal behaviour is also an expression of those same needs and values.[92] Sutherland and his followers plotted the workings of differential association in white-collar crime[93] (a phrase invented by

[91] L. Wirth, 'Culture Conflict', 237–8.
[92] E. Sutherland and D. Cressey, *Principles of Criminology*.
[93] E. Sutherland, *White Collar Crime*.

Sutherland himself), professional crime,[94] embezzlement,[95] and even seemingly motiveless crime. An absence of motives, it was claimed, was a powerful source of motive that was itself learned. Ironically, perhaps, those studies are now valued not so much for their examination of differential association but for their original ethnographic detail.

The theory of differential association insisted on the ordinariness of the processes by which deviance arose. It located those processes in mundane social settings. It argued that deviance evolves in transactions with others. It emphasized the central part played by meaning and motive in the formation of deviant projects. And its acceptance by a number of energetic scholars ensured that some major part of criminology would continue to explore deviance as embedded, shared, symbolic experience changing over time.

Few would now wish to defend the more grandly ambitious claims of differential association theory. The theory promised a kind of specious precision which could never be realized. How would it ever be possible, worthwhile, or desirable to add up and evaluate all the competing definitions of law that one is likely to meet in one's formative years? The theory is riddled with escape clauses and qualifications that diminish its power to predict. Thus, it could always be argued that a great mass of definitions favourable to the violation of law can be outweighed by a few definitions of special intensity, priority, or duration. Unless the theory is trivialized to absurdity, it is not difficult to put forward numerous exceptions to the contention that all crime is learned in association with others. Lemert certainly discovered what appeared to be a major anomaly in his discussion of the naïve cheque forger.[96] Yet differential association theory supported a useful tradition which might otherwise have failed. It stimulated ethnographic work when such work was unfashionable, underpinning what has become, in effect, a continuous social history of crime. And it served as a bridge between the early work of the Chicago School and what was to become subcultural theory, a significant theory which we shall discuss in an independent chapter.

[94] E. Sutherland, *The Professional Thief*.
[95] D. Cressey, *Other People's Money*.
[96] E. Lemert, 'An Isolation and Closure Theory of Naive Check Forgery'.

Exported to Britain, Chicago sociology affected both the ethnographic work of the 1960s and the sociology of urban social problems. There seemed to be a most significant affinity between the turbulent and expanding Chicago of the 1920s and the cities of England. In particular, Birmingham, Liverpool, and Sheffield were subject to the zonal hypothesis. Their inner-city areas were similar to the zone in transition of an earlier Chicago: they were composed of a fluid, immigrant population; they were characterized by all the conventional signs of social pathology; they were in ill-repute and physically deteriorating. English analysis added an English emphasis on the interplay of social classes, denying the spontaneity and unplanned qualities of the natural area and stressing the political economy of housing. Much was made of the organized struggle for space waged between the different 'housing classes', classes which were distinguished by their access to and occupation of distinct styles of residence. Not all the urban sociologists remained at the level of the political economy of the city. Some turned to more focused studies of the politics and history of special areas, concentrating on the growth of communal reputations. Thus it has been argued that contingency or the deliberate concentration of 'problem families' can stigmatize particular neighbourhoods, affecting official policies and police strategies. The inhabitants of those areas may encounter distrust and hostility. They may be identified as deviants. Exposure to such definition, restricted opportunity, and enmity may engender self-fulfilling prophecies which perpetuate collective deviance.

Criticism

We have not discussed many of the more specific arguments offered by Chicago sociologists of the 1920s and 1930s. For instance, Anderson's *The Hobo* is a most important work, but we have chosen to ignore it. There are others which we have neglected. Our intention has been merely to review those arguments which reveal the more important themes of Chicago sociology and, in particular, those arguments which have attracted criticism.

Such criticism must be examined rather circumspectly. Like

much other censure in sociology, it sometimes reveals more about its author's position than about ideas that were developed in Chicago itself. After all, criticism is usually advanced to promote a particular purpose, and the theories that are attacked often seem to become distorted in the process. Thus, Matza praised *The Hobo* as a major innovation which developed 'appreciative' analysis and the sympathetic interpretation of the actor's own stance. Indeed, Matza depicts *The Hobo* as the major achievement of the Chicago School. Faris, by contrast, states: '*The Hobo* achieved most of its contribution by way of informal descriptions, using informal research technique and yielding no new sociological principles.'[97] Criticism is rarely disinterested.

Criticism of the Chicago School may be grouped into three broad parts: there are reproofs for asking questions ineptly, reproofs for accepting wrong answers, and reproofs for not putting other questions in their place. In the main, the exploratory and unformulated character of field-work has attracted a censorious response. Those who take to a natural-scientific model of research find the Chicago ethnographic tradition to be strangely loose, imprecise, and muddled. They argue that there is no clear investigation of hypotheses, no specification of objectives, and no means of finding that a theory is wrong. For instance, Davis remarked: 'in the naturalist's tradition, description for its own sake often superseded theoretical rationales for data analysis.'[98] Similarly, Shils observed that the Chicago School failed to 'set out to demonstrate any explicitly formulated sociological hypotheses.'[99] What these critics demand is a neat theory, a neat and articulate method, and a neat conclusion. They are frequently taxed by the Chicago sociologist's reluctance or inability to provide coherence.

In its defence, it could be argued that the imprecise character of Chicago sociology stems quite intelligibly from the pragmatic conception of knowledge as an evolving, grounded, and open-ended process. It will be recalled that the pragmatists held that hypotheses should not be too organized or explicit at the very beginning of research. On the contrary, firm expecta-

[97] R. Faris, *Chicago Sociology*, 66.
[98] N. Davis, *Sociological Constructions of Deviance*, 53.
[99] E. Shils, *The Present State of American Sociology*, 9.

tions would only prevent the sociologist from seeing and responding to phenomena and events as they arise. Theory must not anticipate, deform, or obscure the facts. It must be allowed to emerge as research advances. In a sense, it may even be argued that the Chicago School's description of research is little more than an unusually honest account of what many sociologists actually experience in the field. Work often seems to develop in a confusing and pragmatic manner.[100] How could it be otherwise? Research almost invariably propels one into the unknown, for which one can never be fully prepared. Sociologists are generally constrained to adopt Plummer's *Ad Hoc* Fumbling Around or AHFA technique,[101] whatever their claims may be before or after the event. Some are in fact content to dismiss the idealistic recipes of methodologists as 'lies'[102] which their authors mouth but cannot implement. The advocates of those recipes could well retort that it is not remarkable that the unprepared become confused, and it is indeed quite likely that there are many different worlds of research. There is no good reason to imagine that the cautious survey researcher will experience work in just the same fashion as the ethnographer or the forensic psychiatrist. But the critics have none the less tended to represent Chicago sociology as if it were unnecessarily disorganized, a product of some silly carelessness or oversight rather than a carefully resolved strategy.

Criticisms of the substantive work of the School chiefly turn on the usefulness of the ecological model. Some have observed that the city is *not* an ecological system but that it is regulated and directed by processes unknown to the biologist and botanist.[103] Although Roderick McKenzie occasionally offered himself as a legitimate butt for such an attack, we have stressed how Park, Wirth, and others expressly acknowledged the limitations of the ecological model: they too were aware that the city cannot be completely explained in such fashion. It is true, however, that their protestations of awareness may not have been enough: they did sometimes present ecology as a system of iron laws which contradict the more indeterminate themes of

---

[100] See P. Hammond (ed.), *Sociologists at Work*.

[101] *Ad Hoc* Fumbling Around: mentioned in conversation. See also his *Documents of Life*.

[102] See S. Cohen and L. Taylor, *Psychological Survival*.

[103] See T. Morris, *The Criminal Area*.

ethnography.[104] Ecology actually enjoys a fluctuating importance in the works of the Chicago School. In some passages it is
a central topic and means of explanation, in others it is
neglected altogether.

More minutely, it has been alleged that persistent reference
to the community and communal group imposed a misleading
simplicity and distinctness on phenomena which were actually
muddled and ill-defined. Thus Suttles insists that 'natural
areas' were very rarely natural. Instead of being unplanned and
unanticipated, the early Chicago neighbourhoods *were*
planned with great deliberation. Chicago was laid out on the
grid pattern and was regulated by copious statutes and
ordinances. Moreover, the natural areas were frequently
inhabited by heterogeneous populations who shared no
consensus and common identity. When social networks *did*
emerge, they could well have been shaped by influences other
than the occupation of a shared territory.[105] Indeed, Pahl
observes: 'Any attempt to tie particular patterns of social relationships to specific geographical milieux is a singularly fruitless exercise. Some people are of the city but not in it, whereas
others are in the city but not of it . . .'.[106]

Dissatisfaction with conceptions of the relation between
community and territory have stemmed from or prompted an
alternative phrasing of urban processes. It has been claimed
that the mere fact that events occurred in a physical setting
could not justify the deduction that the setting was chiefly
important in affecting those events.[107] Instead, it has been
proposed that the idea of community be dissolved, and
replaced or complemented by class, race, or political economy.
Classes and similar groupings have been put forward as more
significant actors in urban life.[108] It was class that dictated the
allocation of housing and the uses of space.[109] In short, certain
criminologists have moved the abandonment of social ecology
and the adoption of other theoretical systems. Their arguments
are not without merit. The Chicago School did neglect the

---

[104] Cf. N. Davis, *Sociological Constructions of Deviance*, 46.
[105] G. Suttles, *The Social Construction of Communities*.
[106] R. Pahl, *Whose City?*, 101.
[107] See M. Alihan, *Social Ecology*.
[108] See M. Davie, 'The Pattern of Urban Growth'.
[109] See J. Rex and R. Moore, *Race, Community and Conflict*.

social history of the business district and the zone in transition, representing their evolution as if it were practically free of human agency:

Their interpretation stopped abruptly at the point at which the relationship between industrial expansion and high delinquency areas could have gone beyond the depiction of the two as coincidentally adjacent to one another geographically. The interpretation was paralysed at the communal level, a level which implied that either the residents were responsible for the deteriorated area, or that communities collapsed on their own account. Instead of turning inward to find the causes of delinquency exclusively in local traditions, families, play groups and gangs, their interpretation might have turned outward to show political, economic and historical forces at work, which would have accounted for both social disorganisation and the internal conditions, including the delinquency.[110]

Suttles's answer would be that there is worth in criticisms made of the Chicago School but that *community* is none the less a useful idea which cannot be reduced down to other elements: 'unfortunately, this style of research fail[s] to capture what some thought essential to communities, particularly their reputational content and the ethos of local culture.'[111] Chicago sociologists may have been deficient in their analysis of 'master institutions and contradictory systems of social relations',[112] but their apparent deficiency does not warrant the wholesale abandonment of ecology. Ecology might well be amended. It confronts particular problems and not others. On occasion, it could be supplanted by more practically useful approches. But it does analyse features of community and territory with considerable competence.

The Chicago sociologists themselves might well have been more robust in their own defence. Pragmatists especially would have maintained that 'contradictory systems of social relations', classes, and 'class struggle' are ideas which have no readily observable referents. One cannot see, touch, smell, or hear a contradictory system. It is an inference most commonly made from a theoretical system. Members of the Chicago School tended to suspect such a priori schemes, arguing that

110 J. Snodgrass, 'Clifford R. Shaw and Henry D. McKay', 10.
111 G. Suttles, *The Social Construction of Communities*, 14.
112 N. Davis, *Sociological Constructions of Deviance*, 49.

they had a superficial persuasiveness but no anchorage in an empirical world which could actually be studied. Class, society, and allied terms were handled circumspectly:

Society is of course but the relations of individuals to one another in this form and that. And all relations are *interactions*, not fixed moulds . . . I often wonder what meaning is given to the term 'society' by those who oppose it to the *intimacies of personal intercourse*, such as those of friendship . . . We should forget 'society' and think of law, industry, religion, medicine, politics, art, education, philosophy— and think of them in the plural. For points of contact are not the same for any two persons and hence the questions which the interests and occupations pose are never twice the same.[113]

There was a preference for the materials of experience, materials which were lodged in people's attempts to handle specific problems in specific settings. Of course, that preference jarred with ecological themes, but it kept much abstraction at bay.

Conclusion

Chicago sociology was a major co-operative enterprise which launched an intellectual assault on the study of the city. Part of that assault was occupied with social problems, and social problems were typically confined to particular districts. The explanation of crime and deviance centred on the peculiar conditions of the zone in transition, a turbulent area which appeared out of joint with the rest of the city. Delinquency was an effort to restore order and opportunity to disorganization, and it could become the content of a stable tradition transmitted on the streets. Personal documents, anthropological field-work, and the analysis of census and court records were linked together to aid exploration.[114] The outcome was the production of a detailed contemporary social history of deviance. It prepared the basis for some of the principal sociological stances that were to come. Ethnography endured to become the 'neo-Chicagoan' Symbolic Interactionism of the 1940s,

---

[113] J. Dewey, quoted in C. Mills, *Sociology and Pragmatism*, 426, 430.
[114] Some kinds of evidence were inexplicably ignored. Newspapers and literary reports, for instance, were almost never used.

1950s, and beyond. The investigation of the distribution of social phenomena became sociological epidemiology: research into the connections between events in time and space. And urban sociology grounded in the Chicago School's writings persisted.

4
Functionalism, Deviance, and Control

Introduction

In the period from the late 1930s to the late 1950s, functionalism came as near as any perspective before or since to constituting sociological orthodoxy. Since that time, it (or, rather, the variety of approaches that were so labelled) has not only fallen from grace, it has been 'every year, every Autumn term, . . . ritually executed for introductory teaching purposes . . . the demolition of functionalism is almost an initiation rite of passage into sociological adulthood or at least adolescence.'[1] In the same vein, Percy Cohen remarked that 'it frequently looks as though anyone in search of theoretical acclaim has only to discover one more defect in functionalism to achieve it'.[2] It seems necessary to point out why, if such is the case, we think it worth while to devote a chapter to the subject.

Firstly, in common with most other approaches, but perhaps to an even greater extent, owing to its former domination over the field, functionalism has all too often been vulgarized by its critics. At times, a package deal is presented in which functionalism, positivism, empiricism, evolutionism, and determinism are collectively linked with a 'consensus' approach to social problems and a conservative approach to their solution. For example, in Douglas's critique of the structural-functional perspective on deviance,[3] the absurdities of such an approach are regarded as by now self-evident, and the contrast is dramatically made with the 'emerging sociological perspective on deviance', which is mercifully free from such errors. (These are usually listed as the uncritical acceptance of official statistics, the permeation of a uniform value system throughout society,

---

[1] H. Martins, 'Time and Theory in Sociology', 246.
[2] P. Cohen, *Modern Social Theory*, 47.
[3] J. Douglas, 'Deviance and Order in a Pluralistic Society', ch. 14.

and a conception of deviance as pathological rather than problematic.) Without wishing to claim that functionalists have
altogether avoided such formulations, we see functionalism as
offering an altogether more sophisticated and subtle model of
deviance and control than emerges from such critiques.
Secondly, deviance and control have long been implicated with
functionalism, at least since Durkheim chose to demonstrate
the 'rules of sociological method' by asserting that crime had to
be regarded logically as not only an inevitable but as a normal
and even healthy social phenomenon. This argument put functionalism in bad odour with criminology (as distinct from
sociology)—John Mays[4] could remark that, taken literally, it
was a 'morally repugnant' argument. Hence, the limited forays
into the analysis of crime and deviance by such American functionalists of the inter-war and post-war period as Kingsley
Davis, Daniel Bell, and Robert Merton, with the exception of
the latter's theory of anomie, barely impinged on criminology.[5]
The more recent revival of functionalist arguments, by Erikson
and Scott, has fared similarly.[6] Despite this neglect, the functionalist approach to crime and deviance continues to survive,
and to raise questions of an intellectually radical kind that as
yet no other perspective deals with at all adequately. At the very
least, it can be argued, with Matza,[7] that the functionalist
approach to crime has contributed significantly to the 'emerging sociological perspective on deviance' to which Douglas
referred as its very antithesis.

The Sociological Background

The main tenets of functionalism seem uncontentious enough:
they are that societies can, for all analytical purposes, be treated
as systems whose parts (the institutions of production, education, human relations, belief, etc.) should be examined not in

[4] J. Mays, *Crime and the Social Structure*, 67 ff.
[5] K. Davis, 'The Sociology of Prostitution', 444–55, and 'Illegitimacy and the Social
Structure', 221–33; D. Bell, *The End of Ideology*, chs. 7–9; R. Merton, *Social Theory and
Social Structure*; and R. Merton and R. Nisbet (eds.), *Contemporary Social Problems*.
[6] K. Erikson, *Wayward Puritans*, and (with R. Dentler) 'The Functions of Deviance in
Groups', 98–107; R. Scott, 'A Proposed Framework for Analyzing Deviance as a
Property of Social Order'.
[7] D. Matza, *Becoming Deviant*, 31–7, 53–62, 73–80.

isolation but in terms of their interrelationships and in terms of their contribution to the society in general. Thus, for example, it would be pointless to a functionalist to study family and kinship simply in terms of their forms and structures, as an end in itself: to do so would be to fail to grasp the significance of family and kinship for other institutions and vice versa. It follows that changes in any one institution have implications for change in others, though no simple 'functional reciprocity' can be assumed: a change in the distribution of wealth may have immense implications for leisure, but a change in patterns of leisure may have negligible impact on the distribution of wealth. If this were all that functionalists contended, then it would be difficult to dispute Kingsley Davis's assertion that, far from being one school within sociology, sociology and functionalism are virtually one.[8]

Functionalists in general, we argue below, have pushed the argument further, and have begun to detach the 'needs' of the social system from the 'needs' of the individuals who, notwithstanding analytical purposes, compose it: this is most obviously the case with Talcott Parsons.[9] Alternatively, they have collapsed the 'needs' of society back onto the 'needs' of individuals, but in a somewhat circular way: this is most evident in Malinowski's 'cultural-functionalism'.[10] Further, they have postulated an evolutionary trend, for example, from simple agrarian to complex industrial societies, with respect to which some institutions are viewed as functional and others not: this is most marked in the case of Durkheim. It should be stressed, however, that functionalist methods vary quite considerably, and different theorists by no means share the same assumptions about different problems. Malinowski, for example, viewed functional analysis as an alternative to evolutionary schemata, not as a tool for their elaboration. All tended, however, to conceive of society as a 'whole' (hence 'holism'), a construction that lent itself to grand and abstract theorizing that, at its worst, and with its schematization way beyond any possibility of empirical validation (as in the work of Talcott

[8] K. Davis, 'The Myth of Functional Analysis as a Special Method in Sociology and Anthropology'.
[9] See in particular T. Parsons, *The Social System*.
[10] See in particular B. Malinowski, *A Scientific Theory of Culture*.

Parsons's middle phase), does indeed deserve the strictures that Douglas, C. Wright Mills, and many others have heaped upon it.[11]

It is as well to begin with the problem defined as central by these theorists, lest it be thought bizarre to be so obsessed with the shortcomings of the founding fathers. Durkheim's main intellectual concern, at the turn of the century, was to analyse the possibilities of securing social cohesion in the face of rapid social and economic change. This problem had been central to social and political theory for much of the nineteenth century: what was novel about Durkheim's formulation was his rejection of purely economic solutions (as, in his view, Marx had proposed), and of leaving things be at all costs (as Spencer had advocated), in favour of what we might now define as a 'corporate state' solution. The division of labour had outstripped the capacity of existing institutions (such as the Churches) to promote moral regulation: yet its function was ultimately the nurturing of co-operation and the lessening of conflict by increasing resources. (Its cause, by contrast, was contentiously assigned by Durkheim to increased population pressures.) The division of labour would therefore ultimately promote moral regulation on the basis of newly emergent 'occupational associations', although this could occur only if the fit between talents and occupations could be 'spontaneously' wrought, rather than 'forced': hence his preference for inherited wealth to be abolished, along with other forms of privilege which intervened between ability and assignment to roles. Sociology's task was to clarify the problems facing industrial society, and to further that end, the 'rules of sociological method' were designed to operate on lines of scientific objectivity. No topic was sacred: to emphasize that point Durkheim would frequently choose themes designed to shock; indeed, the 'sacred' became his culminating topic. In 'The Elementary Forms of Religious Life', he analysed religion (in the form of aboriginal ritual) as the collective representation of the social: 'Society' was God. The function of religion was the celebration of the social group. How primitive man had accomplished so sophisticated a solution to the problem of social order was left unresolved.[12]

[11] J. Douglas, 'Deviance and Order'; C. Mills, *The Sociological Imagination*, ch. 2.
[12] S. Lukes, *Émile Durkheim: His Life and Work*, is the fullest, and A. Giddens's

Malinowski addressed this problem much more directly, professing himself at odds with Durkheim's notion of the 'group-mind', as he put it, and also attacking the quite separate practice of the 'hearsay' method in anthropology, whereby the anthropologist stayed only long enough to write down what his informants told him about native customs and belief. Proper field-work involved the ethnographer's tent in the background, and a prolonged period of observation of what actually went on, as distinct from, though complementing, what was said to go on. In this context, functionalism enabled one to map social reality as it unfolded. Forms of conduct unintelligible in themselves took on meaning within the context of the patterns of reciprocity and exchange of kinship and tribe. 'Culture' could be itemized: 'it was possible to correlate one aspect of culture with another and show which is the function fulfilled by either within the scheme of culture.'[13] It should be stressed that Malinowski took pains to oppose the 'seamless web' conception of culture so often associated with functionalism. The unity of the clan is 'a social institution of great complexity'; native law is a set of ideals, 'only rarely attained in practice';[14] 'human culture is not a consistent logical scheme, but a seething mixture of conflicting principles',[15] and so on. The functionalist method of rendering culture intelligible *without* resort to an evolutionist schema was its whole point: that did not, however, imply a resistance to acknowledging the reality of change. Fletcher has stressed, in a forceful attack on the tendency to caricature functionalism as capable only of a *static* portrayal of societies, that both 'synchronic' and 'diachronic' accounts are seen as essential by Radcliffe-Brown, and that both are recognized as *processes in time*.[16] This does not resolve the logical problem of how, if society 'hangs together' via mutually sustaining functional elements, change is allowed to occur.

The same problem recurs in the most ambitious conceptual attempts to map the 'functional requisites' of social order and

Introduction to *Émile Durkheim: Selected Writings*, the most succinct account of Durkheim's work.

[13] B. Malinowski, *Crime and Custom in Savage Society*, 128.
[14] Ibid. 119–20.   [15] Ibid. 121.
[16] R. Fletcher, 'Evolutionary and Developmental Sociology', 42.

the 'structure of social actions' in the work of Parsons. Parsons's work is so little wedded to empiricism and ethnography, by contrast with Malinowski and Radcliffe-Brown, that only their underlying shared emphasis on functional relationships enables them to be bracketed together at all. Parsons's aim was to combine a 'voluntaristic theory of action' with a model of the social system that would apply to any society. Hence, he propounded his notion of the 'pattern variables', a five-fold set of 'value-orientations' to action, which matched actors' appropriate behaviour and expectations with socially structured role prescriptions. The relationships of husband and wife, doctor and patient, teacher and pupil are broadly scripted: the individuals improvise the fine detail for themselves. These broad structural constraints are theorized as varying by the type of society, and in accordance with the 'functional requisites'—system 'needs' which any viable society must meet.[17] This is not the place to attempt a detailed sketch of Parsons's 'grand theory'. As critics have been keen to point out, it topples over, especially in its stress on the internalization of common values by the individual, its near-deterministic profiles of human type-casting, and near-tautologous portrayals of social systems endlessly reproducing themselves. The first and second reduce the social to the sociable,[18] and nowhere convey, or allow for, the active struggle involved in, for example, simply bringing up children, even under relatively favourable conditions; the third hardly allows for the brute facts of conflict, power, and subordination.[19] Deviance is poorly dealt with, either as the product of system malintegration at the margins, or as that of inadequate socialization in childhood. What Parsons does achieve, however, is a sense of the magnitude of the accomplishment of social order, even if it is at the expense, as Wrong so eloquently put it, of an 'over-integrated' view of society and an 'over-socialised' conception of man.[20] It remains the only attempt since the classical theorists to link the processes of interaction on the face-to-face level with the

---

[17] For an analysis of the problems associated with this theme, see L. Sklair, 'The Fate of the "Functional Requisites" in Parsonian Sociology', 30–42.

[18] A Gouldner, *The Coming Crisis in Western Sociology*, 425–8.

[19] See in particular D. Lockwood, 'Some Remarks on "The Social System"', 134–46; J. Rex, *Key Problems of Sociological Theory*; and Gouldner, op. cit. pt. II.

[20] D. Wrong, 'The Oversocialized Conception of Man', 183–91.

institutional constellations at the macro level worthy of the undertaking itself.

It was an attempt, however, that failed, and attempts to supplant it with a superior theory, or indeed to patch it up, have preoccupied sociologists for the past thirty years. It accounts for the revival of Marxism(s), the popularity of French structuralism, the passion for symbolic interactionism and allied approaches: sociology abhors a vacuum. Marxism and structuralism indeed have great affinities with Parsonian structural–functionalism: compare Hawthorne's summary of Althusser with Parsons's mode of explanation: '. . . modes of production . . . furnish the limits within which institutions and individuals can act, and in that extremely weak sense determine that action. But . . . in any place at any time anything may be more immediately determinant, or "dominant".'[21] Functionalist currents also pervade symbolic interactionism. Goffman, for example, in his essay on gambling, falls back ultimately on the notion that 'Character is gambled . . . We are allowed to think there is something to be won in the moments that we face so that society can face moments and defeat them.'[22] This should not surprise us: Mead, the founding father of interactionism, contributed a major essay on the functions of punishment for social structure. It begins to look as though functional analysis refuses to be struck from the sociological canon.

The Functions of Deviance and Control

Durkheim and Mead. Durkheim's view of the proper rules of sociological method was based on a forthright positivism: the astonishing success of the natural sciences could be matched by the social sciences, provided that similar methods were adopted. The classification of social phenomena could match the taxonomies of the natural sciences. The social world could be investigated using concepts similar to those of health and disease employed in the anatomization of living organisms. 'Normalcy' and 'pathology' could be empirically established by reference to the generality of phenomena in societies of com-

---

[21] G. Hawthorne, *Enlightenment and Despair*, 229.
[22] E. Goffman, 'Where the Action Is', 237–9.

parable development and complexity: divergence from the average would indicate degrees of pathology. Two steps were involved in the assessment of normalcy: firstly, it could be empirically established whether or not a phenomenon existed throughout the range of known societies: if so, then its normalcy could be presumed, and the sociologist was alerted to its likely functional character. Secondly, the contribution of the phenomenon to the 'conditions necessary for group life' had to be established. Only if both steps were accomplished could functionality be inferred, and a yardstick for the assessment of pathology set up.

The illustration of these methods with reference to crime led Durkheim to make his most contentious assertion that 'crime is normal . . . It is a factor in public health, an integral part of all healthy societies.'[23] Its universal character pointed to its functionality, but Durkheim could only secure his conclusion by stating the manner of the contribution that crime makes to social stability. This ensues, he argued, from the response that crime (or, by extension, deviance in general) elicits from the group or community: it serves to 'heighten collective sentiments', sharpen perceptions of moral imperatives, more tightly integrate the community against the transgressor—in short, to clarify and reinforce the norms and values of the group. A certain amount of crime is therefore functional, too little or too much is pathological: 'There is no occasion for self-congratulation when the crime rate drops noticeably below the average level, for we may be certain that this apparent progress is associated with some social disorder.' By the same logic, 'excess [when the crime rate is unusually high] is undoubtedly morbid in nature'. The former implies that the forces of social control have become too strong, that too great a social investment is being made to eliminate it: the result is social stagnation. The latter implies that it is swamping the group's capacity to respond collectively to it, and that social cohesion is gravely at risk. Commonly accepted beliefs about crime are much more likely to agree with the second rather than the first assertion, and Durkheim employed all his customary eloquence to make the argument hold: 'Imagine a society of saints, a perfect cloister

[23] É. Durkheim, *The Rules of Sociological Method*, 67.

of exemplary individuals. Crimes, properly so called, will there be unknown; but faults which appear venial to the layman will create there the same scandal that the ordinary offence does in ordinary consciousness.'[24] Durkheim would no doubt have seen what Stanley Cohen[25] has termed 'moral panics' as necessary forms of communal consciousness-raising to reactivate social controls. Such panics seem subject to eternal recurrence. As Pearson has commented: 'The terms and limits within which the problems of lawlessness are understood and acted upon are established within a form of public discourse which has been with us for generations, each succeeding generation remembering the illusive harmony of the past while foreseeing imminent social ruin in the future.'[26] To a functionalist, such continuities are the stuff of which social order is made.

A 'crime-free society' is therefore a contradiction in terms, since to bring about the elimination of all crime would entail such a massive heightening of collective sentiment against it that currently trivial deviations would become magnified to take their place. The attempt to eliminate them would produce a further twist in the spiral, to the point where social life logically seized up. This does not, of course, imply that Durkheim approved of all crime or all punishment; nor does it obviate debate about the most desirable 'cutting-point' at which societies should accept some crimes, but not others, as the norm. What it does insist on as an argument is the impossibility of eliminating crime (or equivalently sanctioned forms of deviance) from social life altogether.

In an article entitled 'The Psychology of Punitive Justice', Mead developed a complementary theme to that of Durkheim.[27] It is quite inadequate, he argued, to account for the social organization of justice by reference to such justifications of punishment as retribution and deterrence. These would as well be served by lynch law. The ritual solemnities of the criminal law reflect rather the community's need for the criminal to be subjected to a form of punitive justice in which

---

[24] É. Durkheim, *The Rules of Sociological Method*, 66–72 and *passim*. For excellent discussions, see M. Phillipson, *Sociological Aspects of Crime*, ch. 3; and A. Cohen, *The Elasticity of Evil*.

[25] S. Cohen, *Folk Devils and Moral Panics* and chs. 6 and 7 below.

[26] G. Pearson, *Hooligan: A History of Respectable Fears*, 229.

[27] G. Mead, 'The Psychology of Punitive Justice'.

the re-establishment of social order is enacted in dramatic form. The two major functions fulfilled by the criminal law are the stigmatization of the offender and the reinforcement of inhibitions against law-breaking among the community at large. The hostility towards the criminal derives from his challenge to the moral boundaries with which the members of the community identify, and this hostility cannot be reconciled with the desire to 'reform' or 'treat' the offender. 'It is quite impossible psychologically to hate the sin and love the sinner.' Contemporary unease about the grafting of rehabilitative measures on to the criminal justice system seem clearly presaged in these arguments. It is not, however, entirely the case, as Phillipson suggests, that Mead and Durkheim are implicitly at one in their penal theories. Phillipson argues that, to Durkheim, in his *Moral Education*, 'the essential function of punishment is not simply retributive, nor is it to produce individual atonement, nor is it to deter the offender, but rather it is to demonstrate the inviolability of the rule broken by the offender'.[28] If the punishment *is* secondary to the reaffirmation of the rule, then the way remains open for alternative measures to the sheerly punitive.

What those alternatives might be was hinted at elsewhere in Durkheim's work.[29] In his evolutionary perspective, he saw 'repressive' justice as yielding progressively to 'restitutive' justice as society moved from 'mechanical' to 'organic' modes of social solidarity. In the former, uniformity of consciousness could accommodate deviance only by strongly punitive responses. In the latter, social order is secured by a more 'spontaneous' division of labour, and restitutive justice—the minimum of reparation needed to restore harmony—becomes more apt. While Durkheim's chronology has been invalidated by modern anthropology, his ideal types of justice retain their analytical force, and can be seen at work in all modern criminal justice systems.[30]

Developments in American Sociology. Despite the radicalism of their tone and style, Durkheim and Mead did not go much

[28] See M. Phillipson, op. cit., 70.
[29] Lukes and Scull, *Durkheim and the Law*.
[30] E. Lemert, *Human Deviance, Social Problems and Social Control*.

beyond asserting, once cant and hypocrisy were swept aside, the inevitability of crime and punishment as properties of social order in at least the societies of their day (and by extension all societies based upon known principles of social organization). Tone and style aside, the American sociologists who took up the functional analysis of crime and deviance came much closer to justifying the pursuit of specific forms of deviance as positively serviceable to the social order.

The growth of a sociological view of deviant phenomena involved, as major phases, the replacement of a correctional stance by an *appreciation* of the deviant subject, the tacit purging of a conception of pathology by new stress on human *diversity*, and the erosion of a simple distinction between deviant and conventional phenomena, resulting from more intimate familiarity with the world as it is, which yielded a more sophisticated view stressing *complexity*.[31]

Appreciation carries the risk of a seeming complicity with the deviance under scrutiny, which is probably the main reason for its relatively later adoption as a method. But there is no reason for appreciation to imply approval: to empathize is not necessarily to sympathize. Appreciation in this sense is a mere research tool used to enhance the study of any group.[32] However, Matza credits functionalism with playing a major role in the growth of 'naturalism' in the sociology of deviance. By searching for the hidden contributions that deviant phenomena might make to the social order, 'some functional analyses sound suspiciously like the justifications of phenomena rendered by the deviant subjects who exemplify and perpetrate them'. Though this appreciation was usually 'from a distance',[33] it was still appreciation. Thus, Kingsley Davis's analysis of prostitution, first appearing in 1937, is remarkably similar to the more recent demands for a 'new deal' by prostitutes in the 1970s and before in the US and most Western European countries. It is claimed, for example, that prostitution operates as a social service for those unable to achieve sexual satisfaction in any other way, thus acting as a safety valve for potential sexual aggression. In Davis's view, this is ulti-

[31] D. Matza, *Becoming Deviant*, 10, also 31–7, 53–62, 73–80.
[32] See, for example, N. Fielding, *The National Front*.
[33] D. Matza, op. cit. 32.

mately the reason why prostitution can never be eliminated, short of abolishing the sanctity of monogamous marriage, and requiring 'mutual complementariness' of sexual desire throughout society.[34] In this sense, prostitution complements the institution of the monogamous nuclear family. Both are threatened by the rise of more widespread sexual freedoms: but to push the latter too far would presumably lead to a Hobbesian state of sexual promiscuity which would chronically affect the social order. Hence, some prostitution is a good thing, an argument taken up and developed with reference to pornography some thirty years later by Polsky.[35] In a fashion analogous to prostitution, pornography canalizes into a purely commercial transaction a welter of sexual gratifications that, by comparison with adultery, for example, pose no threat to family ties.

Appreciation appears a mixed blessing for sociology. The injunction to empathize with the internal and subjective realities of a phenomenon is not entailed in classical functionalism. Its appeal is most obvious in the more exotic but victimless forms of deviance such as smoking marihuana or joining a nudist colony. In cases of victimization it carries the aura of a spiritual collaboration: to 'appreciate' Fascism, however, is not to condone it. Matza's argument that to apprehend the world as it is involves taking that risk is best exemplified by Daniel Bell's portrayal of the racketeering in New York's dockland. Addressing the problem of why the New York rackets should flourish long after they declined elsewhere, Bell conveys the distinctive character of the operations there as a stable organization that actually copes relatively efficiently with the unusually intricate nature of the New York dockside. That the price is graft, corruption, and exploitation does not detract from the 'beauty' of the racket, which 'provided extraordinary gain on almost no investment other than muscle-men for intimidation . . .'.[36] As Matza comments: 'Such a truth is obviously partial, but it is necessary to begin there. Otherwise, the coherence, form, texture, and even utility of deviant phenomena cannot become evident.'[37]

[34] K. Davis, 'Prostitution', 286.   [35] N. Polsky, *Hustlers, Beats and Others*.
[36] D. Bell, 'The Racket-Ridden Longshoremen', *The End of Ideology*, 187.
[37] D. Matza, *Becoming Deviant*, 37.

Still pursuing Matza's scheme of things, in which—it should be stressed—his major aim is to chart the development of naturalism in the study of deviance, and not to adjudicate on the validity or invalidity of theories, we are shown a second by-product of functionalism to be the purging of pathology. This is no small achievement, since the classical functionalism of Durkheim rested upon just such a conception. The purging is best exemplified in the work of Merton, who distinguished between manifest and latent functions in order to stress the ways in which social phenomena, however 'immoral' or 'unhealthy' on the surface, may actually contribute to the social order. In fact, there was nothing apart from the terminology employed that was especially new about the idea of latent function. For Durkheim, all functions were latent; he called those that were manifest (to Merton) purposes. However, in his analysis of the political machines which were a byword for corruption and graft in American life, Merton sought to establish unintended and unnoticed virtues. These reside largely in the capacity of the political machines, directed by the local Boss, to deliver actual results, against the grain of legal constraints and democratic convolutions. 'The functional deficiencies of the official structure generate an alternative (unofficial) structure to fulfil existing needs somewhat more effectively.'[38] Once learnt, this analytical model can appear to justify practically anything, a deficiency Merton sought to remedy by introducing the concept of 'dysfunction' to complement that of function. However, Davis, Bell, Merton, and others in the 1930s, 1940s, and 1950s were primarily concerned with the functions of the deviant: the dysfunctions of the conventional were merely the mirror-image that supplied a certain analytical symmetry in principle. The question, much the most deadly, which they rarely raised was 'At whose expense?', and its corollary, 'Functional for whom?' Their intention was not, however, to produce a functionalist theory of deviance, but to use deviance on occasion as a hard case for the exemplification of functionalist strategies.

The third achievement of functionalism, in Matza's view, was to accelerate the movement away from a view of deviance

---

[38] R. Merton, *Social Theory and Social Structure* (1949), 73.

and, by extension, society as essentially simple, to an awareness of its complexity. 'Overlap' and 'irony' are terms
employed to convey the processes involved. Deviant phenomena overlap with conventional: the same motives, the
same organizational principles, even the same morality, can
inspire deviant and conformist alike. In this sense, Al Capone,
as Merton stressed, was a model American capitalist. Racketeering was illegal, but in all other respects it conformed to the
canons of good business practice. The irony employed by the
functionalists was perhaps less novel than Matza implies:
after all, novelists and satirists from Swift and Fielding on,
and dramatists as celebrated as Shakespeare and Shaw, had
employed the device on these very issues to matchless effect.
Mandeville, in his *Fable of the Bees* (1714) had argued that the
practice of virtue was incompatible with commercial prosperity, which can flourish only in a context of pride, greed,
and emulative luxury. The use of irony in sociology, however,
was decidedly novel. 'By the idea of irony, the functionalists
revealed social process as *devious*, and thus increasingly complex.'[39] Thus Merton: 'A cardinal American virtue, ambition,
promotes a cardinal American vice, deviant behaviour.'[40]
Thus Davis: 'If we reverse the proposition that increased
sexual freedom among women of all classes reduces the role
of prostitution (as Kinsey's findings suggest), we find ourselves admitting that increased prostitution may reduce the
sexual irregularities of respectable women.'[41] That deviance
could operate as a blessing in disguise was, as Bell put it,
nevertheless bought 'at a high price'—a double irony that
stemmed from virtue's dependence on evil for the performance of necessary services.

In all of this, the American functionalists (Davis apart) were
prone to neglect the second stage of Durkheim's methodology.
Sheer persistence of a phenomenon was not sufficient to secure
functionality: the ways in which it necessarily contributes to
group life tended to be taken for granted. It is in this sense that
Erikson's work represents a return to Durkheimian orthodoxy.

[39] D. Matza, *Becoming Deviant*, 77.
[40] R. Merton, *Social Theory and Social Structure* (1949), 137.
[41] K. Davis, 'Prostitution', 283–4.

But it is an orthodoxy which he takes as a beginning rather than an end of enquiry:

This [approach] raises a delicate theoretical issue. If we grant that human groups often derive benefit from deviant behaviour, can we then assume that they are organised in such a way as to promote this resource? Can we assume, in other words, that forces operate in the social structure to recruit offenders and to commit them to long periods of service in the deviant ranks? . . . Deviant forms of conduct often seem to derive nourishment from the very agencies devised to inhibit them. Indeed, the agencies built by society for preventing deviance are often so poorly equipped for the task that we might well ask why this is regarded as their 'real' function in the first place.[42]

If this is so, it may help account for the surprising symmetry between the deviant and the conformist, a symmetry far more striking when scrutinized from a distance: 'A twentieth-century American is supposed to understand that larceny and other forms of commercial activity are wholly different, standing on "opposite sides of the law". A seventeenth-century American, on the other hand, if he lived in New England, was supposed to understand that Congregationalism and Antinomianism were as far apart as God and the Devil.'[43]

His argument culminates in the linkage of the fear of deviance with the processes whereby that very thing is created: 'If deviation and conformity are so alike, it is not surprising that deviant behaviour should seem to appear in a community at exactly those points where it is most feared. Men who fear witches soon find themselves surrounded by them; men who become jealous of private property soon encounter eager thieves.'[44] And the point of this exercise in 'self-fulfilling prophecy' returns us to the most ancient antinomy of all: that good can be known only in relation to evil, its mirror image. 'In the process of defining the nature of deviation, the settlers were also defining the boundaries of their new universe.'[45]

Two subsidiary themes also occur to Erikson. He argues that the volume of deviance has more to do with the community's capacity to handle it than with the inclinations towards deviance among its members. Social control agencies tend to

---

[42] K. Erikson, *Wayward Puritans*, 283–4.
[43] Ibid. 21.   [44] Ibid. 22.   [45] Ibid. 23.

regulate rather than attempt to eliminate deviance, whatever they claim rhetorically about the 'war against crime'. Stabilization seems to be preferred to elimination partly because the control agencies demand some predictability of employment, but also because the very definitions of the problem adjust to fit the community's calibration of its control machinery. As a corollary, societies develop appropriate 'deployment patterns' to negotiate the optimum volume of deviance that it 'needs' for boundary maintenance. Here Erikson propounds what is virtually a 'conservation of energy' theory of deviance containment. Rag-days, charivari, festivals, provide outlets for the ventilation of deviance in licensed form. Certain age-grades are extended a heightened degree of tolerance: the young are expected to 'sow their wild oats', 'get out of hand', and generally 'raise hell' from time to time, though the tolerance is finely tuned to curb those who go 'too far'. In sum, Erikson is probing, so to speak, for a deep structure of deviance and control beneath the myriad forms they assume in history and from society to society.

Functionalists from Durkheim to Erikson tend to treat social cohesion, and the need for boundary maintenance, as their ultimate data. But why the need for boundaries at all, and what does it mean to assert that societies must 'cohere'? In what remains the most recent comprehensive attempt to address those questions, Robert Scott draws not only on the work of the functionalists, but also on that of the philosopher of science, Thomas Kuhn, on the anthropologically based analyses of rules and meanings of Mary Douglas, and on the social phenomenology of Berger and Luckmann.[46] From Kuhn, he takes the idea that people explain the world to themselves in terms of a 'paradigm', a self-contained model which is relatively immune to change, except in the form of very rare 'paradigmatic revolutions' which overturn established ways of apprehending reality and replace them by ones emergent from the new paradigm. From Mary Douglas he takes the axiom that cultures cannot explain everything, but what cannot be explained is treated as anomalous, as something that 'should

---

[46] R. Scott, 'A Proposed Framework for Analyzing Deviance', T. Kuhn, *The Structure of Scientific Revolutions*; M. Douglas, *Purity and Danger*; P. Berger and T. Luckmann, *The Social Construction of Reality*.

not be there': 'Dirt is matter out of place' is her vivid metaphor. From Berger and Luckmann, he takes the notion of 'world-openness', the absence for man of an environmental stability: thus, 'men require a symbolic framework for ordering social reality'. Social order is man's creation of 'world-closedness' against the void, a construction to ward off the chaos of nature; it is therefore always precarious and besieged by countless 'alternative' realities. The development of social order is made possible only by man's capacity to symbolize, and thus to habitualize actions, which by repetition and reinforcement become reified, 'real', 'social things', as Durkheim called them, with the potency of exercising constraint over generation after generation. The legitimation of such patterns lends them moral meaning and the patina of 'naturalness'; the integration of such legitimations provides an overarching symbolic framework. Social and cultural cohesion and coherence are achieved when the group as a whole takes a particular system as *the* institutional pattern, in which 'everything makes sense'. In complex societies, many sub-universes of meaning can coexist, but the dominant order is generally adhered to with a deep conservatism and resistance to change. Gellner assigns the term 'ironic cultures' to those forms of belief which do not ultimately challenge the dominant symbolic order, except at the surface of appearances: people may 'believe' in astrology, but they do not commonly entrust themselves to astrologers for brain surgery or bridge-building.[47]

Social order is set in a field of force which has the capacity to overwhelm it. Chaos holds the potential to confront us with things that literally should not exist if the concept of reality that is embodied in our symbolic universe is true. Yet cultures exhibit great resilience in the face of such threats to their integrity. Just as scientific paradigms can bracket away, as anomalous, events which science itself postulates ought not to exist, or which it has classified and categorized wrongly, so cultures can deploy mechanisms for smoothing out and resolving threats posed by anomalies. Deviance enters in as a property of social order to serve as a category for the anomalous. Other mechanisms exist that perform complementary functions. *Misperception* can quite genuinely occur, so that

[47] E. Gellner, *Legitimation of Belief*, 191–5.

anomaly is simply not noticed. *Debunking* can flatten anomaly into the everyday. *Normalizing* can redefine it as not really what it seems, as—for example—in the anxiety to cure the deviant whose 'real' problem is something else. If recalcitrant, deviance can be coercively *controlled*. If unduly defiant and threatening, *nihilation* can occur, the 'conceptual liquidation' of the deviant's definition of reality. Finally, *change* to accommodate the deviance can occur, but Scott (following Kuhn) views this as extremely rare. In sum, deviance is not just what is left over from conformity: it is inextricably bound up with the preconditions for conformity to exist.

Criticism

In a formidable summary of the strengths and weaknesses of functionalism, Percy Cohen lists three species or levels of criticism, logical, substantive, and ideological.[48] Of these, the logical criticisms are by far the most severe. Firstly, functionalist theories are viewed as taking a teleological form which is ultimately unacceptable, despite plausible justifications for this form of argument in the human, as distinct from natural, sciences.[49] Teleology consists in the imputation of cause to beneficial consequence: e.g. religion originates in the need for social cohesion. It can be argued that this presents no real problem: men have purposes, and put them into effect collectively by trial and error. In other words, they have the consequences in mind as an anterior condition of behaviour. The problem here is that functionalism was created in the teeth of the complexities of social life that could not be accounted for in terms of intended consequences. As Cohen argues:

many, if not most, social phenomena are the product of the *unintended* consequences of social actions; these social actions are themselves purposive; but many of their consequences have no direct connection with these purposes. Thus, men may participate in their religion in order to achieve a state of salvation; if this widespread participation has consequences for the moral order, this may be quite unconnected with the purposes envisaged by the participants. This is not to deny that men sometimes set out to create or destroy social

[48] P. Cohen, *Modern Social Theory*, ch. 3.
[49] See, for example, A Stinchcombe, *Constructing Social Theories*, ch. 3.

phenomena ... But whatever men do in this respect, they always unintentionally produce certain social and cultural items which, though they appear to have been devised for certain purposes, were not.[50]

The problem then becomes how to avoid a purely circular explanation, in which the grounds for the existence of the phenomenon are simply read into the alleged functions it serves. For example, it is one thing to assert that crime can be made to serve some social end or other *once it has occurred*, e.g. to heighten solidarity by uniting against the offender. It is another step altogether to explain crime as promoted in advance by society to bring about that end. There are examples of the latter, to be sure: witch-hunting, scape-goating, and the activities of *agents provocateurs* are not least among them. But in such cases it is normally particular groups seeking specific ends, and not some emanation from the social processes of the group as a whole, that seem the more plausible causal agency.

We do have our own misgivings about Cohen's stress on the unanticipated consequences of social action. Indeed, we would argue that there must be quite substantial resort to teleology in a discipline devoted to human activity. People do have purposes and they are quite perceptive and far-sighted. They often seek what functionalists describe as unintended ends. Functionalist analyses of deviance actually give us very little evidence about stated intentions. They do not busy themselves with what people *say* they are doing. Yet it is never very difficult to find someone, somewhere, on the social scene who is capable of putting an identifiable version of the functionalist case. After all, judges themselves state that they try to promote solidarity amongst the virtuous; prostitutes that they are performing a vital social service; and organized criminals that they are exemplary capitalists, mediators, and patrons. No scholar is required to point them to the latent functions hiding beneath the manifest surface of things. And once the pointing occurs, functionalism becomes self-falsifying. When a description of the unintended and latent functions of action is published, it can no longer be safe to assume that the literate are innocent about the consequences of their behaviour. The

---

[50] P. Cohen, op. cit. 49.

result has been an odd, distorting view of social life that removes much that is purposeful and recognizable about conduct. Mary Douglas has put the argument well:

[Functionalism] proposes an unacceptable view of human agency. . . . The argument depends on a form of sociological determinism that credits individuals with neither initiative nor sense. It was partly for this failing that sociological functionalism has been in low repute for the last thirty years. It had no place for the subjective experience of individuals willing and choosing. To suppose that individuals are caught in the toils of a complex machinery that they do not help to make is to suppose them to be passive objects, like sheep or robots.[51]

Another vexing problem concerns the testability of the theory. How could one possibly falsify a functionalist proposition? In the case of crime, for example, it may be possible to apply the normal/pathological distinction to different societies on the basis of their crime rates. The USA would undoubtedly emerge at the pathological end of any such spectrum, which indeed might point to the myriad defects which socialists have long noted as built into American society. But functionalism at this point offers an embarrassing number of solutions to the problem of accounting for those defects.[52] The high levels of deviation may be a 'warning light'; but they could also be a 'safety valve', a price to be paid for the maintenance of valued institutions, such as a relatively strong commitment to 'free enterprise'. They may be the 'functional equivalent' of what, in other societies, appear as high rates of political oppression, religious fanaticism, or mental illness. Similarly, religion has divided communities as well as united them: but this is viewed as confirming its unifying function, albeit within each sub-community. Nothing can ever be disproved, nor can the promise of comparative analysis be fulfilled, since items can only be evaluated in their own context.

Finally, functionalism promotes holism, the tendency to analyse societies as 'wholes' or systems, which inhibits the exploration of just how a phenomenon affects different groups within it. In asking 'Functional for whom?' the bottom falls out of the functionalist case. For what is functional for one group

---

[51] M. Douglas, *How Institutions Think*, 32.
[52] For an enumeration of such functions, see A. Cohen, *Deviance and Control*, 6–11.

may well be dysfunctional for another, even though this may not always be so—institutions may be functional for very large numbers. Functionalists recognize this problem, but hope to overcome it by a complicated cost–benefit analysis in which the functions and dysfunctions for various groupings are somehow totted up to produce a sociological balance sheet. Functionalism in this sense is, as Gouldner has noted, no more than sociological utilitarianism,[53] in which it is quite proper for a minority to suffer, in principle, for the social cohesion of the majority. As a *New Yorker* cartoon might put it (we do not know if one has), the victim of muggers should be gratified that he has played his part in reactivating social solidarity. The main logical defect of such a position is that the vantage-point from which such a cost–benefit analysis proceeds is inescapably value-laden.

Empirically, the grounds for opposing functionalism are mainly that its logical problems are so pronounced that little empirical work has been mounted to test its core assumptions. Erikson is the main exception in the sociology of deviance, but his chosen ground—Puritan New England—is lacking in that very complexity towards which functionalists point as the chief characteristic of modern societies. As Gellner has stressed, structurally simple and small-scale societies allow more scope for 'functionalism as a doctrine' because the problem of feedback of unintended beneficial consequences is minimized.[54] When applied to modern societies, Erikson's assumption of constancy in the crime rate looks almost bizarre. Moreover, the effect of crime is often the reverse of that assumed in functional analysis: far from drawing together 'upright consciences', it all too often triggers off a retreat into isolationism. The community in which the 'In Cold Blood' murders occurred reportedly withdrew from any semblance of social life in the aftermath of those murders. The Bradford 'Ripper' murders allegedly had the same effect on the social life of women. 'Indifference' phenomena are widely reported in the States in the context of the seemingly intractable deterioration in inner-city victimization. All this may be wild exaggeration: it is unfortunate that the main tenets of functionalism have not prompted more empirical work in this field.

Functionalists perhaps stand accused most powerfully of

[53] A. Gouldner, *The Coming Crisis*.   [54] E. Gellner, 'Concepts and Society'.

ignoring conflict, failing to explain change, and employing conservative ideology as a consequence. These criticisms can on the whole be discounted as misconceived or beside the point. Conflict can be regarded as functional and, indeed, Simmel[55] and Coser[56] have produced lengthy essays arguing that a period of open conflict can resolve otherwise gnawing strains in society; that conflict promotes the social solidarity of those who are bound together to confront a common enemy; that conflict is a clear warning of the presence of social problems; and that conflict is often surprisingly orderly, a social process locked into other social processes, and less disruptive than naïve spectators might suppose. Where conflict is not regarded as functional, it can be described as the outcome of 'malintegration'. Change is no less well accounted for than persistence and, as Merton pointed out, to assert that things 'hang together' in society as an argument against reform tends as much to revolution as to preserving the status quo. Merton observed that if social structures are as integrated in functionalist analysis as its critics maintain, all change, however petty, would indeed be revolutionary because no part would remain untouched. Indeed, functionalists are the defenders of no one form of political or social order. They are interested in very abstract and general principles of structural organization, principles so abstract that they are intended to apply to Utopia as well as to hell. Finally, the allegation that functionalism must be dismissed because it is conservative is itself an ideological rather than a sociological response. It assumes that conservatism is indisputably at fault, and that is not an assumption that can be made on safe philosophical or empirical grounds. The merit of conservatism is a metaphysical matter. If it is found to be the case that functionalism is well-argued and solid, and if the theory makes conservatism intellectually compelling, then its critics should reconsider their position on conservatism instead of using it as an argument for the rejection of functionalism.

Finally, none of the above applies to functional analysis as a method where the purposes of institutional arrangements and their effectiveness in terms of specific aims are concerned; nor

[55] G. Simmel, *Conflict and the Web of Group Affiliations*.
[56] See, for example, L. Coser, *The Functions of Social Conflict*.

are the unintended side-effects of phenomena any less central a topic if functionalism is abandoned. As a part of sociological enquiry, functional analysis remains in order. 'It is essential to evaluate the functionalist method, in the sense that it suggests to us where to look, in isolation from the functionalist doctrine, that tells us what we will find there.'[57]

As long as it is maintained that certain institutions 'fit' other institutions more than others, and some minimal congruence is suited to human association, functionalism is in principle a better guide than other approaches to many sociological questions. As soon as it is admitted, say, that modern industrial society requires some kinds of family structure, or certain types of education, rather than others, the functionalist method is also admissible. It may be that functionalists have tended to overplay their hand, but at least they appear to be playing the right sort of game. And it should be noticed, too, that functionalism still seems to be persuasive and pervasive enough to surface in a variety of disguises throughout sociology. There may be very few sociologists who would now advertise themselves as functionalists. But there are many calling themselves by other names who resort to functionalist ideas. When a radical criminologist like Stuart Hall or Steven Box proclaims that the effect of publicized working-class crime is to support capitalism by deflecting attention from the doings of the powerful, functionalism is being advanced. When a structuralist like Mary Douglas states that the suppression of deviance promotes the integrity of cognitive orders, functionalism is being advanced. When a phenomenologist like Jack Douglas points to the symbolic interdependencies of good and evil, deviance and respectability, functionalism is being advanced. In short, there is a tacit but perfectly virile functionalism still lurking in much of the sociology of deviance.

[57] L. Sklair, 'The Fate of the "Functional Requisites"', 40.

5

Anomie

Introduction

Anomie theory is distinctly out of fashion, perhaps permanently so. Like functionalism, from which it derives, it has
become a routine conceptual folly for students to demolish
before moving on to more rewarding ground. The critical
onslaught has been particularly fierce in the case of Robert
Merton's version of anomie theory, the turning-point being
Clinard's collection of critical essays on this theme in 1964.[1] By
contrast, Durkheim's original statement of anomie as a source
of deviant behaviour has received more sympathetic treatment,
largely because Durkheim is so central a figure in sociological
history, and anomie is so central a concept in his thought. That
is not the same thing, of course, as continuing to take it
seriously. However, both Lukes and Horton, for example,
discern in Durkheim's conception of anomie a philosophical
critique of capitalist society in relation to which Merton's
theory of anomie is at best confused and at worst 'dehuman-
ised'.[2] Other critics are prone to dimiss both as seriously
defective; Douglas attacked the entire methodology on which
Durkheim's sociology rested; Rex views Merton's central idea
as 'extraordinarily over-simplified' and seeks to rescue the bulk
of Durkheim's sociology from its damaging association with
the former's use of anomie; in Clinard's book, Lemert,
Gagnon, and others dealt a seemingly terminal series of blows
at both the theoretical and empirical weaknesses of the theory.
By the 1970s, Paul Rock and Mary McIntosh could refer
prosaically to the 'exhaustion of the anomie tradition'.[3]

---

[1] M. Clinard (ed), *Anomie and Deviant Behavior*.
[2] S. Lukes, 'Alienation and Anomie'; J. Horton, 'The Dehumanisation of Alienation
and Anomie'.
[3] J. Douglas, *The Social Meanings of Suicide*; J. Rex, *Discovering Sociology*, 234 ff.;

If only for its centrality to the sociological tradition of theorizing about deviance, however, anomie theory deserves recovery.
Among its strengths are a focus on the implications for deviance of one of the defining features of capitalist societies, that is,
the fostering of the propensity to consume *irrespective of* the
material possibilities of such a course; a meta-theory which is
capable of application to societies other than those of the
capitalist world; and the capacity, never greatly elaborated
upon since Durkheim's day, of addressing the conditions that
may suffice to determine the breakdown of social order.[4] So
powerful a theory cannot be disregarded. It was something of a
sociological counterpart to the cosmological Big Bang and its
effects have been both diffuse and lingering. Anomie theory was
at first thought to be so compelling that it was subject to
unusually sustained elaboration. After Durkheim and Merton,
there followed Cloward and Ohlin, Spergel, Downes, and
others working in a kind of tacit co-operation that appears only
rarely in sociology. Much of the theory still remains undeveloped, but it has been expanded to become one of the most
ambitious single attempts to explain deviance. (We shall
pursue the application of that attempt to deviant subcultures in
the next chapter.) More, anomie theory was under cultivation
at a time of energetic social engineering in the United States,
and it was appropriated to give intellectual coherence and
legitimacy to Mobilization for Youth.[5] It thereby became one
of the few well-documented instances of the sociology of deviance achieving a major impact on policy formation. And,
thirdly, it may be remarked that sociologists have not yet
proved able to relinquish such a pivotal part of their thought.
However much they may have protested about anomie theory,
it has been reincarnated again and again. It has an anonymous
presence in Jock Young's essay in labelling theory, *The Drug-
takers*. It is the invisible prop to the Birmingham Centre for
Contemporary Cultural Studies' radical work on class, youth,
and deviance in Britain. Indeed, just as Karl Mannheim was

Clinard, *Anomie and Deviant Behavior*; and P. Rock and M. McIntosh (eds.), *Deviance and
Social Control*, xi.

[4] Though see, in particular, P. Berger and T. Luckmann, *The Social Construction of
Reality*, and K. Erikson, *In The Wake of the Flood*.

[5] See Mobilization for Youth, *A Proposal for the Prevention and Control of Delinquency by
Expanding Opportunities*.

called the *bourgeois* Marxist, so Hall, Clarke, and Hebdige of Birmingham could be labelled the radical anomie theorists. Extensive echoes of the Big Bang will be discerned in any sensitive reading of the contemporary sociology of deviance.

Durkheim's Theory of Anomie

There are two distinct usages of anomie in Durkheim. Lukes restates them as follows:

> In the 'Division of Labour in Society', it [anomie] characterises the pathological state of the economy, 'this sphere of collective life which is in large part freed from the moderating action of [moral] regulation', where 'latent or active, the state of war is necessarily chronic' and 'each individual finds himself in a state of war with every other'. In 'Suicide', it is used to characterize the pathological mental state of the individual who is insufficiently regulated by society and suffers from 'the malady of infinite aspiration' . . . It is accompanied by 'weariness', 'disillusionment', 'disturbance, agitation and discontent', 'anger' and 'an irritated disgust with life'. In extreme cases this condition leads a man to commit suicide and homicide.[6]

As this passage makes clear, a shift is already under way from anomie conceived of as a constant property of industrial society, to anomie as a variable with social–psychological implications. It is by no means the case, as Davis, for example, asserts, that this process originated with Merton's later adaptation of the concept.[7]

Durkheim's conception of anomie must be set in the context of his theory of social evolution. In his first use of the concept, it is in the transition of society from mechanical to organic solidarity that the division of labour assumes an anomic form. In the former state, the division of labour is minimal, and the term 'mechanical' is paradoxically employed to refer to the uniformity of consciousness in the simplest societies. A single normative system holds absolute sway. In the latter, it is assumed that (for no society has yet attained this state) the division of labour, though highly differentiated, has generated mediating institutions that assure social cohesion despite marked moral diversity. In the transition, however, anomie results from the

[6] S. Lukes, 'Alienation and Anomie', 138–9.
[7] N. Davis, *Sociological Constructions of Deviance*, 109.

rapid growth of the economy without a corresponding growth in the forces that could regulate it. 'Sheerly economic regulation is not enough . . . there should be moral regulation, moral rules which specify the rights and obligations of individuals in a given occupation in relation to those in other occupations'— 'occupational groups' were somehow to be the source of this control.[8] A prerequisite is for the division of labour to assume a 'spontaneous' form, that is, individuals must be able to fill occupational positions which accord with their talents and which, therefore, they will accept as legitimate. This cannot prevail where the class system (or, presumably, any other form of stratification) inhibits the chances of large numbers of people attaining positions that fit their abilities. Such a 'forced' division of labour can only be abolished if all 'external' inequalities are ended, e.g. the hereditary transmission of property. It is in this sense that Taylor, Walton, and Young refer to Durkheim as a 'biological meritocrat', for he assumes an ideal correspondence is possible between 'internal' qualities and social position.[9] 'Labour is divided spontaneously only if society is constituted in such a way that social inequalities exactly express natural inequalities.'[10]

Anomie, then, is the peculiar disease of modern industrial man, for it is accepted as 'normal, a mark of moral distinction, it being everlastingly repeated that it is man's nature to be eternally dissatisfied, constantly to advance, without relief or rest, towards an indefinite goal'. Religion, governmental power over the economy, and occupational groups have lost their moral sway. Thus 'appetites have become freed of any limiting authority' and 'from top to bottom of the ladder, greed is aroused without knowing where to find ultimate foothold. Nothing can calm it, since its goal is far beyond all it can attain.'[11] In this analysis, class conflict and industrial crises are a symptom, not a cause, of anomie. Marx is reviewed as reversing the true causal priority, and, as a result, as proffering a false resolution of the problem, a purely economic cure.

In his second usage of the concept, in *Suicide*, Durkheim

---

[8] A. Giddens, *Émile Durkheim: Selected Writings*, Introduction, 11.
[9] I. Taylor *et al.*, *The New Criminology*, 81 ff.
[10] É. Durkheim, *The Division of Labor in Society*, 377.
[11] É. Durkheim, *Suicide*, 256.

elaborates on the sources of variation in the experience of anomie. In this pioneering study, the techniques of multi-variate analysis are deployed for sociological ends—it can hardly be maintained that Durkheim simply treated anomie as a constant and invariant property of industrialism. His argument rests on the crucial nature of the distinction between social *integration* and social *regulation*, which—largely independently of each other—are viewed as causally related to different forms of suicide (see accompanying table):

	Types of suicide	
	---	---
	Integration	Regulation
Too strong	Altruistic	Fatalistic
Too weak	Egoistic	Anomic

With certain exceptions, the excessive strength of integration and regulation are linked with pre-industrial societies, and the types of suicide characteristically prevalent, such as the honorific and the ritualistic, derive from the excessive subordination of the individual to the group. The reverse obtains in the case of industrial societies.

The egoistic form of suicide was seen by Durkheim as the product of excessive individuation, or the 'cult of the individual', which he saw as the moral counterpart of a specialized division of labour. It was exemplified by the higher suicide rate among Protestants as compared with Catholics; among the unmarried compared with the married; and among the childless as compared with parents. The force of the thesis was most strikingly displayed by the explanation Durkheim gave of the lower rates that obtained at times of political crisis compared with periods of political stability, as in France in 1830, 1848, and 1870. 'Great social disturbances', he argued, 'and great popular wars, rouse collective sentiments, stimulate partisan spirit and patriotism and, concentrating activity towards a single end, at least temporarily, cause a stronger integration of society.'[12] Suicide,

[12] Ibid. 208.

therefore, varies inversely with the degree of integration of society.[13]

Economic crises produced the contrary effect, a sharp increase in the suicide rate. This, argued Durkheim, is *not* due to the sudden loss of livelihood or amenities, for an increase in prosperity produces the same result as a decline. Also, suicide rates were at their lowest in the poorest regions of Europe, e.g. Calabria. (These also were the most Catholic, but Durkheim was not equipped statistically to avoid confounding possibilities of this sort.) To account for this phenomenon Durkheim invoked the concept of anomic suicide, that which flows from the disturbance such crises create in the regulatory aspect of social activity. Subject to deregulation in such crises, people's aspirations overshoot socially contrived limits, and fix on the unattainable. Durkheim spent a great deal of time accounting for people's inherent capacity to adopt this course *unless* they are curbed by social regulation. In striving to convey the character of anomie, Durkheim was driven to his most rabbinical purple passages: 'To pursue a goal which is by definition unobtainable is to condemn oneself to a state of perpetual unhappiness.'[14] It occurs because 'nothing appears in man's organic nor in his psychological constitution which sets a limit to such tendencies', i.e. the 'quantity of well-being, comfort or luxury legitimately to be craved by a human being'. 'It is not human nature which can assign the variable limits necessary to our needs. They are thus unlimited so far as they depend on the individual alone.' Hence, people must receive such regulation from 'an authority which they respect, to which they will yield spontaneously': such can only be provided by society. Hence, economic disasters and sudden surges in prosperity alike disrupt the capacity of society to exercise this influence

[13] A recent and striking confirmation of this aspect of Durkheim's theory is provided by P. O'Malley, 'War and Suicide'. O'Malley argued that, if Durkheim was right, then the rate of suicide among Australian women should have fallen significantly at three points in Australia's involvement in World War II: her entry into the War, her defeats with other Allies in North Africa, and the fall of Singapore—a real threat to the Australian mainland. The theory was sustained by the available evidence. The only alternative explanation might lie in the processes whereby the definitions of suicide were contrived, and it is conceivable that coroners in wartime are swayed from such definitions for patriotic reasons—suicides betoken demoralization, etc. But no data exist to substantiate or refute this alternative.

[14] É. Durkheim, *Suicide*, 248 ff. for this and subsequent quotations.

and—for a time—all regulation is lacking. 'Consequently, there is no restraint upon aspirations . . . At the very moment when traditional rules have lost their authority, the richer prize offered these appetites stimulates them and makes them more impatient of control. The state of de-regulation of anomie is thus further heightened by passions being less disciplined, precisely when they need more discipline.' The causal flow is from the prior fracturing of social regulation, to the adoption of unattainable goals, to suicide.

It is essential, in Durkheim's view, to avoid confounding that type of suicide stemming from the 'malady of infinite aspirations' with that resulting from the weakening of the social bond, in which the individual is 'detached from life because, seeing no goal to which he may attach himself, he feels himself useless and purposeless'. The two types also display distinctive psychological states at the point of suicide, and affect different groups in society. Egoistic suicide is associated with lassitude, weariness, goallessness, and has its principal victims among those in intellectual careers, the world of thought; anomie is associated with irritation, self-disgust, normlessness, and draws its recruits from the industrial and commercial world in which anomie is endemic and 'chronic'.

Despite Durkheim's eloquence, his attempts to differentiate egoism and anomie—and integration and regulation—strike many observers as overdone,[15] and, indeed, as beside the main point: that is, the tendency for industrialism to lead to what Weber termed the 'disenchantment of the world', with all that that implies by way of existential doubts and insecurities. A separate issue is: is a state of normlessness conceivable? This is, after all, an extremity beyond anarchy which is, properly conceived, the relatively simple notion—by comparison with anomie—of a society without government. A society without norms seems, on the face of it, a contradiction in terms. (There is also the problem of how, once deregulated, norms are reconstituted.) In general, cases where such extremes are approached empirically are infrequent: in the very young and the very old; there are very few even among those designated mentally ill. The feral child, the senile dement, the psychopath are our only approximations to the anomic in everyday terms.

[15] See S. Lukes, 'Alienation and Anomie', 139, n. 14.

There are, however, a few good descriptions of societies and communities that come close to Durkheim's conception of the anomic. Thus, Rainwater's *Behind Ghetto Walls*[16] depicted the mistrustful, nasty, alienated, and fragmented world of the Pruitt-Igoe housing development in St. Louis, Missouri. So suspicious and isolated had the tenants of the estate become, that there was no longer anything approaching a viable social life. Neighbour preyed on neighbour. People were reluctant to leave their homes for fear of others breaking in. They were loath to ask one another to keep an eye on their apartments because everyone was a potential predator. In time, the municipal authority concluded that existence in Pruitt-Igoe was so intolerable that the apartment blocks would have to be physically destroyed by dynamite. A second example has been given by a major neo-Durkheimian, Kai Erikson. *Everything in its Path* (published in Britain as *In the Wake of the Flood*[17]) narrates the devastation caused by the collapse of a dam in the mining community of Buffalo Creek, West Virginia, in 1972. As 132 million gallons of mud rushed down the creek, it carried away houses, people, roads, and possessions. Many were killed and a once orderly chain of communities was radically disrupted. Neat settlements were replaced by a haphazard trailer camp that incorporated no substantial social and architectural organization. There was an accompanying loss of moral regulation, a decline in co-operativeness, a pervading sense of meaninglessness, and a lack of purpose. Many people retreated inwardly, ceasing to busy themselves with one another. And there is yet another society that could be described as anomic, the Ik of Northern Uganda, as documented by Turnbull.[18] These 'mountain people' were subjected to a sudden deregulation born of economic catastrophe, when their traditional hunting grounds were designated a national park. Though Turnbull does not invoke Durkheim, he lists a mixture of Ik characteristics reminiscent of both egoism and anomie: 'acrimony, envy and suspicion' even among (illegal) hunting parties;[19] 'excessive individualism, coupled with solitude and boredom';[20] 'lassitude and inertia'.[21] Children over the age of

[16] L. Rainwater, *Behind Ghetto Walls*.   [17] K. Erikson, *In the Wake of the Flood*.
[18] C. Turnbull, *The Mountain People*.   [19] Ibid. 239.
[20] Ibid. 238.   [21] Ibid. 253.

three, and the old or disabled, were abandoned or robbed: 'without killing, it is difficult to get closer to disposal than by taking the food out of an old person's mouth, and this was primarily an adjacent-generation occupation, as were tripping and pushing off balance. Moreover, I confess they never expressed any intent to kill; it was all good, clean fun.'[22] The extremities of hunger and dispossession, such as the industrial West has not experienced outside the concentration camps (since even in prison regular food and shelter are to be had), lead Turnbull away from moral censure. Like Durkheim, he is concerned to stress the similarities between the anomic and the lives that we lead (overdrawn as some of these are by Turnbull: leaving children to the bush is hardly the same as sending them to summer camp[23]). But he notes the extent to which, in a context of plenty unknown to the Ik, we countenance suffering at home and starvation abroad. However, in other respects, Durkheim's analysis does not fit the Ik. They did not lack a goal (as in egoism) for their goal was survival; nor did they 'aspire infinitely' (as in anomie) for they aspired very specifically towards such mundane goals as food and water. Yet, in key respects, Durkheim offers more of a vocabulary for the understanding and prediction of the Ik than other classical theorists. And though the Ik cannot be said to represent pure anomie (in which, presumably, no rules of conduct can obtain, and people resemble dements), they come sufficiently close for credence to be granted the proposition that 'sudden deregulation' may bring social disaster—though not necessarily so, since other peoples in the region of the Ik had prospered through relocation. The irony is that the best-documented example of this 'disease' of modern industrial man should be a pre-industrial people. As Turnbull stresses in perhaps too melodramatic a way, however, the parallels are all too close.

Merton's Theory of Anomie

Merton took the conception of anomie as a starting-point for fresh theorizing, rather than as an end-product to be embellished.[24] The very different context in which he was writing, the

---

[22] Ibid. 252. [23] Ibid. 234.
[24] R. Merton, 'Social Structure and Anomie'.

America of the immediate post-Depression years, provides the
main clue to the divergent course he took. For Merton, the key
feature of his society of the 1930s was the contrast between the
American Dream and the enduring reality of harsh economic
inequality. The difference between that society and the France
of the 1890s, in which Durkheim had written, lay chiefly in the
Dream and not the inequality. In Europe, centuries of inequality were institutionalized in the complexities and subtleties of a
class society that re-formed rather than changed in any
dramatic way. Despite 1789, hereditary privilege and status still
counted. By contrast, as the floods of immigrants to the New
World testified, America still held out the promise of an open
society. At some point before 1917, even Lenin and Trotsky
had contemplated emigration to the USA. In America, no
hereditary aristocracy held even vestigial sway. There was Old
money and New money, but in the end it was simply money
that counted. Hence there was the American Dream, open to
all, given hard work and the opportunity to realize one's
talents.

In this context, Merton argued, the condition of anomie
which Durkheim had regarded as exceptional, as visited upon
people in boom and slump but as otherwise held at bay by
social regulation, becomes routine, a built-in feature of the
social world. In this respect, he came closer to Durkheim's first
Hobbesian depiction of anomie as endemic in industrial
capitalism.[25] But the *source* of anomie for Merton was not the
asymmetry between talent and reward; it lay rather in the lack
of symmetry between the culture and the social structure. The
'culture' of the USA was taken to be, at bottom, the American
Dream; but the social structure, however rapidly and widely it
spawned and spread prosperity, could not yield limitless
opportunities for all. Only a minority could enjoy the reality of
superabundance. As a process, however, 'Americanization'
pivoted on the hope that ultimately all could attain levels of
prosperity unknown by all but the tiny aristocratic and
bourgeois élites of old Europe. 'Infinite aspirations', far from
being released only under the shock of economic disturbance,
were the very seam of the cultural fabric of the American way of

[25] Durkheim also regarded the state of anomie as 'chronic' in the 'sphere of trade
and industry' in his analysis in *Suicide*; see especially 254–8.

life. Such a phenomenon was unprecedented, since only in America were the conditions of advanced industrial society combined with a distinctive ideology of classless egalitarian democracy; for this reason, Merton regarded his theory as applicable only to America. The basic argument on which it was based, however, i.e. the consequences of disjunction between goals, and the means of goal attainment, could be applied to any social context where the same type of disparity arose.

The pursuit of infinite aspirations was not seen by Merton as an innate human tendency, that emerged whenever social regulation was weakened. It was, rather, the product of a particular culture that needed incessant nurture if it was to persist and develop. A key feature of Merton's theory is his sensitivity to the dramatic growth of advertising in the inter-war period; a necessary adjunct to the growth of mass production and mass distribution was mass consumption. In this respect, Merton is—as Gouldner has noted—at one with Marx.[26] The fostering of the propensity to consume, with its creation of wants and dissatisfactions, is basic to economic growth in 'free market' economies. American ideology supplied the cultural counterpart of economic accumulation: fluid social mobility, the capacity to make it from Log Cabin to White House, was transmitted as a core value by the churches, the schools, and the mass media. The 'success' goal was sacred, failure profane: but in a society founded on the repudiation of monarchy and aristocracy, success came to be symbolized by sheer material gain (a future predicted with some assurance by de Tocqueville a century earlier). 'Money-success' was coined by Merton as *the* core value of American society, a 'cultural goal' extolled above all others.

For Durkheim, deregulation led to infinite aspirations; for Merton, infinite aspirations led to deregulation. The result, for both, was the same: high rates of deviation. The 'strain to anomie' crystallized in Merton's view in four types of deviance, differentiated by their combination of either acceptance or rejection of the goal and the means for realizing the goal (see the accompanying table).

---

[26] See Gouldner's Foreword to I. Taylor *et al.*, *The New Criminology*, x–xi.

	Culturally prescribed goal	Institutionally available means
Conformity	acceptance	acceptance
Deviant adaptations:		
Innovation	acceptance	rejection
Ritualism	rejection	acceptance
Retreatism	rejection	rejection
Rebellion	replacement	replacement

Despite the formidable strain to anomie, the majority of the population adhered, in Merton's view, to conformity. The mass of middle America remained small-town Puritans, wedded to cautious advancement but with an eye to the main chance. Their conformity ensured some social stability. For those unable to hold the socio-cultural tensions in balance, however, four 'deviant adaptations' were available. The first of these, 'innovation', basically involved the adoption of illegitimate means to the attainment of the cultural goal, 'money-success'. Crime, as Bell was later to put it, was a 'queer ladder of social mobility' in American life. The rackets were the deviant response to the small-town puritans' recipe for conformity, Prohibition. But any chicanery in politics or worldly affairs would exemplify deviant innovation just as well. Its mirror-image, 'ritualism', entailed the elimination of the goal and an obsessive attachment to the institutional means: here Merton is attempting to capture the ultra-conservative response to social tension, the celebration of sticking to the rules, of 'being in a rut', of staying put, that characterizes much of respectable lower- and middle-class life. 'Retreatism' involves the rejection of both goals *and* means, by dropping out of conventional society and yet not consciously striving to construct one afresh: the tramp, the hobo, the drug-taker are his key examples. Finally, 'rebellion' is seen as the rare attempt to resolve the tensions by not only rejecting both aspects of the status quo, but also actively seeking to replace them by alternative goals and means. Merton illustrated his thesis with a wealth of symbolic reference to key cultural myths. Empirically, his central conclusion was that, owing to the more intense and widespread experience of the disparity between the goal and the means at the bottom of the social hierarchy, deviance is inversely related to social status. Again, Durkheim had argued the reverse, for in his view, the social pressure exerted by the layers above them acts to limit the aspirations of the lower orders. 'Those who have only empty space above them are almost inevitably lost in it . . .'.[27] By contrast, Merton writes:

Of those located in the lower reaches of the social structure, the culture makes incompatible demands . . . In this setting, a cardinal American virtue—'ambition'—promotes a cardinal American vice—'deviant behaviour' . . . Within this context, Al Capone represents the triumph of amoral intelligence over morally prescribed 'failure' when the channels of vertical mobility are closed or narrowed in a society which places a high premium on economic affluence and social ascent for *all* its members.[28]

Merton's brief statement of anomie theory was first published in 1938, and revised and somewhat expanded versions were included in the four editions through which his major textbook has passed over the last fifty years. For almost half that period, it received almost uncritical acceptance; since the early 1960s, it has been overcritically rejected. Before going on to the criticisms that have real substance, it is useful to look at those which appear misplaced. The first of these is that Mertonian anomie theory presumes a simple consensus about the primacy of 'money-success' as a cultural goal. It is necessary to point out that sharing a goal does not imply simple consensus: the sharing of goals can generate the most bitter conflict. Hence, anomie theory does not collapse when confronted with the realities of class and value conflict, since class divisions and value conflicts may be framed in terms of inequalities of access to material wealth which all (to varying extents) desire. In his analysis of class and class conflict in Britain, for example, Westergaard documents the division of life-chances that persists along class lines, in terms of wealth,

[27] É. Durkheim, *Suicide*, 257.
[28] R. Merton, *Social Theory and Social Structure*, 145–6.

income, health, educational achievement, and mobility, and even access to welfare. He cites as an aggravating feature of class conflict the very 'revolution in rising expectations' which has often been equated with the 'withering away' of class: such expectations tend to surpass the material possibilities of their fulfilment, and promote what Marshall termed 'mild economic anomie'.[29] The fostering of the propensity to consume means that all come to share the aspirations once appropriate only to the élite: 'the luxuries of today become the necessities of to-morrow'. This process is entirely in accord with that of Merton's theory: though it is clear that class loyalties may profoundly modify the strain to anomie, they hardly negate it.

A second such criticism is that, in a diverse and complex society, 'money-success' is not the only goal; it merely competes with myriad other goals for a claim on energy and time; or it is itself mainly a *means* to quite different goals, such as family support and well-being. To pursue a variety of goals is not, however, to transcend the goal of 'money-success', which is at its most potent when legitimized by 'higher' things: the 'family' is as important to the 'Godfather' as to the early settlers. It may well be that it is successfully resisted by a minority of active 'rebels'; but so all-pervasive is the cash-nexus that such 'rebellion' is rare, and may well be replaced by an equally exclusive 'cultural goal', such as membership of a religious 'elect' or of a 'party' élite that are in themselves anomie-promoting. The abolition of private property has not abolished, but has heightened, the attractiveness of the perquisites of high office in State socialist societies.

A third, vivid criticism is that Merton's theory is both ahistorical and lacking in critical perspective. Laurie Taylor compares Merton's image of society to that of a giant fruit-machine,[30] whose pay-outs are rigged, but which most players delude themselves into perceiving as fair. The deviants are those who try to rig the machine to *their* advantage; who play it blindly and obsessively; who ignore its existence; or who smash it up and seek a better model. Nowhere, however, says Taylor, does Merton tell us who is taking the profits, and who put the

[29] T. Marshall, *Sociology at the Crossroads*; J. Westergaard, 'The Withering Away of Class'.
[30] L. Taylor, *Deviance and Society*, 148.

machine there in the first place. This telling criticism applies more to Merton's exposition of his theory than to the validity of the theory itself, for it would strengthen the theory rather than the reverse if it were to be prefaced by a history of American capitalist exploitation, and a synopsis of who owns what.

Anomie and After

Merton would never have described himself as a criminologist or sociologist of deviance: his interest lay elsewhere, in formal theorizing and in the sociology of science and knowledge. Although his account of anomie was to be so very central to the analysis of deviance, it was also oddly brief and uncherished. Anomie was discussed in two essays which were never lengthy or expansive enough to develop more than a few of its possibilities. There was to be no reply to many of the criticisms subsequently levelled at his thesis. It would not have been difficult to form a response or adapt his theory, but ideas were left in limbo.

In a sympathetic but critical reappraisal of Merton's theory, Albert Cohen noted that its author had laid it out in a surprisingly insulated fashion, not only from the allied work in the sociology of deviance in the 1920s and 30s, but also from his own contributions to general sociology: reference group theory and role theory.[31] Reference group theory has alerted us to the limited social worlds in which people invest their energies, and the generally limited horizons which mark them out. We typically compare ourselves, not with the upper echelons or the supremely successful, but with the peer groups of our own age, sex, and approximate social position. Among others, Runciman has demonstrated this effect for a variety of groups in Britain: manual workers tend to compare themselves with other manual workers, rather than with dukes.[32] Role theory is concerned with the kinds of people it is possible to be in a society, and with how roles are allocated and taken on; but, again, we are mostly preoccupied wth roles that are accessible to us, and not with those beyond our reach. Knowing this, asks Cohen, how could Merton propound so individualistic a

[31] A. Cohen, 'The Sociology of the Deviant Act', 5–14.
[32] W. Runciman, *Relative Deprivation and Social Justice*.

theory as anomie, as if people exercise choice in a kind of social vacuum, save for their sense of strain born of a heightened awareness of success-goals? Had Merton combined these different aspects of his own theorizing, he would surely have made a more realistic thesis. As it stands, anomie theory is static, individualistic, mechanistic, and focused on 'initial states and deviant outcomes rather than on processes whereby acts and complex structures of action are built, elaborated and transformed'.[33] People do not jump from conformity to deviance without, typically, 'a tentative, groping, advancing, backtracking, sounding-out process' going on. Cohen's own seminal contribution to meeting this difficulty, whilst retaining the strengths of the goals—means formulation, was the concept of subcultural process,[34] and it is in the development of different versions of subcultures of deviance that anomie theory has persisted most influentially.

Otherwise, anomie as a concept has been little more than marginal in the development of post-war theories of social problems, and almost totally absent from theories of social structure. Parsons[35] and Rex used it to mean imperfect understanding.[36] Empirically, despite many attempts, it did not lend itself to survey work or field methods of observation.[37] Becker parodied the theory in guying students who failed to find it on visits to car factories.[38] Like phlogiston in eighteenth-century physics, it increasingly appeared to be an artefact of an outmoded view of the social universe. The few serious attempts to measure its incidence have not established support for the theory in any direct sense. Stinchcombe found the strongest pressures for 'rebellion' lay among middle-class boys in high school, whose commitment to success goals was most marked and whose failure to achieve the most resented.[39] This finding has implications for any theory which invokes anomie and/or subcultural variants as an explanation for lower-class delinquency, but undermined confidence in Merton's overall theoretical emphasis on high rates of deviance among the lower

---

[33] A. Cohen, 'The Sociology of the Deviant Act', 9.   [34] See Chapter 6.
[35] T. Parsons, *The Social System*, 39.   [36] J. Rex, *Key Problems*, 177.
[37] See the formidable inventory compiled by S. Cole and H. Zuckermann in Clinard, *Anomie and Deviant Behavior*, 243–83.
[38] H. Becker, 'Labelling Theory Reconsidered', 50.
[39] A. Stinchcombe, *Rebellion in a High School*.

classes. Mizruchi complicated the model further by suggesting that middle-class anomie ('boundlessness') differed fundamentally from working-class anomie ('bondlessness').[40] Srole's 'anomie scale' employed questions designed to elicit the extent to which people felt at home in the world, but items such as 'little can be accomplished in a society which is seen as basically unpredictable and lacking order' appeared more as tests of political orthodoxy than existential unease.[41] Such overschematic tests were so reliant on ambiguous indicators and almost infinitely elastic and subjective measures of 'deviance' that the theory faded from serious consideration.

Criticism

'These facts', Durkheim stated characteristically, in a crucial passage in *Suicide*,[42] 'are susceptible of only one interpretation . . .'. Durkheim's passion for facts, his demand that 'social facts' should be 'treated as things', is the basis for his particular form of sociological positivism. But even the most sympathetic reader of *Suicide* cannot fail to be struck by Durkheim's boldness in bending 'the facts' to suit his theory. 'Crises' are classified as such on several occasions to suit the suicide rate, rather than being allowed to stand as anomalies. For example, the unification of Italy is treated as an economic, not as a political, event, primarily—one suspects—because it coincided with a rise rather than a decline in the suicide rate. Certain elections which produced, in Durkheim's view, a change in the suicide rate comparable in scale and intensity to the major crises of 1830, 1848, and 1870 lead him to comment: 'Mild as they are, mere election crises sometimes have the same result (as crises of war and revolution).'[43]

Douglas has argued that Durkheim's whole approach (and, by extension, that of positivism in general) was based on a methodological fallacy.[44] The flaw can be illustrated by Durkheim's treatment of the different suicide rates of Protestants and Catholics, of fundamental importance for his

[40] F. Mizruchi, *Success and Opportunity*.
[41] See the comments by Merton in Clinard, *Anomie and Deviant Behavior*, 227–8.
[42] É. Durkheim, *Suicide*, 208.   [43] Ibid. 204.
[44] J. Douglas, *The Social Meanings of Suicide*; and also in A. Giddens (ed.), *The Sociology of Suicide*.

concept of egoism. Durkheim asserted that *both* groups
strongly opposed suicide on theological grounds, and therefore
the differences between the two groups' rates of suicide could
not be accounted for in terms of their belief structures. Rather,
it was the Protestant emphasis on free enquiry that attenuated
the social bond and promoted greater strain towards egoistic
suicide among Protestants. Douglas criticizes Durkheim for
not going beyond sheer assertion on so crucial a point, since the
particular form of Catholic doctrine concerning suicide, which
entails eternal damnation, is far more emphatic than Protestant
doctrine. The point for Douglas, however, is not simply that
Durkheim was wrong on a specific point, however crucial; it is
that his method of reliance on official rates eliminated the possibility of eliciting such meanings from individuals.

Differences in the official rates of suicide were taken by
Durkheim to be social facts *sui generis*. Douglas asserts by
contrast that they are prone to all the weaknesses inherent in
official statistics, and are most prone to distortion in just those
respects where differences in the rates are most crucial, e.g. in
the case of Protestants and Catholics, or at times of crisis.
Against this view, Durkheim tried to guard himself against the
charge that many of the variations he noted were administrative artefacts, as, for example, may be caused at points of
revolutionary change by the disruption of the administrative
machinery for the registration of suicides. Were this the case,
Durkheim argued on several occasions, the rates would be
affected only in the areas where disruption was located,
whereas in reality the variations were far more widespread.
Douglas, however, is most concerned to stress the ways in
which officials are themselves influenced by the social meanings of suicide. For example, the view that certain social
situations, such as social isolation, may promote suicide, may
influence coroners in returning such a verdict in otherwise
ambiguous cases. Researchers then proceed to establish isolation as a 'cause' of suicide, and the theory appears confirmed.
Social meanings also pervade the presentation of death in
everyday life: Durkheim's confidence in the suicide statistics is
summed up in his phrase 'a corpse is a corpse', but if, for
example, some groups rather than others, for doctrinal and/or
social reasons, have a strong interest in concealing or disguising

suicides, the official rates may compound this practice. Durkheim himself allowed for the passive as well as the active suicide—the man who fails to stop himself falling as distinct from jumping—but arguably failed to follow this insight through to a radical enough extent. In his Table XXX, of suicides as classified by manner of death, such processes as drowning, leaping from a high place, and self-strangulation by hanging far outnumber poisonings and other forms of self-inflicted destruction less amenable to ready classification as suicide.[45] Douglas's alternative approach, the close scrutiny of suicide notes and allied correspondence, was expressly ruled out by Durkheim as unrepresentative. This exclusive reliance on official rates was assumed by Durkheim to be valid because of the regularity and stability of such rates: but if errors fit stable patterns, and are routinely reproduced, this assumption is invalid. The fallacy is to presume that official rates and indices are somehow constructed independently of social meanings.

This criticism was employed with even greater force against the assumption of Merton that the lower class were pressurized into higher rates of deviance than the middle and upper classes. 'Anomie theory stands accused of predicting far too little bourgeois criminality and too much proletarian criminality.'[46] This time it is the acceptance of the official rates of crime and delinquency, rather than that of suicide, which is seen as unwarranted. In Box's view, by accepting a simple inverse relationship between deviance and social status, Merton reduces anomie theory to that of 'relative deprivation'.[47] The entire house of cards collapses once this prop is removed, and the theories which base themselves upon it can be seen as mystifications blurring our view of 'deviance, reality and society'. Such a perspective is reproduced in police practices, which focus far more on working-class than on middle- or

[45] É. Durkheim, *Suicide*, 291.

[46] I. Taylor *et al.*, *The New Criminology*, 107.

[47] S. Box, *Deviance, Reality and Society*, 105–6. Box bases his case on the much more random distribution of criminality to be inferred from 'self-report' studies. For a critique of such studies, see A. Reiss, 'Inappropriate Theories and Inadequate Methods as Policy Plagues: Self-Reported Delinquency and the Law', 21–22. Reiss argues *inter alia* that police practices are largely *reactive*, and therefore have little probable impact on crime rates.

upper-class criminality. These practices naturally lead to official statistics which lend credence to the theory, and so, in a self-confirmatory circle, a politically innocuous conception of deviance is propagated.

Lindesmith and Gagnon note the severe limitations of both Merton's theory of anomie and one of its variants, the 'double failure' hypothesis of Cloward and Ohlin, in accounting for the social character of addiction.[48] Merton had typified addicts, along with vagrants, inebriates, and psychotics, as retreatists, i.e. 'as non-productive liabilities' and as 'asocialised persons who are *in* society but not *of* it', who have both 'relinquished culturally prescribed goals and abandoned the quest for success'.[49] Even if it is conceded that not all anomie produces deviance, and not all deviance flows from anomie, Lindesmith and Gagnon argue that the theory fails to specify clearly *which* forms of addiction may flow from anomie; or to confront the reverse proposition, that addiction may led to anomie; or to square with the specialized social skills that addicts must develop if they are to survive the control measures against them, and finance a highly expensive habit; or to convey the complexity of the social worlds constructed by the diverse groups so readily tagged 'asocial'. The application of anomie theory to a specific form of deviance raises, in short, the most fundamental doubts about its capacity to either explain or enhance our understanding of the origins, consequences, and processes of development of deviance in general.

In the same volume, Lemert argues that the theory 'strains credulity' for reasons that go beyond the purely logical or empirical. Firstly, the very terms so confidently used by Merton to sustain his theory are highly problematic: 'social structure' and 'culture' are at best abstractions that are exceptionally difficult to differentiate in terms of data, at worst reifications that derive from the fallacy of misplaced concreteness. 'Inescapable circularity lies in the use of "culture" as a summary to describe modal tendencies in the behaviour of human beings and, at the same time, as a term of designating the causes of the modal tendencies.'[50] The same term, 'culture',

---

[48] A. Lindesmith and J. Gagnon, 'Anomie and Drug Addiction'.
[49] R. Merton, *Social Theory and Social Structure*, 142–4.
[50] E. Lemert, 'Social Structure, Social Control and Deviation', 60.

tends to be applied across the board to the small-scale, relatively unified society (such as Tikopia) and to the highly differentiated agglomeration of often diverse sub-societies, such as the USA.

It is theoretically conceivable that there are or have been societies in which values learned in childhood, taught as a pattern, and reinforced by structured controls, serve to predict the bulk of the everyday behaviour of members and to account for prevailing conformity to norms. However, it is easier to describe the model than to discover societies which make a good fit with the model.[51]

Lemert prefers a model of a pluralistic society, in which different groups and associations negotiate compromises and reach contingent accommodations that derive, if at all, only at several removes from a consensus over some ultimate values.

One objection to Merton's view of choice and action by individuals is that it simplifies something enormously complex. Instead of seeing the individual as a relatively free agent making adaptations pointed toward a consistent value order, it is far more realistic to visualise him as 'captured' . . . by the claims of various groups to which he has given his allegiance [familial, occupational, religious, ethnic, and political ties are what Lemert has in mind, *inter alia*]. It is in the fact that these claims are continually being preemptively asserted through group action at the expense of other claims, frequently in direct conflict, that *we find the main source of 'pressures' on individuals in modern society*, rather than in 'cultural emphasis on goals'.[52]

It is possible to refine Merton's conception to take account of Lemert's quite distinct model of social structure and culture: but only at the cost of reducing the intensity of the 'strain' induced by the goals—means discrepancy to far milder levels than he proposed.

Secondly, Merton's theory neglects altogether the implications of social control for the shaping of deviant behaviour. Lemert's critique takes two major forms: one, the need to allow theoretically for the promotion of 'active' as well as 'passive' social control; and two, the need to differentiate between 'primary' and 'secondary' deviation. 'Active social control' refers to the growing organizational tendency in complex industrial societies with a high rate of technologically induced

---

[51] Ibid. 63–4.   [52] Ibid. 68.

growth to regulate activity in purely instrumental ways. For example, the regulation of pollution, industrial safety, traffic, and commercial and financial transactions is only negligibly concerned with the imputation of stigmas and moral evaluations, and is primarily designed to enforce minimum standards of compliance that do not signally interfere with production and profits. Innovation, far from emerging as a 'deviant or nonconforming response of structurally disadvantaged individuals',

has become organised or institutionalised in our society . . . Nowhere is the contingent nature of deviation made more apparent than in the action of government regulatory agencies with adjudicative and punitive powers in situations where they are confronted by consequences of technological and organisational change. Large areas of action to do with business, finance, health, labor, housing, utilities, safety and welfare are subject to control through administrative rules discontinuous in origin and form from the culturally derived norms which impressed Merton and others seeming to favor a conception of passive social control.[53]

In other words, an increasing proportion of control activity is 'active' and cannot be seen to flow in any simple or direct fashion from 'the norms' that are presumed to inhere in patterns of childhood socialization.

'Passive social control', however, still operates in the sphere of the 'sacred': and it is in this respect still potent in the operation of the criminal justice system. Moral character and 'status degradation' remain part of the armoury that produces 'secondary deviation', i.e. 'how deviant acts are symbolically attached to persons and the effective consequences of such attachment for subsequent deviation on the part of the person'.[54] In such secondary deviation, 'the original "causes" of the (primary) deviation recede and give way to the central importance of the disapproving, degradational, and isolating reactions of society'.[55] Lemert holds this to be 'pragmatically the more pertinent' a research problem, and one to which anomie theory has as yet contributed nothing. To put it

[53] E. Lemert, 'Social Structure, Social Control and Deviation', 89–91.
[54] Ibid. 82.
[55] Ibid. 81; see also chapter 7 of the present text on interactionism.

crudely, it may be that the majority of people 'steal', but only a minority become processed as 'thieves': anomie theory alerts us to possible reasons for the former, but precludes analysis of the processes underlying the latter proposition.

In a more structurally inclined critique of Merton, Gouldner makes the point that more follows from the malintegration of goals and means than appears in even the revised statements of the theory.

The allocation of the means to succeed and, with this, of position in the class system, is in appreciable part a function of the institution of private property and its hereditary or testamentary transmission. Thus the distribution of anomic responses is a function of this institution. But it does not follow that those on the top of the class system are less anomic, if by this is meant that they have more of a genuine belief in and devotion to their culture's moral values. Indeed, there is reason to predict that their genuine commitment to these moral values is undermined by the very institution from which they derive their advantages. For this institution makes it possible for them to sever the connections between gratification and conformity to cultural values . . . In short, the spoiler of the society's morality is . . . 'vested interest', the right to do something for nothing.[56]

To this critical catalogue, we would wish to add only three more problems. Firstly, although he later attempted to plug the gap,[57] Merton ignored the reverse situation to the malintegration of goals and means that occurs when results *exceed* expectations. The 'anomie of success' is again more prevalent at the top than the bottom of the system, and applies whether the success is 'earned' or not. The overnight 'star', the unexpected 'bestseller', the 'pools winner' are arguably candidates for anomie just as much as the relative failures (though data exist which cast doubt on this response for one group of pools winners in Britain[58]). A second problem is the difficulty of conceptualizing the chronology of anomie and deviance. Once formulated, deviant adaptations exist in the world as social institutions possessing some degree of stability and continuity. They may be encountered before any exposure to the 'strain to anomie' has occurred. However, if the 'solution' is

---

[56] A. Gouldner, *The Coming Crisis*, 325.
[57] R. Merton, in M. Clinard, *Anomie and Deviant Behavior*, 219–22.
[58] S. Smith and P. Razzell, *The Pools Winners*.

embraced before the 'problem' is encountered, as described, for example, in Whyte's depiction of neighbourhood rackets in an Italian–American slum, then the experience of anomie is pre-empted.[59] It becomes a purely structural property without subjective counterpart. The problem of investigating anomie empirically may therefore elude available methodologies, since the only indicators of anomie that remain are its presenting symptoms, such as high rates of crime and delinquency.[60] The circularity is well demonstrated in Lander's study of Baltimore, in which the best predictors of delinquency could not be adequately disentangled from the best predictors of anomie. And, finally, there is the problem raised by Albert Cohen and Arthur Stinchcombe. Anomie seems to be conceived as the outcome of a yawning gap between aspiration and the prospect of final achievement. It is presumably most grievous in its effects on ambitious but disadvantaged young people who cast ahead to gauge their life-chances. But it appears that people actually tend not to project their lives very far ahead. Indeed, Stinchcombe argued that adolescents plan only a little into the future.[61] Expectations and motives are frequently confined to limited periods of time, shifting with each significant turning-point in the life cycle. Experiences, perspectives, projects, and acquaintances interact and evolve continuously, and ambition and explanations of failure are significant parts of that phased growth. They are not usually set but emergent, they are often short-term, and anomic disjunction itself may not be as profound as Merton claimed. To be sure, there are groups whose deprivation is so great that their frustration can never be modulated. But it is not clear whether anomie theory is intended to refer chiefly to them or to others whose lives are rather too complicated to be captured so simply.

Conclusion

It may well be the case, as Douglas argues, that Durkheim's methodology is flawed, but that does not invalidate the general

---

[59] W. Whyte, *Street Corner Society*.

[60] Merton and Srole distinguished *anomie* as a systemic property from *anomia* as a psychological state. This differentiation does not resolve the problem as we see it here.

[61] A. Stinchcombe, *Rebellion in a High School*.

support for his theory that can be drawn from a revised view of the official statistics. Douglas's alternative method 'for determining and analysing the communicative actions which can be observed and replicated in real-world cases of suicide' remains obscure, beyond the examination of suicide notes, and the like. Indeed, it was the limitations of such methods that led Durkheim to focus on the rates as alone capable of providing sufficient evidence for analysis. The two methods are, in certain respects, quite compatible. As Atkinson's recent work testifies, however, there are perhaps intractable problems involved in a reliance on the rates alone.[62] While empirical support for Durkheim's theory remains mixed, it is still a formidable source for theory and research.

Merton's application of the concept draws both its strengths and its weaknesses from his Americanization of anomie. The weaknesses stem from too facile an acceptance of the official rates of deviance, and too standardized a view of the prevalence of the American Dream. But 'Americanization' remains a real phenomenon, as generations of immigrants from diverse cultures were and are subject to a relatively unbridled ideology of egalitarian consumerism. The content and consequence of these processes have been, if anything, too little researched and explored. Jules Henry echoed Merton and elaborated on the theme of 'money-success' in writing: 'In contemporary America children must be trained to *insatiable* consumption of *impulsive* choice and *infinite* variety.'[63] The impact and nature of the collective representations of advertising remain relatively unknown, but such evidence as we have gives point to Merton's thesis. Nor is the imputed effect confined to America: all consumer societies have experienced rising rates of crime and delinquency in the context of growing affluence; and anomie theory remains one of the most plausible attempts to account for this seeming paradox.[64] In the most systematic review of the

---

[62] M. Atkinson, *Discovering Suicide*.   [63] J. Henry, *Culture Against Man*, 70.

[64] The British experience may offer a test of sorts by which to compare the effectiveness of Merton's as against Durkheim's version of anomie. In the austerity of the immediate post-war period, crime and delinquency rose. In 1951, rationing ended, and a newly elected Conservative government encouraged consumption by fiscal measures. The crime and delinquency rates, along with the rate of strikes, fell during the next few years, to increase from the mid-1950s onwards. Durkheim would have predicted an immediate rise in crime following the 'end of austerity' that regulated life in Britain from 1945 to 1951. Merton, however, would have predicted a rise in deviance only after

evidence to date, Braithwaite concluded that it supported 'a strong *prima facie* case . . . that reducing inequalities of wealth and power will reduce crime.'[65]

Lemert may be right in proposing the general inadequacy of anomie theory in any simple sense to convey the processes involved in deviance and control. His own critique, however, fails to differentiate between social change resulting from innovation that falls *within* the realm of institutional means, and social change resulting from innovation which does not. An example of the latter is the extent to which the 'hidden economy' is producing considerable distortions in taxation and consumption by comparison with the 'formal economy'.[66] Lemert seems in this and other respects to miss the point of Merton's analysis. Even planned social change can disrupt lives for the worse, for example, the unemployment that can result from technological obsolescence falls unevenly on the population, and for those adversely affected, the goals–means equation is arguably subject to sharp deterioration. It remains an empirical question as to whether that promotes higher rates of deviance, of whatever kind. In sum, though substantial revision is in order, there is a great deal of unexplored mileage in anomie theory, whichever version we prefer.

a time-lag, during which advertising and the greater availability of goods stimulated aspirations beyond the modest levels to which people had become habituated during the war and its aftermath.

[65] J. Braithwaite, *Inequality, Crime and Public Policy*.
[66] See, for example, S. Henry, *The Hidden Economy*.

6

Culture and Subculture

Introduction

Attempts to explain and understand social deviance, in particular juvenile delinquency, in terms of adherence to distinctive cultural patterns, have developed rapidly over the past few decades. In the 1950s and most of the 60s, it was considered somewhat novel even to link the two concepts. It was also considered scientific, in so far as sociologists, with respectful nods in the direction of anthropology, sought to divide up the population in relation to their parent class cultures, varieties of subcultures, and burgeoning counter-cultures, each with their distinctive norms, values, and beliefs, each with a clear-cut relationship to the others, all invested with a degree of clarity which consigned any lingering doubts about the reality of all this cultural attribution to the margin. It is all too easy, in retrospect, to see this body of work as a somewhat mechanical attempt to pin down the unpinnable: cultures as they are lived. But there were real gains none the less, not least the establishing of the proposition that the most apparently senseless and meaningless forms of aggressive delinquency could be rendered intelligible and rational by taking account of their authors' 'definitions of the situation', and by conceiving of delinquency as a solution, rather than as a problem, to dilemmas that they faced.

We shall argue that there was an excessively schematic quality about the subcultural theories of delinquency of this period. It was held that society, whether American, as in the work of Albert Cohen, Cloward and Ohlin, and Miller, or British, as in the work of Mays, Downes, and Hargreaves, could be clearly layered and categorized into classes, sectors, age-groups, and sex-roles.[1] Overall, especially in Cohen's influential work, there

[1] A. Cohen, *Delinquent Boys*; R. Cloward and L. Ohlin, *Delinquency and Opportunity*;

loomed in stable ascendancy the 'dominant' culture: White Anglo-Saxon Protestant culture, the ascetic, achievement-orientated, highly competitive, middle-class way of life. To this centre of cultural gravity everyone was pulled: none could escape its clutches, though in line with the model underlying Merton's theory of anomie, those most embroiled in the system's imperfections could kick against it in various ways. Deviant subcultures could be originated in reaction against it; once in being, they in themselves became a form of constraint. Delinquents acted out delinquent subcultures: the real analytical problem was to theorize why such deviant solutions could be generated in the first place. The sociologist, in short, was the dispassionate observer and analyst of deviant behaviour, albeit one who credited that behaviour with a version of rationality, collective problem-solving, and group process.

The break with these variations on the 'delinquent subculture' theme came with the work of Matza.[2] It was a partial break only, for—as we shall see—Matza retained certain features of these theories in his own work. But he helped to open up, along with the exponents of labelling theory, a Pandora's box whose contents—the emphasis on free will, the argument that all prior theorizing had 'over-predicted' delinquency, the rejection of the attempt to differentiate deviants from non-deviants as a fruitful mode of enquiry—swamped the neat boundaries between this subculture and that which were the hallmark of existing approaches. By no means all of this was incompatible with the theories under attack. For example, the focus of labelling theory on such variables as police bias against gang compared with non-gang boys rather neatly complemented them.[3] Even so, the later phase of work in the cultural and subcultural vein shifted away in the 1970s to markedly different theories and methods.

After 1967, subcultural theory languished. For five years or so no substantive work appeared which derived from its central

W. Miller, 'Lower Class Culture as a Generating Milieu of Gang Delinquency', 5–19; J. Mays, *Growing Up in the City*; D. Downes, *The Delinquent Solution*; D. Hargreaves, *Social Relations in a Secondary School*

[2] D. Matza, *Delinquency and Drift*.

[3] See, for example, I. Piliavin and S. Briar, 'Police Encounters with Juveniles', 206–14; also C. Werthman and I. Piliavin, 'Gang Members and the Police'.

tenets or which developed its major propositions. Its similarities with anomie theory subtly became more obvious, and the critical exposure of the defects of anomie theory was extended to subcultural theory. Both rested on the assumption that deviant behaviour originated in socially induced 'strain' or 'tension'. Underlying that 'strain' was the image of society as basically stable and consensual, though flawed by remediable inequalities of opportunity. Such an image was unattractive both to the labelling theorists, who favoured a more pluralistic model of society as a mosaic of disparate social worlds; and to the more radically inclined sociologists of deviance who sought to base their theories on the central assumption of class struggle. It was not until 1972 that a perspective emerged that was capable of accommodating such diverse strands. Phil Cohen's analysis of working-class youth cultures in East London emphasized the latter approach to such effect that it became the basis for the substantial work on deviance and control by the Birmingham Centre for Cultural Studies, under the directorship of Stuart Hall.[4] Their work concentrated in general on the interplay between class conflict, youthful rebellion, and media presentations, and did not entail first-hand ethnographies. Paul Willis's work at the Centre was somewhat exceptional. He engaged with the complexities of field-work, not in the traditional manner of the theorist out to prove or refute a theory, but in the mode that Jules Henry has termed 'passionate ethnography'.[5] He attempted with rare success to describe and analyse the subjective unfolding of 'contradictions and problems' as they are 'lived through to particular outcomes'.[6] The result was a series of re-creations of 'cultures' (Willis significantly did not use the term subculture at all, preferring the term 'subordinate cultures'), which could hardly have been accomplished if Willis had been preoccupied by formal theory-testing. His work has, none the less, a real significance for theories of culture and subculture.

From 1972 to date, a flood of work has appeared in Britain which takes as its axis the need to 'capture' cultural meanings yet also to contextualize their source in the larger social

[4] P. Cohen, 'Working Class Youth Cultures in East London'.
[5] J. Henry, *Culture Against Man*, 3.
[6] P. Willis, *Profane Culture*, 1. See also his *Learning to Labour*.

structure, usually in terms of its contradictions. The works of *inter alia* Murdock, Pearson, Corrigan, Cohen and Robbins, Hebdige, Brake, and Pryce share this broad perspective. Important exceptions such as Parker, Gill, and Marsh, draw more comprehensively from labelling theory and earlier socio-logical and subcultural approaches while achieving consider-able observational records.[7] Overall, the priority accorded formal theory-testing has receded, perhaps too much so, in the face of an unprecedented enthusiasm for more extensive explorations of diverse social worlds.[8] The materials gathered in the process have enhanced the possibilities for cultural and subcultural theories to develop in a less constricted way than in the past. Such possibilities, however, have yet to be realized.

Strain Theories

The first truly systematic use of the concepts of culture and subculture in the explanation of delinquency occurs in the work of Albert Cohen. The problem, as he stated it, was that previous theories had made only a limited, and largely circular, use of such concepts. To say that delinquency was 'part of' a culture, or was 'culturally transmitted', did not take one very far. What was needed was a theory of the *origins* of such culture. Again, the delinquency previously theorized about had been mainly of the acquisitive kind, akin to adult forms of theft and robbery. Yet the more puzzling forms of delinquency were primarily expressive in character. Violence, vandalism, joy-riding: these kinds of activity were simply not addressed by existing theories (though he made little reference to the work of Thrasher in this respect). Cohen argued that an adequate

[7] G. Murdock and R. McCron, 'Youth and Class; The Career of a Confusion'; G. Pearson, '"Paki-Bashing" in a North East Lancashire Cotton Town'; P. Corrigan, *Schooling the Smash Street Kids*; P. Cohen and D. Robins, *Knuckle Sandwich; Growing up in the Working Class City*; R. Hebdige, *Subculture; The Meaning of Style*; M. Brake, *The Sociology of Youth Culture and Youth Subcultures*; K. Pryce, *Endless Pressure: A Study of West Indian Lifestyles in Bristol*; H. Parker, *The View From the Boys*; O. Gill, *Luke Street*; P. Marsh *et al.*, *The Rules of Disorder*.

[8] This has not been so in the case of traditional criminology, or in the USA. See, for example, D. West, *Present Conduct and Future Delinquency*; D. West and D. Farrington, *Who Becomes Delinquent?*, and *The Delinquent Way of Life*; also M. Hindelang, 'The Social versus Solitary Nature of Delinquent Involvements', 167–75; and D. Elliott and H. Voss, *Delinquency and Dropouts*.

theory should address itself to both the character and social distribution of the most serious forms of delinquency; and also employ the concept of culture in ways which specify the functions it performs, and the problems it solves, for the groups whose behaviour it allegedly influences so strongly.

This conception of culture is characteristically functionalist. Culture enables people to solve the problems created *for* them by the social structure. Culture consists of 'traditional ways of solving problems' or of 'learned problem solutions' which are transmitted through the processes of childhood socialization. Cohen was concerned to address the problem of why, if such a strong basis for conformity is provided by cultures, there should be any possibility of innovation. The answer he supplies is reminiscent of Merton's anomie theory, and consists of accepting that, at some points in the social system, normative conflict is possible. Structure and culture make incompatible demands, and it is at these points of pressure that subcultures are evolved to 'solve' the problems that arise. Subcultures typically borrow elements from the larger culture and rework them into distinctive forms. Such elements (e.g. violence, hedonism) are available to all: but not everyone is a bearer of a subculture which gives them unusual predominance. 'The crucial condition for the emergence of new cultural forms is the existence, *in effective interaction with one another, of a number of actors with similar problems of adjustment*.'[9] Cohen vividly conveyed the scope for distinctive subcultures to emerge as solutions to problems posed for different groups. 'Each age, sex, racial and ethnic category, each occupation, economic stratum and social class consists of people who have been equipped by their society with frames of reference and confronted by their society with situations that are not equally characteristic of other roles.'[10] The task was to theorize 'the role of the social structure and the immediate social milieu in determining the creation and selection of solutions' in a manner applicable to gang delinquency.[11]

The main plank of Cohen's own theory was his characterization of gang delinquency, and his assumption that it amounted to a 'way of life' in downtown metropolitan and inner urban

[9] A. Cohen, *Delinquent Boys*, 59.
[10] Ibid. 54.   [11] Ibid. 55.

neighbourhoods. This pattern of delinquency could be sum-marized as displaying the following six characteristics: (*a*) non-utilitarianism: even in the case of thefts, economic rationality seemed rarely to prevail, since goods would be stolen 'for kicks', and given away, discarded, or destroyed, rather than consumed or sold for profit; (*b*) malice: a thread of destructive-ness ran through the delinquency which seemed quite distinct from damage wrought as a by-product of sheer skylarking (for example, the apparently wanton vandalism that accompanied some break-ins); (*c*) negativism: much delinquent behaviour seemed not simply at odds with respectable values, but their inversion; (*d*) short-run hedonism: the cult of instant gratifica-tion 'reached its finest flower' in the delinquent gang; (*e*) versatility: the gang's activities ran the gamut through theft, vandalism, aggression, and general hell-raising (by contrast the delinquency of girls seemed more aligned with sex-role expectations, as manifested in such offences as shop-lifting clothes and cosmetics); (*f*) group autonomy: gang loyalty came first, all other allegiances being subordinated to it.

This profile of the delinquent subculture did not aim to be an exhaustive catalogue of all delinquency, but an inventory of the most serious forms that group delinquency took. It should also be stressed that Cohen was accentuating tendencies which occasionally became 'reality', rather than a set of everyday activities. Criticisms of the theory which caricature it for conjuring up an image of incessant warfare between youth and the adult world often ignore its 'ideal-typical' character.

The explanation of such delinquency was sought by Cohen in terms of the initial conformity of youth to the established cultural order. However, in the case of subordinate groups in a society stratified along lines of social class, the very process of adhering to the values of the dominant culture makes for the creation of problems rather than their resolution. The rationale for the apparently motiveless and meaningless behaviour of delinquent gangs is to be found in the problems faced by the sector of society apparently most involved: lower-class, male, urban adolescents. For Cohen they commonly experience great tension and strain in handling the paradoxical many-are-called-but-few-are-chosen nature of democratic schooling. Schools exist to *make* children care about social status and academic achievement, but on terms which effectively deny them to all but a minority of the working class. Faced with a common 'problem of adjustment' caused by school failure, the rejected evolve the delinquent gang solution as a means both to acquire status in a more accessible form, and to hit back at the system that has branded them as failures. The gang takes the rules of respectable society and turns them upside down: the D stream's revenge. The theory is neatly tailored to account for the much lower rates of such delinquency among the middle class (they are far more likely to attain success by the conventional route); girls (they value marriage to an occupationally successful male far more highly than 'making it' in career terms themselves—a proposition that in turn would predict relatively more female delinquency as that tradition weakens); and in non-urban areas (schools hold less sway as the route to honoured crafts and trades). It seemed to 'fit the facts' extremely well; to aid in both explaining and understanding the group character of most delinquency; and to go beyond previous theories whilst retaining their more valuable insights.

The theory quickly stimulated variants of much the same model, and a plethora of essays at empirical testing. The most sympathetic work to that of Cohen was Cloward and Ohlin's study.[12] They proposed much the same structurally generated model of delinquency causation as Cohen, but argued that he had seriously underrated the degree of *specialization* that existed, and overrated the role of the school as the crucible of delinquency. They discerned three types of delinquent subculture arising in different types of neighbourhood: criminal (gangs pursuing quite utilitarian forms of robbery and theft); conflict (fighting gangs); and retreatist (drug-using gangs). The major source of variation was the presence or absence of stable recruitment into adult criminal enterprises in the local community: where such patterns existed, the criminal gang would predominate; where not, the conflict gang. Boys failing to succeed either legally or illegally in any context would slough off this 'double failure' by resorting to drug-using and 'hustling'. The root cause of the original emergence of delinquent subcultures was not so much the school—largely an irrelevance to the downtown street-corner youth—as the economic pursuit

[12] R. Cloward and L. Ohlin, *Delinquency and Opportunity*.

of 'money-success' earlier emphasized by Merton in his anomie theory, and reinstated by Cloward and Ohlin as the prime source of embittered frustration in the metropolitan slums. In some of the ghetto areas, youth unemployment reached the level of 40–50 per cent and, although Cloward and Ohlin did not see ethnicity as a significant causal variable, their approach does make some sense of the 'fact that homicide is the leading cause of death among young black males in the USA'.[13]

Empirical studies based on the testing of these two theories became a major factor of criminology in the late 1950s to mid-1960s. The main conclusions to emerge from the most meticulous of these projects, that of Short and Strodtbeck in Chicago,[14] inclined towards Cohen's more generalized characterization of gang delinquency, but rejected his emphasis on the oppositional character of the subcultural values that supported it. Situational elements were acknowledged: the precipitating motive for gang fights supplied by the fact that threats to the leader's status loomed larger at street level than in theory: the part played by sheer contingency in dragging large numbers of otherwise only marginally delinquent youth into the fray; and the disconcerting ability to accommodate apparently quite contradictory 'value systems' shown by gang boys, who gave more support than non-gang boys to values favourable to delinquency without significantly disaffiliating from the values of conventional society. A major problem in all of this was the sheer difficulty of testing more than a few facets of the theories in other than a somewhat mechanical fashion: but the data pointed to the inescapable conclusion that delinquency was far more autonomous and contingent than earlier theories had allowed.

The work of David Matza made rather more impact by achieving a partial critical break with the underlying assumptions of strain theory and by proposing an alternative theory of delinquency. His theory is nowhere presented as a coherent whole, but is to be assembled, albeit with some inconsistencies, from several sources.[15] He roundly condemns strain theorists

---

[13] V. Fuchs, *Who Shall Live? Health, Economics and Social Choice*, 40.

[14] J. Short and F. Strodtbeck, *Group Process and Gang Delinquency*.

[15] David Matza's work on delinquency and deviance emerged chronologically as

(along with virtually all prior work) for 'over-predicting' delinquency, for accounting for far more of it than exists. At the same time, he retains some of strain theory's central features, notably the stress on group process, and—in his assertion that 'preparation' and a sense of 'desperation' are preludes to delinquency in certain areas—he conjures up an implication of strain akin to the earlier subcultural theorists. Matza's major achievement is to build his theory around the axiom that delinquency is *willed* behaviour, and is in general 'intermittent' and 'mundane' as well as subject to a sharp diminution with the onset of adulthood. The idea that delinquency flowed from a deeply held commitment to a set of oppositional values embodied in delinquent subcultures could not account for these patterns. Instead, he proposed that a state of drift typically precedes delinquency. Drift entails a loosening of controls from which delinquency is only *one* possible outcome. 'The delinquent transiently exists in a limbo between convention and crime . . . postponing commitment, evading decision.'[16] Delinquency, however, does not occur in a vacuum. It is facilitated by a 'subculture of delinquency' comprising a set of precepts that both release the delinquent from the constraints of law and custom, and caricature commonly held values rather than representing an inversion of them. 'Techniques of neutralization' solve the problem of moral scruples: 'I didn't mean to do it', 'They had it coming to them', 'Everybody does it', 'Nobody got hurt', and 'I only did it for my friends' are commonly held justifications for deviance rather than the peculiar preserve of offenders. Similarly, delinquency is rendered attractive, not by adherence to a bizarre morality unique to young offenders, but by their exaggerated valuation of widely circulating 'subterranean' values: the pursuit of excitement, the disdain for routine work, and the equation of toughness and masculinity. This combination encourages males in the 'limbo' of adolescence to manufacture excitement by law-breaking. The process of drift helps account for the episodic and generally 'mundane' character of delinquency. The closeness of the

follows: with G. Sykes, 'Techniques of Neutralization', 1957; 'Subterranean Traditions of Youth', 1961; with G. Sykes, 'Delinquency and Subterreanean Values', 1961; *Delinquency and Drift*, 1964; *Becoming Deviant*, 1969.

[16] D. Matza, *Delinquency and Drift*, 28.

delinquent's values to those of conventional society helps account for the relative ease with which maturation out of delinquency is accomplished with the onset of adulthood and more structured role-playing in work and family life. Unfortunately, in setting out to remedy theories which he saw as 'over-predicting' delinquency, Matza over-corrects to the point at which his own theory *under-predicts* both its scale and, in particular, its more violent forms. In his discussion of violence, Matza employs the idea of 'desperation', but the theme is left relatively unexplicated. 'The drifter is not less a problem than the compulsive or committed delinquent even though he is far less likely to become an adult criminal. Though his tenure is short, his replacements are legion.'[17] It is as if, in crucial respects, Matza is addressing a different problem to the earlier theorists, who focused on the 'committed' rather than the 'mundane' delinquent. Also, the notions of 'compulsive' and 'committed' delinquency retain the links with positivism that Matza had been concerned to repudiate.

Matza actually devoted rather little space to the examination of evidence about rates of delinquency. He appears to have proceeded on the basis of surmise instead. What we do know is actually less certain and rather graver than Matza supposed. For example, Britain is a country whose volume of delinquency seems to be lower than that of the United States. Yet, almost all the British youths in West and Farrington's and Belson's self-report studies had engaged in crime. To be sure, much of that criminality was petty enough, but there was violence too. By the time they are 28, some 30 per cent of men in England and Wales have appeared before the courts.[18] And we know very little about what happens to delinquents as they grow up and become young men and women. What unpublished work by Janet Foster on south London makes plausible is the possibility that they do not cease breaking rules altogether but start to break new rules more discreetly. They come off the streets where they are the highly visible perpetrators of public order and status offences and become deviant in sheltered places. It would not do to underestimate the scale of crime and delinquency in the West.

[17] D. Matza, *Delinquency and Drift*, 30.
[18] See *Home Office Statistical Bulletin*, 7/85.

One virtue of these theories was that they seemed to lend themselves well to comparative work. The causes of delinquency that they specified were not to be found in the USA alone. In varying degrees, they exist in all industrial, urban societies with democratic political institutions. However, despite being, if anything, more urbanized than the USA, British patterns of crime and delinquency appear far milder and less prevalent. Even including as homicides all the deaths attributable to the political situation in Northern Ireland, the murder rate for Britain is startlingly lower than that for the States. Part of the contrast may be explained by the differential availability of hand guns (although Switzerland, with its citizen Army and widespread dispersal of guns, has the lowest rate of all[19]). And, with the possible exceptions of Glasgow and some groups of football supporters,[20] the violent fighting gang has not emerged as a phenomenon in Britain. Three main structural and cultural differences may help explain this variation, all of which can in turn be related to the apparently stronger class allegiances that obtain in Britain as compared with the USA. Firstly, there is a much more moderate adherence in Britain to the theme of individual success or failure; secondly, there is still a relative absence of minority group loyalties based on ethnicity that cut across class allegiances to any significant extent; and thirdly, post-war 'affluence' has been combined with relatively full employment. These last two points of difference have recently lost much of their force, and there have been corresponding changes in crime and delinquency that may be partly attributed to this development.

Class identity as a variable which diminished the strain to anomie loomed large in Downes's observations of delinquency among a small number of adolescent boys in East London in the early 1960s, and recurs in similar respects in Wilmott's study in Bethnal Green at much the same period.[21] 'Status frustration', 'alienation', and 'delinquent subculture' were concepts that did not seem to fit descriptions of boys involved intermittently in offences of the fighting/joy-riding/theft/vandalism variety. Typically, they were not members of structured

---

[19] See M. Clinard, *Cities with Little Crime*.
[20] See D. Robins, *We Hate Humans*; J. Patrick, *A Glasgow Gang Observed*.
[21] D. Downes, *The Delinquent Solution*; P. Wilmott, *Adolescent Boys in East London*.

delinquent gangs, with a marked sense of territory, leadership, hierarchy, and membership. Delinquency was a *fact* of life, but not a *way* of life. Educationally, their talk of school implied dissociation from its values rather than embitterment at academic failure. Occupationally, aspirations and expectations were pitched realistically low, consistent with their experience of a succession of 'dead-end' jobs. Early marriage and 'settling down' were already in view. In a negative sense, though, the theories could be regarded as validated since the conditions they held to be essential for the emergence of gang delinquency were largely absent. In a study carried out within a school in a comparable inner-city area, Hargreaves found that C and D stream boys engaged in behaviour analogous to that described by Albert Cohen, but of a milder 'delinquescent' character. Copying, cheating, messing, and rowdyism were the converse of the 'pupil' ideal, but in general fell short of full-blown delinquency.[22]

The question that remains in the British context is to account for delinquency at all, given the rough correspondence between aspirations and expectations. It is at this point that Matza's theory seems to have most to offer. The most frequent of the reasons quoted by the boys themselves for their delinquency was boredom, a word that takes on additional meaning when used with reference to leisure—the one domain in which they have the opportunity to express their character through action. Because their fatalism about school and work is so entrenched, leisure assumes immense significance, not least when the expectation of action is met with the reality of 'nothing going on'. It is out of their response to this impasse that not only much delinquency, but also the successive styles of youth culture have emerged, particularly since the post-war employment boom for young workers led commercial interests to develop the lucrative 'teenage market'. Even so, for working-class adolescents in particular, leisure is too often a counterpart of work: a dreary 'caff', nowhere to go, too little cash for the 'good times'. In this context, delinquency is a repertoire of possibilities for the display of toughness, daring, and panache. The streets, soccer matches, the law itself provide the settings and raw materials for action: delinquency is 'something

[22] D. Hargreaves, *Social Relations in a Secondary School*.

happening'. The meanings and forms are immensely varied
—from 'weird ideas' that emerge from hanging about 'doing
nothing', to clashes between groups contriving different expressive styles, Mods against Rockers, Skinheads against
Greasers, to more ambitious enterprises. 'One has to strip *all* the
hub caps off *every* car in a parking ground, one has to wait until
the last *possible* moment before dropping an object from a
bridge onto the railway line, one has to paint a slogan on the
opposite wall of the underground train tunnel.'[23] There are by
now at least three linkages between delinquency and excitement: delinquency is the *means* to buying excitement: the
Round House boys bought the good times (pubs, girls, motors,
pot) with the proceeds of the theft of car radios;[24] delinquency
is the raw material of excitement (Matza's view); and delinquency is a *by-product* of the pursuit of actions that are exciting
in themselves (smashing milk bottles is Corrigan's example).[25]
There seems no particular reason to regard these as self-
cancelling alternatives: at different times and places, one
option may be preferred to another. An affinity with strain
theory is that excitement tends to be assumed as a taken-for-
granted goal of young male adolescents: and strain theorists
tend to assume that this is only so in leisure because other
valued goals have been denied them in school and at work.
With the rise of forms of deviance among relatively privileged
youth groups in the 1960s, such as drug-use among middle-
class hippies, and student 'violence' in universities and polytechnics, these theories lost some of their force. Labelling
theory assumed greater plausibility.

Labelling theorists[26] do not particularly address themselves to
the 'causes' of delinquency, since they are far more concerned
to develop a missing dimension in previous theorizing: the
impact of social reactions to deviance. But the tradition from
which labelling theory emerged, symbolic interactionism,
supplied a number of insights which could only enrich analysis.

Becker, Lemert, Cicourel, and other theorists in the labelling
tradition, broadly conceived, were the first to approach the

---

[23] S. Cohen, 'Directions for Research on Adolescent Group Violence and Vandalism', 337.   [24] H. Parker, *The View From the Boys*.
[25] P. Corrigan, *Schooling the Smash Street Kids*.   [26] See Chapter 7.

social reaction to deviant behaviour as a *variable*, not a constant; and to argue that the relationships that developed
between deviants and social controllers are in themselves
important influences that help to shape and transform deviant
phenomena.[27] Dramatic analogies played a major part in the
models of deviance and control that flowed from this perspective: the process of *becoming* deviant was conceived in terms
of the gradual construction of a role and an identity that
mirrored the conventional career. The early emphasis was on
the amplificatory potential of social control for deviance: the
agencies of the State could create far more deviance than would
otherwise exist by criminalizing morally disturbing activities
(for instance, certain forms of drug use); by mobilizing bias and
unduly heavy penalties against groups low in power and status;
by attributing quite spurious and stigmatizing features to
deviant groups, and so on. As Young stressed, the media in
particular could be singled out as promoting stereotypical
images of the deviant, which are then contrasted with a picture
of 'normality' that is over-typical.[28] The result is to polarize
society into a conforming majority and a deviant minority, a
dynamic process that helps create a self-fulfilling prophecy,
since those to whom deviance is attributed become both objectively and subjectively more at risk: they are subjected to forms
of exclusion (from jobs, housing, recreation) that worsen their
situation; and they are under pressure to collude with the
majority view that they are 'essentially' deviant.[29]

British sociologists have contributed strongly to this perspective, and in Stan Cohen's study of the 'moral panic'
induced by the Mods and Rockers conflicts in the mid-1960s
we have a repository of the nuances of social control of at least
one moment in British social history.[30] Loose stylistic associations were metaphorically transformed by the media into
tightly knit gangs. Ideal-typical 'folk-devils' were created: the
youth who offered to pay his fine by cheque was parodied as a
symbol of youthful affluence, defiance, and indifference to
authority. His actual inability to pay attracted less publicity.

[27] For references, see Chapter 7. for a comprehensive analysis of their work, see
R. Ericson, *Criminal Reactions*.
[28] J. Young, 'Mass media, Drugs and Deviance', 241.
[29] D. Matza, *Becoming Deviant*, 179.
[30] S. Cohen, *Folk Devils*.

Even non-events were news: towns 'held their breath' for invasions that did not materialize. Cohen argues that the sensationalistic treatment of the initial events sensitized far more adolescents on the fringes of the Mods and Rockers scene to a novel form of action than would have been the case with more modest and realistic reportage.

More recent work in this perspective has tended to ally it with class conflict and culture conflict theories,[31] or with functional approaches.[32] All stress the inadequacy of labelling theory alone to account for the phenomena concerned, but see it (as Becker originally did) as addressing an essential dimension missing from previous theorizing. Thus, Gill is concerned to trace the emergence of 'Luke Street' as a delinquency area from the initial policy which allocated a cluster of larger than average, publicly owned houses in one small neighbourhood to families already classified as 'problems'. These families faced considerable difficulties owing to their large size, low incomes, and high unemployment. Adverse labelling impinged on the lives of the relatively large number of adolescents who came of age together in this context in various cumulative ways. Coming from the 'worst' area of Liverpool, they found even 'dead end' employment withheld; episodes of street delinquency were given wide press coverage which reinforced the stereotype; local youth clubs banned them; they felt subject to unusually fierce police harassment. Gross exclusion fuelled a sense of local territoriality which in one episode, on Bonfire Night, escalated into a running battle with the police. It is improbable that any wider youth culture had very much to do with Luke Street delinquency.

For all its concern to avoid it, Gill's study still conveys a sense of determinism. It is as if the fate of Luke Street was sealed the moment the Housing Authority decided to allocate a critical mass of the housing to large poor families. The press, the police, and the authorities in general closed the trap progressively over time. Lashing out was the boys' only resource, apart from passively sinking into apathy. In another Liverpool study of a contrasting form of delinquency 'on the move', the systematic pilfering of car radios, Parker perhaps demonstrates

---

[31] S. Hall *et al.*, *Policing the Crisis*; O. Gill, *Luke Street*.
[32] P. Marsh *et al.*, *The Rules of Disorder*.

most plainly the problems of applying the concepts of 'culture'
and 'subculture' to the explanation of delinquency.[33] This
emerges most of all because of the strengths of his observational
work. The boys' 'conversation culture' is depicted with
immense sensitivity and skill. The rapport that Parker established allowed him to sustain his role for three years. He
observed both major and minor changes in the boys' views of
themselves and the world. Yet no clear-cut picture of their
'culture' emerges because their 'culture' is not clear-cut.
Parker's methods are those of interactionism, and he is alert to
the qualities of improvisation, negotiation, and the genuine
'emergence' of new ways of defining the situation and moving
on to different ways of handling it. But the boys' autonomy was
bounded by the rules of the larger society, and eventually they
acceded to that power, after a calculated appraisal of the risks
which was worthy of Bentham. Theoretically, the study shows
affinities with strain theory (the 'good times' must be wrung
from a penny-pinching society); with labelling theory (the subjective shift from a sense of apartness to a sense of alienation
results from first-hand experience of the police and the courts);
with control theory (the 'streetwise' involvement in trouble
from early childhood, and the eventual decision that the costs
outweigh the benefits); and conflict theories (the 'iron cage'
which ultimately clamps down on their horizons and life
chances). It is because the nuances of meaning are so well conveyed that 'capturing' their culture seems a scholastic irrelevance.

Nevertheless, certain themes recur in different studies of
boys engaged in alternative forms of trouble that seem to reaffirm the reality of subculture. In their study of soccer hooliganism, Marsh and his colleagues argue that such behaviour is
basically a ritualized form of aggression ('aggro') which would
only contingently escalate into real violence were it not for the
disruption of group-controlled processes by outside agencies,
particularly the police. In a particularly shrewd assessment of
the dynamics of such hooliganism, they explain the fans'
apparently 'schizoid' accounts of their behaviour in terms of a
'conspiracy'. Fans claim that those they oppose 'get their heads

---

[33] H. Parker, *The View from the Boys*.

kicked in': but miraculously the boys so kicked are 'all right—usually anyway'.[34]

In conspiring to construct a reality which seems to be at variance with their tacit knowledge of orderly and rule-governed action, fans are engaged in the active creation of excitement. For fans, regularity and safety are things to be avoided . . . What the soccer terraces offer is a chance to escape from the dreariness of the weekday world of work or school to something which is adventurous and stimulating. But in order to achieve the contrast it is necessary to construe, at least on one level, the soccer terraces as radically different from the weekday world.[35]

The media collude with the conspiracy. The police play a more complicated role, since the fans script them in to defuse a situation without loss of face to themselves. Should the police either over- or under-react, by implications, things go awry. This chimes extremely well with Matza's notion of delinquency as the 'manufacture of excitement'. In the case of soccer hooliganism, however, the delinquency is mainly a matter of rule-governed symbolization and fantasy.

Culture conflict theories are based on the idea that the clash of conduct norms has a central role to play in the explanation of crime. Such a view was presented in succinct form by Thorsten Sellin: 'If the conduct norms of a group are, with reference to a given life situation, inconsistent, or if two groups possess inconsistent norms, we may assume that the members of these various groups will individually reflect such group attitudes.'[36]

The most obvious conflicts of conduct norms arose in the process of migration to the USA of people from an immense variety of cultural backgrounds. As the process of acculturation developed, criminological interest shifted towards the cultural conflicts that arose from social structural sources, and away from the issue of disparate geographical origins. The model could be adapted to explain aggressive delinquency by invoking the sheer magnitude of the cultural differences between the middle and working classes (without implying any necessary built-in antagonism, as do class conflict theories; and without

[34] P. Marsh *et al.*, *The Rules of Disorder*, 82.   [35] Ibid. 97.
[36] T. Sellin, *Culture Conflict and Crime*, in M. Wolfgang *et al.* (eds.), *The Sociology of Crime and Delinquency*, 228.

implying that working-class adolescents are significantly influenced by middle-class culture, as do (some) strain theorists). They share with control theorists a definition of the
dominant society as unable to gain any effective purchase on
the 'hearts and minds' of the working class. They hold that
working-class culture is profoundly lodged (in Miller's words)
in a 'generations-old shaking-down process' born of industrialization and urbanization, and that it is little affected as yet
by the changes and reforms which are so often heralded as
the promoters of classlessness,[37] such as the 'Welfare State',
the 'affluent society', and other alleged diversions from a
distinctive class consciousness.

Miller's theory (in many ways the inheritance of Thrasher's
portrait of the gang) simply argues that lower-class group
delinquency, far from representing a 'counter-culture', is the
direct, intensified expression of the dominant culture pattern
of the lower-class community: 'a long-established, distinct-
ively patterned tradition with an integrity of its own'. This
culture comprises six 'focal concerns' to whose polarities each
individual can, in principle, orient himself somewhat idiosyn-
cratically. They are: trouble (the tension between law-abiding
and law-violating behaviour); toughness (masculinity–effem-
inacy); smartness (sharp-wittedness–dull-wittedness); excitement   (activity–passivity);   fate   (luck–being   unlucky);
autonomy (independence–dependency). For Miller, engagement with these 'concerns' tends to involve lower-class adolescents in a head-on clash with a dominant society whose
legal code is underwritten by middle-class values. The delinquent gang intensifies such commitment, since its members
are likely to be socialized in female-based households where
little reliance is placed on the stability and earning power of
the male. The gang helps resolve sex-role problems by providing a vehicle for the pursuit of masculine status and reassurance. Miller claims much empirical support for this theory,
notably the high proportion of aggressive acts in street-corner
groups that are intra-group, verbally expressive of his focal
'concerns' alone, and rarely directed against middle-class or
even adult targets: signs that ambivalence about status in those

[37] W. Miller, 'Lower Class Culture', and in M. Wolfgang *et al.* (eds.), op. cit. 267–76,
and (with others) 'Aggression in a Boys' Street-corner Group'.

terms is negligible. Most delinquency is non-violent. Theft accounts for a far higher proportion than any kind of assault: such delinquency is, however, rare in itself. Violence, when it does occur, is a response to perceived insults and/or rejection by specific others, not a random outpouring of 'senseless' aggression. It is a source of group cohesion and an affirmation of group values, rather than a springboard for hostility against 'society', the 'adult world', or 'middle-class values'.

A similar type of explanation is afforded by Oscar Lewis's concept of the culture of poverty. Generated by the experience of poverty, this culture takes much the same form whatever the national or structural context.[38] Whether it is studied in Buenos Aires, Glasgow, or New York, the same combination of values is observed: it includes, *inter alia*, a refusal, amounting to inability, to defer gratification; a stress on machismo or the primacy accorded the sexual prowess of the male; and a profound fatalism about the possibility of influencing events. Violence, particularly as an outcome of the impugning of masculinity and honour, finds fertile soil in such values. Adherence to this culture alone would vitiate any prospect of betterment.

There are several counterparts of these theories. Indeed, the theme of masculine consciousness as a legitimation of crime and delinquency recurs from the work of the Chicago School onwards. The ideas of John Mays in Liverpool are akin to those of Miller. John McVicar describes 'crude machismatic values' as central to his boyhood. He claims that it was not material gain but prowess which attracted him to the delinquent subculture.[39] Similarly Paul Willis discerns throughout the culture of motorbike boys a concern with the elaboration of masculine imagery, an imagery that 'owed nothing to the conventional

[38] O. Lewis, *Five Families: Mexican Case Studies in the Culture of Poverty*; also *The Children of Sanchez*, and *La Vida: A Puerto Rican Family in the Culture of Poverty*. In his introduction to *La Vida*, he made it plain that poverty and the 'culture of poverty' are not mutually inclusive terms. For example, the Jews of Eastern Europe were very poor, but their literacy and religion insulated them from the culture of poverty. However, despite some disclaimers on both parts, the culture of poverty corresponds closely with Liebow's observations of one group of the urban poor in the USA (E. Liebow, *Tally's Corner: Negro Street-corner Men in Washington, D.C.*). For a discussion, see C. Valentine, *Culture and Poverty*. For a criminological statement of much the same position, see M. Wolfgang and F. Ferracutti, *The Subculture of Violence*.
[39] J. Mays, *Growing Up in the City*; J. McVicar, *McVicar by Himself*.

notion of the healthy masculine life . . . Valued tenets of this code . . . such as impudence before authority, domination of women, humiliation of the weaker, aggression towards the different, would be abhorrent to traditional proponents of honour, and labelled criminal by agents of social control.'[40] In early rock and roll, they found a musical form that corresponded perfectly to their self-image. The motor bike was culturally appropriated rather than just mechanically used.

There are naturally a host of criticisms that have been directed against the conception of working-class culture propounded by Miller and others, and some have held that it is highly dubious to attribute the toughness and defiance of authority found among the 'roughest' communities to the working class in general. However, it must be remembered that part of that criticism may flow from a misreading of Miller. Miller had written about 'lower class culture' and, in American speech and possibly in American sociology, the lower class is *not* the same as the working class, but a small, lumpenproletarian, chiefly Black, segment of it.

There is also an element of tautology in reading behaviour culturally (Barbara Wootton once referred to it as the thesis that a way of life may be explained by a way of life). Nevertheless, scientifically unsatisfying as they may be, these approaches do 'resonate' with some aspects of the more serious forms of violence in a way that the more abstract Mertonian theories do not.

Class conflict theories basically apply much the same set of ideas to the explanation of crime and delinquency as do other theorists; but they do so within a broad Marxian framework which takes it as an axiom that class conflict is inevitable in capitalist societies, and that the dynamics of such conflict must be related to issues of deviance and control. This does not necessarily mean that delinquency is simply 'decoded' as a symptom of class warfare; or that delinquents are seen as fighting 'the system', albeit in a regressive way. But it does mean that connections are sought between the structural 'contradictions' of capitalist societies and the forms assumed by deviance and control.

The concept of subculture, for example, has been applied by

[40] P. Willis, *Profane Culture*, 29–30.

Phil Cohen to innovations in youth culture.[41] Those innovations are seen to emerge where the contradictions of capitalist
political economy work their chief effects—in the working-class
inner city. Post-war changes in housing, transport, and technology have, despite some gains in affluence, served to fragment working-class community. The costs of the faltering of
the machinery of prosperity have fallen quite disproportionately on working-class youth and on immigrant minorities.
The inability of the 'parent' working-class generation to cope
with these problems means that they are refracted, already
freighted with associations of class defeat, onto the young.
Their response to the resultant family tensions, fragmented
community, and economic insecurity is necessarily symbolic.
It is to create a succession of subcultural styles which 'express
and resolve, albeit "magically", the contradictions which
remain hidden or unresolved in the parent culture'. Thus, for
example, the Mod style could be interpreted as an 'attempt to
real-ise, *but in an imaginary relation*, the conditions of existence
of the socially mobile white-collar worker. While their argot
and ritual forms stressed many of the values of their parent [i.e.
working class] culture, their dress and music reflected the
hedonistic image of the affluent consumer.'[42] The skinhead
style was an attempt to recover and assert the traits associated
with hard manual labour under threat from technological
change. And if there is a certain uniform pattern to the rise and
fall of successive styles—Teds, Mods, Rockers, Skinheads,
Punks—this is because revolts into style (in Melly's phrase[43])
can only ever retranscribe, and not resolve in any structural
sense, the set of contradictions that gives rise to them.

Stuart Hall and his colleagues have applied much the same
model to the issue of delinquency in general, and to middle-
class expressive movements in particular, since the war.[44] The
rise of the hippy 'counter-culture' is attributed to the growing
incompatibility between the traditional puritan ethic and the
newfound affluence and consumerism of the expanding middle
class. The breakdown of traditional middle-class constraints
began from *within* the dominant class. It was then transformed
and pushed to expressive lengths, in both the hippy and

[41] P. Cohen, 'Working Class Youth Cultures in East London'.   [42] Ibid. 23–4.
[43] G. Melly, *Revolt Into Style*.   [44] S. Hall *et al.* (eds.), *Resistance through Rituals*.

student protest movements. So lodged, it was perceived as a threat to social order. The authors are aware of the pitfalls of giving too ideological a reading to youthful styles, since 'disaffiliation' is frequently short-lived and some phenomena are so ephemeral that it strains credulity to invest them with much symbolic significance. While that awareness is only parenthetic, and class conflict approaches are as likely to 'overpredict' as strain and culture conflict theories, there are some safeguards in the ethnographic work which the Birmingham School has evolved.

In his study of 'how working class kids get working class jobs', Willis tackles a subject that is almost worn out by the sociological repetition of the observation that schooling is perceived by such youths as a massive irrelevancy. His work gains a wealth of insight by combining interviews and observations of a small group of boys in a typical comprehensive during their last year at school and first year in work. What they revealed above all was their clear sense of their limited life-chances in the industrial division of labour, and the implications of that sense for their resistance to schooling. Their own hidden curriculum was a timetable of 'skiving', 'dossing', and 'having a laff'. Their culture stressed 'the perennial themes of symbolic and physical violence, rough presence, and the pressure of a certain kind of masculinity'.[45] 'Sexism' and 'racism' are part of the price to be paid for the accomplishment of a form of masculine self-image which renders the prospect of routine manual work palatable, and which sets off the alternative major grouping in the school, the 'ear'oles' who are destined for superior skilled manual or technical jobs, as cowed conformists. Willis undercuts the moral condemnation of their culture by making the profound point that only such a willed appropriation of labouring saves a liberal society from forced labour.

Willis uses the terms 'culture' and 'counterculture' in a far more 'dialectical' sense than occurs even in the work of most other class conflict theorists. His main concern is to convey the 'profane creativity' of subordinate cultures as the 'only route for radical cultural change'.[46] By implication, earlier approaches

---

[45] P. Willis, *Learning to Labour*, 36. The colloquialisms roughly translate as work-dodging, cat-napping, and fooling about.   [46] P. Willis, *Profane Culture*, 1.

define cultures as 'simply layers of padding between human beings and unpleasantness'.[47] The active appropriation and reworking of cultural items junked by capitalist commodity fetishism can provide the materials for at least temporary challenges to the cultural dominance of the bourgeoisie. Willis's analysis of the cultures of motor-bike boys and hippies, and Hebdige's of punks, share a view of profane culture as a refusal to be silenced by superior cultural forces.[48] In his study of the school counter-culture and shop-floor cultures, Willis goes further. He acknowledges that 'it would be wrong to impute to "the lads" individually any critique or analytic motive', yet 'their collective culture shows both a responsiveness to the uniqueness of human labour power and in its own way constitutes an attempt to defeat a certain ideological definition of it'.[49] Though he fights shy of using the term 'alienation'[50] he is in effect applying Marx's original use of that term to the realm of cultural production. Capitalism ultimately determines the conditions whereby the limited 'penetrations' the lads collectively make into the mysteries of bourgeois ideology become a weapon for their own willed subordination. They in no sense collude, or merely collide, with bourgeois ideology. They fashion their own independent critique of the system—the higher values placed on manual labour in particular—the logic of which is their eventual entrapment in labouring. The system wins, though a certain autonomy at the cultural level is salvaged.

Corrigan adds a historical dimension to the seeming paradox that the long struggle to win the right to schooling for working-class children is so largely wasted on the supposed beneficiaries. We should not be too surprised about the result, he argues, in view of the fact that what has been won is the right to a form of schooling originally *imposed on* the working class (the term used by Forster was 'gentling the masses') in a struggle that robbed them of their own emergent educational institutions. Corrigan also proposed a different interpretation of Matza's idea that much street delinquency is the 'manufacture

---

[47] P. Willis, *Learning to Labour*, 52.
[48] R. Hebdige, *Subculture: The Meaning of Style*.
[49] P. Willis, *Learning to Labour*, 132.
[50] Ibid. 143, n. 22.

of excitement' in a context of 'nothing going on'. The elaboration of 'weird ideas' as a feature of apparently 'doing nothing'
involves frequent rule-breaking. But the 'rules are not broken
specifically because they are rules; rules are broken for the most
part as a by-product of the flow of activity engaged in by the
boys'.[51] Again, the class context both limits and subverts
autonomy.

Criticism

The promise of subcultural theory was that it would be better
than any other at 'fitting the facts' of the problem it was
designed to explain. Those 'facts' clustered around one central
assumption: that the most serious forms of delinquency are to
be found in highly localized form in one sector of the social
system, that of the male, lower-class, urban adolescent. A basic
problem from the outset was that the prevalence of delinquency was far from general, even in this sector. The problems
allegedly encountered by members of this category plainly led
only a minority to serious delinquency, and only a minority of
a minority to serious *gang* delinquency. Yet the other options
open to such boys, the 'college' (upwardly mobile) and the
'corner boy' (respectable, working-class) 'adaptations', were
never successfully differentiated causally from the delinquent
option. The question 'Why should similarly situated youths
sometimes choose delinquency and sometimes the alternatives?' was left open, so that subcultural theory became all too
vulnerable to David Matza's criticisms that it 'over-predicted'
delinquency by accounting for far more than actually existed.
Later subcultural theories of the Marxist school are open to the
same criticism: though Matza's own approach, with its characterization of most delinquency as 'mundane' and 'periodic',
veers towards the opposite fault of 'under-prediction'.

A related problem in the assessment of the theory revolves
around its dependence on the official criminal statistics. Numerous self-report studies threw serious doubt on the subcultural
theories' identification of the more serious forms of delinquency
with lower-working-class, male, urban adolescents. The more
sophisticated studies, such as that by Martin Gold, narrowed the

51 P. Corrigan, *Schooling the Smash Street Kids*, 140.

differentials between male–female and lower class–middle class to something approaching unity.[52] Moreover, throughout the 1960s, forms of social deviance such as drug-use and even instrumental violence became associated with just those groups that were theoretically most immune to delinquency: the middle-class 'college boys'. It began to look as if subcultural theories were addressing a non-problem and were incapable of addressing emergent ones.

A third difficulty was that the theories had always relied heavily on analytic imputation. Subcultures were alleged to arise in situations of socially structured 'strain' or, in the Marxist version, in situations where the 'contradictions of capitalism' were experienced most intensively. This search for correspondences between 'problems' and 'solutions' could lead all too easily to the circularity of explanation already familiar to students of the 'social disorganization' and 'functionalist' schools. The saving grace of earlier subcultural theories had been an insistence on evidence that adherents to a subculture should be aware, however dimly, of the problems to which it was a response, and the values around which it was held to cohere. In later subcultural theories, this safeguard has been eclipsed all too frequently by the methodology of 'decoding' subcultural style into what are assumed to be its immanent properties.

Attempts to solve the problem of analytical imputation— that is, to establish whether or not the distinctive meaning systems of the various subcultures are in reality those imputed to them—have taken successively complicated forms. In David Maurer's classic early work, subculture was inferred from the distinctive linguistic vocabulary used by pickpockets and sneak thieves.[53] The homology between language and practices was complete. A self-enclosed, relatively unchanging, and antique way of life was depicted. Such unity was never established in the more variegated instances of expressive delinquency.[54] Early subcultural theorists sought to link distinctive sets of

[52] For a comprehensive review of such studies, see S. Box, *Deviance, Reality and Society*; and M. Gold, *Delinquent Behavior in an American City*.

[53] D. Maurer, *Whiz Mob: A Correlation of the Technical Argot of Pick-pockets with their Behavior Pattern*.

[54] Though Willis establishes a considerable symmetry in the relations between life-styles and musical forms in his studies of 'profane cultures'.

norms, values, and beliefs to allegedly distinctive types of delinquent subculture. The work of Cloward and Ohlin is a prime example. In such work, the relationship between the parent culture and deviant subcultures was essentially static. The only source of change was the apparently growing instability of the inner city. Hence, it was appropriate to attempt to 'trap' subcultural norms by standard techniques of interview and survey methods. Labelling theory introduced a fresh source of change, the nature of the social reaction. A certain dynamism was lent to the somewhat static conception of subculture, but the gain was limited. Social reaction could reinforce subcultural cohesion, as in Young's depiction of the impact of police harassment on drug users.[55] Such work tended to complement earlier approaches, though the preferred method of the labelling theorists, participant observation, could enrich available accounts of cultural meanings. Sources of change in delinquency still seemed inadequately explained by such methods, however. This failing was most pronounced in the analysis of what Hebdige has termed the 'spectacular subcultures' of adolescence that periodically emerged in Britain as apparent symbols of youthful defiance: Teds, Mods, Rockers, Skinheads, Punks. The introduction of a fresh dynamic, developments in class conflict in post-war Britain, promised a means of accounting, at several removes, for the shape such subcultures took. New methods were employed, in particular semiotics, to capture the nuances of each successive style as a *mélange* of signs, or *bricolage*, as Lévi-Strauss would call it: but the problems of imputation have become, in the process, more rather than less evident.

In a searching critique of the work of the 'new' subcultural theorists, Stan Cohen addresses the problem of imputation at three levels of analysis: structure, culture, and biography.[56] At the level of structure, the main innovation has been an appeal to history. In the work of such theorists as Phil Cohen, Corrigan, and Pearson, working-class delinquency is placed in the context of class struggle. This perspective enables the theorist to analyse both continuity and change afresh. The daily toll of routine delinquency (which may be termed the 'unspec-

[55] J. Young, 'The Role of the Police as Amplifiers of Deviancy'.
[56] In the Introduction to the revised edition of his *Folk Devils*.

tacular' subcultures) can be related to the reproduction of order by repressive means: in Gouldner's terms, 'normalised repression'. The innovations or 'spectacular subcultures' can be related to crucial 'moments' or 'conjectures' in the class struggle. For example, the Skinhead style emerged in the attempt to retrieve traditional symbols of working-class cohesion devalued by post-war 'affluence'. The problem, however, is that such an approach assists 'an over facile drift to historicism . . . In each case the connections sound plausible. But in each case, a single and one-directional historical trend is picked out—commercialisation, repression, bourgeoisification, destruction of community, erosion of leisure values—and then projected onto a present which (often by the same sociologists' own admission) is more complicated, contradictory or ambiguous.'[57]

At the level of culture, these new approaches

are massive exercises of decoding, reading, deciphering and interrogating. These phenomena *must* be saying something to us—if only we could know exactly *what*. So the whole assembly of cultural artefacts, down to the punks' last safety pin, have been scrutinised, taken apart, contextualised and re-contextualised. The conceptual tools of Marxism, structuralism, and semiotics, a Left Bank pantheon of Genet, Lévi-Strauss, Barthes and Althusser have been wheeled in to aid this hunt for the hidden code.[58]

The dominant themes of *resistance* (to subordination) through *ritual* (symbolic displays of various kinds) typically confront the awkward problem of intra-group or minority group victimization by the notion of 'misrecognition'. The real enemy (the bosses/State/dominant class) remains unscathed. The essentially 'subversive' nature of the subcultures can be inferred from their styles. As Hebdige put it: 'These "humble objects" (bikes, clothes, make-up) can be magically appropriated: "stolen" by subordinate groups and made to carry "secret" meanings which express, in code, a form of resistance to the order which guarantees their continued subordination.'[59] This may, as Stan Cohen puts it, be 'an imaginative way of reading the style; but how can we be sure that it is also not

---

[57] Ibid. viii–ix. [58] Ibid. ix
[59] R. Hebdige, *Subculture: The Meaning of Style*, 18.

imaginary?'.[60] Ultimately, this approach finesses the problem of intent. Symbols may mean what they appear to mean; they may, by exaggeration or parody, be taken to mean the opposite, as Hebdige claims they should in the case of the punks' wearing of the swastika emblem; or they may represent a latent intentionality. At this point, the method comes close to producing a cultural Freudianism.[61]

At the level of biography, much the same problems recur, in a fashion akin to earlier subcultural theory. With delinquency as with other phenomena, many are called but few are chosen or self-elected. The subcultural activists are greatly outnumbered by the conforming majority, despite their common exposure to similar pressures. No fresh insights are offered as to which variables might intervene to differentiate the two. In this respect, there is continuity with, but no significant improvement on, earlier cultural approaches: that delinquent and troublesome youth cultures signify 'a reaction (with more or less degrees of commitment, consciousness and symbolic weight) to growing up in a class society'.[62]

A final criticism of subcultural theory in general applies with particular force to the exponents of the various class conflict approaches. It may be termed differential magnification, the tuning of the analytical lens to an almost exclusive degree on the 'subordinate cultures', with a corresponding neglect of the 'dominant' or 'subaltern' cultures. In these works, the worlds of teachers, social workers, policemen, prison officers, employers, and even academics are treated with the very disregard for ambiguity, complexity, and resistances to ideology that would be (rightly) impugned if applied to working-class or delinquent cultures. This massive over-simplification is at times justified in

[60] S. Cohen, *Folk Devils*, xv.

[61] As, for example, in Hebdige's assertion that 'Everytime the boot went in, a contradiction was concealed, glossed over or made to "disappear"' (op. cit. 60). The drift to a facile idealism recalls Zilboorg's Freudian explanation of why pickpockets plied their trade at public hangings. 'This was their revenge for their own vicarious execution.' As Maurer notes, Barrington, the famous eighteenth-century thief, gave a sounder explanation: 'Everybody's eyes were on one person, and all were looking up' (D. Maurer, *Whiz Mob*, 14–16). In this case, however, a clear-cut purpose was involved: thieving as a trade. Expressive 'spectacular subcultures' do not lend themselves so readily to instrumental accounts, so that Hebdige's approach is correspondingly more defensible, and in general his methods lend themselves to a more rigorous use of evidence than the above might imply.

[62] S. Cohen, *Folk Devils*, xxv.

terms of structuralist method: whatever they think they are doing, those in authority are doomed to support the system. Such an assumption can only be supported on a historicist basis. The limitations of this position could be overcome by extending to these groups the forms of research reserved as yet for 'subordinate cultures'. the idea that upper- and middle-class cultures comprise merely 'stultification, reification and pretence' merits sceptical examination.[63]

In counter-criticism, it could be contended that subcultural theories, broadly conceived, have furnished the elements for a fully sociological theory of much collaborative deviance. Causal explanation and interpretative approaches have both been addressed, though the focus has been almost invariably limited to juvenile delinquency and adolescent trouble-making.[64] Criticisms of the factual basis for much theorizing in this vein have in their turn been subjected to substantial attack, not least for their tendency to overstate the impact of selective forms of policing on the construction of delinquency.[65] Certain basic assumptions have resisted invalidation.[66] Above all, perhaps, the logic of subcultural theories predicted with some success, albeit imprecisely, such developments as the emergence of a 'hustling' culture among West Indian youth, and the appeal of extreme authoritarianism among the most disadvantaged white adolescents.[67] It may well be that such predictions are eminently possible without the aid of subcultural theory. But they at least afford support for the view that such theories have barely explored strengths as well as demonstrably glaring weaknesses. Finally, despite the obvious dangers of overstretched antennae, the work of the 'Cultural Studies' School has reanimated the possibilities of making 'culture' more than a synopsis of the very problems it is employed to explain.

[63] P. Willis, *Profane Culture*, 5.

[64] An exception is K. Plummer, *Sexual Stigma: An Interactionist Account*.

[65] A. Reiss, Jun., 'Inappropriate Theories and Inadequate Methods as Policy Plagues'; and R. Mawby (ed.), *Policing the City*.

[66] M. Brake, *The Sociology of Youth*. Brake demonstrates that there is greater agreement over views of the self, other groups, and society, within as compared to between the youthful subcultures of Skinheads and Hippies.

[67] See, for example, D. Downes, *The Delinquent Solution*; S. Cohen, 'Directions for Research'.

7
Symbolic Interactionism

Introduction

The University of Chicago sociology department was paramount in the United States for some two decades. Its students
were to set the agenda for the evolution of American sociology,
which remained virtually unchallenged until the appearance of
structural-functionalism at Harvard in the late 1930s. As work
proceeded and scholars dispersed, the various strains of
Chicago sociology tended to undergo separate development.
Ethnography became associated with one wing, subsequently
described as symbolic interactionist. The connection and continuity have been real enough for some to call interactionists
'neo-Chicagoans'.[1]

Interactionists were to be overshadowed during the 1940s
and 1950s, the period of rampant functionalism.[2] Sutherland,
his colleagues, and his students did continue to explore crime
and deviance as instances of differential association, writing
about embezzlement,[3] drug addiction,[4] professional crime,[5]
the crimes of business corporations,[6] and deviant motivation.[7]
Everett Hughes wrote about matters that were of some oblique
interest to sociologists of deviance, and in particular about the
moral division of labour into clean and dirty work, with its
accompanying stocks of innocent and guilty knowledge about
the world.[8] One man, Edwin Lemert, was to be recognized
later as a vital forerunner of the interactionist sociology of deviance. He borrowed from symbolic interactionism to construct a

[1] See D. Matza, *Becoming Deviant*.
[2] Cf. K. Davis, 'The Myth of Functional Analysis'.
[3] See D. Cressey, *Other People's Money*.   [4] A. Lindesmith, *Opiate Addiction*.
[5] See E. Sutherland, *The Professional Thief*.
[6] See E. Sutherland, *White Collar Crime*.
[7] See D. Cressey, 'Role theory, Differential Association and Compulsive Crimes'.
[8] E. Hughes, 'Good People and Dirty Work'.

general theory of social pathology.[9] But all this work seems to have been identified at the time as rather peripheral to the main body of American sociological writing.

It is not at all clear why the Chicago School should have been eclipsed.[10] Neither is it clear why its heir, symbolic interactionism, should have come to prominence in the criminology of the 1960s. Symbolic interactionists were a little bemused themselves: and Howard Becker, the man held chiefly responsible for the renaissance, expressed considerable surprise at his own influence.[11] It must be recalled that the possibilities of the functionalist and anomie models had not been exhausted. Indeed, they had never been fully exploited in criminology. By contrast, it cannot be alleged that the Chicago School had practised a kind of withdrawal and return. There had been no willing retreat. Neither had there been any lack of work on deviance. Re-adoption may have to be explained by what seems to be the inevitable half-life of sociological fashions: there is an ingrained impatience with the old which condemns every set of ideas to a limited vitality. It may also have to be explained by the great expansion of higher education which took place in the 1960s, an expansion which disrupted routine and introduced marginal academics to teaching and research. It may have been connected with what were thought to be some of the distinctive qualities of the decade: the flowering of expressive deviance, the novel sense of openness, and a toying with what Horowitz has called the politics of experience.[12] There was indeed something of an affinity between a particular social world and a particular kind of writing. Interactionism was held to be an existential sociology which had animation and openness enough to capture the new *demi-monde*. Interactionists themselves were called *demi-mondaines*. Thus Gouldner argued:

This group of Chicagoans finds itself at home in the world of hip, Norman Mailer, drug addicts, jazz musicians, cab drivers, prostitutes, night people, drifters, grifters, and skidders, the cool cats and their kicks. To be fully appreciated this stream of work cannot be seen solely in terms of the categories conventionally employed in

---

[9] See E. Lemert, *Social Pathology*.
[10] See A Reiss and M. Tonry, Preface to *Communities and Crime*.
[11] See J. Debro, 'Dialogue with Howard S. Becker'.
[12] See I. Horowitz, 'The Politics of Drugs', 165.

sociological analysis. It has also to be seen from the viewpoint of the literary critic as a style of genre and particularly as a species of naturalistic romanticism.[13]

Although interactionism was actively pursued long before the emergence of the special low life of the 1960s, and participation in that life was no prerequisite to becoming an interactionist, a number of interactionists have apparently accepted a history of themselves as crypto-deviants.[14] They have not vociferously rejected the biographies which were constructed for them. And interactionism did suddenly seem to loom large. It became sovereign for a while. Sections of certain works have been described as 'catechisms' for the sociology of deviance.[15] One book in particular, Becker's *Outsiders*, was to become one of the two most frequently cited of all American criminological writings in the period between 1945 and 1972.[16]

Symbolic interactionists take part of their job to be a formal description of the little social worlds that constitute a society. Schools, gangs, families, pubs, and hospitals are not unlike the natural areas of the Chicago School. They are bounded social situations, created by people who experience them as sets of changing resources, opportunities, contexts, and constraints. Any social situation will be a blend of activity, history, and material props which achieves its definition and coherence from shared symbols. It is to be anticipated that some features of those worlds will be familiar and general, and that others will not. How they combine and under what conditions can never be clear until they have been examined. Indeed, interactionists would say that an explorer can never know what he or she is exploring until it has been explored. It requires a particularly patient, cautious, and attentive methodology to chart such a delicate and complicated process as social life. It is all too easy to impose an alien explanatory scheme that obscures vision, ignores problems, and pre-empts solutions. Above all, it is held that analysis must grasp the meaning that animates and shapes

---

[13] A. Gouldner, 'Anti-Minotaur: The Myth of a Value-Free Sociology', 209.

[14] S. Cohen, 'Criminology and the Sociology of Deviance in Britain'; I. Taylor and L. Taylor (eds), *Politics and Deviance*; N. Polsky, *Hustlers, Beats and Others*; J. Weis, 'Dialogue with Matza'.

[15] G. Pearson, *The Deviant Imagination*, 52

[16] See M. Wolfgang *et al.*, *Evaluating Criminology*.

social activity. Consequential meaning is that employed by the social actors themselves, not by the sociologist, and interactionism is designed to take the observer and an audience inside the actors' own perspectives on selves, acts, and environments. Interactionists thus tend to practise the anthropology of participant-observation, an anthropology which marries surveillance to a busy involvement in the affairs of a social world. The resulting reports cannot but be limited, dwelling on the particular character of one constellation of events, but they should be able to reproduce what is both intricate and subtle.

Symbolic Interactionism and Deviance

There is a modest compatibility between interactionism and deviance which stems from the propensity of rule-breakers to gather in the small, bounded social worlds which interactionist ethnography can map. Heroin-users, thieves, and prostitutes may draw themselves apart, seeking those who share common problems, experiences, and solutions. Together, they create a series of strange groupings whose peculiarities can stimulate the sensitivities which are indispensable to interactionism.

We have already argued that ethnography requires sociologists to reconcile the two contradictory states of participation and observation. They must so distance themselves that they can define commonplace actions and utterances as problematic, yet their knowledge must be intimate enough to permit a reasonable interpretation of the meanings of those selfsame actions and utterances. Deviant phenomena can take the form of people doing extraordinary things in an ordinary and familiar world, and they lend themselves to special study. Theft, drug-taking, and prostitution are a useful blend of the common and the uncommon which permits the sociologist to be both provoked and appreciative.

Deviance itself is defined as a product of the ideas which people have of one another. It is argued that social action cannot be a response to people as they 'really' are and in every detail. After all, much is unknown, concealed, irrelevant, or ambiguous. People are constrained to react to a filtered, adapted, and limited conception of themselves, each other, and the situations in which they meet. Activities are necessarily grounded in working definitions which are situated and negotiable. Central to such conceptions are the names and symbols upon which definitions are built: as names change, so do actions. For a while, the naming associated with deviance was held so important to its interactionist analysis that the entire approach was generally, if misleadingly, termed 'labelling theory'. Frequently cited are the remarks of Becker, Kitsuse, and Erikson:

Social groups create deviance by making the rules whose infraction constitutes deviance, and by applying those rules to particular people and labeling them as outsiders. From this point of view, deviance is *not* a quality of the act the person commits, but rather a consequence of the application by others of rules and sanctions to an 'offender'. The deviant is one to whom that label has successfully been applied; deviant behavior is behavior that people so label.[17]

I propose to shift the focus of theory and research from the forms of deviant behavior to the processes by which persons come to be defined as deviant by others. Such a shift requires that the sociologist view as problematic what he generally assumes as given—namely, that certain forms of behavior are *per se* deviant and are so defined by the 'conventional or conforming members of a group'.[18]

The critical variable in the study of deviance . . . is the social audience rather than the individual actor, since it is the audience which eventually determines whether or not an episode of behavior or any class of episodes is labeled deviant.[19]

There is a recommendation in all three remarks that the sociologist should concentrate on the work that naming accomplishes. Deviance is held to be a kind of description used in the conversations that order social life. Conversations have distinct and analysable qualities, and it is those qualities which organize some of the character of deviance. In the first instance, interactionists do not take conversation to be confined entirely to activities outside the self. Their discussion of deviance hinges on a larger conception of names, selves, and conversations. It is imperative to turn to that conception before the more focused analysis becomes clear.

[17] H. Becker, *Outsiders*, 9.
[18] J. Kitsuse, 'Societal Reaction to Deviant Behavior', 19–20.
[19] K. Erikson, 'Notes on the Sociology of Deviance', 11.

Chief amongst the problematic objects confronting an observer is the self. Unlike the phenomenologists, interactionists maintain that people lack a sure knowledge of what they are and what they can accomplish. New problems and settings pose new tasks and it is not certain that one is equal to them. It is not even certain that one can repeat past achievements. Indeed, one expriences oneself as a somewhat erratic and shadowy entity: one can let oneself down, surprise, and embarrass oneself. Every situation has the capacity to establish, educate, and redefine the self.

Any action requires an appraisal of one's capacities and of the action's implications for oneself. There are certain things one can or cannot do; certain things which might seem incongruous with past performances, or which humiliate or elevate the self. It follows that monitoring and assessment of the self are indispensable to any intelligent social strategy. A mind must scan itself just as it scans other objects in its environment. Only then will it be able to form conjectures about what it appears to be, what an environment will permit it to do, and how it may work back on the environment to shape it to its will. In all this activity, it is evident that there is a vital division within consciousness. One phase or aspect of reasoning becomes a surveying subject, the other becomes a surveyed object. Bending their minds back on themselves, people become an observing 'I' and an observed 'me'. Activity may then be likened to a kind of intellectual acrobatics in which mind becomes contorted in an effort to view itself.

The internal gyrations of the self would be virtually impossible without language. Words have a power to fold back on the speaker with a special force: a man cannot see himself, but he can hear himself speak, and it may well be that his hearing is not too dissimilar to the hearing of others. Speaking, he can become his own stimulus: he is able to act and then react to himself. In this fashion, speech encourages a sense of self-estrangement, an opening-up of the I and the me, which allows a man to become his own audience. Words have an additional power, in that they tend to be relatively anonymous, accessible to anyone. Describing oneself, one is required to employ terms which are universal and universalizable. Those terms transform private experience into a public matter, making the unique general and social. As one uses words, so particular circumstances receive a common classification. Further, that public currency of speech is also used by those about one. It becomes possible to imagine some of the responses which others make to one's action and projected self.

An imagination of others' replies is the vital prerequisite of social action. It distinguishes the mere emission of actions from concerted and co-operative behaviour. And imagination permits the construction of the 'significant gesture', a gesture which is at the very core of all sociability. A person who acts is rarely heedless of the effects of what he does. Whether his action is benevolent or malevolent, it is normally intended to achieve some response. In turn, the planned action must be tailored to the anticipated reply which others might make. Anticipation requires one to take the role of another, to envisage how he views one's display and predicts one's intentions. It forces one to mould one's gestures so that their significance is properly and efficiently conveyed.

The work of composing a significant gesture is yet further complicated. It entails rehearsing one's own reply to the other's reply, conceiving the other's answering response, and so on. It also entails a running interpretation of the complementary activities which the other does. Imaginations thus become intertwined, mingled in a common social undertaking. The private and subjective are locked into a wider structure. It does not follow that one's interpretation of the other is 'correct'. Indeed, there is no sure method of establishing the inner meaning of one's own and another's acts. But all joint behaviour rests on a series of working conjectures and definitions.

Life is thereby patterned by symbolic indications. People continuously interpret themselves, their settings, and their partners. They must make sense of the past, make plans, and infer intentions. Indications are predominantly linguistic, although gestures, expression, clothing, and context also convey meaning. Language permits the identification and stabilization of social affairs. It allows one to assume persistence and similarity so that responses become available. It is the common medium which integrates the public activity.

It is in this sense that the self has been compared to a dialogue within consciousness. The I and the me talk to one another, stimulating one another, interpreting one another, and relying on words for their understanding. The process of recognizing and negotiating deviance is thus importantly merged with the inner world of the self. Decisions about future conduct turn on readings of the meaning of deviance, the acceptability of deviant identity, the significance of particular acts, and the possible responses of others. They revolve around the character of potential selves and they are all transacted within the self. Thus an early and important article by Becker traced some of the stages of one such private conversation.[20] It discussed the manner in which the marihuana user came to terms with known and likely definitions of drugs. When the article was written, marihuana was thought to be a dangerous substance with massive moral implications for its consumer. The prospective user was obliged to consider what kind of person he might become. His plans were moulded by his acceptance, rejection, or redefinition of stigmas. His management of the problem had little to do with the social control emanating from direct confrontations with other people, the police, or courts. But it did centre on the social control embedded in the meanings of deviation and the self.

The experience of oneself as free to deviate depends in part on access to appropriate names and explanations.[21] Doing something is eased by sympathetic description. When acts and states can be reassessed as worthy or innocuous, when they can be presented as not 'really' deviant, it is a little easier to accept them. Arguing that deviation requires a mastery of guilt, Sykes and Matza listed the techniques of neutralization which offer more or less honourable motives for dishonourable acts.[22] An appeal to higher loyalties or the denial of injury can exculpate the deviant and permit a drift into rule-breaking. The very absence of an apparent motive can itself become a motive, liberating the offender from personal responsibility for his conduct.[23]

It is when deviance ceases to be the subject of purely private

[20] H. Becker, 'Marihuana Use and Social Control'.
[21] Cf. C. Mills, 'Situated Actions and Vocabularies of Motive'; M. Scott and S. Lyman, 'Accounts, Deviance and Social Order.
[22] G. Sykes and D. Matza, 'Techniques of Neutralization'.
[23] Cf. D. Cressey, 'Role Theory'; L. Taylor, 'The Significance and Interpretation of Replies to Motivational Questions'.

contemplation that it becomes qualitatively transformed. One is then required to rehearse and provide an account to those who may be offended, perturbed, or charged with the enforcement of rules. The account must not only satisfy oneself but also the suspicious outsider. Strategies are routinely employed to contend with the problems which deviance brings in its train. Amongst them is penitence and the acknowledgement of fault.[24] Not all deviation is magnified when it is confronted by accusation or sanction.[25] On the contrary it may decline: the rule-breaker can feel shame or fear. And there are the alternative strategies of denying blameworthiness, representing deviance as some other phenomenon, or deflecting attention away from treacherous signs.[26] Quite commonly, problems are solved by retreating to the company of those who are similarly beset. When deviance is co-operative, dependent on joint activity or on a division of labour, it is especially likely that errant subworlds will emerge.[27] In those subworlds, pretences may be partially abandoned, unwelcome relationships avoided,[28] skills learned, and supportive interpretations acquired.[29] Deviant subcultures represent limited answers to the difficulties of living in a hostile and discouraging world. Over time, they can come to offer a modest refuge, providing new meanings to overcome the opprobrium which deviance attracts. Such subcultures have come to be the special province of the interactionist. His research is replete with the histories of small deviant circles.

In the main, it is the public meanings and structures of deviation which interactionists choose to study. Not only does interactionism deny the sociologist a capacity to reach the inaccessible processes which make up a subjective experience.[30] It also asserts that it is recognized deviance that is the proper topic for sociology. Deviance enters social life when it receives a response. Accordingly, interactionists may be a little indifferent

[24] See M. Cameron, *The Booster and the Snitch*.
[25] See H. Parker, *The View From the Boys*.
[26] See F. Davis, 'Deviance Disavowal'; E. Goffman, *Stigma*.
[27] See M. Leznoff and W. Westley, 'The Homosexual Community'.
[28] See D. Tanner, *The Lesbian Couple*.
[29] See A. Lindesmith, *Opiate Addiction*; E. Schur, *Narcotic Addiction in Britain and America*; K. Plummer, *Sexual Stigma*.
[30] Cf. H. Becker, 'The Self and Adult Socialization'.

to first causes. In the analysis of mental illness, for example, there are those like Thomas Scheff who argue that origins are diffuse, numerous, and often untraceable. The sociological problem is not the explanation of ultimate origins but the fashion in which mental illness becomes identified and shaped in public interaction.[31] Similarly, Lemert observed that rule-breaking is commonplace in everyday life. Sociology should not focus on the multiplicity of petty, undistinguished, and unacknowledged breaches. It should analyse the forms which they take when there is some reaction. Deviance then intrudes into the public arena to become a socially consequential event.[32] In a supporting illustration, Becker returned to Malinowski's description of the Trobriand Islander who had committed incest.[33] The incest was tacitly condoned until denunciation made it inescapably public. Advertisement transformed what had been a tolerated, private act impelling the Islander to face an untenable situation and kill himself.[34]

It is quite important to note that a concentration on public response does not entail the claim that there is no deviation without labelling by others. Considerable confusion has arisen from the belief that interactionism treats public labelling as a fundamental prerequisite of deviance. Indeed, some critics have maintained that 'hidden' or 'secret' deviance poses insuperable problems for the interactionist.[35]

It can very easily be demonstrated that interactionism does indeed recognize the way in which people answer and adapt to their own private descriptions of self without any intervention from outsiders. And interactionism has shown that the consequences of such self-labelling are real enough. But interactionists do attach uncommon significance to the public recognition of deviance. When rule-breaking receives a reply from the outside world, it must be defended, ended, or disguised. It must be altered to cope with novel, often painful restraints. The deviant may have to contend with the imputation of sinister intentions, the awarding of an unpleasant identity, and social placement with pariahs. Just as important, such deviation can become a feature of others' lives. Their

---

[31] T. Scheff, *Being Mentally Ill*.   [32] E. Lemert, *Social Pathology*.
[33] H. Becker, *Outsiders*.   [34] B. Malinowski, *Crime and Custom*.
[35] See J. Gibbs, 'Conceptions of Deviant Behaviour'.

conception of the world, its character and dangers, will be framed by knowledge about publicly-ratified transgressions. There is thus a significant difference between the experience of one who has 'merely' stolen and one who is certified a thief. Stealing might not have been incorporated into core definitions of the self. It might have been construed as a lapse or atypical adventure, an act that was rather peripheral to the kind of person that one is. Proclamation can translate that stealing into a pivotal feature of the offender's personality. It will affect the manner in which he is treated by others. The thief may become obliged to reconsider who he is and what he might do in time to come. There is, Lemert argues, the possibility of a symbolic reorganization of the self: 'When a person begins to employ his deviant behavior or a role based upon it as a means of defense, attack, or adjustment to the overt and covert problems created by the consequent societal reaction to him, his deviation is secondary.'[36]

Secondary deviation can occur in any of the transactions which centre on the overt deviance of a person. It may arise in informal relations. Indeed, official intervention by the police and other agents being relatively uncommon in social life, it is the informal response which is most frequently encountered. Quite crucial will be the general and local assumptions which people apply to detected deviation. It is evident that much rule-breaking is tolerated providing secondary rules are themselves observed. There is theft at work. There is lying in everyday life. Sexual transgressions occur. It is not every instance of such rule-breaking that becomes reported to law enforcement agencies. Some is condoned, some falls outside the aegis of law, and some is thought insufficiently vexatious to merit action. It is equally evident that what is intolerable in one group can be approved in another. Trivially, what is proper in a bar is not always proper in a lecture theatre. Deviation is defined by its situation, by its perpetrators, and by its audience. In the course of a day, a person will pass through innumerable settings and the rules of one will not be the rules of another. The conventional order of a family does not apply to relations between strangers in the street or to the organization of a work-place. More dramatically, there may be quite marked discontinuities

---

[36] E. Lemert, *Social Pathology*, 76.

between worlds, discontinuities which turn 'normal' order upside down. For instance, Barbara Heyl has described how the madam of an American brothel educated novice prostitutes by attempting to insulate them from the universe of 'squares': there was a systematic inversion of strategic sexual and social conceptions about men, money, and intercourse.[37]

It is not the simple presence of deviance but its quality, scale, and location which typically shape a reply. Very often, deviation will be 'normalized' and accommodated,[38] built into the fabric of accepted life. It is only when it is inexplicable, disorganized, or threatening that a gross reaction can take place. Crisis occurs when others cannot or will not cope. Its precipitation hinges on prevailing ideas about propriety, the social structure of the audience, and the appreciation of possible remedies. Some groups are tightly organized, others have a loose order, and others little apparent order at all. In turn, there is a great variation between the schemes which confer coherence on the world and between the abilities of people to monitor one another. Thus the army is regulated by elaborate, interconnecting, and precise rules of conduct. It assigns special personnel to the business of administering order and judging disputes. By contrast, a group of youths who 'hang out' on a street corner inhabits a rather simpler world: it *is* rule-governed, but its rules are often implicit, negotiable, and unenforced. And remedies are also coloured by social organization. There is an appreciable difference between the punishments inflicted by an army, a street-corner group, and a therapeutic community. Each punishment mirrors something of the symbolic vision of those who impose it. For example, a Quaker body might use discipline to underscore the importance of forgiveness and tolerance.[39] An army might use it to emphasize the need for complete compliance. Even so connections are rarely simple and uniform. Quakers *do* expel membes and call upon the police. The army *does* exercise clemency, recognize religious objections to certain practices, and make use of psychiatry.

The interplay between social control, social organization,

[37] B. Heyl, *The Madam as Entrepreneur*.
[38] See S. Cavan, *Liquor License*.
[39] See R. Dentler and K. Erikson, 'The Functions of Deviance in Groups'.

deviance, and identity is neatly illustrated by Scheff's *Being Mentally Ill.* It is Scheff's contention that mental illness is a social role. Initially a disconcerting and anomalous breach of an unnamed, 'residual' rule, mental illness is given form by lay and professional stereotypes of madness. There are abundant labels and definitions which describe the character and behaviour of the mad. They are available to those who witness strange conduct. They are also available to those who have otherwise inexplicable and disturbing experiences. Labels may not be applied immediately. They may not be accepted without qualification when they *are* applied: there is often some scope for negotiation.[40] But labels do embody general and seemingly objective ideas. They make sense of problems, suggesting ways in which one can and should go mad. In particular, they inform psychiatric practice, providing a basis for diagnosis and treatment. Scheff would argue that much psychiatry is devoted to the 'apostolic mission' of persuading people to accept one of a limited number of mad roles. Patients are encouraged to comply with therapeutic authority, gain insight, and accept an appropriate definition of themselves. It is a paradox that those who reject diagnoses are taken only to confirm the astuteness of the diagnostician.[41] It little matters whether psychiatric analyses are 'correct' or not. The social consequences of analysis would remain the same. The sociological import of labelling is that mad behaviour is rewarded. People learn to be mad, confirming the validity and utility of the original stereotypes.

Partly because of its sheer accessibility, formal social control has been subjected to some considerable analysis by the interactionists. It was interactionism that enlarged the task and complexity of criminology by insisting on the creative role played by outsiders in the production of deviance. Scheff and others demonstrated that it was difficult to explain the social organization of deviance by referring to properties of the offender alone. Deviance is identified, answered, and formed by those who deal with rule-breakers. The character of the

---

[40] T. Scheff, 'Negotiating Reality: Notes on Power in the Assessment of Responsibility'.

[41] See E. Goffman, 'The Moral Career of the Mental Patient'; D. Rosenhan, 'On Being Sane in Insane Places'.

answer given by bailiffs,[42] the police,[43] psychiatrists,[44] magistrates,[45] and doctors[46] will provide the materials for the
deviant's own significant gestures. At the very least, the deviant
will be obliged to construct his or her actions around the probable reaction that they will elicit.

It must be emphasized that the violation and enforcement of
rules are contingent upon place, time, and character. Law
officers are not automata. They are also responsive to setting
and organization, behaving rather differently in the slum, the
office, and the suburb.[47] When offences are comparatively mild
(and the definition of mildness is itself contingent), much may
hinge on the demeanour and response of the deviant. Whilst
compliance and deference might bring about a decision not to
charge a person, surliness and tardiness can hasten action.[48] All
this will be negotiated in a shifting context of plans and
relations. An individual policeman might be just about to come
off his shift, he might seek overtime work, he might be under
scrutiny for poor performance or for excessive zeal.[49]

There is thus a tendency to treat rules as *resources* rather than
as binding instructions. It is a tendency that creates considerable flexibility in the organization of relations between deviants
and agents of control. Rule-breakers may be co-opted as allies
or informants,[50] they may become part of a game-like and well-
regulated exchange,[51] they may be effectively ignored, or they
may be pursued with great vigour. Typically, for instance, it is
so difficult to obtain information about activities that have no
willing complainant that the police have to offer a licence to
insiders.[52] Drug-suppliers may trade information for immunity.[53] And relations may also change over time: shifts in personnel, policy, or politics can introduce pressures to abandon old

[42] See P. Rock, *Making People Pay*.   [43] See D. Bordua (ed.), *The Police*.
[44] See E Goffman, *Asylums*.
[45] See R. Emerson, *Judging Delinquents*; P. Carlen, *Magistrates' Justice*.
[46] See E. Freidson, *Profession of Medicine*.
[47] See E. Bittner, 'The Police on Skid Row'; A. Stinchcombe, 'Institutions of Privacy
in the Determination of Police Administrative Practice'.
[48] See C. Werthman and I. Piliavin, 'Gang Members and the Police', J. Wilson,
Varieties of Police Behavior.
[49] See J. Rubinstein, *City Police*.
[50] See G. Marx, 'The New Police Undercover work'.
[51] See H. Sacks, 'Notes on Police Assessment of Moral Character'.
[52] See J. Skolnick, *Justice Without Trial*.
[53] See B. Cox *et al.*, *The Fall of Scotland Yard*.

strategies or adopt novel ones. In one celebrated instance, the appointment of a new chief constable led to a wholesale transformation in the control of homosexual importuning. What had been neglected became a target for energetic prosecution.[54] More minutely, there is a great scope for injecting variety *within* relationships. Thus Willis observed that there was no uniform suppression of drug use in one English town. On the contrary, users and members of the local drugs squad appeared to enjoy a symbiotic relationship: the police arresting those whose offences were relatively flagrant and substantial, and the users themselves reporting 'pushers' whose behaviour was held to be exploitative and bullying. Most consumers were allowed to proceed undisturbed, coexisting quite amiably with the police.[55]

The orderly production of deviance and deviants therefore hinges on an extraordinarily complicated set of interchanges. It cannot be distilled down into a series of mechanical and predictable processes. Interactionism is accordingly somewhat reluctant to rely on schematic descriptions of social control. Instead, it turns sociology towards the detailed analysis of specific events. General themes *do* dominate that analysis but they are not held to have the character of iron laws. On the contrary, outcomes are treated as uncertain and possibly surprising.

Scott's *The Making of Blind Men* is an important demonstration of the intricate and largely unexpected forms that social control can take. It stresses the interdependence of control and deviation, proclaiming that the blind are manufactured by the special agencies which care for them. Organizations must achieve a limited success, displaying their capacity to train blind people for work and activity in the world of the sighted. Not every blind person is educable. Only a few are eligible as candidates for transformation into the acceptably functioning blind. It is those few who are heavily recruited by the voluntary agencies for redemption. They are the 'blind children who can be educated and the blind adults who can be employed. The system largely screens out the elderly, the unemployable, the uneducable, and the multiply-handicapped—in other words, the vast bulk of the blindness population.'[56]

[54] See *Police Review*, 3 August 1963.
[55] P. Willis, *Profane Culture*.
[56] R. Scott, *The Making of Blind Men*.

Blindness is rarely a total loss of vision. Many of those in the charge of American blindness agencies can see a little. They are methodically encouraged to play the blind *role*, relinquishing any use of sight and adopting the methods of the utterly sightless. They are required to learn incapacity, conforming to embedded institutional definitions of blindness. In this fashion, skills and senses are surrendered, being replaced by an orderly incompetence:

The disability of blindness is a learned social role. The various attitudes and patterns of behavior that characterize people who are blind are not inherent in their condition but, rather, are acquired through ordinary processes of social learning. Thus, there is nothing inherent in the condition of blindness that requires a person to be docile, dependent, melancholy, or helpless; nor is there anything about it that should lead him to become independent or assertive. Blind men are made, and by the same processes of socialization that have made us all.[57]

The special selection of the blind and the special meanings of blindness appear to flow from the agencies' dependence on a continuous production of conspicuous and sympathetic successes. Their dependence, in turn, stems from a need to secure funds and carve out satisfying professional careers. The malleable and changed are more impressive work materials than the intractable and recalcitrant: they provide a clear justification for expenditure and effort.[58]

The awarding of deviant identity cannot then be portrayed as an elementary reflex action on the part of the State or powerful institutions. To be sure, the State does have considerable power to describe its subjects. It is a power which sometimes allows the subject little scope for negotiation or rebuttal. In many transactions, the authoritative expert on control or treatment can impose his or her will on the deviant. Yet the definitions offered vary and they may have remarkable consequences. Becoming deviant is not always a progression into evil or wickedness. The rule-breaker may be coaxed into any one of a number of roles, wickedness being ascribed only when an agency or witness holds to ideas of free will, when the

[57] Ibid. 14.
[58] See also J. Roth and E. Eddy, *Rehabilitation for the Unwanted*.

offender was thought to know what he was doing, and when he could have done otherwise.[59] Equally available are penitent, sick, or probationary roles.[60]

Central will be the agencies' intentions and capacities. Certain enforcement institutions are geared to regulating occupations or industries, and their prime objective is not to punish but to transform behaviour. The Oxford Centre for Socio-Legal Studies has produced a spate of studies of those who employ such 'compliance strategies'. Hawkins, for instance, has examined the control of the industrial pollution of water;[61] and Hutter has written about environmental health officers. The business of an environmental health officer is not to pronounce on immorality or to outcast and penalize those who produce contaminated food. It is to stop contamination. Yet, when people resist reasonable attempts to make them comply, they may well be treated as conventional deviants. In all those studies are to be found distinct pariah roles conferred on those who persistently, flagrantly, and disrespectfully ignore compliance strategies. A neutral enforcement process will then give way to moral outrage.

Other institutions lack the power or means to manage deviants as outsiders. They will create identities which are expressly designed to ease their work. Being unable to control hostile and estranged people, they will emphasize the normality of those whom they privately define as abnormal. In the case of debt-collection, for example, enforcement procedures are designed to persuade defaulters that they are fundamentally honest, albeit forgetful, people. Were enforcement to antagonize them, collection would become impossibly expensive and inefficient.[62] For rather different reasons, it was the policy of a home for unwed mothers to convince its clients that pregnancy was a misadventure which should not be blamed on them.[63] In both instances, the regulation of deviance contributed roles which protected the rule-breaker. In the latter instance, the proffered role restored innocence to the deviant and permitted further drift into deviation.

[59] See P. McHugh, 'A Common-Sense Perception of Deviance'.
[60] See J. Gusfield, 'Moral Passage'.
[61] K. Hawkins, *Environment and Enforcement*.
[62] See P. Rock, *Making People Pay*.
[63] See P. Rains, *Becoming an Unwed Mother*.

We have used the language of role and role-playing, and there is some little confusion in the suggestion that the world is neatly scripted and organized for dramatic purposes. As Goffman observed, 'all the world is not a stage—certainly the theater isn't entirely'.[64] Roles are adapted and created in use, breaking down their stereotyped character and replacing it by innovation.[65] Deviant roles themselves resist precise classification. Increasingly, interactionists have begun to write of homosexualities instead of homosexuality, stressing the wealth and diversity of sexual deviation. And it would be misleading to argue that the business of deviating consists merely of stepping into an arranged part. Interactionism casts deviance as a process which may continue over a lifetime, which has no necessary end, which is anything but inexorable, and which may be built around false starts, diversions, and returns. The trajectory of a deviant career cannot always be predicted. However constrained they may seem to be, people can choose not to err further. Phillipson has likened the process to a long corridor with numerous doors: one is not compelled to travel the entire length but may leave at any stage.[66]

Becoming deviant is itself described dialectically as a series of phases which supersede one another, each phase reworking the significance of what has gone before. In turn, each phase is held to be causally important in its own right. It is not enough to describe the initial conditions of rule-breaking (be they social disorganization, conflict, or defective personality), it is also necessary to appreciate the evolving character of the deviant career as it emerges in time. Thus Lindesmith and others have been somewhat scathing about psychiatric analyses which presume that traits diagnosed in treatment were somehow invariant dimensions of personality. They insist, instead, that those traits may have arisen in the treatment or control of deviation. Homosexuals or drug addicts may not have been passive or inadequate when they made their first moves towards deviation. Becker accordingly stressed the need to employ a model of sequential causation which can comprehend the developing, staggered, and changing qualities of

---

[64] E. Goffman, *Frame Analysis*, 1.
[65] See R. Turner, 'Role-Taking: Process versus Conformity'.
[66] M. Phillipson, *Sociological Aspects of Crime and Delinquency*.

deviation. It is a model which requires an expenditure of time and patience, coaxing research to monitor or reconstruct events as they unfold. Like its ancestor, the Chicago School, inter-actionism defines research itself as emergent and exploratory. Knowledge about the social world is built up little by little in an active process of enquiry that continually transforms an original problem and the questions that can be asked about it.

Interactionism and labelling theory were given a new and possibly somewhat awkward emphasis in the British sociology of deviance of the 1960s. Independently of and simultaneously with the emergence of 'labelling' theory in the USA, a social statistician, Leslie Wilkins, had drawn certain inferences about the effects of the distribution of phenomena in social space.[67] He had observed that deviants were statistically uncommon, an odd claim unless it was intended to refer to *assumptions* about the frequency of rule-breaking. Wilkins proceeded to argue that there was a tendency for deviants to become structurally isolated from the majority, and this was also an argument that *might* be said to hold about popular *assumptions*. He concluded that information about such an isolated minority was necessarily transmitted over a distance to the majority: it was second-hand and mediated and, being mediated, it was liable to distortion. The effect is deviancy amplification, an amplification effect which resembles the workings of a cybernetic system with inaccurate feedback loops. Amplification occurs when the majority or its agents react to a deforming representation of the deviant minority, creating a new situation, problems, and context for deviation. The answering replies of deviants are again distorted, generating a new response and a new reply. Incorporated by Cohen[68] and Young,[69] amplification theory explained the dialectical progression of deviant processes: action producing reaction in a spiralling chain of ever more alienating gestures. Some slight initial difference in dress, expression, or conduct can lead to a sequence of events which magnifies, exaggerates, and creates deviance. Thus Teddy Boys were given a demonic cast in the England of the 1950s, coming to stand for much that was corrupt and evil.[70] Amplification theory seems to be most telling when it is applied to

---

[67] L. Wilkins, *Social Deviance*.

[68] S. Cohen, *Folk Devils*.

[69] J. Young, *The Drugtakers*.

[70] See P. Rock and S. Cohen, 'The Teddy Boy'.

symbolic or expressive deviation, deviation that is publicly proclaimed and designed to invite a public response; its uses elsewhere are less certain. It is not clear how such amplification cycles start and end, nor is it clear why particular cycles amplify and others serve to reduce visible deviation.[71]

Criticism

As the interactionist sociology of deviance came to the fore, so criticism itself mounted. In part, there was a response from those whose work had been overshadowed. In part, there was a reaction from those who had exploited developments within interactionism, pursued them beyond the limits of interactionist analysis, and returned to interactionism with their new arguments. As Plummer remarked, 'in just ten years, labelling theory has moved from being the radical critic of established orthodoxies to being the harbinger of new orthodoxies to be criticised.'[72] The history of interactionism has thus followed the conventional pattern of much sociology: the extraordinary has become ordinary and then banal.

Attacks have typically been coloured by the parent perspectives of the critic. What one takes to be a conservative stance[73] is thought by another to be radical. Interactionism is defined as overly empiricist by one[74] and insufficiently empiricist by another.[75] Debates about sociology are inordinately complex because they entail a series of interminable questions about the position of the questioners.

The first and most obvious objection to interactionism challenges its scientific standing. Science is held to characterize disciplines which are articulate and reasoned in their methods. Above all, it is held that sociology should proceed by logically scanning problems, formulating hypotheses, and applying them in rigorous fashion. Interactionism is heir to the assumptions and practices of the Chicago School and it is as resistant to an orderly logico-deductive methodology. It patently fails to

[71] Cf. J. Ditton, *Controlology*.
[72] K. Plummer, 'Misunderstanding Labelling Perspectives', 85.
[73] Cf. A. Platt, review of *The New Criminology*.
[74] See I. Taylor *et al.*, *The New Criminology*.
[75] See W. Gove (ed.), *The Labelling of Deviance*.

conform to the strict version of science.[76] It is hesitant about elaborate planning and exposition, arguing that such work blinds one to the possibility of learning in the field. Thus, Laud Humphreys observed 'hypotheses should develop *out of* ... ethnographic work, rather than provide restrictions and distortions from its inception.'[77] Interactionists would preserve their openness to the social world, being educated as they pursue research. Hostile critics find this deliberate lack of preparation intolerable. They portray interactionism as ambiguous, ill-resolved, and evasive. They are particularly distressed by its refusal to offer conjectures that might sustain or falsify its fundamental propositions. Adopting a Popperian philosophy of science,[78] they remark that interactionism is not scientific because it is a closed system which resists falsification. There is merit in the observation: symbolic interactionism has woven such a subtle system of indeterminate ideas that the rejection of one can always be explained by invoking another. Its proponents would retort that science should respect the qualities of the materials which it explores: ambiguity, contradictoriness, and openness distinguish the social world and it would be foolish to impose schemes that block them out. But interactionism is reduced a little in the process. It may well be that sociology cannot be otherwise, that efforts to make it conform to a simplified version of the natural sciences do violence to enquiry, and that society cannot be distilled into clear formulas. It may well be that sociology can never be stereotypically scientific. Yet the appeal of interactionism must retreat towards the sheer persuasiveness of its imagery of people, and it is evident that not all *are* persuaded.

More telling is the phenomenological assertion that interactionism fails even in its core task. If interactionists resist the codification and formalization of their approach, it is because they would faithfully reflect central properties of social order. It is their ambition to capture the workings of symbolic process. To be sure, they recognize that those workings are not 'naturally' reproduced by sociology, that sociology is a distorting activity that answers special purposes and employs a special

---

[76] See J. Huber, 'Symbolic Interaction as a Pragmatic Perspective'.

[77] L. Humphries, *Tearoom Trade*, 22.

[78] See K. Popper, *Conjectures and Refutations*.

language. But there is assumed to be correspondence between the structure of social life and the structure of its reports. Some phenomenologists have argued that that correspondence is less than sure. They claim that there is a problematic gulf between the interactionist vocabulary of 'role', 'deviance', and 'process' and the actual procedures by which people organize their affairs. Cicourel, for instance, questioned whether one does order one's life by role analysis.[79] If one does not, it becomes uncertain what status the word 'role' is supposed to occupy. Roles are sociological inventions, not features of the social world. People presumably turn to different practices and ideas when they behave, and Cicourel would have the sociologist inspect *them* rather than the suspect conception of role itself. We have observed that roles are not discussed as if they were binding instructions to people. We have also observed that roles are imprecise, fluid, and negotiated. Nevertheless, roles appear to be the sociologist's property, not the role-player's. Similarly, Phillipson and Roche have subjected the very term 'deviance' to an examination which suggests that the rules which are broken are those devised by sociologists, not those of people in everyday life.[80] Deviance is *not* a label that people bestow on one another very freely. One may be identified as a 'hippy', a 'punk', a 'cad', or a 'reprobate'.

There may be some formal similarity in the consequences of such identification. But the overarching term 'deviance' is more generally a sociological artefact which stems from an unspecified theory; it is not just a natural phenomenon which the sociologist discovers in an undisturbed state. Interactionists are relatively unprepared to develop that unspecified theory—to do so would compound the error which the phenomenologists have already emphasized. *Deviance* is tacitly taken to be a 'sensitizing concept': 'Hundreds of our concepts—like culture, institutions, social structure, mores and personality—are not definitive concepts but are sensitizing in nature. They lack precise reference and have no bench marks which allow a clean-cut identification of a specific

[79] A. Cicourel, 'Interpretative Procedures and Normative Rules in the Negotiation of Status and Role'.

[80] M. Phillipson and M. Roche, 'Phenomenology, Sociology, and the Study of Deviance'.

instance, and of its content. Instead, they rest on a general sense of what is relevant'.[81]

Little intellectual capital has been sunk in the interactionist idea of deviance. The idea maps out a vague idea and propels sociologists towards it. It does not inform them about what exactly they will find there. Such information would be misleading: by definition, it would make research redundant. *Deviance* has become a loose working conception whose details have been progressively supplied by studies of concrete events. The interactionist would not care to amalgamate or sift all those details. Rather, the conception is built up 'crescively'[82] and gradually, including marginal and perhaps absurd cases. It has come to include dwarfs, giants, stutterers, prostitutes, strippers, and thieves. Whether those disparate figures do share a list of common properties which exclude all ambiguous cases is thought to be analytically unimportant. More significant is the utility of an approach that employs the term and ideas of deviance. Interactionists maintain that cross-reference and comparison have been helpful, that prostitutes can be understood by applying analysis derived from studies of drug-addicts. They are unconcerned about the ownership of the idea of deviance, and equally unconcerned about its precision, arguing that precision cannot and should not be the end of sociology.

Quite different criticisms have flowed from radical criminology and its sympathizers. We shall discuss how radical criminologists seek to place the analysis of specific and general events in the context of a particular master vision of society. It is a vision which borrows heavily from Marxism and the sociology of conflict. Every individual phenomenon is thought to acquire its significance from the whole and from its contribution to the whole. Radical criminologists dwell on the structures and transformations of capitalism, relating crime and its control to the larger organization of capitalism itself. Sociological theory is also given meaning by that organization, regarded as a political process in its own right. It is alleged that criminological ideas should be assessed as participants in a wider struggle for power and authority. They are not simply

[81] H. Blumer, *What is Wrong with Social Theory?*, 148.
[82] Cf. A. Rose, Preface to *Human Behavior and Social Processes*.

dispassionate commentaries which can be examined for their logicality, coherence, and appropriateness.

Thus defined, the business of criminology is very unlike the interactionist project. It is concerned with a critical mapping of the major systems of power and their interconnections with the State and its enforcement apparatus. Interactionism does touch on power and it has offered histories of law-making and control. But it also refrains from translating such work into a schematic or revolutionary theory of society. Indeed, it has little commerce with conceptions of global structure. The interactionists hold that the sociologist is offered only a series of partial glimpses which may lack overall unity. Thus delinquent groups change from time to time, situation to situation, and place to place. The intensive study of a delinquent group does not provide truths about all delinquents. It certainly does not furnish information about the most important inner workings of capitalism.

Interactionists and radical criminologists have melded many of their ideas,[83] but there remains an irreconcilable gulf between them. In particular, there is no agreement about the character or very existence of social structure. Whilst radical criminologists hold to a view of structure that supports strong political recommendations, interactionists would doubt that there is a self-evident structure that can be investigated by defensible empirical means. Their doubts would be encouraged by the marked absence of consensus amongst sociologists themselves. Sociology cannot agree on the nature of society: it is far from apparent that there is one version of structure that all recognize. Although radical criminologists may allege that interactionism ignores or evades questions posed by their conception of society, the problem does seem to involve much more than deferring to a bald and obvious truth. There are matters still to settle.

Conversely, a strong radical politics is not regarded as compelling or proven by all interactionists. They are unbowed when they are admonished about the political repercussions of their position because they do not share a common vision of their work and its consequences. More, they would argue that it is not the sociologist's primary job to produce a congenial

[83] Cf. R. Scott, *Why Sociology Does Not Apply*.

politics but an adequate sociology, that the two are not necessarily compatible, and that a sound sociology with an unpopular politics is preferable to a weak but politically approved sociology. Indeed, a weak sociology would almost certainly engender a weak politics. As we shall argue in a later chapter, radical criminology was itself to fork on that issue in the 1980s, some radicals altering their politics to accommodate new sociological evidence, others ignoring the evidence in order to conserve their politics.

Interactionism has also been subjected to more minute criticisms—a response to the central importance which some have awarded labelling. Studies of police and judicial reaction have been taken to argue that there would be no deviance without formal intervention. Further, it has been thought that such deviance cannot but be a steady progression into ever increasing alienation. Thus Gouldner stated that interactionism has 'the paradoxical consequence of inviting us to view the deviant as a passive nonentity who is responsible neither for his suffering nor its alleviation—who is more "sinned against than sinning" '.[84] Akers, too, observed: 'one sometimes gets the impression from reading this literature that people go about minding their own business and then—'wham'—bad society comes along and slaps them with a stigmatized label.'[85] There are certainly strains within the interactionist sociology of deviance which encourage such opposition.[86] On occasion, deviants are presented as if they were the innocent targets of signification. But those strains are not necessary or widespread. We have remarked that deviation can take place without the manifest interference of others. We have also remarked that the effects of labelling are not at all determinate: they are contingent and variable, having no predictable outcome in individual cases. Criticisms of the species offered by Gouldner really reflect a response to only the most narrow version of interactionism.

Conclusion

Symbolic interactionism held sway over the sociology of deviance in the 1960s and early 1970s. Antipathetic to systematic

[84] A. Gouldner, 'The Sociologist as Partisan', 38.
[85] R. Akers, 'Problems in the Sociology of Deviance', 463.
[86] Cf. T. Scheff (ed.), *Mental Illness and Social Processes*.

theorizing and insistent on empirical research, it emphasized the active discovery of knowledge in the research setting. Some interactionists have correspondingly denied that they possess a 'theory' at all. Instead, they insist that theirs is a perspective which enables them to venture out into society to observe people doing things together.[87] One of the prime contributions made by interactionism is its compilation of detailed information about deviant practices. Its practitioners are not content to speculate about how deviance is transacted. On the contrary, they have been urged on by an active curiosity. Returning with focused descriptions, they have presented deviance as a series of complicated processes without a fixed structure. The deviant is one who constructs activities and assesses meanings in the company of others. He is not always constrained. Neither is he utterly free. He is restricted by circumstances, by the significance which behaviour can possess and by his ability to negotiate meaning. The interchanges in which he engages have a spatial and temporal dimension so that rule-breaking is not the same in Moscow and in Hemel Hempstead, in 1900 and in 1980. Interactionists do not claim to manufacture grand theory. They do not answer all the pressing social problems which bedevil people. They proceed more modestly and slowly. As Plummer suggests, 'symbolic interactionism is only one theory that need be used within the labelling perspective, but it has an affinity with the study of marginality and deviance, and it is a useful corrective to grander, more general theories. It has a useful role to play.'[88]

---

[87] H. Becker, 'Labelling Theory Reconsidered'.
[88] K. Plummer, 'Misunderstanding Labelling Perspectives', 119.

8

Phenomenology

The safeguarding of the subjective point of view is the only but sufficient guarantee that the world of social reality will not be replaced by
a fictional non-existing world constructed by the scientific observer.

A. Schutz, 'The Social World and the Theory of Social Action'.

Introduction

Phenomenology came out of a great mass of debates about the
character, scope, and certainty of knowledge. Those debates
have only a remote bearing on our theme and we shall not
explore them in any detail. It is enough to recall that, although
there have always been some misgivings about our ability to
make sense of the world, a severe doubt became central to the
writings of particular English empiricists and German philosophers at the beginning of the nineteenth century. The claim
was made that observation and the methods of science
provided no foundation for iron laws of nature and science. It
was even argued that observed objects are not necessarily what
they seem.

Let us reconstruct one version of that argument. It was stated
that observation is manifestly constrained. It is affected by the
physical capacities of the body and brain, by assumptions
about the patterning of things, and by memories of past connections. One does not usually see confusion but order, and it
is difficult to determine how that order arose. At the very least,
perspectives are shaped by a rank inability to attend to more
than a limited range of sensations at any one time and in any
one place. Order may inhere in the world but things cannot be
grasped without the active workings of consciousness; consciousness moulds what may be known, and it is impossible to
disentangle features which 'belong' to objects from those which
are bestowed by their observers. In particular, appearances are

structured by the present and future purposes of the observer, by experience, and by stocks of knowledge. What is known hinges on practical objectives. A desert is simply not the same thing to oil prospectors, readers of *Dune* and *The Seven Pillars of Wisdom*, ecologists, botanists, painters, Bedouin, and tourists. It is not even the same thing to an oil prospector over time. It is a *phenomenon*, a phenomenon being 'that which appears to be the case, that which is given in perception or in consciousness, for the perceiving and conscious subject'.[1] Phenomena are those organized experiences which are available to us as we explore the world with our senses and imagination. They are utterly distinct from *noumena*, the undeformed, unchanging, and absolute essences of things. It was held to follow that the world can never be understood immediately, and without interference: its distorted appearance is uncertainly related to its unobserved, uninterpreted, innocent, and 'real' state. Indeed, is it possible to conclude only that the true nature of a thing is unascertainable.

Phenomenology explicitly addresses the possibilities of phenomena. It represents a series of answers to the problems posed by the sheer inaccessibility of sure knowledge about things as they 'really' are. In response to an apparently inescapable uncertainty, some of its authors proposed that philosophy should turn away from the search for an impeccable truth about the external world. They proclaimed their belief that that search was absurd, unprofitable, or profitable only with unconventional methods. It was their arguments that one can never know something which is uncontaminated by its own investigation. All that remain are phenomena and the processes which give them birth. Phenomenology accordingly tended to redefine the proper business of philosophy as a descriptive analysis of how things are grasped by consciousness. It directed attention at a relatively certain area whose limits are the limits of effective knowledge itself. It no longer enquired whether knowledge was correct but how it came into being. By extension and with a little irony, a number of phenomenologists could proceed to argue that almost all knowledge becomes correct in context. After all, there is no deeper, higher, or more

[1] M. Phillipson and M. Roche, 'Phenomenology, Sociology and the Study of Deviance', 126.

fundamental truth with which it may be compared and revealed as false.

Phenomenology was to become a substantial intellectual enterprise. Like any such enterprise, it acquired its own peculiar conflicts and ambiguities. Not only does it encompass what might be described as rather marginal and inconsistent themes,[2] it is not always clear what unites those who call themselves phenomenologists. There are profound contradictions between the ideas of Hegel, Heidegger, Scheler, and Schutz: they share few ambitions and methods. Indeed, much of the argument we have advanced should actually be qualified to incorporate the dissenting statements of major phenomenologists. There is not one important proposition with which all would agree.

Happily, what passes for phenomenological sociology is a most partial interpretation of the opportunities offered by the school. Many complexities have never been imported to affect the analysis of deviance. Thus no criminology has yet been grounded in the writings of Husserl, Jaspers, and Merleau-Ponty. But disharmony inevitably remains and it should be stressed that disagreement *has* been taken into criminology. Moreover, the exponents of different versions have not even been entirely faithful to their own principles. Phenomenological sociology does not offer an integrated logic and methodology. Rather, it forms a loose collection of observations which sometimes fail to support one another. Applied to deviant phenomena, those observations tend to provide irreconcilable perspectives and recommendations. It is important to be alert to the result which is both inconclusive and fragmentary. An expectation of coherence would only be confounded.

Phenomenology and Sociology

There are outcrops of phenomenology scattered throughout sociology, but their distribution and character are a little capri-

---

[2] An instance is the debate about whether significant differences exist between phenomenology and symbolic interactionism. See G. Mead, *The Philosophy of the Act*, esp. 360; D. Miller, *George Herbert Mead*; B. Meltzer *et al.*, *Symbolic Interactionism*; J. Douglas (ed.), *Understanding Everyday Life*, chs. 1, 11, and 12.

cious. The very resort to phenomenology suggests that some sociologists had identified social meaning as a subject or problem. Such an identification is more likely to be made when there is a deliberate attempt to comprehend the social organization of particular styles of thought: the sociologies of religion, ideology, knowledge, science, and literature being obvious instances. Phenomenology is manifestly busier in the study of religion than in the study of the State. But the connection between topic and interpretation is not at all straightforward. Not every sociologist of religion would find phenomenology persuasive although he or she may have to contend with its arguments. Those who do turn to phenomenology can move in quite different directions. And it could be argued that the sociology of the State would be enhanced by an injection of phenomenology.[3] After all, phenomonologists can claim that *every* topic is a problem in the explanation of consciousness. The State, it would be maintained, is not independent of the imagination. As Berger asserted, 'the "stuff" out of which society and all its formations are made is human meanings externalized in human activity. The great societal hypostases (such as "the family", "the economy", "the state", and so forth) [should be] reduced by sociological analysis to the human activity that is their only underlying substance.'[4] Thus conceived, the 'state' is an aspect of consciousness and it is to consciousness that the phenomenologist would go.

The appropriateness of phenomenology does not reside in the subject but in the sociologist's knowledge and sense of what is fitting. Deviance itself is not taken by all sociologists to be so infused with problems of meaning that it must be submitted to phenomenological analysis: it may be thought that meaning is unimportant or that it is 'objective' enough to forestall the demands of phenomenology.[5] Indeed, the definition of deviation as a process rooted in symbolism and consciousness typically stems from a prior commitment to phenomenology or interactionism. Most criminologists lacked that commitment,

---

[3] Works which point to the kind of analysis that might ensue include M. Edelman, *Politics as Symbolic Action*; W. Lippmann, *Public Opinion*; J. Douglas, *American Social Order*; P. Manning, *The Narc's Game*.

[4] P. Berger, *The Social Reality of Religion*, 18.

[5] Cf. L. McDonald, *The Sociology of Law and Order*, 18.

and criminology was pursued for decades before it experimented with phenomenology. The experiment was rather short-lived and it was confined to a peculiar, slender version of phenomenology which had been exported to America in the 1930s, remained unnoticed for some while, and was rediscovered and put to use in the California of the late 1950s and early 1960s.[6] The phenomenological sociology of deviance is principally the work of Cicourel, Douglas, Bittner, Sudnow, and a few others. Reimported into Europe, it has also been developed by Atkinson, Phillipson, Coulter, and Drew. It is that joint work which we shall describe.

Our description of phenomenology is simplified and limited. It is confined to a few arguments which are at the centre of the imported version accepted by criminology. The imported version is an incomplete reflection of the wider span of phenomenology but its framework is orthodox enough. It is designed to explore the practical knowledge which people have of their social world, knowledge which is awarded a paramount significance. Society is not taken to be something apart from practical consciousness. Rather, it is represented as an object or process which exists in, wells up from, and *is* the workings of common sense. It cannot be analysed or considered until it is experienced. Experienced, it becomes a phenomenon. It must be examined as a facet of thought.

The sociological phenomenologist is particularly concerned about the nature and ownership of the experiences which make society available to consciousness. Those experiences are not entirely and always his or her own. Approaching phenomena outside the social domain, the philosopher need reflect only on his own responses and the responses of some imaginary and typical other introduced to generalize his observations. Approaching social materials, it is apparent that reflection is directed at the responses and reflections of others. Those others may not share the phenomenologist's sensibilities. They are independent of his will. In this sense, sociological phenomenology is a reaction to others' reactions, a consciousness of others' consciousness, a knowledge of others'

[6] One of the very first references to phenomenology made by those who would later affect the sociology of deviance is to be found in A. Cicourel and J. Kitsuse, *The Educational Decision-makers*, 11.

knowledge. Schutz emphasized its character by distinguishing between constructs of the first and second degrees, arguing that social phenomena are chiefly shaped by constructs of the first degree:

[The social scientist's] observational field, the social world, is not essentially structureless. It has a particular meaning and relevance structure for the human beings living, thinking, and acting therein. They have preselected and preinterpreted this world by a series of common-sense constructs of the reality of daily life, and it is these thought objects which determine their behaviour, define the goal of their actions, the means available for attaining them. . . . The thought objects constructed by the social scientist refer to and are founded upon the thought objects constructed by the common-sense thoughts of man living his everyday life among his fellow-men. Thus, the constructs used by the social scientist are, so to speak, constructs of the second degree, namely constructs of the constructs made by the actors on the social scene.[7]

Social reality must be real for someone somewhere and its reality must be publicly endorsed and publicly visible. It may be presented as a system of running descriptions which receive life only in the activities of people in the everyday world. It is those activities which create and animate social phenomena, not the analysis of the phenomenological observer. The description offered by the phenomenologist is secondary and removed, and phenomenology is actually a rather pallid facsimile of reality devised for special purposes unrelated to most practical action. Social reality appears when people decipher their environment; put forward proposals and inter-pretations; respond to their own and others' constructions; modify, accept, or reject what is about them; and thereby build a world for themselves. In this manner, description, describing, and described are much the same. What gives them authenti-city and solidity, making them properly social, is recognition and ratification by others. The phenomena of society emerge when they are given public response. In Berger's words, they are sustained in conversation.

The phenomenological project is almost wholly taken up with discussing the manufacture and application of measures to

[7] A. Schutz, 'Common-sense and Scientific Interpretation of Human Action', 5–6.

enter and reproduce the subjective experience of others. In practice these measures tend to consist of an amalgam of intro-spective, functionalist, literary, and observational techniques. Particularly important is introspection, defined by the phe-nomenologist as the phenomenological or eidetic reduction. Mind is turned back on itself, examining its own processes and replies to the world. Read as a practical demonstration of method, much phenomenological writing becomes an exam-ination of how its author imagines he understands his reactions to his surroundings. It stands as a distillation, a stripping-away of the inessential and the murky, which reveals the formal rules and procedures of the conscious mind. The only mind nakedly before the phenomenologist is his own. Others are opaque, impatient, and fleetingly present. Hence the practices of people in the social world are almost inevitably portrayed as identical to the phenomenologist's own conduct, conduct which is subject to unusual scrutiny. Phenomenological analysis is a projection or working extension of a private world. Its authority rests in large measure on an appeal to plausibility and a community of experience. It is as if the author had added a rhetorical preface which not only asserted that things could not possibly be other-wise but called upon the reader's own memory and sensibility to confirm everything that is to come. Such a preface is supported by the implicit functionalism of much phenomeno-logy. Many of the more general treatises tend to assemble a list of rules and qualities which are indispensable to a viable exist-ence in society. It is not that the phenomenologist can prove or observe the presence of all the phenomena he described. But he can quite cogently announce that these phenomena *must* be if people are to live with one another. An instance is Berger's claim that social order is an overarching canopy of objectified beliefs which keep madness at bay.[8] Another instance is Schutz's observation that one must make certain assumptions before any social conduct emerges. Those assumptions are identified by Schutz as 'pragmatically motivated basic con-structions', constructions which are brought into being so that action can go forward. They include the belief that people tend to exchange perspectives when they exchange positions ('the idealization of the interchangeability of standpoints'); the belief

---

[8] P. Berger and T. Luckmann, *The Social Construction of Reality*.

that people interpret the world in much the same way despite their diverse personal histories ('the idealization of the congruence of relevance systems'); and the synthesizing belief that 'the life-world which is accepted as given by me is also accepted by you, indeed, by us, fundamentally by everyone . . .'.[9] Schutz could never offer an indisputable demonstration of these propositions. He *could* argue that it is difficult to imagine or plan a social world constituted in any other fashion.

Schutz did not often obey his own injunction to move beyond introspection to a properly described and close observation of behaviour. But a number of phenomenologists have become empirical of late. Variously referring to themselves as ethnomethodologists, existential sociologists, and sociologists of everyday life, they rely less obviously upon a search within. They have undertaken meticulous examinations of the conduct of conversation, believing that talk makes a social world.[10] They have staged frightening or disconcerting encounters which are designed to make subjects and themselves newly aware of rules previously taken for granted.[11] They have improved new methods for alienating people from themselves, forcing a self-consciousness and a production of accounts which had hitherto been undemanded.[12] All this work is directed at the same ends as those of the phenomenologists of the reduction: there is a quest for knowledge about interpretative practices that are so familiar and understated that they are normally beyond the reach of the conscious mind.

Phenomenology, Sociology, and Deviance

Phenomenologists tend to be preoccupied with the general and formal properties of rules. The use of rules in any concrete setting may provide an oportunity for empirical work, but its exploration is unlikely to detain the phenomenologist for very long. Few phenomenologists attach themselves permanently to one substantive area. Reluctant to become sociologists of education, politics, or development, they flit from site to site.

[9] A. Schutz, *The Structures of the Life-World*, 61.

[10] See M. Atkinson and P. Drew, *Order in Court*.

[11] See H. Garfinkel, *Studies in Ethnomethodology*.

[12] See R. Hill and K. Crittenden, *Proceedings of the Purdue Symposium on Ethnomethodology*.

Indeed, there is a strain which encourages the recognition of two distinct kinds of rule, variously defined as 'deep' and 'surface' or 'syntactic' and 'semantic'. Deep rules regulate the construction of phenomena: they permit one to constitute 'teachers', 'students', and 'lessons'. Surface rules are directed at the understanding and manipulation of intact phenomena: enabling a teacher and students to embark on a lesson. In the main, phenomenology is thought to be taken up with an analysis of deep rules. The phenomenology of deviance is accordingly a somewhat vulnerable enterprise, which is more concerned with the manufacture of deviant phenomena as phenomena than with the relations of deviance themselves. That manufacturing process is held to be substantially similar to any other: the peculiar facts of deviance are not so peculiar that they demand specialized attention. It was in this sense that Phillipson argued:

[we should] turn away from constitutive and arbitrary judgements of public rule breaking as deviance towards the concept of rule itself and the dialectical tension that ruling is, a subject surely more central to the fundamental practice of sociology where men and sociological speakers are conceived as rule makers and followers. What is now the sociology of deviance might then be pushed to the margins of sociological discourse as a museum piece to be preserved perhaps as that antediluvian activity which sought to show oddities, curiosities, peccadilloes and villains as central to sociological reason.[13]

Such disdain for matters of the surface has prevented the emergence of a dedicated phenomenological criminology. None the less, curiosity about the conditions of rules and rule-observance has produced a limited affinity between criminology and phenomenological sociology. At some phase in their lives, many phenomenologists flirted with the sociology of deviance. An important generation of American West Coast sociologists passed their apprenticeship in symbolic interactionism before the refinding of Alfred Schutz in the 1960s. Interactionist work on symbolism, meaning, and rules fostered a sensitivity to interpretative analysis. Those who became thus sensitive might have found themselves impelled to proceed to phenomenology.

[13] M. Phillipson, 'Thinking Out of Deviance', 5–6.

But their early research experience may well have been grounded in an interactionist study of deviance.

Empirically and methodologically, the investigation of rules can lead to those marginal and strange situations where the constitution of social life seems particularly stark. Phenomenological sociologists are especially interested in common-sense reasoning. Precisely because it *is* common sense, it is prone to appear natural, familiar, and unproblematic. It is liable to be approached with what Schutz called the 'natural attitude', an attitude which does not question or disbelieve. The phenomenology of Schutz recommends the suspension of the natural attitude. It proposes that the ordinary should be treated as if it were extraordinary, that mundane phenomena should be regarded with an anthropological naïvety that refuses to take the world for granted. Any suspension of the natural attitude is precarious and difficult. It is almost impossible to cease believing in the objectivity, solidity, and permanence of the social world. Disbelief may have to be forcibly secured by jolting those who trust. Thus, Garfinkel invited his students to haggle over prices in supermarkets and to behave as if members of their family were strangers. Creating 'trouble' is a method of disrupting normal appearances and flouting normal expectations. It can lay bare that which is usually so silently presupposed that it is unnoticed.[14] It is also a form of mild deviance and the deviant, like the blind, are customarily endowed with a special vision. They are offered unusual perspectives on social phenomena. They are beset by questions which little affect others, questions about the character and presentation of the normal. It was Garfinkel too who went to a hermaphrodite to learn about sexual meanings.[15] He maintained that marginality imposes an awareness of commonplace social arrangements. Agnes, his hermaphrodite, had something of a sensitivity to phenomenological issues. She seemed to have suspended the natural attitude. It could not be argued that Garfinkel is a criminologist, yet he sought out deviant occasions because they nursed the sensibilities which Schutz and Husserl had praised.

Deviance is even more intimately implicated in the phenomenological conception of rules. It is held that the social world is

---

[14] H. Garfinkel, *Studies in Ethnomethodology*, ch. 2.   [15] Ibid. ch. 5.

constituted by rules of description and classification, that classification is a process whose formal properties can work back on the world, and that an understanding of the power of classification can disclose the forms which society will assume. Mary Douglas has observed that a 'heavy social load . . . is carried by apparently innocent-looking taxonomic systems'.[16] We have already illustrated the character of that load in our discussion of functionalism. Functionalism, structuralism, and phenomenology are indistinguishable at points. But the topic is important enough to warrant some repetition and amplification.

It has been remarked that phenomenological sociology argues that society can be analysed only as a set of experiences, that experiences are ordered by consciousness, and that order is built on a vital framework of categorization and sifting. In some of its guises, phenomenology would proceed to argue that social order is a fragile human accomplishment achieved in the face of meaninglessness. If the universe is not intrinsically significant but has meaning heaped upon it by people, any system or set of phenomena is an area of organization carved out of disorganization. Society itself can be defined as sense surrounded by things which make no sense. More complexly, there is not merely one society but a number which crowd upon each other. The order of one may be the disorder of another. Any classification system must recognize its own. The integrity, clarity, and coherence of society must be defended against threats to meaning and, indeed, against the very collapse of meaning. Minor instances of such collapse have been documented: societies can seem to lose corporate identity and purpose.[17] But some phenomenologists would claim that death, nightmare, and madness present glimpses of the unreason that lurks at the boundaries of society:

Society is the guardian of order and meaning not only objectively in its institutional structures, but subjectively as well, in its structuring of individual consciousness. It is for this reason that radical separation from the social world or anomy, constitutes such a powerful threat to the individual . . . He becomes anomic in the sense of

---

[16] M. Douglas, Preface to *Rules and Meanings*, 11.
[17] See K. Erikson, *In the Wake of the Flood*; T. Shibutani, *The Derelicts of Company K*.

becoming worldless. . . . The socially established nomos may thus be understood, perhaps in its most important aspect, as a shield against terror. The ultimate danger of . . . separation is the danger of meaninglessness. This danger is the nightmare *par excellence*, in which the individual is submerged in a world of disorder, senselessness and madness. Reality and identity are malignantly transformed into meaningless figures of horror.[18]

Those who deny or defy important separations and definitions within society do more than merely break a rule. They may be thought to challenge the very legitimacy and structure of order, becoming agents or instances of chaos. Homosexuality or madness can become laden with a significance which bears on the entire project of maintaining social order. Describing that project as a programme, Berger observed that serious deviance 'provokes not only moral guilt but the terror of madness. . . . The so-called "homosexual panic" may serve as an excellent illustration of the terror unleashed by the denial of the programme.'[19] Deviance is translated into a symbolic refutation of organization, an affirmation of meaninglessness, which demands control and suppression. Its forms may be interpreted as phenomena which borrow from the particular fears and order of a society: when threats to sense are countered they typically take the shape imposed by the sense that is under assault. Thus Erikson described a symbiotic relation between ideas, ideology, and deviance. He asserted that the crime waves of the early Massachusetts Bay Colony mirrored central disturbances in the society's classification scheme: Quakers, witches, and Antinomians were the unreason of one small seventeenth-century community.[20] They would not be so now. Again, Shoham claimed that the Nazi stereotype of the Jew was a simple antithesis of the Teutonic Superman.[21] The Jew owed less to the social organization of Jewry than to the structure of Nazi cosmology. The system of belief manufactures its own deviants. Men 'covenant implicitly to breed a host of imaginary powers, all dangerous, to watch over their morality and to punish defectors'.[22]

[18] P. Berger, *The Social Reality of Religion*, 30, 31, 32.
[19] Ibid. 33, 34.
[20] K. Erikson, *Wayward Puritans*, 7–8.
[21] S. Shoham, *The Mark of Cain*, 7–8.
[22] M. Douglas, *Implicit Meanings*, xiv.

When eruptions from without are identified as dangerous, it becomes evident that danger, its forms, and its magnitude will be affected by the character of the frontiers which must be breached. All societies are defined but they are not identically marked-off from what is about them. Mary Douglas would argue that they may be ranked by the emphasis which they place upon their boundaries. Those which stress their apartness will generate a distinct kind of explanation for deviance. Deviants will more commonly be presented as outsiders to the virtuous group. Evil itself is not produced by the group but by a dangerous environment. The weakly-bounded, however, tend to lodge the origins of deviance in their own community, looking to their fellows as a source of danger.[23]

Deviance is sometimes more than a simple threat of disorganization. It can also take the guise of an orderly and solid enough antithesis to familiar morality. Part of the fascination of strangers is that they are outsiders who not only confirm our own identity but also offer glimpses of a tantalizing freedom. Societies are defined by what they are not, and we can only know what we are by identifying things that negate us. We have already reported that Jack Douglas argued that good and evil, God and Satan, morality and immorality are inseparable twins. Meaning and social organization would be impossible without the continuous presence of their contrasts. Communists draw symbolic sustenance from capitalists, and capitalists from communists. Indeed, the contradictions of politics often seem staged to dramatize rectitude and confirm organization. The far left and the far right *need* one another. Moderates require extremists. The manner in which they portray one another depends more on the dialectics of the political process and the ideology of the definer than on any 'real' or 'independent' properties of the defined. They create one another. And that work of creation is never a fixed or stable activity. As a society changes and its moral frontiers move, so its companion forms of deviance will also shift. Thus Davis maintained that pornography will always be discovered just outside the boundaries of conventional sexuality, and that it changes with every alteration of convention.[24]

Internally, the defence of social order rests upon the preser-

<hr>

[23] See M. Douglas, *Natural Symbols*.   [24] M. Davis, *Smut*.

vation of neat distinctions between the classes and phenomena which constitute a society. Those things and processes that are recognized as detached must retain their separation. Confusion would erode social organization, and the chief instruments of confusion are ambiguity and anomaly. Following Douglas and Berger, Scott states 'no social order can survive unless it develops mechanisms for protecting the symbolic universe against the threats that chaos and anomaly present to it. ... The property of deviance is conferred on things that are perceived as being anomalous from the perspective of a symbolic universe.'[25] It is Scott's contention that danger emanates from those who seem responsible for blurring and disrupting the outlines of categories. Thus the hermaphrodite is neither male nor female but a disturbing exception.[26] So, too, witches, homosexuals, and the mad do damage to the socially-constructed world. They cannot be contained but threaten to expose the fragility of conventional meanings. Significantly, those who straddle categories are sometimes awarded non-human or superhuman qualities. Witches were once thought able to assume the shapes of beasts. The mad were thought to be possessed. They were described as the inhabitants not only of the ruled world of human beings but also of the chaotic world of unruled nature. It was their conceptual unruliness which chiefly required discipline: they could be avoided, interpreted as innocuous, destroyed, or labelled as dangerous.[27] Perhaps the very starkest example of the man who straddled boundaries was Oedipus, the parricide and incestuous lover of his own mother, who was so abominably unnatural that he brought a plague on Thebes and had to be banned or killed before the pestilence abated. All classification systems must engender anomalies because none can be exhaustive. It is intrinsic to organization that it produces the unmanageable cases that subvert it.

Much of this phenomenological analysis lodges the roots of deviance in the formal properties of classification. It is not the contents of a scheme but its structure which creates deviation.

[25] R. Scott, 'A Proposed Framework for Analyzing Deviance', 22.
[26] See R. Edgerton, 'Pokot Intersexuality'.
[27] See M. Douglas, *Purity and Danger*.

The cleavages, links, and limits of systems are thought to be important in their own right. Thus the very existence of internal differentiation can work characteristic effects upon deviance. Douglas has argued that 'sets of rules are metaphorically connected with one another, allowing meaning to leak from one context to another along the formal similarities that they show'.[28] Such leakage is admirably exemplified by the influence exerted by hierarchy. Social phenomena tend to be ranked, ranking tends to be a moral matter, and matters clustered around the various ranks tend to borrow their moral meanings. In aggregate, stratification by social class can be so dominant that it absorbs other major systems of classification. Classes can become morally meaningful categories which colour the artefacts and conduct of those who are assigned to them.[29] Thus Duster has asserted that opiate addiction carried little stigma when it was widely dispersed amongst the different classes of nineteenth-century America. It was only when middle-class addiction was confined in discreet private clinics that drug use became identified with the disreputable and was held to be disreputable itself.[30]

It will have been marked that the work which we have reviewed is ambitious, devoted to the resolution of grand questions about cosmology and the fabric of the social universe. It is representative of one tradition of speculative phenomenology associated with the New School for Social Research in New York and the anthropology of Mary Douglas. In the main, criminologists have either ignored its arguments or regarded them as somewhat tangential to the central problems of their discipline. Criminology is probably the poorer for their neglectfulness. If it does recognize phenomenology, it is a different tradition that receives acknowledgement. That tradition, based largely on California, has preserved an emphasis upon the futility of a quest for absolute and fixed truth. It focuses on the phenomena which have been constituted by consciousness. However, the contexts and phenomena which it describes are superficially rather distinct. The criminologically-

---

[28] M. Douglas, *Rules and Meanings*, 13.

[29] See J. Douglas, 'Deviance and Respectability', in J. Douglas (ed.), *Deviance and Respectability*, 6–7.

[30] T. Duster, *The Legislation of Morality*.

ratified phenomenologists have concentrated upon small, observable settings. Their work dwells on interchanges between probation officers and delinquents and between prostitutes and their clients, on the physical design of abortion clinics, on the structure of homosexual encounters, and on the social order of nude beaches. It would appear to be a more humble, exact, and empirical enterprise. Yet, in one important sense, its goals and ideas are quite consistent with the more speculative analysis. Both are firmly anchored in phenomenology. Both explore the constitution and operation of rules. Both display some indifference about the specific phenomena that rules produce. A juvenile delinquent and a cosmos are equally the artefacts of interpretative practices.

What made the second tradition significant to criminology was its commentary upon the constitution of official criminal statistics. We have argued that those statistics have always served as an important resource for theorization and inference. It had long been understood that they were atypical of the larger 'real' population of criminals and criminal incidents. There *was* a worrying dark figure which had to be ascertained in some fashion. Different stages *had* been mapped in the flow of decisions that make up the criminal justice system. But the statistics themselves were defined as independent of theory, acting as an objective and precise check on conjecture, disclosing patterns, and suggesting associations. The phenomenological excursion into the social construction of crime rates was thus unexceptional phenomenology but strategic to criminology. Rates were treated as phenomena, produced as all phenomena are by interpretative work and social organization. Crime rates were no different from the rates of academic success and failure manufactured by schools.[31] However, what was relatively unremarkable in other spheres became the catalyst of considerable debate and revision in criminology. The solid facts of crime seemed to melt into a rather fluid and unreliable subjectivity.

Kitsuse and Cicourel had argued 'in modern societies where bureaucratically organized agencies are increasingly invested with social control functions, the activities of such agencies are centrally important "sources and contexts" which generate as

[31] See A. Cicourel and J. Kitsuse, *The Educational Decision-Makers*.

well as maintain definitions of deviance and produce populations of deviants.'[32] Theories and hypotheses employing crime statistics became redefined as constructs of the second degree. Rates were seen not as the raw, unprocessed indices which Émile Durkheim and Louis Chevalier had supposed them to be. On the contrary, they were themselves condensed interpretations of the world. They were embedded in background information and contexts of meaning which often remained unanalysed. They compressed numerous decisions, preoccupations, and practices. As Douglas stated, 'once we follow . . . "disembodied numbers" back to their sources to see how they were arrived at and what, therefore, they actually represent, we find that they are based on the most subjective of all possible forms of activity.'[33] Thus the categories of 'juvenile delinquent' and 'thief' do not emerge quite spontaneously and immediately from the doings of everyday life. Work has to be done before they are animated and applied. They reflect practical assumptions about troublesome behaviour, rules of classification, and the assignment of people to different classes. Clustered together and given a numerical form, those categories are more or less unintelligible unless those who scan the statistics are aware of the manner in which they were put together. The language, conceptions, and knowledge of those who encode and tabulate statistics must be available to those who decipher them: 'sociologists have been slow to recognise the basic empirical issues that problems involving language and meaning pose for all research.'[34]

Borrowing from Mannheim,[35] ethnomethodologists[36] have adopted the word 'indexical' to refer to the dependence of meaning on environment. They define the social world as 'awesomely indexical'. All utterances and signs are to be understood as indices which point to and stand for the wider and fuller situations in which they arose.[37] Suicide rates, for

[32] J. Kitsuse and A. Cicourel, 'A Note on the Uses of Official Statistics', 139.

[33] J. Douglas, 'Understanding Everyday Life', in J. Douglas (ed.), *Understanding Everyday Life*.

[34] A. Cicourel, *The Social Organization of Juvenile Justice*, 331.

[35] See K. Mannheim, 'On the Interpretation of "Weltanschauung"'.

[36] 'Ethnomethodology' is the study of the common-sense practices or methodologies which ordinary people employ to make sense of the everyday world.

[37] See A. Cicourel, *Method and Measurement in Sociology*.

instance, incorporate the lay and scientific reasoning of those who determine the cause and character of death. They reflect shorthand definitions of typical motives, circumstances, and courses of action.[38] Similarly, judicial statistics record the routine practices and conceptions of the courtroom. The staff of busy courts tend to standardize their tasks, establishing patterns of co-operation, a division of labour, and sets of stereotyped operations. Those operations, in turn, can be performed only when the work material is itself stereotyped and standardized. Cases must be predictable, simple, and repetitious, enabling the ordinary activity of the court to go on. They will become 'normal cases',[39] those unambiguous and elementary scenes which can be efficiently produced by the existing organization of the court. In those jurisdictions which rely heavily on plea-bargaining and 'negotiated justice',[40] there will be a systematic strain towards the discovery and creation of such normal cases. Defendants or incidents which are anomalous may be subject to an unusual pressure to undergo redefinition. In all this, the phenomenologist is concerned to investigate 'the processes by which persons come to be defined, classified, and recorded in the categories of the agency's statistics'.[41] His concern is part of a wider interest in the social production of knowledge. Only rarely will it be confined merely to the problems of those who compile and consume statistics. His concern is also part of a more general campaign against the procedures and claims of 'orthodox' sociology. Phenomenology, and ethnomethodology in particular, is forwarded as a rival to sociology and not as a complement or source of correction.[42]

It would be rather misleading to portray the phenomenology of deviance as a sociological perspective that focuses solely on the more significant repercussions of official social control. Limited work has been done on the negotiation of social order in settings that are subject to little formal discipline. Jack Douglas, Peter Manning, and others have been especially active in charting deviant worlds. Their writing is occasionally

[38] See J. Douglas, *The Social Meanings of Suicide*; M. Atkinson, *Discovering Suicide*.
[39] See D. Sudnow, 'Normal Crimes: Sociological Features of the Penal Code'.
[40] See J. Baldwin and M. McConville, *Negotiated Justice*.
[41] A. Cicourel and J. Kitsuse, *The Educational Decision-Makers*, 9.
[42] Cf. W. Sharrock, 'Ethnomethodology and British Sociology'.

indistinguishable from the ethnography of symbolic interactionism, dwelling upon the manufacture and preservation of
eccentric styles of life.[43] What it does contain is a reproduction
of the deviant's vision. On occasion, anomalies, ambiguities,
and areas of disorganization in systems of representation are
complemented by the deviant's own sense of absurdity or flux.
Deviance is sometimes depicted as a response to the apparent
disorderliness of everyday life. There are innumerable settings
which seem to be governed by no consistent rules, and where
any conduct is forced to become the breach of some precept or
principle of order.[44] Moreover, there are many settings which
possess a moral integrity and coherence that are condemned by
those who don the trappings of an absolute morality. Dis-
inclined to subscribe to a single, absolute, and unequivocal
truth, the phenomenologists of deviance are prone to describe
society as a welter of competing and inconsistent worlds which
constitute no unified whole.[45] Deviance documents a diversity
which others would suppress in the name of an oppressive
uniformity.

Criticism

Perhaps the most telling criticism of phenomenological work
on deviance proceeds explicitly and implicitly from phenomenology itself. We have related how importance is attached to
understanding and describing constructs of the first degree.
The phenomenologist would learn how his subjects make
sense of themselves and their world, reproducing their own
procedures and assumptions. It is apparent that utter fidelity
can never be attained: any piece of written analysis must
change and distort its object. Indeed, the business of analysis is
largely unfamiliar in everyday life. There is seldom time to
'stop and think'; thinking does require the interruption of
stopping, and thinking is rarely trained on phenomenological
ends. Analysis embodies practices, ideas, and objectives that
are necessarily different from those of the natural attitude.
Phenomenology must deform if it is to advance at all. What

---

[43] Cf. J. Douglas (ed.), *Research on Deviance*.
[44] See J. Douglas, 'The Experience of the Absurd and the Problem of Social Order'.
[45] See J. Douglas, *American Social Order: Social Rules in a Pluralistic Society*.

phenomenologists do is to advocate the use of one or more tests of adequacy which might help to undo some of the deformations imposed by their own sociology or philosophy. One such test is the provision of an effective scheme of translation which could eventually permit the subject to recognize himself or herself in any description that has been offered. It is the test that is most seldom applied[46] and its results could not but be uncertain. Translation transforms meaning: what is recognizable might not be phenomenology, and what is phenomenology might not be recognizable. The subject is unlikely ever to have pondered about the constitution of his consciousness in the intense manner of the phenomenologist. What he would be offered could thus be 'correct' but still almost wholly foreign. And the subject could as readily be converted by a description as recognize himself in it. Descriptions work on people and change them. In all this, the gap between constructs of the first and second degree remains unbridged. But the phenomenological sensitivity also remains to trouble those who examine their own and others' accounts.

Cicourel, for example, turned on the sociology of deviance and enquired what was intended by central phrases that had never been properly amplified or explained: 'recent advances recognizing the problem of how members of a group come to be labelled as "deviant", "strange", "odd", and the like, have not explicated terms like "societal reaction" and "the point of view of the actor", while also ignoring the practical reasoning integral to how members and researchers know what they claim to know.'[47] Applied liberally, such observations are likely to lead to the demise of much of what passes for the phenomenology of deviance itself. The use of words like 'rules', 'deviance', and 'social order' is as vulnerable to the accusation that they are unexplicated. After all, the experience of everyday life does not encompass many of the ideas lodged in contemporary phenomenology. Any investigation of the basis of that experience is calculated only to move one from deviance to an

[46] The major example was conducted not by a phenomenologist but by a Marxist anthropologist, Paul Willis, in *Learning to Labour*. Willis presented his subjects with the somewhat abstract and abstruse commentary which he had constructed to explain their conduct. They flatly refused to accept it as a proper or appropriate analysis.

[47] A. Cicourel, *The Social Organization of Juvenile Justice*, 331.

analysis of quite different phenomena and problems. In practice, that move has taken place. Phillipson, Cicourel, and
others have deserted deviance for the more fundamental problems of deep rules. They tend to represent deviation as a
clumsy idea that belongs neither to phenomenology nor to lay
experience.

External responses to ethnomethodology and the phenomenology of deviance have been somewhat scarce. Criminology itself tends to remain an eclectic discipline which
subordinates an activity called 'theorizing' to practical ends.
Theory is sometimes taken to be an encumbrance which is
independent of policy, methodology, and serious problems.
Theory which muddles and complicates analysis is a distraction. 'Reflexive' theory which urges the theorist to study himself as he theorizes is held to be especially burdensome. Having
noted the mass of phenomenological observations about the
significance of data, the criminologist might exhort people to
be cautious in their interpretation of official criminal statistics.
Little else is stated. Phenomenology is not represented as particularly salient to the resolution of critical criminological problems. In the division of intellectual labour, phenomenology is
assigned to others. It is 'bracketed away' as an interesting,
irrelevant, and possibly rather fanciful enterprise. Some sociologists, indeed, would dismiss ethnomethodology altogether as
a piece of Californian silliness that will pass:

The 1960s were indeed a revolutionary and romantic period, for well
known reasons, at least on the major campuses and in California. If
one wanted to project or translate its distinctive mood, the cult of
subjectivity, the rejection of external structures, into the language
and *problematik* of sociology, then one should quite naturally end up
with something just like Ethnomethodology. So this movement
would be the manner in which subjective, 'Californian' mood enters
the otherwise sober, scientifistic, sociological segments of the groves
of academe.[48]

Other sociologists describe phenomenology and ethnomethodology as substantial projects but join with Gellner and the
criminologists to define them as not quite pertinent to their

---

[48] E. Gellner, 'Ethnomethodology', 435.

work. Thus McDonald introduced her study of crime rates by asserting:

What the phenomenologists do is change the level of inquiry. It is not just that they do their research in a different way, but they ask different sorts of questions—*how* social control agencies work, *how* officials and the public interact, as opposed to *who* becomes a client of such an agency in the first place and *why*. . . . Questions as to why certain societies have high crime rates and full prisons, and others do not, cannot be addressed with phenomenology, and this is the sort of question I wished to entertain.[49]

It is apparent that the major critical drift is to present phenomenology as marginal to 'real' issues in the 'real' world. McDonald actually advanced her own argument by turning to Lenin. She acknowledged that Lenin 'came on strong'[50] but did not seem to disapprove of his statement that 'ideals of causality, necessity, law, etc. are a reflection in the human mind of laws of nature, of the real world'.[51] Neither does she dissent from Lenin's belief that 'the mastery of nature manifested in human practice is a result of an objectively correct reflection within the human head of the phenomena and processes of nature, and is proof of the fact that this reflection . . . is objective, absolute, eternal truth'.[52] Radical criminologists now echo Lenin, repeating his accusation that phenomenology obstinately refuses to know the setting in which it is lodged. Quinney attacked 'the epistemological assumption of a social constructionist thought [phenomenology] . . . that observations are based on our mental *constructions*, rather than on the raw apprehension of the physical world'.[53] And Taylor, Walton, and Young would also restore an absolutist conception of the social order, a conception which deferred only to one essential and true description of society. They would refrain from delegating authentic experience:

In essence the ethnomethodological critique of sociology . . . is that our shorthand concepts like alienation, class, deviance, etc. are either meaningless or if they do have meaning, they are no more meaningful than the generalization made by members. . . . Our final assessment of ethnomethodology's contribution to the study of deviance is

---

[49] L. McDonald, *The Sociology of Law and Order*, 18.   [50] Ibid. 279.
[51] V. Lenin, *Materialism and Empirio-criticism*, 15.   [52] Ibid. 190.
[53] R. Quinney, 'Crime Control in Capitalist Society', 184.

that in 'bracketing' away the question of social reality, it does not allow of any description of *the social totality* we assert to be productive of deviance.[54]

Allied to this argument about reality as absolute is a companion criticism of the absurdity of reflexive analysis. Phenomenologists would have sociologists examine their own practices as they examine the practices of their subjects. They have proposed that methodology and theory bend back on themselves, becoming their own topics. The radical and absolutist maintain that interpretative analysis is foolish, and that an interpretative analysis of interpretative analysis is doubly foolish. Borrowing from attacks on the sociology of knowledge, they raise the spectre of the infinite regress of reflexivity. The observed observer would have to be observed by one who was himself observed in an endless chain. The inconvenience, pathos, and folly of the regress are thought to be potent reasons for avoiding reflexivity and interpretative work altogether.[55]

The phenomenological reply might well ask questions about the ownership of conceptions of 'social reality', 'social totality', the 'real world', and the like. Critics do not seem prepared to trust ordinary people or one another with a sense of the real. Ernest Gellner and Richard Quinney berate ethnomethodology for its subjectivism, but they would fail to agree on the nature of the objective and the real. Phenomenologists themselves would not accept Quinney's or Gellner's description of reality. It is apparent that social reality is not really self-evident but contingent on description, describer, purpose, experience, time, and place. The reality of one person is the fantasy of another. It is perhaps barely possible that one definition is correct and all others are false. But the acceptance of that one definition has not yet been unanimous and could be secured only by force. Its production requires construction like the production of any other definition. In short, 'reality' is inescapably mediated, and Quinney has offered no recipe for arriving at this raw apprehension of the physical world. He would have one know without any of the processes associated with knowing. A mediated reality requires the exploration of its

[54] I. Taylor *et al.*, *The New Criminology*, 199, 208.
[55] See B. Hindess, *The Use of Official Statistics in Sociology*.

mediations and that exploration is phenomenology. Those who maintain the dignity of sociology by avoiding that which is absurd have not refuted reflexive work. They have merely pronounced it disagreeable. A priori, there is no reason why sociology and social life should not be a little absurd.

Our own reservations about the phenomenology and ethnomethodology of deviance centre on one pivotal problem. Gellner phrased the matter well when he described 'the scandal of undemonstrated privacy'.[56] The inner subjectivity of the phenomenologist's mind is held to be a model for all practical analytic purposes. It has a plausibility for many. It awakes a shock of recognition. Indeed, much of it seems convincing to us. But it is not accepted by all, and their refusal invites a phenomenological demonstration of the cogency of the phenomenological sensibility. No such demonstration has or could be made. The Freudian, the Jungian, the Adlerian, the Marxist, and the interactionist would assert their difference from phenomenology. Their reasoning is not the common sense of Schutz's life-world; they may be wrong, although 'wrongness' does not appear to be a useful term in this context; they may not have deployed the phenomenological method well enough. But there is a priori evidence that they have not found the case for phenomenological method persuasive enough to experiment with it. In short, phenomenology is a metaphysics which lacks disciplined, examinable procedures for building its constituent arguments. Some of the applications of that metaphysics cannot be so criticized: conversational analysis, for example, *is* explicit, methodical, and refutable. But the conversational analysts are singular in their commitment to demonstration. Some ethnomethodologists and phenomenologists are blandly indifferent to demands for standard sociological checks on speculation. In the past, their indifference has been compounded by a conception of indexicality which insists on the situational embeddedness of phenomena. If utterances and processes achieve meaning in context, they tend to lack general or abstract meaning which is independent of context.[57] There is thus something of a resistance to the asking of questions about the typicality,

[56] E. Gellner, 'Ethnomethodology', 431.
[57] Of course, thre are major exceptions to the insistence upon the utter indexicality of everything. Merleau-Ponty is an important instance.

distribution, and incidence of objects described. That resistance is quite intelligible. After all, the phenomenological method directs one at focused, meticulous work which cannot and should not be generous in scope. Perhaps the phenomenologists are justified in their tacit assertion that it is impermissible to confront the problem of generalization. But that assertion is contradicted by others which present arguments as if they were universal. It is not alleged, for example, that sectors of society are exempt from the processes described by phenomenology. Neither is it suggested that instances of analysis should be regarded as temporally, socially, or spatially limited. It is as if Sudnow's courtroom were an archetype for all courts everywhere, Agnes had a mandate to proclaim the character of all American sexuality, and abortion clinics must be as Ball's own was.[58] Much analysis is placed in a limbo from which it is difficult to retrieve it. It really is most important to learn whether Agnes's perspective is unique, whether Sudnow's courtroom is typical, and what uniqueness and typicality signify. There is no provision of statements of scope. Neither is the idea of 'context' very clear. Contexts can be shifting and personal, of indefinite scope and uncertain meaning. By extension, it is difficult to know how analysis should be assessed and what it is intended to accomplish. Phenomenology offers no formulas for illuminating or clarifing the question. It merely leaves its objects uncertain.

[58] See D. Ball, 'An Abortion Clinic Ethnography'.

9
Control Theories

Introduction

Control theories have a formidable pedigree. They can be traced back through Durkheim to Hobbes and to Aristotle: 'It is in the nature of men not to be satisfied . . . The fact is that the greatest crimes are caused by excess and not by necessity.'[1] The curbing of desires, and not the equalization of property, was the appropriate remedy. Hobbes's question, 'Why do men obey the rules of society?' he himself answered in terms of 'fear . . . It is the only thing, when there is appearance of profit or pleasure by breaking the laws, that makes men keep them.'[2] Similarly, Durkheim wrote in *Suicide*: 'It is not human nature which can assign the variable limits necessary to our needs. They are thus unlimited so far as they depend on the individual alone. Irrespective of any external regulatory force, our capacity for feeling is in itself an insatiable and bottomless abyss.'[3] Bentham and the utilitarians followed Montesquieu in seeking to base social and legal controls on the principle of rational calculation. The 'felicific calculus' presumed the human capacity to align actions with whatever course would maximize pleasure and minimize pain, a premiss which opposed overly severe, as well as too lenient, penalties for infraction.[4] In short, control theories are rooted in fertile and popular philosophical soil: householders who lock their doors at night are articulating one aspect of such theories, the belief that *opportunity* in itself is a cause of crime.

How, then, do we account for the fact that, until very recently, control theories have been virtually discounted in

---

[1] Aristotle, *Politics*, quoted in L. McDonald, *The Sociology of Law and Order*, ch. 2.
[2] Hobbes, *Leviathan*, 195; also the discussion in T. Hirschi, *Causes of Delinquency*, 4–6.
[3] É. Durkheim, *Suicide*, 247.
[4] For a useful discussion, see L. McDonald, *The Sociology of Law and Order*, ch. 2.

sociological theorizing on deviance and control? Even in more orthodox criminological work, they have been accorded a rather marginal role. The most plausible explanation would turn to the sheer obviousness of control theories. Science at large, and sociology in particular, has a tendency to interest itself in the unexpected. Many sociologists, Karl Marx and Émile Durkheim amongst them, proclaim that science should busy itself with the unintended and latent consequences of social action. They hold to the belief that consequential discoveries are those which lay people cannot make for lack of skill. It is a mark of science that it surprises common sense.[5] Control theories are not likely to confound common sense at all. On the contrary, they confirm it and, in doing so, they lose some of their sociological appeal.

In criminology, the neglect of control theory may also have been due to the unpopularity in liberal sociological circles of work which appears to support discipline, punishment, and regulation. Far more congenial are ideas which debunk control strategies. Unpopular too has been the work of the Gluecks,[6] whose attempts to predict delinquency in the 1930s, 1940s, and 1950s became associated with the sociological equivalent of Original Sin—a stress on the pathological, the individualistic, and the psychological. The three variables which they came to employ in their predictive studies—mother's affection for the child, mother's supervision of the child, and family cohesion—have now resurfaced in modified forms in the work of Hirschi and Harriet Wilson;[7] although the methodological and theoretical problems of the Gluecks' work perhaps led to the neglect of such variables in the 1960s, their centrality to the revived forms of control theory cannot be denied. Some criminologists remained interested in this approach even in the days of the ascendancy of strain and labelling theories: Reckless, for example, elaborated the notion of 'self-concept' as an 'insulating factor' in delinquency.[8] Such work was largely ignored, however, in the sociological reaction against the more psycho-

---

[5] See M. Davis, 'That's Interesting!'.

[6] Chiefly in S. and E. Glueck, *Unravelling Juvenile Delinquency*.

[7] T. Hirschi, *The Causes of Delinquency*, and H. Wilson and G. Herbert, *Parents and Children in the Inner City*.

[8] See W. Reckless *et al.*, 'Self-Concept as an Insulator against Delinquency'; and W. Reckless, *The Crime Problem*.

analytical and family-centred explanations of delinquency, which in the post-war period were viewed as the somewhat dated products of the 1920s and 30s. That period had also produced the main sociological version of control theory, Shaw and McKay's concept of 'social disorganization', as the principal cause of high rates of crime and delinquency, a theory that Albert Cohen temporarily eclipsed with his argument that the absence of controls cannot explain the presence of stable and recurring deviant phenomena.[9]

The undertow of dissatisfaction with the strain theorists' tendency to place virtually the whole weight of explanation on the sheer intensity of deviant motivation led to several attempts to give some emphasis at least to control variables. Sykes and Matza argued that delinquents commonly adhered to much the same set of values as everybody else. Deviants differed chiefly in their invocation of 'techniques of neutralization' which freed them from guilt and shame, and which temporarily neutralized the social bond to enable them to engage in delinquent activities. Sykes and Matza acknowledged, however, that these rationalizations hardly accounted for the attractiveness of delinquency in the first place; and in accounting for that[10] their theorizing overlapped far more with strain theories than they were prone to acknowledge at the time. Jackson Toby, a trenchant critic of the Gluecks for their 'theoretical blindness',[11] proposed a more sociological version of control theory by asserting that delinquents were chiefly to be distinguished from non-delinquents by their minimal 'stake in conformity'; in this approach, the common impetus to deviate interacts with varying commitments to conformity stemming from family as well as school and work experiences and opportunities.[12] A more sophisticated version of this argument was presented by Briar and Piliavin, who added the notion of 'situational inducements' as a fresh motivational angle.[13] The combination of variations in the inner commitment to conform and

[9] See Chapter 3, and A. Cohen, *Delinquent Boys*, 33.
[10] See Chapter 6.
[11] J. Toby, 'An Evaluation of Early Identification and Intensive Treatment Programs for Pre-delinquents'.
[12] J. Toby, 'Social Disorganization and Stake in Conformity'.
[13] S. Briar and I. Piliavin, 'Delinquency, Situational Inducements, and Commitment to Conformity', 35–45.

the external opportunities to deviate was already furnishing an alternative, however rudimentary, to the by now over-elaborate 'motivation' offered by the strain theorists.

Though few explicit links were fashioned, the work of Homans and Blau[14] in sociological theory provided a model for the analysis of the individual in society that corresponded in its essentials with the work of control theorists in criminology. In 'social exchange' theories, a sociological version of Economic Man is approximated. It is held that human behaviour is best explained by the individual gratifications that 'exchange' provides, and moral values are themselves emergent from ongoing exchanges. One of Homans's key examples is drawn from the famous Westinghouse Electrical Company study, in which informal group norms emerged to restrict production to levels set by the workers and not the management: deviants (rate-busters) were sanctioned to enforce group conformity. The pay-off for the group as a whole was perceived to be superior to that which would accrue from outright individualism. More generally, social behaviour is seen as grounded in quite tangible forms of exchange which provide the bases for rational choice. Accordingly, men should be 'brought back in' to social theories in a far fuller sense that was imaginable in the Parsonian 'social system': in this respect, Homans in particular is close to the symbolic interactionists.[15] He and Blau differ from interactionists chiefly in their relative indifference to meanings and interpretations: Homans's view of people is more attuned to the behaviourism of Skinner than to the interactionism of Mead. To Gouldner, his 'is the most unabashedly individualistic utilitarianism in modern sociology'.[16] People do what they do to maximize pay-off, whether it takes the form of material well-being, status, or affection. The approach is somewhat unforthcoming on how people choose *between* different pay-offs. Also, as Heath points out, 'Skinnerian man is based on the common pigeon. He is not a forward-looking maximiser endowed with sophisticated reasoning powers but a practical creature who learns from experience, avoiding what has proved

---

[14] G. Homans, 'Social Behavior as Exchange', 597–606; P. Blau, *Exchange and Power in Social Life*.

[15] G. Homans, *The Human Group*, and 'Bringing Men Back In', 809–18.

[16] A. Gouldner, *The Coming Crisis*, 140.

painful in the past, and seeking out what has proved reward-ing.'[17] The implications for crime and its control are not as stark as this might imply, but the scope for applying exchange theory to these phenomena has often suffered critically from guilt by association: it is assumed that any truck with Skinner, pigeons, and control must be bad for any criminological theory. The most recent forms of control theory have been keen to avoid such imputation.[18]

Sociological Control Theories of Deviance

Hirschi states that the common property of control theories at their simplest level is their assumption that 'delinquent acts result when an individual's bond to society is weak or broken'.[19] But what are the elements of the social bond? He specifies four elements which he terms attachment, commitment, involve-ment, and belief. 'Attachment' to others is viewed as prior to caring about their opinions and wishes. It is therefore a variable superior to the 'internalization of norms' since 'to violate a norm is to act contrary to the wishes and expectations of other people. If a person does not care about the wishes and expectations of other people, that is, if he is insensitive to the opinions of others, then he is to that extent not bound by the norms. He is free to deviate.'[20] 'Commitment' signifies that

the person invests time, energy, himself, in a certain line of activity, say, getting an education, building up a business, acquiring a reputa-tion for virtue. When or whenever he considers deviant behaviour, he must consider the costs of this deviant behaviour, the risk he runs of losing the investment he has made in conventional behaviour ... Most people, simply by the process of living in an organised society, acquire goods, reputations, prospects that they do not want to risk losing. These accumulations are society's insurance that they will abide by the rules.[21]

'Involvement' is the behavioural counterpart of commitment: 'A person may be simply too busy doing conventional things to find time to engage in deviant behaviour ... To the extent to

[17] A. Heath, *Rational Choice and Social Exchanges*, 171.
[18] See, for example, the opening section of H. Wilson, 'Parental Supervision: A Neglected Aspect of Delinquency'.
[19] T. Hirschi, *Causes of Delinquency*, 16.   [20] Ibid. 18.   [21] Ibid. 20–1.

which he is engrossed in conventional activities, he cannot even think about deviant acts, let alone act out his inclinations.'[22] Finally, the assumption that delinquents and non-delinquents alike share a common value-system is not the same as insisting that their 'belief' in the rules derived from it attains a common intensity. 'We assume that there is *variation* in the extent to which people believe they should obey the rules of society, and that the less a person believes he should obey the rules, the more likely he is to violate them.'[23] These four variables interact to produce an ideal-typical portrait of a non-delinquent who is strongly attached to conventional others, strongly committed to conventional activities, heavily involved in them, and imbued with a strong belief in the need to obey the rules. The delinquent is relatively free from such controls, and hence more at risk of deviation. Such deviation is not, however, automatic or determined: it is simply no longer ruled out as a possibility.

As Hirschi acknowledged, the most disconcerting question remains: 'Yes, but *why* do they do it?'. He accepts the force of Cohen and Short's criticism of control theories that they explain delinquency in the absence of effective controls, and accordingly imply 'that the impulse to delinquency is an inherent characteristic of young people and does not itself need to be explained; it is something that erupts when the lid—i.e. internalised cultural restraints or external authority—is off'.[24] Hirschi's reaction is to accept that this is indeed the case, and that while certain motivations of a situational character are consistent with control theory, they are 'by no means deducible from it. . . . The question 'Why do they do it?' is simply not the question the theory is designed to answer. The question is, "Why don't we do it?".'[25] Kornhauser is even more dismissive of the motivational issue: 'The question is not whether control theory can account for the motivation of delinquency, but whether it is necessary to specify the motivation of delinquency in order to explain its occurrence.'[26] The problem of motivation is resolved by its redefinition as a non-problem.

[22] T. Hirschi, *Causes of Delinquency*, 22.
[23] Ibid. 26.
[24] A. Cohen and J. Short, Jun., 'Juvenile Delinquency', 106.
[25] T. Hirschi, *Causes of Delinquency*, 34.
[26] R. Kornhauser, *Social Sources of Delinquency: An Appraisal of Analytic Models*, 154.

The strength of Hirschi's work, however, is empirical rather than theoretical. Much of *The Causes of Delinquency* is taken up with testing a variety of propositions derived from subcultural theory (in both its 'strain' and 'cultural deviance' forms),[27] and finding them wanting. For example, he shows social class to be related only very weakly to delinquency; and adherence to the 'values' most commonly cited as 'working-class' (such as 'smartness' and 'fatalism') is in Hirschi's data most remarkable for its lack of relation to class. On the other hand, control variables correlate with delinquency quite closely and consistently. For example, parental supervision was measured by the extent to which parent(s) knew where and in what company boys were, when away from home; the results for non-delinquents ranged from none reporting 'low' to 63 per cent 'high' supervision; for relatively serious delinquents, 55 per cent reported 'low' and only 12 per cent 'high' supervision, results which are corroborated by Wilson's English study.[28] 'Intimacy of communication' and 'affectional identification' with parents showed similarly strong links with delinquency: the less the child's reported bonds with his family, the greater his involvement in delinquency. Findings on links with the school and teachers showed the same trend. Hirschi's data were based on a large-scale self-report survey of over four thousand children aged 12–17 sampled from a predominantly urban-industrial area, and the population surveyed seems about as representative of American society as possible. Although the self-report technique is open to question (as indeed are official criminal statistics), the results were the first substantial sign that the most attractive approaches theoretically were the weakest empirically, and vice versa.

The study by Steven Box[29] went some way towards redressing the more glaring theoretical deficiencies of control theory, whilst retaining its basic tenets. Firstly, he sought to align control theory with labelling theory; and secondly, he furnished a theory of delinquency congruent with control theory but sensitive to the issue of motivation. The need for the alignment with labelling theory stems from Box's attempt to explain how and why social class and ethnicity have such weak relations

[27] See Chapter 6.
[28] T. Hirschi, *Causes of Delinquency*, 89, Table 18; and H. Wilson, 'Parental Supervision'. [29] S. Box, *Deviance, Reality and Society*.

with delinquency in self-report studies, and such strong links in official statistics. The answer he proffers is that the first capture 'primary' and the second 'secondary' deviations.[30] By the processes of official intervention, at every stage of which the more powerful members of society are relatively advantaged, the raw data of primary deviation are filtered, screened, and negotiated to produce predominantly lower status and Black populations of 'secondary' deviants—the probationers, prisoners, and ex-cons who come to represent collectively the 'crime problem'. Labelling processes interact with control variables to make matters worse for those defined as deviant: such bonds as they already had with conventional society are attenuated even further. Their exposure to the risks of fresh deviations is correspondingly heightened. At each stage of the spiral, a greater feat of self-redefinition is needed if the deviant is to conform.

Motivation looms larger for Box than for earlier control theorists. 'Whether or not an individual with the option to deviate decides to, depends to some extent on what he makes of the issue of *secrecy*, *skills*, *supply*, *social* and *symbolic support*.'[31] The first relates to chances of concealment; the second to the knowledge required for deviance; the third to the necessary equipment; the fourth to the support of associates; and the fifth to that drawn from the wider culture. A pot-smoking campus party scores highly on all points, at least in 1980: in 1950, it would have been almost impossible, in England at least, to secure the vital ingredient. These elements, however, are little more than those termed by Briar and Piliavin 'situational inducements': they do little to suggest why some individuals, and not others, would choose to take up this particular option.

Box makes more extensive attempts to develop a theory of the will to delinquency in discussing the work of Albert Cohen and Matza.[32] Cohen, he argues, portrays the delinquent as both frustrated by, and resentful of, the experience of school failure. But his eventual theory stresses status frustration at the expense of sheer resentment, since the former implies at least some prior internalization of middle-class norms, while the latter implies only that boys cannot be indifferent to the im-

---

[30] See Chapter 7.
[31] S. Box, *Deviance, Reality and Society*, 150.
[32] Ibid. 106–9 and 122–33.

putation of failure. The former leads to 'reaction formation', the denial of a (real) attachment by the ostentatious display of rule-breaking. The latter leads to behaviour which seeks to assert independent standards. Cohen employs a logic which forces him to accept the first, but not the second, route to delinquency, yet it is the latter which in Box's view is far more in line with social reality. The weight of the evidence on this point is against Cohen, though it might be remarked in passing that the delinquent subculture, as he conceived it, has a dual functionality: the restoration of status, and the collective provision of social means to hit back at the source of imputed failure. Phenomenologically, it seems eminently possible to be frustrated in terms of social status, *and* resentful about even caring about status in the first place.

A similar criticism is made of Matza's attempt to depict the delinquent as *both* aiming at restoring 'the mood of humanism' *and* rationalizing his delinquency away as the result of being 'pushed around'. These, says Box, are incompatible: either you are restoring the mood of humanism and meaning it, or you genuinely feel pushed around and 'objectified'. Box prefers to treat the second technique as a purely situated account in the context of arrest. Again, the logic of strain theory is pitted against that of control theory. In strain theory, to which Matza partially adheres, delinquents care about breaking the law: hence they invoke 'techniques of neutralization' to justify their deviations ('I was pushed', etc.). To control theorists, no such commitment to the rules exists in the first place, hence 'I was pushed' is a sheerly *ex post facto* excuse which offenders hope will evoke leniency. There is no way of settling this issue here, particularly as the negligible amount of empirical evidence is indecisive, but again it could be added that the appeal of Matza's 'techniques' lies in their dual functionality: they both express an existential state of mind, and assist in self-exculpation.

Harriet Wilson's study of socially deprived families in inner Birmingham has produced findings which are strikingly in line with the tenets of control theory. An index of 'chaperonage'[33] was developed to measure the degree of protection given to their children by parents to ensure their safety. Scores were

[33] First employed by J. and E. Newson, *Seven Years Old in the Home Environment*.

allocated to parents on such items as fetching children from school, allowing them to roam the streets, and whether or not there were rules for coming in at night. Though the numbers involved were very small (fifty-six families in all) the families were selected to share certain characteristics, including intact family status, having five or more children, and residing in old housing in a deprived inner-city area. Within this group, the 'chaperonage' variable sharply distinguished delinquents from non-delinquents, whereas other factors, such as the 'happiness' of the home atmosphere, did not. 'Chaperonage' was related to 'strict' rather than 'permissive' standards of morality: ' "strict" parents insist on a degree of tidiness and cleanliness in the home, they tend to discourage or punish genital play, children looking at each other when undressed, or giggling over the toilet, and parents tend to avoid undressing in the children's presence.'[34]

The families who exercised chaperonage and who tend to adhere to traditional standards of strictness are motivated in many different ways, but they share the belief that the deprived neighbourhood and its inhabitants are bad and that their children need protection against this badness . . . These parents were driven into applying child-rearing measures which, under more normal conditions in a friendly and known neighbourhood they would not be likely to apply. They kept their children indoors or under close supervision in the back yard; they accompanied them to and from school; they forbade them to play with undesirable youngsters in the streets. If the boys played out their mothers knew where to find them. These measures are applied at great cost to themselves.[35]

In a further study Wilson extends the support for this conclusion, but she is careful to state that

the essential point of our findings is the very close association of lax parenting methods with severe social handicap. Lax parenting methods are often the result of chronic stress, situations arising from frequent or prolonged spells of unemployment, physical or mental disabilities among members of the family, and an often permanent condition of poverty . . . If these factors are ignored, and parental laxness is seen instead as an 'attitude' which by education or by punitive measures can be shifted, then our findings are being misinterpreted.

[34] H. Wilson and G. Herbert, *Parents and Children*, 176.
[35] Ibid. 177.

measures can be shifted, then our findings are being misinterpreted. It is the position of the most disadvantaged groups in society, and not the individual, which needs improvement in the first place.[36]

In this analysis, a control theory of delinquency is combined with a strong sense of structural context.

Without assuming anything like the ascendancy of strain theories in the 1950s and early 60s, or labelling theories in the following decade, control theories are beginning to attract a considerable following. Such textbooks as those by Nettler and Hagan[37] argue that they provide the most promising foundation for criminological theory. Hagan, Simpson, and Gillis have proceeded to explore the impressive potential of control theory for the explanation of gender differences in criminality; their work is discussed in Chapter 11. Their appeal has strong implicit links with the growing opposition to rehabilitation and the call for a return to sentences based upon untrammelled 'due process' based upon 'harm done', i.e. retributivism. Patricia Morgan[38] argues that delinquency is fostered by the fashion for permissiveness in family life, education, and crime control, a vogue bolstered by labelling theory. In her view, adolescents have too much, not too little, freedom to act out their fantasies. In even sterner vein, James Q. Wilson argues that incapacitation alone provides a guarantee against criminality: he calls for unrepentant incarceration of offenders as a costly but sure means of combating crime.[39] This is not to say that control theory is a package deal, committing its adherents to the 'war against crime' and punitive sentencing: the work of Harriet Wilson and James Q. Wilson is not so easily merged. But there is little doubt that control theory lends itself to the technology of crime control, and chimes with lay theories of crime as caused by inadequate preventative measures, affinities that alternative approaches do not share. The most obvious links in these respects are indeed quite explicit in 'situational' control theories.

[36] H. Wilson, 'Parental Supervision', 233–4.
[37] G. Nettler, *Explaining Crime*; J. Hagan, *The Disreputable Pleasures*.
[38] P. Morgan, *Delinquent Fantasies*.
[39] J. Wilson, *Thinking About Crime*. A Home Office study questions the feasibility of this approach: S. Brody and R. Tarling, *Taking Offenders Out of Circulation*.

'Situational' Control Theories

The case for this form of control theory is succinctly made by Clarke:

Criminological theories have been little concerned with the situational determinants of crime. Instead, the main object of these theories (whether biological, psychological, or sociological in orientation) has been to show how some people are born with, or come to acquire, a 'disposition' to behave in a consistently criminal manner. This 'dispositional' bias of theory has been identified as a defining characteristic of 'positivist' criminology, but it is also to be found in 'interactionist' or deviancy theories of crime developed in response to the perceived inadequacies of positivism . . . In fact . . . a dispositional bias is presented throughout the social sciences.[40]

The immediate stress of situational control theories, by contrast, is on the purely technical, cost–benefit-ratio aspects of crime: the opportunities for crime available in the environment, and the risks attached to criminal activity. Both variables are—in his view—more amenable to change than those policy recommendations that flow from dispositional theories, which lead people to suggest 'methods of preventive intervention precisely where it is most difficult to achieve any effects, i.e. in the relation to the psychological events or the social and economic conditions that are supposed to generate criminal dispositions'.[41] The argument is significant not only because of its content but also because of its provenance. Clarke was to become Head of the Home Office Research and Planning Unit for a while, and he was able to influence the making of policy and the funding of research in England and Wales. When Clarke declared that policy-relevant research should focus on containment, deterrent sentencing, police effectiveness and crime prevention, his ideas were unusually consequential.[42] One outcome was the establishment of the Home Office Crime Prevention Unit in 1983 and the commissioning of a series of research reports on small practical campaigns to modify crime. Situational theories are not limited to purely technical and

---

[40] R. Clarke, 'Situational Crime Prevention', 136.
[41] Ibid. 137.
[42] See R. Clarke and D. Cornish, *Crime Control in Britain*, 41.

mechanistic manipulations of the environment; they are consonant with a model of the offender as capable of rational choices and decisions. Indeed, the representation of criminals as reasoning people implicated in chains of decisions lent itself remarkably well to research conducted within and for government. Much control theory may be found in and around the boundaries of official action. It was 'intended to locate criminological findings within a framework particularly suitable for thinking about policy-relevant research.'[43] Rational criminals confronting critical choices are fairly readily susceptible to intelligent control strategies. Moreover, the presumption of rationality had a common-sense appeal: that is how most people would care to explain their own and others' behaviour. It seemed to have support in 'the evidence of ethnographic studies of delinquency[44] [which] strongly suggest that people are usually aware of consciously choosing to commit offences.'[45] It is, in short, in line with theories of social learning and rational exchange; and it has no difficulty, unlike dispositional theories, in accepting that 'the bulk of crime—vandalism, auto-crime, shop-lifting, theft by employees—is committed by people who would not ordinarily be thought of as criminal at all.'[46] Far from narrowing the scope of criminological hypotheses, it enriches its possibilities: 'First, explanation is focused more directly on the criminal event; second, the need to develop explanations for separate categories of crime is made explicit; and, third, the individuals' current circumstances and the immediate features of the setting are given considerably more explanatory significance than in "dispositional" theories.'[47]

Measures for crime prevention have two linked emphases: reducing the physical opportunities for offending, and increasing the risk of an offender being caught. The first embraces such examples as the replacement of vulnerable coin-boxes with stronger ones, which virtually eliminated theft from telephone kiosks; and the dramatic fall in the Birmingham suicide rate when supplies of non-toxic (North Sea) gas were installed in

---

[43] D. Cornish and R. Clarke, *The Reasoning Criminal*, 1.
[44] The reference is to H. Parker, *The View from the Boys*.
[45] R. Clarke, 'Situational Crime Prevention', 138.
[46] Ibid. 137. [47] Ibid. 139

people's homes.[48] Several well-researched instances of specific successes in crime prevention can be adduced to bear this proposition out. There is Laycock's demonstration that acceptance of the advice of police officers on target hardening led to a decline in burglaries from pharmacies;[49] and that property-marking schemes reduced residential burglary in an experimental site in Wales. Possibly the most exciting application of this approach has been the attempt made by Bennett, Wright, and others to reconstruct the environment as potential predators see it. They conducted extensive interviews with burglars, using videotapes of residential housing and venturing on tours with an accompanying commentary from experienced criminals, in order to establish how surroundings are interpreted. It has become clear that signs of occupation, surveillance by neighbours and ease of access are critically important in the decision to break in to a house.[50] By contrast, the activities of the police are relatively inconsequential.

There has been an increasingly meticulous mapping of the visual controls built into space. It is as if every part of the built environment can be transformed by control theory into a bundle of observed possibilities for offending. One clever demonstration of those links between design and crime may be found in a study of burglary in schools. Hope contrasted two different styles of school building in Britain—the large, modern and sprawling schools which were often set in spacious grounds and the small, old, and compact schools with only a modest amount of space around them. Between 1977 and 1978, the average number of burglaries in his sample were 7.9 for the large and sprawling and 2.2 for the small and compact schools. Having explored rival explanations, it was his conclusion that

---

[48] Sainsbury (1986) has questioned the inference that trends in the detoxification of gas supplies to domestic consumers in England account for the sharp decline in the suicide rate between 1963 and 1975. He notes the similarity between rates of suicide in a number of towns in England and Wales, and provinces in Holland, despite dissimilar phasing of the detoxification process. Clarke and Mayhew (1988, and forthcoming) rebut this criticism by reference to inadequacy of the data for Holland and their inconclusive nature for England and Wales, owing to the small number of towns sampled (1988, p. 130). The balance of evidence now seems to favour control theory on this issue, whose significance as a test of displacement makes it a priority for further research.

[49] G. Laycock, *Reducing Burglary*.

[50] T. Bennett and R. Wright, *Burglars on Burglary*.

the differences in burglary rates could be attributed to features of design: the small schools were less accessible to predators and afforded 'greater opportunities for surveillance by the public and by school caretakers'.[51]

The second prong of the preventive approach builds on the assumption that there is 'a good deal of unrealised potential for making use of the surveillance role of employees who come into regular and frequent contact with the public in a semi-official capacity.'[52] Control theory has translated the physical environment into a terrain patrolled, watched, and guarded by numerous official and unofficial custodians. Door-men, bus-conductors, car-park attendants, caretakers, and the like have been shown to make a considerable impact on specific crime rates. For example, on double-decker buses without conductors, areas of least supervision attracted most damage: drivers could monitor behaviour on the lower deck but not on the upper, and 'there was about 20 times as much damage on the upper as on the lower deck.'[53]

An allied example is that of the municipal housing estates in England and Wales whose structure and administration are becoming ever more frequently examined for their impact on deviance and conformity. During the 1960s, a drive for economy and rationalization removed administrative and maintenance work from the estates and centralized it in main offices. Repairs and caretaking tasks were undertaken by mobile teams. Latterly, however, and partly as a result of the movement towards centralization, a number of housing estates have become identified as something of a social problem. To the Department of the Environment, they are the 'hard-to-let' estates. To the Home Office they are a new kind of criminal area. The beginnings of a political response may be seen in the estate improvement schemes run by the National Association for the Care and Resettlement of Offenders and the Department of the Environment's Priority Estates Projects, schemes encouraging a return to decentralized maintenance, lettings, and administration. In the process of devolution, it has been discovered just how much informal social control can be exercised by local caretaking staff.

[51] T. Hope, *Burglary in Schools*.
[52] R. Clarke, 'Situational Crime Prevention', 142.
[53] P. Mayhew *et al.*, *Crime as Opportunity*, 26.

Resident caretakers play 'a key role in helping to reduce vandalism, patrolling public areas and supervising the cleaning of them and dealing at first hand with tenants' problems'.[54]

The most discussed, if not best attested, theory in this vein is Oscar Newman's study, *Defensible Space*. His work attracted a great deal of attention because he claimed to have demonstrated the link between high-rise public sector housing and increased rates of crime and delinquency. Jane Jacobs had laid its foundation in her classic lament for the rapidly disappearing intimacy and diversity of city life,[55] a lament which chronicled the progressive extinction of the street as the urban form most in harmony with human scale. The street had evolved as an arena for diverse activities and safe associations, particularly for children at play, and was enhanced by passersby, the presence of traders and news-vendors, and ease of surveillance from houses and shops. The high-rise housing complex has planned these features of urban concourse away. As a result, social processes have been squeezed out by built forms. It was Newman who then proceeded to describe how areas of space of an 'indefensible' character have been created, consisting of deserted through-ways and under-passes, unobservable lifts and stair-wells. Entrances to buildings are used by so many people that it is no longer certain who has a right to pass through them and who has not, who is reputable and who is not. In particular, there has been a proliferation of 'confused' and anonymous areas which belong to no one and are cared for by no one. It has become impossible to decide who has a reasonable claim to be present in a tract of land or a building. In turn, people are unable to establish practical or symbolic boundaries around territory which is their own or to exercise informal social control within them. The result has been a great increase in rates of crime. Ironically, inner-city building that was planned to pack the maximum number of people in to the minimum permissible amount of space, in part to prevent the suburban drift of workers essential to the political economy of the city, has accentuated problems which hasten that very process.

Subsequent criticisms have dented Newman's authority

---

[54] Department of the Environment, *Reducing Vandalism on Public Housing Estates*.
[55] J. Jacobs, *The Death and Life of Great American Cities*.

somewhat,[56] although the criticisms themselves are not without flaw. In Britain, especially, the argument has been put that Newman neglected the social effects of communal reputation on the behaviour of those who lived in crime-ridden neighbourhoods: people who are part of a morally stigmatized area are alleged to experience discrimination, impaired life-chances and unsupportive neighbours (a criticism that is not universally borne out). There has been the charge that Newman was insensitive to the effects of different policing strategies: the high crime rates of the problem estates, it is said, reveal police assumptions and policies as much as real variations in behaviour (although later work disclosed how such estates seem to be *under-policed*[57]). It has been argued that Newman ignored housing allocation policies: a community's characteristics reflect letting and transfer decisions. It has been suggested that Newman made the improper assumption that criminals do not belong to an area but are outsiders against whom space can successfully be defended. But his work was original, stimulating and politically timely, and it did succeed in drawing together a number of strands usually considered in isolation from each other by urban planners, criminologists, and environmentalists. Moreover, although it focused on the control aspects of the environment, his theory implicitly raised questions of a more symbolic character. There is an extensive and as yet largely unanswered programme of questions to be asked about the features which enhance the social sense of 'belonging' to a neighbourhood and make for a feeling of involvement rather than indifference. In this respect, his work combines both situational and sociological control variables.

Perhaps the most direct application of Newman's concept of 'defensible space' has been the work done by the Land Use Research Unit at King's College, London. *Utopia on Trial* reports a massive survey of 4,099 blocks of flats, listing those design features which seem to correlate with such measurable signs of disorder as graffiti, litter, vandalism, and the number of children in care.[58] The assumption has been that it is poor physical design that causes social breakdown by estranging

[56] See, for example, the review by A. Bottoms.
[57] See, for example, F. Reynolds, *The Problem Housing Estate*.
[58] A. Coleman, *Utopia on Trial*.

members of a community from one another, by letting
marauders in, and by preventing an effective response. Crime
itself is believed to flow from the uncontrolled circulation of
strangers along the walkways of poorly planned estates; from
the residents' loss of a sense of territoriality; from an abundance of escape routes for predators; and from inadequate
opportunities for surveillance. It can be reduced by redesigning
portions of estates so that entrances can be controlled, the
movement of strangers restricted, spatial ambiguity reduced,
and monitoring improved. In newly-created small, private, and
enclosed areas of residence, outsiders may imagine that they
are more conspicuous and insiders that they have a greater
stake in territory. Alice Coleman has given an insistent
emphasis to the importance of design, tending to devalue social
variables, and she has attracted the ire of critics who defend
social explanation and critics who do not. The most strident
has been Hillier who maintained roundly that 'her method of
quantification of malaise is flawed, her correlations largely
illusory and her attempt to test for social factors desultory.'[59]
Hillier objects that many of Coleman's correlations between
malaise indicators and design may actually be explained by the
effects of increasing population density in flats. Design features
and signs of malaise are both likely to vary with the size of
blocks. Others have repeated the criticisms that were first
directed at Newman, arguing that Coleman neglects the influence of stigma, social organization, and formal social control.
Yet there does remain a provocative line of reasoning whose
potential is far from exhausted.

Miscellaneous Theories of a Control Character

'Control' is a term of such common currency in criminology
and the sociology of deviance that it is essential to distinguish
between three separate usages. Firstly, there are control
theories, discussed above, which take control variables, of different kinds, to be the most significant *causes* of deviance.
Secondly, there is control as a substantive phenomenon in its
own right, i.e. the sanctions that are brought to bear against
deviancy. Thirdly, there is that aspect of all theories of deviance

[59] B. Hillier, 'City of Alice's Dreams'.

that deals with control, either implicitly or explicitly. In strain theories, for example, that aspect is largely unexplored, but a generally neutral set of control responses to deviance tends to be assumed. In labelling theories, controls that are differentially and often maladroitly applied paradoxically are viewed as a major source of deviation ('secondary' deviation). In some culturally framed theories, which site the causes of deviance in 'culture conflict' (Sellin) or 'cultural diversity' (Miller, Mays, Oscar Lewis), the strength of the controls exerted by the dominant (generally middle-class) culture are seen as weakened by the offenders' adherence to an exaggerated form of alternative culture ('lower-class culture', 'the culture of poverty', etc.); in Sutherland's theory of 'differential association', variation in exposure to such alternative cultures is viewed as sufficient to explain different rates of deviance.[60] The concept of 'social disorganization' of Shaw and McKay also rests on the premiss that lax controls generate deviance. Durkheim's theory of anomie alone discerns greater attenuation of controls at the top, rather than the bottom, of the social hierarchy. In general, however, it would be inappropriate to call the third set of theories 'control theories', since the weakness or absence of controls is caused by adherence to alternative cultures or subcultures, rather than (as in control theories properly so described) by contingent or random events that serve to deregulate individual families or careers, or that exist as a built-in feature of certain milieux.

In the realm of psychological theories of deviance, however, virtually all approaches arguably rest on the efficacy of psychodynamic controls. Various explanations are proffered by different schools of psychology and psychoanalysis for their strength or weakness. While it is an over-generalization to see the control variable as predominant in all psychological theories[61] there are certain instances where it is unequivocally so. Perhaps the archetypal example is Eysenck's theory of crime and personality, and its social psychological variant,

[60] T. Sellin, *Culture Conflict and Crime*; W. Miller, 'Lower Class Culture'; J. Mays, *Growing Up in the City*; O. Lewis, *The Children of Sanchez*, xi–xxxi; E. Sutherland, *Principles of Criminology*, first published in 1924, and since 1955 extensively revised by D. Cressey.

[61] As A. Cohen implies in his trenchant critique 'Seven Limitations of Psychodynamic Control Theories', in his *Deviance and Control*, 59–62.

Trasler's explanation of criminality in terms of 'inadequate socialisation'.[62] The main premiss of Eysenck's theory is that extroverts are more resistant to conditioning (a crucial element of social learning) than introverts, and that logically it is to be inferred that, in all contexts save a criminal sub-society, extroverts will tend to be more amenable to criminality than introverts. It is also argued that neuroticism interacts with extroversion to heighten the likelihood that inhibiting responses will be overwhelmed by excitation. Trasler argued that in addition the techniques of child socialization employed by lower-class families were less efficient than those used by the middle class in the reinforcement of inhibition. The typical delinquent on this basis would be the lower-class, neurotic extrovert, though it should be added that even on unrepresentative populations, such as prisoners and institutional youths, these propositions have not, in general, been confirmed. Cochrane[63] listed some twenty tests of Eysenck's theory which in all cases but one falsified rather than verified the central point of his theory concerning extroversion. It remains a classic instance of a control theory, however, not least for Eysenck's proposal that 'conscience is a conditioned reflex'. It may none the less be the case that certain social contexts do indeed produce neuroticism in more extroverted children. Harriet Wilson quotes one telling example: 'Some permissive mothers have quiet, withdrawn children who give little cause for friction, and if parental demands are minimal, conflicts rarely arise. Others reported much trouble, which they linked with explanations of their temperament: "He's got a terrible temper, if you cross him he throws things—you've got to get round him." "If he can't have his own way, he shouts and kicks the furniture—in the finish I give him his own way—I have to".'[64] It may well be that, in the contexts of poverty and overcrowding, the more extroverted children are socialized into neuroticism, not so much because that is an innate condition, more because—faced with intolerable physical constraint—they cannot withdraw into protective apathy as do their more

---

[62] H. Eysenck, *Crime and Personality*; G. Trasler, *The Explanation of Criminality*.

[63] R. Cochrane, 'Crime and Personality: Theory and Evidence', 19–22; and H. Eysenck, 'Crime and Personality Reconsidered', 23–4.

[64] H. Wilson and G. Herbert, *Parents and Children*, 177.

introverted siblings. In these instances, however, the social context appears to be the most salient causal variable.

Criticism

Control theorists are quite open about the most telling criticism of their approach: 'I have frequently heard the statement "it's an absence of something explanation" used as an apparently damning criticism of a sociological theory. While the origins of this view are unknown to me, the fact that such a statement appears to have some claim to plausibility suggests one of the sources of uneasiness in the face of a control theory.[65] Earlier, Hirschi asserted: 'The primary virtue of control theory is not that it relies on conditions that make delinquency possible while other theories rely on conditions that make delinquency necessary. On the contrary, with respect to their logical framework, these theories are superior to control theory, and, if they were as adequate empirically as control theory, we should not hesitate to advocate their adoption in preference to control theory.'[66] As these passages make clear, there is a tendency to overdraw the differences between what are presented as the empirically sound but modest claims of control theory and the empirically unsound but more pretentious alternatives.[67] Leaving aside for the moment the question of whether or not such theories do indeed 'make delinquency necessary', the chief point at issue is how far these theories are addressing the same problem as control theory. In one respect, there is agreement: all theories attempt to explain the social distribution of delinquency, much as that might vary according to the indicators used. In other respects, there is substantial

[65] T. Hirschi, *Causes of Delinquency*, 32–3, n. 44.   [66] Ibid. 29.

[67] Since control theorists make so much of the strength of their case empirically, it is worth noting that in certain respects Hirschi's data strain credulity—a pleasant change from theories producing that effect. His definition of serious delinquency is weak in the extreme: any two or more of six offences—theft of under $2; theft of $2 to $50; theft of over $50; joy-riding; 'banging up something that doesn't belong to you'; and, not counting fights with a brother or sister, the beating up or hurting of anyone on purpose. How is it that over 50 per cent of Hirschi's Californian sample of White boys are non-delinquent by these standards throughout adolescence? Presumably they put their own interpretation on minor vandalism and fighting, in which case we need to know what implicit standards they are employing. This, needless to say, is *the* major problem with self-report studies of this kind. (Another reason may be that school drop-outs did not fill in the questionnaire.) Ibid. 54 ff.

divergence, for the equally important aim of alternative sociological theories is to account for the *character* of delinquency,
one principal aspect of which is to attempt to construct models
of motivation which correspond with its typical forms. It is
hardly adequate for control theorists to assert that 'we would all
be deviant, if we dared'. Deviant in what ways? Shorn of any
meaning, for control theory deprives it of such, deviance is
presumably pursued for the sheer gratification of appetites—
acquisitive, aggressive, and sexual. If this is indeed the case,
then we are certainly wasting our time in pursuit of some
Weberian ideal of *verstehen*. But it is also difficult to account for
the very phenomena that theorists of other persuasions set out
to explain: why delinquency is so often non-utilitarian; why
aggression is so frequently ritualized and non-violent in its outcome; why sexual gratification takes such complex forms. In
short, control theorists make far too little of both deviance and
conformity: as Kornhauser put it, why bother with motivation?

Small wonder, then, that control theorists dismiss as of negligible impact the role that norms and values play in social
behaviour. These are viewed as almost entirely dependent on
attachments to those whose opinions we value. Weaken or
remove those attachments and we feel free to deviate. It may
well be that Parsons's assumption that, once adequately intern-
alized, norms and values are with us for life is hopelessly over-
blown; that it constitutes, in Dennis Wrong's memorable
phrase, an 'oversocialized conception of man'. Nor would we
wish to dissent from the view that norms and values are fluid,
negotiable, and subject to constant revision. But to link adherence to norms and values so strongly to personal attachments,
whether to families or to institutions, is to go too far towards a
purely 'other-directed' and 'under-socialized' view of man.
Norms may be shed, and values revalued, but that can take
place in the context of strong attachments, as well as in their
absence. Rates of deviation may rise after marital break-up: but
most divorcees remarry. School failures may resent the school
(as Box suggests), but it has not yet been established that they
do so without reference to an alternative set of norms and
values. In sum, norms and values are not so easily reducible to
attachments as control theorists contend.

Situational control theorists are also well aware of the weak link in their arguments. Clarke argues that 'the specificity of the influences upon different criminal behaviours gives much less credence to the "displacement" hypothesis; the idea that reducing opportunities merely results in crime being displaced to some other time or place has been the major argument against situational crime prevention'.[68] He argues that 'displacement' is least likely in cases of 'opportunistic' crime, most likely in cases of professional crime. Even for the bulk of offences that arguably lie in between these extremes, he cites success in specific cases (e.g. kiosk design and vandalism; or the West German installation of compulsory steering locks and theft of cars). In other cases, there is more doubt about the claims made for situational control. Apart from the non-toxic gas example quoted above there is also some doubt that gun-control would do much to lower levels of violent crime in the USA—though one would welcome its implementation. As Clinard has pointed out, guns are present in most homes in Switzerland, owing to the system of citizen defence, yet the rate of crimes of violence is very low.[69] The vast differences in rates of criminal violence between the USA and Switzerland can hardly be accounted for in terms of the availability of firearms: presumably socio-cultural differences play a more considerable causal role.

Control theorists would doubtless reply that it is easier to control firearms than to 'Helvetianize' America, and it would be absurd to deny that certain control measures demonstrably deter certain offences at what Matza has termed the 'invitational edge'. Yet there are dangers that situational crime control may prove counter-productive in unanticipated ways. Firstly, as Clarke acknowledges, there is the danger that it acts *repressively*, subjecting the population as a whole to surveillance techniques which constrict freedom of movement, privacy, or action. Clearly, circumstances alter cases, and few airline passengers now resent screening for firearms or explosives. On the other hand, similar-sounding arguments can be advanced for fingerprinting the entire population. Secondly, it may operate *regressively*, as the bill for semi-officialdom to monitor shops, public buildings, and transport systems is heaped on the

[68] R. Clarke, 'Situational Crime Prevention', 138.
[69] M. Clinard, *Cities with Little Crime: The Case of Switzerland*, 114–15.

consumer regardless of ability to pay. Thirdly, it may deflect attention from attempts to engineer those difficult social and economic changes that control theorists regard as too remote for contemplation, such as the reduction of inequality. And yet, as the 'race riots' of the past two decades have borne witness, steering locks do not prevent police cars being overturned and fire-bombed. The 'technological fix' is double-edged; it may ease the crime problem in certain specific respects, but also blunt our awareness of the need to examine the more fundamental causes of high rates of crime. Housing built on the cost–benefit principle, without regard to the human factor, cannot be rescued by cost–benefit crime control.

One of the most pressing problems of control theory stems from its propensity to combine assumptions about the rationality of behaviour with the measurement and comparison of objective behavioural indicators. It is as if a sensible criminologist knows all there needs to be known about the processes and phenomena that link the two. Control theory operates with tacit arguments about how reasonable people conduct their affairs, stealing, burgling, surveying, interpreting, and controlling. It seems to be assumed that we are quite familiar with the routine practices of residents, caretakers, and others as they go about such tasks as looking out of their windows and making sense of the social scene. It also seems to be assumed that we have an adequate comprehension of the way in which predators decipher their environment and formulate plans, being deterred or seduced by signs, obstructions, and possibilities.[70] There is almost no warrant for those assumptions. Control theorists have done little to observe ordinary behaviour, they have no evidence that it is as they describe, and their analyses and inferences are correspondingly suspect. Supposition has been allowed to replace observation. To be sure, their supposition is often highly intelligent, but people do untoward and surprising things and supposition is not enough. One of the central tasks of a sociology of deviance is to replace wild or informed guesses about conduct with more reliable charts of the social world. A beginning has been made with Walsh,[71]

[70] See, for example, R. Taylor and S. Gottfredson, 'Environmental Design, Crime, and Prevention: An Examination of Community Dynamics'.
[71] See D. Walsh, *Break-Ins* and *Heavy Business*.

Bennett, and Wright's interviews with burglars and robbers. Joanna Shapland of the Oxford Centre for Criminological Research has undertaken important but as yet unpublished research on the informal social control practised by people in everyday life. But it is only a beginning, and quite an edifice has been built on a foundation of unsubstantiated surmise about the invasion and defence of territory, the creation and loss of attachments, and mutual surveillance.

It can be asserted in reply to some of the earlier criticisms that control theorists do not wish to rule out the search for patterns of motivation that help us to understand deviance: they merely argue that no theories so far advanced actually work. Situational controls need not rule out the search for dispositional causes: they merely help us cope with the crime problem we face here and now. At the least, both aspects of control theory point to a dimension that is missing from existing theories, and which needs to be included. The relative novelty of the approach in its present forms should not incline us to premature dismisal: it harbours potential for considerable development.

10

Radical Criminology

Introduction

At the time of its emergence (the early 1970s) the very phrase
'radical criminology' seemed a contradiction in terms. There
had, after all, been a concerted attempt to differentiate 'criminology' (which was associated with political orthodoxy and
'positivism') from the 'sociology of deviance' (which espoused a
more 'radical' definition of the subject and a preference for
methods, in particular that of participant observation, which
were of reputedly marginal scientific status).[1] To reintroduce
the term 'criminology' seemed to fly in the face of much that
had been symbolically gained over the previous decade. To
yoke it to the term 'radical' (or 'new', 'critical', or Marxist)
seemed both perverse and over-ambitious. The directive in the
phrase, however, was clear: to break with the seeming limitations of the 'sociology of deviance' without a regress to conventional criminology.[2]

What had led, in so short a time, to so signal a break in the
ranks of those who had collectively opposed traditional criminology? In criminology, as in sociology and the humanities
more generally, the answer must lie at least partly in the
context of the times. In the USA, and more mutedly in Britain,
the late 1960s produced a significant minority of students 'rad-
icalized' by the Vietnam war, racial conflict, and a host of more
minor issues, such as those surrounding new forms of drug use.
A fierce impatience was expressed with the gradualism of

[1] See, for example, S. Cohen's Introduction to *Images of Deviance*; and M. Phillipson,
Sociological Aspects of Crime and Delinquency, chs. 1 and 2. For a more detailed account of
developments from this perspective, see S. Cohen, 'Criminology and the Sociology of
Deviance in Britain'.

[2] See the discussion in Chapter 1, 16–20. The operative image of conventional
criminology was of activity almost exclusively geared to the more precise measurement,
prediction, and control of criminality without regard to wider social and economic
contexts, and by quantitative methods. The reality was naturally more diverse.

liberal, social-democratic politics. Both the American 'War on Poverty' and the Labour Government in Britain were seen as failing crucially to correct structural inequalities of class, status, and power. At this point, the longer-standing project of the New Left, to dissociate Marxism from the 'State Socialist' regime of the USSR, and to regenerate it as a critical force, bore fruit. May 1968 came to symbolize the possibility of revolutionary change in affluent, Western societies. A variety of neo-Marxist philosophers reinterpreted Marxist theory to attempt to account for the crises that arose, the inability of capitalism to resolve them, and the inevitability of new and more devastating conflicts.

Against the appeal of Gramsci, Habermas, and Althusser[3] the work of even such gifted interpreters of deviance as Matza and Becker seemed tame, and that of Merton and Albert Cohen positively antediluvian. Whereas the latter offered tentative 'processual' models for an enhanced understanding of 'becoming deviant', or theories aimed at explaining lower-class forms of delinquency, the former seemed to provide a basis for grasping the 'total inter-connectedness'[4] of crime and capitalist society. The appeal of the application of Marxist theory and method to criminology was also increased by the growing visibility of what came to be termed 'crimes of the powerful'. None of the theories in vogue in the 1950s and 60s addressed white-collar crime and the crimes of corporations at all satisfactorily. To adapt Sutherland's dictum about the limitations of psychoanalytical theories of crime, it seemed absurd to regard Investors Overseas Services as suffering from 'status-frustration', or the corporations involved in the 'great Electrical Conspiracy' as victims of 'secondary deviation' or undue stigmatization.[5] The problem is neatly summarized by Taylor,

---

[3] The work of Antonio Gramsci and Jurgen Habermas has no direct connection with criminological issues, but had by the late 1960s an immense significance for the New Left. See in particular *Selections from the Prison Notebooks of Antonio Gramsci* (ed. and tr. by Q. Hoare and G. Nowell Smith); and, from Habermas's continuing work, *Legitimation Crisis*. Major themes from their work are closely integrated in S. Hall *et al.*, *Policing the Crisis*, which also deploys some conceptions from Althusser. The structuralist Marxism of Althusser had elsewhere been viewed as incompatible with the study of crime, deviance, and allied concerns. See P. Hirst, 'Marx and Engels on Law, Crime and Morality'.

[4] I. Taylor *et al.*, *The New Criminology*, 278.

[5] For documentation of these cases, see C. Raw *et al.*, *Do You Sincerely Want to be Rich:*

Walton, and Young's criticism of earlier theories as 'predicting too little bourgeois, and too much proletarian criminality'.[6] Such theories could not be readily adapted to resolve their shortcomings: a new paradigm, a fresh 'problem-shift' was called for. The adequacy of the Marxist criminology that emerged as an alternative to other perspectives forms the subject of this chapter.

The 'New' Criminology

The most vigorous attempt to supplant existing approaches by a neo-Marxist alternative occurs in the work of Taylor, Walton, and Young (1973, 1975). In their first book, a comprehensive appraisal of the full range of theoretical approaches in criminology is made. The main criterion by which such approaches are evaluated and, in general, found wanting, is their capacity to provide what the authors term, in the book's subtitle, a fully 'social theory of deviance'.[7] Their own model for a fully social theory is Marxism, but it is the Marx of the *Economic and Philosophical Manuscripts of 1844*, as well as of *Capital*, which they commend: Marx the dialectician rather than the determinist, Marx the action theorist as much as the analyst of political economy, who was concerned with alienation and consciousness as much as modes of production.[8] To establish the new criminology as superior to the old involved a ground-clearing critique, a critique which forms the bulk of the 1973 book and which is concerned to salvage certain elements from prior theorizing for integration into an improved Marxist criminology.

In nine chapters, issue is taken with eight major approaches and their variants, and a synthesis of their most useful insights is attempted in the ninth. Thus, in the first chapter, the philosophical bases for liberal criminology are located in the work of

Bernard Cornfeld and IOS: An International Swindle, and G. Tyler, 'The Great Electrical Conspiracy'.

[6] I. Taylor *et al.*, *The New Criminology*, 107.

[7] See, for example, ibid. 281–2.

[8] This brought them quickly into dispute with Hirst, whose Althusserian Marxism stressed the latter, and largely excluded the former concerns. See Hirst, 'Marx and Engels', and the reply by Taylor and Walton in I. Taylor *et al.*, *Critical Criminology*, chs. 8 and 9.

Hobbes, Locke, Bentham, and the utilitarian tradition. This 'classical criminology' and its neo-classical variants are viewed as incapable of reconciling forms of inequality rooted in property relations, and the extension of rationality (as distinct from responsibility), to those who offend against the law.[9]

In Chapter 2 the 'appeal' of positivism is viewed as residing in its claim to be capable of accounting for criminality in neutral, scientific terms which situate pathology in the individual offender, and deflect attention from the social context of unequal social relations which basically frame the offence. The third chapter is perhaps the most crucial, for in it they challenge the conventional image of Durkheim as a functionalist who argued that crime is both inevitable and necessary if society, *any* society, is to survive. They argue instead that Durkheim restricted his view of the functionality of deviance to societies that fell short of true 'organic' solidarity. On this reading of Durkheim, the proposition that 'crime is normal' need not inhibit the pursuit of a 'crime-free' society.[10]

The next five chapters deal critically with ecological and anomie theories; labelling theory; what are termed American naturalism and phenomenology; Marx and Engels's own view of crime, and the lone attempt of Bonger to apply formal materialism to its study; and to the conflict theories of Turk and Quinney.[11] All are found wanting in terms of their potential as a basis for a 'fully social' theory of deviance, either because they dehumanize the deviant, or fail to furnish an adequate context of political economy, or both. Ecological theory is valued for its move away from individualistic accounts, but placed far too great an emphasis on purely urban processes, such as the emergence of 'natural' delinquency

---

[9] 'The "solution" in social contract to the problem of inequality . . . is an evasion, and is best seen in Locke. He makes a distinction between those numbers of the poor who have chosen depravity and those who, because of their unfortunate circumstances, were unable to live a "rational" life. Thus, crime is *either* an irrational choice (a product of the passions) *or* it may be the result of factors militating against the free exercise of rational choice. In neither respect can it be fully rational action in the sense that conforming action is invariably seen to be.

These two alternative views of criminal motivation have dominated criminology (surviving the attack of positivism) ever since.' I. Taylor *et al.*, *The New Criminology*, 6–7.

[10] See Chapter 4.

[11] References here are primarily to W. Bonger, *Criminality and Economic Conditions*; A. Turk, *Criminality and the Legal Order*; and R. Quinney, *The Social Reality of Crime*.

areas, divorcing these from the play of economic forces. Anomie theory—and its subcultural variants—related crime and deviance to the social structure, but reduced the deviants themselves to purely reactive or adaptive, and therefore not creative, people. Labelling theory made a crucial break with positivism by treating deviance and control dialectically, as variable and dynamic processes implicated one with the other, but ultimately merely transposed one over-simple model for another: control leading to deviance, and not the reverse. Images of deviance remained flawed as a result, since deviant motivation was reduced to passive resistance to or acquiescence in the superordinates' definitions of reality: in Gouldner's phrase, the deviant is regarded as 'man-on-his-back' rather than 'man-fighting-back'.[12] American naturalism attempted to restore a more humanistic model of deviance, but 'appreciation' as a method merely gave unwarranted primacy to the deviants' own view, thus abdicating the sociological task of mediating the relations between that view and those from other vantage-points. Phenomenology moved even further away from a concern with the social context to a preoccupation with individual perceptions of deviance and control. Even Marx and Engels, in the occasional passages where they focused on crime, were prone to a determinism at odds with the role accorded creativity and consciousness elsewhere in Marx's work, a mechanistic lapse mistaken for a truly Marxist approach to crime by Bonger and other formal Marxists. Finally, non-Marxist radical criminologists, in particular Turk and Quinney, whilst attempting to relate crime to the structural sources of conflict in advanced societies, confused authority relations with power relations, thus obscuring their actual foundation in class conflict.

In all these approaches, partial gains are offset by significant flaws that are rooted in their inadequate epistemologies. The last chapter of the book attempts to synthesize the gains and eliminate the flaws by recovering them for a fully Marxist model of deviance and control. It is axiomatic that capitalism is

[12] A. Gouldner, 'The Sociologist as Partisan' in *For Sociology: Renewal and Critique in Sociology Today*, 39; first published in *The American Sociologist*, May 1968, this article formed the basis for much of the critique by the 'new' criminologists of what Gouldner termed the 'zookeepers of deviance', that is, the work of Howard Becker and the symbolic interactionists. See Chapter 7.

criminogenic, as are all societies based on exploitation and oppression. The only form of society which in principle holds out any possibility of being crime-free is a society embodying the principles of 'socialist diversity'. 'Socialism' entails an absence of material differences, and a willed commitment to equality. It removes the rationale for crimes against property, the bulk of offences in any capitalist society. 'Diversity' entails a commitment to the toleration of minority beliefs and activities which many formally socialist states proscribe, such as drug use, sexual deviance, and gambling. To do otherwise than to work for the demise of capitalism, and the transformation of society to one of socialist diversity, is to implicate oneself in correctionalism, i.e. the coercive use of the criminal sanction to 'correct' behaviour on a personal basis when its roots lie in social structural inequalities of wealth and power. In their introduction to their later work, *Critical Criminology* (1975), these themes are recapitulated but not greatly elaborated, save for the argument by Young that working-class control over policing should be greatly extended.

The 'Birmingham School'

In the 1970s, the Centre for Contemporary Cultural Studies at Birmingham University became, under the aegis of its Director, Stuart Hall, of some consequence in the sociology of deviance and control. While its members' interests were diverse, and embraced the fields of industrial relations, the media, and race relations, the unifying feature of their work was the reproduction of order in capitalist Britain, a theme which they came increasingly to research and theorize in the context of youthful deviance and adult control. This theme had been dealt with by the media and by some sociologists as a product of 'intergenerational conflict', a mode of explanation which the Birmingham School rejected at the outset as misleading. The 'Birmingham School' holds that, in a class society, youthful deviance is most profoundly lodged in the refusal to accept, and the struggle against, relations with 'authorities' which administer, on the State's behalf, institutions based on a rule-bound set of interests which are ultimately those of a capitalist ruling class. Youth is a crucial point of vulnerability for the reproduction of order, for if capitalism allows the members of its subordinate working class a 'moment of truth', it is at the point of entry into the occupational order. Willis is especially preoccupied with the manner whereby that structural problem is culturally resolved by 'the boys' themselves.[13] Phil Cohen supplied the School with a method for bringing class struggle far more centrally into focus in the analysis of youthful sub-cultures than earlier, non-Marxist theorists had envisaged.[14] However, these studies took no more than marginal note of societal reactions to deviance, and of the details of the manifestations, both social and economic, of the 'contradictions of capitalism' to which subcultures were allegedly a symbolic response. In *Policing the Crisis*, Stuart Hall and his colleagues make a most ambitious attempt to integrate these various levels and aspects of analysis around the phenomenon of 'mugging'.

Policing the Crisis is by no means the complete expression of the kind of 'critical' criminology urged by Taylor, Walton, and Young, for it deals only fleetingly with the third and the sixth 'formal requirement' of their 'fully social theory': the 'actual act' and the 'outcome of the social reaction on deviants' further actions'. On the remaining five such requirements, however, it attempts an exhaustive analysis, and thus provides the most sophisticated basis so far by which we might assess the claim that critical criminology is superior to alternative approaches.[15]

The book is divided into four parts, each dealing with a major aspect of 'Mugging, the State, and Law and Order', as the subtitle puts it. Part I deals with the rise of a generalized concern about 'mugging' in England in the early 1970s. Part II follows the particular case which led to three youths from Handsworth, Birmingham, receiving sentences of ten and twenty years imprisonment for their commission of one such offence. Part III sets both the pattern of offences and the official and societal reactions to which they appeared to give rise within the context of the 'crisis of hegemony' afflicting the British State

[13] In his *Learning to Labour*. See Chapter 6.

[14] P. Cohen, 'Working Class Youth Cultures', see Chapter 6.

[15] The formal scope of a fully social theory was held to require coverage of: 1. The wider origins of the deviant act; 2. Immediate origins of the deviant act; 3. The actual act; 4. The immediate origins of social reaction; 5. The wider origins of social reacton; 6. The outcome of the social reaction on deviant's further action; and 7. The nature of the deviant process as a whole. In Taylor *et al.*, *The New Criminology*, 270–8.

in that period. Part IV links these aspects together in the depiction of a 'politics of mugging'. It connects street crime, among Black youth in particular, to what are seen to be the fundamental contradictions of political economy in Britain. It is these which promote the real crisis; street crime is both product and palliative, rather than the source, of intensifying class conflict.

The study opens with a painstaking examination of the 'facts' which were held to justify the importation from the USA of a term, 'mugging', by which to describe crimes of robbery with violence long extant in England. It came to signify a trend which in turn came to justify the creation of 'anti-mugging' squads, or their equivalent, by the transport and ordinary police forces; and in turn to justify sentences far exceeding existing norms for a period in which the length of sentences of imprisonment had been rising anyway. It was widely alleged, by press, police, and judiciary alike, that the ever-rising crime rate was a product of the 'permissive' society, coupled with too lenient a pattern of sentencing; that certain aspects of street crime *were* novel, and that these features had been the subject of rising public anxiety. Hall and his colleagues argue, with considerable evidence, that only the label, not the crime, were new. Different crimes were conflated to give the impression, particularly in the crucial 1972–3 period, of a sharp and unprecedented rise in street crimes of violence. In some instances, even pickpocketing, by definition a crime of stealthy non-violence, was added to the 'mugging' total. They are able to show that the link between the rise in crime and lenient sentencing had no basis even in official facts, since the 1965–72 period saw a *lower* rise in the crime rate than the 1955–65 period, though sentencing in the 1960s was far tougher than in the 1950s; there was no change in the rate of acquittals; and even in the specific case of robberies with violence, there was no uniform or steeper trend in either London or the provinces in 1972–5 than in 1955–65. The much-quoted rise of 129 per cent in 'muggings' in London over the 1968–72 period was derived from figures clouded in ambiguity. Most surprising of all, 'we have never had any figures at all concerning the scale, and rate of increase, of provincial muggings'.[16]

This unpacking of the 'mugging' scare is the foundation for

[16] S. Hall *et al.*, *Policing the Crisis*, 16. But see M. Pratt, *Mugging as a Social Problem*.

all that follows, for it enables the authors to ask: 'If the reaction to mugging cannot be explained by a straightforward reference to the (official) statistics, how *can* it be explained?[17] Their answer is:

> When the official reaction to a person, group of persons or series of events is *out of all proportion* to the actual threat offered, when 'experts', in the form of police chiefs, the judiciary, politicians and editors *perceive* the threat in all but identical terms . . ., when the media . . . stress 'sudden and dramatic' increases . . . and 'novelty', above and beyond that which a sober, realistic appraisal could sustain, then we believe it is appropriate to speak of the beginnings of a *moral panic*.[18]

A 'referential context' is built up in which the 'meaning of mugging' is taken to be the growing social *malaise* of the inner city, a symbol of urban violence long associated with America (to which frequent allusions are made) but now increasingly evident in Britain. The crucial novelty is not the rise in crimes of violence, but the involvement of Black youths and White victims. The orchestration of consensus by police, media, and judiciary now assumes a *vox populi* role, in which the media represent the judiciary as speaking *for* the public, and the judiciary can quote the media as 'evidence' of the strength of public opinion. They interact to produce 'an effective ideological and control closure around the issue'.[19] At which point the media, without any recourse to conspiracy or dragooning, operate as an 'ideological State apparatus'.

The second stage of the analysis concerns the particular response elicited by the case of Paul Storey and two accomplices who 'mugged' an elderly man in Handsworth, and whose sentences were for twenty and ten years imprisonment respectively. The case made for saturation media coverage, in part because the boys returned to inflict further injuries on the victim two hours after the original attack. The age and defence-less character of the victim, the small sum of money stolen, combined with the second assault, were picked up as features of the menace of mugging. In addition, however, Storey was half West Indian, and one of his accomplices was of Cypriot background: the link with 'race' was reinforced. The local press

---

[17] S. Hall *et al.*, *Policing the Crisis*, 16.   [18] Ibid. 16.   [19] Ibid. 76.

treatment of the case is analysed in detail, and while much was made of the associations between deviance and urban decay, lost neighbourhood and family cohesion, and poor recreational facilities, the structural background remained absent from even feature articles. The national press probed no deeper, and the 'liberal' papers, such as the *Guardian*, are defined as largely silent on the issues involved. Letters to the press were analysed, as were anonymous and abusive letters to the Storey family. Certain 'root-concepts' emerge from all sources which can be read as 'English ideologies of crime'. 'Englishness' equals a belief in the necessity for work to be undertaken as a source of livelihood. By contast, crime is parasitic. Certain key symbols recur: the family, the need for discipline, respectability, and decency: the police and the law are seen as the guarantors of these core values, to which the working class adhere as fiercely as others. Detestation of crime transcends and ultimately unites classes in the face of class differences in other respects. The 'Black mugger' is thus the perfect 'folk devil', a scapegoat for all the social anxieties produced by the change to an affluent, but destabilized, society.[20] Unable to generate a political solution to these problems, the working-class response is that of corporate, defensive class consciousness, a regress to *exclusion* and *typification* of a surrogate enemy; that of the lower middle class is to react with moral indignation. Against the full force of English common sense and traditionalism, liberalism wilts and runs for cover.

If crime is one of the few symbolic sources of unity in an increasingly divided and embittered class society—if, moreover, the traditional armoury of consensus (power, deference, fatalism, and external enemies) is exhausted, diminishing, or absent—then it follows that the State, faced with a 'crisis of hegemony', will need little incentive to use the 'war against crime' as a source of re-legitimation. The management of consensus has, in this view, only recently become of truly critical significance for the British ruling class. It may well be that Britain's economic decline can be traced to 1870 and beyond: but it is only in the last two decades that the international context has been so transformed that the decline is now beyond dispute. The breakdown of the machinery of prosperity has

[20] Ibid. 159 ff.

coincided with the loss of empire, a conjuncture that left only one serious candidate for bearing the costs: the working class. Yet the working class have been incorporated into political society, and 'pragmatically accept' the status quo only as long as those conditions hold. As the economic crisis deepens, hegemony becomes increasingly difficult to sustain. The Heath–Wilson years revealed the bankruptcy of Social Democratic reformism in the face of stubborn working-class resistance to a change in the rules of the game evolved over the previous century. Important concessions had been wrung from the ruling class, most notably, the extension of the rule of law to all groups, the guarantee of certain union immunities and rights, and universal suffrage: a host of others, such as universal education, the Welfare State, and an increasingly mixed economy, were administered by a massive increase in the numbers of bureaucratic State employees, who stand in a 'subaltern' relation to the hegemonic class. By the late 1960s, it was evident that the inter-class truce grounded in full employment, free collective bargaining, and rising wages could not be sustained. Working-class resistance to the erosion of first one, and then the other, led most dramatically to the three-day week, the miners' flying pickets, and the fall of the Heath Government, a sequence which coincided with a fresh 'wave' of immigration from Kenyan Asians, and alarm about the numbers of immigrants still 'flooding into' the country as dependants of those already here. 'All four themes (political and economic crisis; ideological struggle; and race) must be understood as unrolling within an organic conjuncture whose parameters are over-determined by two factors: the rapid deterioration in Britain's economic condition; and the maintenance of a political form of "that exceptional state" which gradually emerged 1968–72 and which now appears ... to be permanently installed.'[21] The latter reference is to the increasing readiness to arm the police in the light of terrorist attacks connected with Ulster; an upsurge in armed robbery and hijackings; and to erosions of civil liberties in the process of criminal justice, such as the attempt to instal control units in two prisons. The State's main concern is to define the crisis away, or to set the terms in which it is discussed apart from that of class relations. The crisis is

[21] S. Hall *et al.*, *Policing the Crisis*, 307.

thus defined as a crisis of legitimate authority, prevented from 'doing its job' by deviants: criminals, industrial dissidents (Wilson's 'small group of politically motivated men'), scroungers, or political deviants. Images of deviance become commonplace in the realm of industrial relations. Enough confusion is sown to lead the working class to 'misrecognize' their enemy: the crisis is deflected on to youth, crime, and race, away from class relations and on to authority relations.

Finally, the 'politics of mugging' emerges: policing the Blacks (the poor and the unemployed) amounts to policing the crisis.[22] There is a reality to young Black crime, increasingly so in the wake of unemployment which bites most deeply on the Black labour force—'a super-exploited sub-proletariat'.[23] Hustling, a semi-criminal *mélange* of 'informal dealing, rackets, semi-legal practices and small-time crime'[24] emerges to meet 'sheer, material needs'[25] and in part to service the Black community's leisure in a context where Blacks can less feasibly aspire to a common class identity with Whites. The young, second-generation Blacks experience both exploitation and expendability, but increasingly refuse to accept the 'reserve army of labour' role assigned to them under capitalism. Yet the refusal to carry out 'White man's shit-work' entails a wagelessness that is a forcing-ground for hustling. 'Crime is one perfectly predictable and quite comprehensible consequence of this process.'[26] It is possible, but unlikely, that a new form of political struggle will be evolved to stave off increasing Black criminalization.

Radical Criminology in America

In America, as in Britain, radical criminology moved from a 'radical liberal' stance in the late 1960s to a more thoroughgoing commitment to a Marxist position in the 1970s. The American-based Marxist criminologists are more concerned with a relatively uncomplicated application of Marx's most central concepts to the analysis of crime and crime control, by comparison with the British theorists' attempts to draw more

[22] Ibid. 332.   [23] Ibid. 375.   [24] Ibid. 351.
[25] Ibid. 360.   [26] Ibid. 390.

fully on 'critical' neo-Marxists such as Habermas and Gramsci. This may reflect what is seen as a more obvious and uncomplicated set of relations between American crime and American capitalism. The shift is well drawn out by Klockars, who juxtaposes passages written by Chambliss and Platt in the 1960s which, on republication in the 1970s, have been revised in a Marxist direction: for example, by the substitution of terms like 'ruling class' for the apparently vaguer and more pluralist 'the social order'.[27] There is also, especially in the work of Chambliss and Quinney, a link with the tradition of American populism, and its traditional desire to expose the threat to the integrity of community by the graft and corruption of Big Business, Big Government, Big Unions and (a theme which did not find inclusion in the work of C. Wright Mills, its most celebrated exponent) Big Crime.[28]

In his most recent work, *On The Take*, Chambliss finds the perfect vehicle for an expression of these concerns: the character and social composition of racketeering in Seattle. The book's subtitle, 'From Petty Crooks to Presidents', summarizes its major finding: the 'hidden hand' in organized crime in America is not 'the Mafia' but leading representatives of the city's ruling class. A diagram which resembles at first glance a high school chart of civic worthiness, with its listing of financiers, businessmen, politicians, and law-enforcement officers, is headed 'Seattle's Crime Network'.[29] The evidence for this profile is gathered from several years' participant observation in Seattle, beginning with Chambliss 'hanging around' bars in which gambling, drugs, and vice connections might be made. After several months' involvement in card schools, Chambliss found several contacts with inside knowledge who were willing to talk, and it was from these informants, motivated in part by grievance or substantial experience of victimization, that he pieced together the links between the front-line operators and the more shadowy entrepreneurs who ultimately control the crime networks: key personnel in the police force, the legal profession, business, local government, and the public prosecutor's office. Meyer Lansky is named as the main link with 'a

---

[27] C. Klockars, 'The Contemporary Crises of Marxist Criminology', *Criminology*, 487 ff.
[28] C. Mills, *The Power Élite*.   [29] W. Chambliss, 74.

national crime network, the structure and organisation of the network in Seattle'.[30] Both Nixon and Johnson as Presidents had substantial dealings with men 'whose business profits derived at least in part from illegal business'.[31] In conclusion, 'crime is not a by-product of an otherwise effectively working political economy: it is a main product of that political economy . . . The logic of capitalism is a logic within which the emergence of crime networks is inevitable.'[32] Despite variations, 'such networks are also pervasive in Europe and Scandinavia'.[33] A visit to Poland confirms that there too corruption and profiteering of a systemic kind flourish. 'Does this weaken the argument that it is the structural characteristics of capitalist democracies . . . that create and sustain crime networks? Not at all . . . The kind of "socialism" that is extant in the Soviet Union and Eastern Europe shares with Western capitalism many essential features: a rigid class system, the use of money for exchange, and the alienation of workers from the product of their labour, to mention only a few.'[34] He concludes with the hope that de-criminalizing gambling and drug dependence will mitigate the hold of the rackets on the trade in these illicit goods and services.

Tony Platt is concerned to make much the same connection in almost identical terms with the phenomenon of 'street crime': 'They [US Government-sponsored Victimization Surveys] supported the conclusion that "street" crime is not simply a *by-product* of the capitalist mode of production. . . . Rather, it is shown to be a phenomenon *endemic* to capitalism at its highest stage of development.'[35] Far from seeking to ignore it, glorify it, or minimize it, the Left should recognize that official agencies 'grossly underestimate' such crimes.[36] The Victim Surveys tapped an incidence of street crimes (theft, auto theft, burglary, rape, assault, and armed robbery) almost four times as great as the rate reported to the police. 'Police brutality, corruption, and incompetence' account for much of the difference, particularly as far as working-class and black minorities are concerned. Moreover, such crimes are 'primarily an *intra-class* and *intra-racial* phenomenon. . . . The highest

---

[30] Ibid. 151.   [31] Ibid. 158.   [32] Ibid. 16, 181.
[33] Ibid. 185.   [34] Ibid. 185.
[35] A. Platt, '"Street Crime"—A View from the Left', 29.   [36] Ibid. 27.

incidence of violent and property crime is among the poor and unemployed, specifically, the super-exploited sectors of the working class, young men, and single or separated women.'[37] The death-rate for Black males by homicide is over eight times that for White males: the starkest illustration of the extent to which the costs of crime are regressive in their effects. However, crime is by no means restricted to the poor: the better-off are shown by self-report studies to engage in crime as frequently, if less seriously, than the most disadvantaged. Much the same situation prevailed in the England of the nineteenth century, 'at the peak of industrial capitalism'.[38] The conditions under which crime could assume a semi-political character were destroyed by capitalism: 'social banditry' was purged as a form of crime by the new technologies of control, and superseded as a means of rebellion by the rise of the political organization of the working-class movement. What remains is predatory 'street' crime that offers no hope of a political solution for the 'super-exploited sectors of the working class. Monopoly capitalism emiserates increasingly larger portions of the working class and "proletarianizes" the lower strata of the bourgeoisie, degrades workers' skills and competency in the quest for higher productivity, and organizes family and community life on the basis of its most effective exploitability. It consequently makes antagonism rather than reciprocity the norm of social relationships.'[39]

Allied Approaches

A continuing source of inspiration for Marxist criminologists has undoubtedly been the longer-standing project of socialist historians to recover what has come to be termed 'history from below'. From the work of Hobsbawm, Thompson, and Rudé, on social banditry, machine-breaking, and the London mob, to the detailed documentation of working-class history by the Ruskin History Workshop, the attempt has been made to rescue the lives of people consigned by orthodox scholarship to the margins of history from what Thompson has aptly termed

[37] A. Platt, ' "Street Crime"—A View from the Left', 29.
[38] Ibid. 30. [39] Ibid. 31.

'the enormous condescension of posterity'.[40] However, although any deliberate policy of exclusion has been disclaimed by Hay in a recent volume of essays on crime in the eighteenth century, the focus of such work has so far been almost entirely on those forms of deviance which seem to embody substantial elements of political resistance to ruling-class or State power, rather than more predatory victimization.[41] Perhaps because those who are often cast as latter-day 'Luddites' and 'wreckers' can speak, through the labour movement, quite forcefully for themselves, there are relatively few attempts to apply this approach at all directly to contemporary forms of crime. Pearson has sought to explain violence against ethnic minorities in part by using much the same framework: 'Paki-bashing' in an economically blighted Northern town is related to the resentment felt against immigrants taking jobs and apparently making good in a context of rising unemployment.[42] As we have seen, the work of Phil Cohen, and Stuart Hall and his colleagues, is informed by a similar approach.

An historical approach has also been employed in the analysis of relations between social control and the political economy of the capitalism that emerged from the Industrial Revolution. Scull has viewed the nineteenth-century asylum- and prison-building programmes as functional for the iron discipline that employers enforced in the period of maximum capitalist growth: by comparison, the stagnant capitalist economies of the 1970s and 80s seek to off-load their institutional charges for cut-price 'community care'.[43] Ignatieff has explored the religious mediations between forms of prison discipline and the symbolic order of capitalist political economy.[44] In a series of works, Foucault has employed a 'structuralist' method along similar lines: capitalist industrialism employed a logic which its agencies applied to ruthless effect in one institutional sphere after another—the asylum, the prison, the clinic, the school,

[40] E. Hobsbawm, *Bandits*; E. Thompson, *Whigs and Hunters: The Origin of the Black Act*; G. Rudé, *The Crowd in History*; R. Samuel (ed.), *Ruskin College, History Workshop Pamphlets*.

[41] D. Hay *et al.* (eds.), *Albion's Fatal Tree: Crime and Society in Eighteenth Century England*, 14.

[42] G. Pearson, '"Paki-Bashing" in a North East Lancashire Cotton Town'.

[43] A. Scull, *Decarceration*.

[44] M. Ignatieff, *A Just Measure of Pain*.

and the factory.[45] Charles Dickens had conveyed the same insight with more poetic force, but he believed in the power of the human heart to reform such organized cruelty. Needless to say, the work of Foucault holds no such illusions.

Unlike Scull, Mathiesen and Fitzgerald see the prison as a functional and continuing necessity for capitalist society.[46] Evidence for the use of the prison as an instrument of class oppression is inferred from the relative over-use of the prison for proletarian populations, and its under-use in connection with 'crimes of the powerful'. Even in the courts, allegedly the most neutral and disinterested forum for the promulgation of the rule of law, class bias is seen to persist: Carlen[47] analyses modes of courtroom interaction as functioning to bestow a sense of impotence and inferiority on the largely working-class defendants, and to buttress the superiority of the overwhelmingly middle- or upper-class lawyers and judiciary. The very language of the courtroom polarizes defendants and prosecution along class lines; and Griffith has documented the unified class character of the judiciary, both in terms of its social composition and its ideology.[48]

The 'crimes of the powerful', and their relative immunity from prosecution and the penal sanction, with all due allowance for the occasional exemplary sentence, is a central theme for Marxist criminology, though it is by no means the case that they pioneered its study: that honour must go to Edwin Sutherland.[49] This important topic remains relatively slightly explored. Frank Pearce's *Crimes of the Powerful* is a largely historical study of violations of the Anti-Trust laws in America, and a critique of the Mafia myth. Prior to Chambliss, but drawing on the work of Albini,[50] he argues that organized crime in America is far more subservient to the imperatives of Big Business, to which it stands in a 'servant' class relation (as, for example, in strike-breaking), than contemporary analyses

[45] M. Foucault, *Discipline and Punish*; also *Madness and Civilization*, and *The Birth of the Clinic*.

[46] T. Mathiesen, *The Politics of Abolition*; M. Fitzgerald, *Prisoners in Revolt*, and (with J. Sim) *British Prisons*.

[47] P. Carlen, *Magistrates' Justice*.

[48] J. Griffith, *The Politics of the Judiciary*.

[49] E. Sutherland, *White Collar Crime*.

[50] J. Albini, *The American Mafia: Genesis of a Legend*.

allow. In a somewhat different vein, Colin Sumner has attempted to integrate the emphasis on labelling of the inter-actionists with the stress on class conflict of the Marxists by means of a focus on criminal sanctions as the ultimate means whereby class rule is secured and symbolically expressed through ideology.[51] In sum, in a relatively short period of time, Marxist criminology has sought to redefine and extend the purposes and boundaries of the field. We now turn to the question of how far those processes are themselves adequately grounded.

Criticism

If all that was being asserted by Marxist criminologists were series of propositions to the effect that capitalism and crime were arguably interconnected, that crime tends to assume a distinctive form under capitalism, and so on, then there could be little to object to in adopting such premises as a basis for further analysis and research. The problems that plagued the earlier structural approaches would still need to be sur-mounted—that of reification of 'structure', for example, and the adoption of somewhat deterministic models of criminal-ity—but all approaches linking crime to the social structure share these pitfalls. Indeed, it was only with the advent of an interactionist approach that they were teased out. But the advocates of a Marxian perspective tend to assert far more than this. The 'new' criminologists, for example, assert the 'total interconnectedness' between crime and capitalism. Class con-flict is viewed as *the*, rather than simply one form of, group conflict in advanced industrial societies. As a result, it is regarded as a cardinal error to argue for a modified capitalism and a modified crime problem: for if the former is eliminated, the possibility exists for the elimination of crime as well (or, at least, the bulk of crime which is attributable to social, rather than psychological or biological factors).

The first, and most obvious criticism, is that the search for a 'total interconnectedness' leads to a revival of the more doctrinal versions of functionalism, in which deviance is viewed as an expression of, or resistance to, capitalist exploitation.

[51] C. Sumner, 'Marxism and Deviancy Theory', and 'Ideology and Deviance'.

Correspondingly, control is viewed as functional for the maintenance of bourgeois hegemony.[52] For example, Young has argued that

> when the State of California spends $73 million in 1968 on marihuana control, when more is spent on Social Security prosecutions than has ever been obtained illegally from the State, when supposedly scarce police resources are utilized in the persecution of gays, and when legislation denies women the right to choose whether to give birth or not—all this seeming ruling-class irrationality contributes enormously to the maintenance of bourgeois institutions.[53]

It is far from clear how such 'irrationality' does in practice contribute to bourgeois hegemony: the processes whereby this aim is accomplished are not examined. If certain offences are decriminalized, it can equally plausibly be argued that the purpose is to secure bourgeois domination by 'repressive tolerance'.[54] This form of circular argument is endemic in the search for 'total interconnectedness'.

Underlying this mode of analysis is a 'new' form of determinism and essentialism. Determinism is shifted from the sociocultural context to the realm of political economy. Essentialism inheres in that

> other-worldly realm of real processes which must not be confused with mundane appearance, everyday belief and social phenomena. It cannot be understood by entering the lifeworld of those who actually experience those processes. The consciousness of essential truth is distinct from the false consciousness of ordinary people ... Radical criminology ... rejects a dependence on empiricism and *Verstehen* ... After all, empiricism merely investigates the sensory world, a world which is not metaphysically authentic. *Verstehen*, too, simply reproduces false consciousness and is incapable of explaining what is real.[55]

It would be idle to pretend that 'false consciousness' does not, in some form or other, constitute both a major problem for sociology and its chief justification. If perfect social knowledge could be assumed to exist, then sociology (and Marxism)

[52] D. Downes and P. Rocks (eds.), *Deviant Interpretation: Problems in Criminological Theory*, 12–13.

[53] J. Young, Foreword to F. Pearce, *Crimes of the Powerful*, 18.

[54] H. Marcuse, *One-Dimensional Man*.

[55] P. Rock, in D. Downes and P. Rock (eds.), *Deviant Interpretations*, 75–6.

would be superfluous. However, there is a marked difference between the assumption that knowledge is inadequate or partial and that it is 'false': the one assumes at least a relative openness to fresh information and insights; the other a pre-structured 'falsity' which can be corrected only by a total transformation of consciousness itself. Sociology is, in general, wedded to the former, with its corresponding 'hard core' commitment to some form of 'falsificationism'; Marxism, in general, eludes or rejects that criterion.

This point is germane to consideration of the second issue, the Marxian theory of class conflict as a necessary outcome of capitalist structure. If Marx was correct in identifying the central properties of capitalism, then class conflict will inevitably grow as the crises of capitalism, born of its contradictions, intensify. It might be thought that Marx's clear specification of a particular evolutionary sequence *could* be tested, particularly as—since 1917—societies based upon a socialist alternative have been constructed. Marxism is particularly replete, however, with subsidiary clauses, which protect its theoretical hard core from critical attack. If the proletariat have not been progressively 'emiserated' under capitalism, then that is because their affluence has been secured at the expense of the Third World. If proletariat and bourgeoisie have not as yet been polarized, then that is because, as Marx predicted, the bourgeoisie have exploited to the full the capacities of their technologies to buy time, and buy off opposition, with further dollops of prosperity. Yet that prosperity remains precariously based and, as the proletariat presses home its strategic advantages, it can be sustained only at the cost of successive crises and hidden forms of exploitation, e.g. of migrant labour. Plausible as these arguments may be, their elaboration lends force to Popper's critique of Marxism as non-scientific because unfalsifiable; and the concentration on capitalism entails a corresponding analytical impoverishment in dealing with conflict, deviance, and control in State socialist or communist societies.

This limitation does not extend to alternative theories of conflict, including class conflict, which stem from the sociology of Max Weber.[56] The major difference between Marx and Weber

[56] There is no space here to elaborate on Weber's theories of class and social stratification: see F. Parkin, *Marxism and Class Theory: A Bourgeois Critique*.

lies in their fundamental assumption about the development of capitalism: for Marx, capitalism rests upon a particular mode of exploitation; for Weber, it rests upon a particular form of rationality. These are not mutually exclusive ideas in principle, but in their philosophical development they become so. For Marx, class domination culminates in the revolutionary transcendence of capitalism, and the opportunity to construct, after a transitional 'dictatorship of the proletariat', a classless, free, and equal communism. For Weber, rationality generates bureaucratic authority, which can be harnessed, with immense difficulty, only by the retention of 'charismatic' authority in the framework of constitutional democracy. In a sense, both have been invalidated by history: Marx failed to predict the logic of the Russian Revolution, and its aftermath; Weber the rise of Hitler, and Fascism, the yoking together of charisma and bureaucratic authority.[57] Ultimately, however, if a choice between the two *has* to be made (and many would argue that neither provide a satisfactory framework for explaining these phenomena), Weber at least provides the conceptual vocabulary with which to make sense of such developments, whereas, in our view, Marx does not. The sociology of Weber can 'handle' the growth of State powers, the rise of bureaucracy, the 'routinisation of charisma', the myriad forms assumed by conflict between classes, racial groups, the sexes, religions; Marxian sociology collapses these into endless variations of the class struggle. The appeal of Marxism is clear: it portends the 'good' society, whereas, in Parkin's phrase, Weber (and Social Democracy) can promise at best the 'not so bad' society (see Chapter 13 below). But at least the possibilities for the improvement of the latter can be prescribed with some precision: the former still resides in the realm of pure theoreticity.

The principal gap in Marxism concerns the lack of any political theory of liberty in socialist societies. No general

[57] There is some considerable scope for uncertainty about Weber's capacity to account for German Fascism. Aron states: 'He did not understand the implications of the Bolshevik revolution nor foresee the totalitarian despotism of single party rule. Anxious to spare democracy the reign of politicians without vocation he emphasised the plebiscitary legitimacy of the charismatic leader, unaware of the dangers which the following generation was to experience and suffer.' [i.e. Nazism.] (R. Aron, 'Max Weber and Power Politics', 99.) Yet Weber's sociology is replete with insights into those very dangers, in a way which Marx's is not. As a sociologist, Weber was acutely conscious of problems for which, as a politician, he could not prescribe remedies.

sequence has been offered concerning 'how power should be distributed; how conflicting interests should be represented and resolved, how abuses to socialist legality should be checked . . .' The most developed institutional mode of resolving such problems, parliamentary democracy, is especially anathema to Marxists, Marx himself having dismissed it as 'parliamentary cretinism'. As Parkin points out, the rejection of Marxism in the Western working class is not so very odd, since its members 'might reasonably wonder why, if all known versions of Marxist society are so seriously flawed, and their revolutions always betrayed, the result next time should be any different'. There is no need to invoke 'false consciousness' or the tortuous workings of 'ideological State apparatuses' to account for their reluctance to engage in revolutionary praxis.[58]

The strengths and weaknesses of Marxian sociology are well exemplified in *Policing the Crisis*. Theoretically, the advance made by this book was the attempt to integrate the interactionist insight concerning 'moral panics' with the Marxian insight into the nature of the 'crisis' wrought by capitalism in Britain in the early 1970s. Empirically, however, this integration is not accomplished. The reality of the 'moral panic' is most skilfully analysed and conveyed:[59] but the grounds for asserting that the official reaction sought to promulgate such a panic for larger ideological and political ends are not established. This is not to say that they could not be established, for even if they are unlikely to issue forth from the mouths of the 'master institutions' themselves, they might be inferred from the demonstration that 'crises' and 'panics' are correlated. But this kind of evidence is not advanced: and, indeed, perhaps could not be advanced, without firmer criteria for the identification of 'crises'. Was there a similar panic in 1925–6? Or 1929–30? Or 1966–7? Or, indeed, 1979–80, the winter of strike action affecting hitherto 'sacred' areas of institutional life, such as— with supreme irony—cancer wards and grave-digging? If not, then the theory can be said to 'over-predict' social control,

---

[58] F. Parkin, *Marxism and Class Theory*, 178, 199, and ch. 9, *passim*.

[59] Not all commentators would agree with this view. See, for example, C. Sumner, 'Race, Crime and Hegemony'. One strand in the analysis of Hall *et al.*, the adoption of tougher forms of policing that are more resistant to democratic controls, is forcefully developed by Hall in *Drifting into a Law and Order Society*.

much as earlier structural theories 'over-predicted' delinquency. Indeed, phrases like 'over-determined' crop up quite
frequently in the analysis, a sure sign that rhetoric is replacing
the assurance of evidence. There is also a central inconsistency
in the analysis: young Black second-generation immigrant men
are exonerated from any undue contribution to the rise in
crime, but are simultaneously identified as a 'super-exploited,
sub-proletariat' whose increasing contribution to crime is
defined as 'inevitable'. On inspection, that inconsistency *can* be
resolved, but the main grounds for its resolution in *Policing the
Crisis* seem far less defensible in the light of critical analyses of its
statistical basis. Ironically, the attempt by Hall *et al.* to be more
precise in their definition of a 'moral panic' than was usually the
case opened up that terrain for reappraisal. Locally, Pratt has
shown that the Metropolitan Police kept records of events called
'muggings' in their area, drawing on McClintock's categories of
robbery, and that those events did both increase at the end of the
1960s and also shift in location from the classic sites of skul-
duggery—towpaths, tunnels, and commons—to far less avoid-
able high streets.[60] More significantly, Waddington has shown
that there was a real and continuous national rise in muggings
before the 'moral panic' allegedly arose. There may have been a
slight decline in the *rate* of increase, but there was no decline in
the propensity of street crime to grow steadily and uninter-
ruptedly: 'the only valid conclusion to be drawn from the figures
presented by Hall *et al.* . . . is the opposite one to that drawn by
the authors themselves. It is that crime during the period immediately preceding the onset of concern about "mugging" was
indeed increasing, and doing so by increasing increments.'
Moreover, 'the lack of any criteria of proportionality allows no
distinction to be drawn in general between a "sober, realistic
appraisal" of a problem and a "moral panic".'[61] Reviewing
evidence about the experience of crime in the inner city some
years later, the radical criminologists Jones, Maclean, and
Young were prompted to observe that fears about mugging are
not panicky but sober and sensible: 'people's perceptions of
crime are not based on moral panic . . .'.[62] Suggestive as the

[60] M. Pratt, *Mugging as a Social Problem*.
[61] P. Waddington, 'Mugging as a Moral Panic', 252.
[62] T. Jones, B. Maclean, and J. Young, *The Islington Crime Survey*, 35.

work of Hall and his colleagues remains, one may conclude that, both statistically and conceptually, their interpretation of the social history of mugging is flawed.

Even if one does accept the statistical argument of *Policing the Crisis*, the official reaction can be indicted for a premature rather than a faulty analysis of the situation, which renders the lengthy sentences intelligible in terms of lay sociology, if indefensible in terms of humane legality. Similarly, the media and judiciary are assailed for their frequent invocation of the American comparison as a prefiguration of the inner-city future: yet the authors themselves make much the same comparison, albeit in more sociologically acceptable terms, though the nub of the analysis is the same. This seems to extend to sociology a 'benefit of clergy' denied to those engaged in formal social control. In sum, the prior commitment to a particular version of class struggle 'over-determines' (for the phrase is acceptable in intellectual, if not in empirical terms) the analytical outcome.

In the work of Platt and Chambliss there is above all a conviction that American capitalism is capitalism, that American crime is crime, and that elsewhere may be found less of much the same thing. Platt sees American capitalism as its 'highest' form, though no grounds are given for this assumption. Giddens could equally plausibly make quite the reverse assumption in his study of the 'advanced societies'.[63] In general, however, the main limitation of their work is that no intermediary or distinctive forms of political economy are worthy of analysis save for capitalism and socialism: Social Democracy is lesser capitalism, and State socialism is failed socialism.

The symmetry between crime, control, and capitalism is questioned by comparative work. For example, Hagan and Leon, in a study of juvenile justice in Canada, could find no basis for the links implied by Platt to exist between the reform of the juvenile justice system and capitalist interests in the child labour market in the USA.[64] Clinard, in his study of crime in

---

[63] A. Giddens, *The Class Structure of the Advanced Societies*, Preface.
[64] A. Platt, *The Child Savers: The Invention of Delinquency*; J. Hagan and J. Leon, 'Rediscovering Delinquency: Social History, Political Ideology and the Rule of Law'. See also the reply by Lauderdale and Lemon, and rejoinder, *Am. Soc. Rev.*, 43 (1978), 922–8.

Switzerland, *Cities with Little Crime*, found a surprisingly low rate of working-class criminality in a supremely capitalist society. The marked variations in crime that obtain in widely differing societies of a formally capitalist type seem scarcely addressed by this approach. And if the net is broadened to include State socialist societies, the yield drops even lower. In short, important as it is to seek the connections between crime and capitalism, it does not improve matters to make the fit, in Cicourel's phrase, 'by fiat'.

Finally, we might return to an inspirational source for the 'new' criminology: Gouldner's insistence that criminology should encompass 'man-fighting-back' rather than 'man-on-his-back'. This theme has been embroidered into a rich symbolic tapestry of deviant 'resistance', 'struggle', 'creativity', and the like.[65] It has been argued that the crime rate can be interpreted as an index of 'the credibility of a propertied society at particular stages of its development—the extent to which the distribution of property is latently accepted or rejected amongst certain sections of the working population'.[66] It is difficult to reconcile this political reading of deviance with actual patterns of criminal victimization, which are overwhelmingly intra-group rather than inter-group. Such a reading also obscures the extent to which deviance is only at several removes a problem for the State. It primarily affects communities, whatever their class composition. Crime and its control in effect operate as a regressive tax on the more powerless and vulnerable sections of society. Much evidence suggests that working-class communities desire more, rather than less, policing, and are less critical of police work than middle-class groups.[67] To sustain the case for crime as a 'misrecognition' of the 'real mechanisms'[68] of subordination involves the risk of reducing crime to a 'very bad case indeed of false consciousness'.[69]

In counter criticism, Marxist scholarship is hardly so tied to apriorism as the preceding critique implies. Two outstanding examples of rigorous research, by contrasting methods, would be Thompson's social historical studies and Willis's ethno-

---

[65] See Chapter 6.
[66] I. Taylor *et al.*, *Critical Criminology*, 42.
[67] R. Sparks *et al.*, *Surveying Victims*, 187–8.
[68] P. Cohen and D. Robins, *Knuckle Sandwich*, 113.
[69] S. Cohen, Introduction to *Folk Devils*, xi.

graphic work. Thompson describes his method in *Whigs and Hunters* as resembling 'a parachutist coming down in unknown territory: at first knowing only a few yards of land around me, and gradually extending my explorations in each direction. Perhaps three-quarters of this book is based on manuscript sources. One source led me to the next; but also, one problem led to another.'[70] In his already classic defence of the rule of law, he remarks that the Whig oligarchy employed the law

very much as a modern structural Marxist should expect it to do. But this is not the same thing as to say that the rulers had need of law, in order to oppress the ruled, while those who were ruled had need of none ... Most men have a strong sense of justice, at least with regard to their own interests. If the law is evidently partial and unjust, then it will mask nothing, legitimate nothing, contribute nothing to any class's hegemony ... We reach then not a simple conclusion (law = class power) but a complex and contradictory one. On the one hand, it is true that the law did mediate existent class relations to the advantage of the rulers ... On the other hand, the law mediated these class relations through legal forms, which imposed, again and again, inhibitions upon the actions of the rulers.

His own conclusion is that to dispense with the restrictions of bourgeois legalism, in favour of Utopian projections, 'is to throw away a whole inheritance of struggle *about* law, and within the forms of law, whose continuity can never be fractured without bringing men and women into immediate danger'.[71]

The Emergence of 'Left Realism'

Latterly, in the 1980s, it seems as if some radical criminologists themselves have found their older, rather aprioristic position untenable. Perhaps in response to external critics, and certainly in response to a series of changing circumstances, there has been a revolution within radical criminology itself. Building on the structure created by Taylor, Walton, and Young and members of the Birmingham School, but also reacting against it, there has emerged a new form of pragmatism which is not

[70] E. Thompson, *Whigs and Hunters*, 16; see chapter 6 for references to Paul Willis.
[71] Ibid. 261–7, *passim*.

very different at points from the older, conventional criminology that was deserted in the early 1970s. Jock Young and, to a lesser extent, Geoffrey Pearson, John Lea, and Richard Kinsey are the architects of what Young has called 'left realism', a realism that attempts to insert itself between what is defined as the hysterical over-reaction of 'law and order politics' and the gross insensitivity to crime of the left in Britain. It is an approach with analytic and political promise.

Left realism has diverse social and intellectual roots. One influence must have been the sheer tedium which inventive minds experienced in emphasizing again and again arguments about the class-bound nature of crime, the forgotten importance of political economy, and criminology's scandalous neglect of Marx, Engels, and Pashukanis. As publishers appreciated the academic and commercial appeal of radical criminology, as the Academic Press established its radical *Law, State and Society* series, Macmillan its *Critical Criminology* series, Penguin published books sponsored by the Socialist Society, Martin Robertson its largely radical *Law in Society* series, it became less and less plausible to contend that critical themes were ignored and that *bourgeois* criminology exercised intellectual hegemony. On the contrary, criminology was awash with critical argument. Radical criminology began to seem increasingly scholastic, established, and ritualistic to some of its advocates. There were diminishing marginal returns in calling for a socialist analysis of crime.

Secondly, with advancing age and the transformation of local government politics in Britain, a number of radical criminologists discovered that there were new contexts and opportunities for practical engagement. Some local authorities, and a few inner city councils and the now defunct Metropolitan Authorities in particular, had begun to espouse a politics with a marked affinity to the politics of critical criminology. They were in noisy opposition to the national Conservative Government elected in 1979 and re-elected in 1983. Many of those councils were composed of people who had had some confrontation with radical thought in University and Polytechnic, who were often themselves a new species of radical intellectual activist, and who sought intellectual support from a wider network of the left. In Merseyside, Edinburgh, the Greater

London Council, Islington and Camden Councils a new shadow criminology developed around Police Monitoring Groups, lesbian and gay rights, and the treatment of Blacks. In turn, Jock Young, John Lea, Richard Kinsey, and others received administrative and financial patronage from the new radical councils, and their words and ideas acquired a new political consequence.

Thirdly, the rise of feminism in the 1970s generated a critical attack on critical criminology. In 1977, a student of Ian Taylor's at Sheffield University, Carol Smart, published her *Women, Crime and Criminology*. In the name of radical criminology, she reproached radical criminology for ignoring the politics of gender, for forgetting the extensive victimization of women, and for celebrating what seemed to be patriarchal oppression. Feminists came to analyse rape, sexual abuse, and battering. They were to be radical champions of the *victim*, and there had been little enough radical talk of working-class victims before. Previous description had been piecemeal and unreflective. Some had dwelt on mental illness, prostitution, homosexuality, and drug-taking—all forms of deviance without immediate and visible victims. Some had refrained from discussing victimization altogether, as if deviance occurred in a void. Some had rather grandly presumed that victims were impersonal organizations or members of the property-owning classes and therefore politically peripheral. There had been little attention paid to the ordinary, abundant suffering which working-class crime inflicts on the working class. The criminal had been romanticized and the victim liquidated. The rediscovery of the female victim had momentous consequences:

Studies of domestic violence, rape, and sexual harassment have been central to the feminist case since the mid-sixties. Feminist victimology was to create enormous theoretical problems for the radical paradigm in criminology. . . . Radical criminology had tended to focus on crimes of the powerful and on the way in which vulnerable groups in society are criminalized. All very worthy stuff, but the traditional concern of criminology—crimes occurring within and between the working class—was a conceptual no-go area. This was part of a general tendency in radical thought to idealize their historical subject (in this case the working class) and to play down intra-group conflict, blemishes and social disorganization. But the power of the feminist

case resulted in a sort of cognitive schizophrenia amongst radicals . . .[72]

Left realism then had one beginning in the female victim and
the acknowledgement that it was difficult for radicals to find
anything politically, morally, or intellectually commendable to
say about her condition or her assailant. It had another beginning in the American, Canadian, British national and local
victimization surveys of the 1970s and 1980s. Survey after
survey demystified the radical demystification of crime. It
became increasingly evident that it was not the *bourgeoisie* but
the proletariat who were the victims of crime, that they were
less capable of coping with crime when they *were* victimized,
and that crime was a very major problem in their lives, a
problem that threatened to subvert community and destroy
happiness:

There was a schizophrenia about crime on the left where crimes
against women and immigrant groups were quite rightly an object of
concern, but other types of crime were regarded as being of little
interest or somehow excusable. Part of this mistake stems . . . from
the belief that property offences are directed solely against the bourgeoisie and that violence against the person is carried out by amateur
Robin Hoods in the course of their righteous attempts to redistribute
wealth. All of this is, alas, untrue.[73]

Indeed, chapters of the major manifesto for left realism, Lea
and Young's *What is to be Done About Law and Order?* were
themselves stolen on two separate occasions. Radical criminology had had a brutal confrontation with the facts of victimization.

Left realism has set itself a number of tasks. The first, and
most important, is a programme of empirical enquiry. It is no
longer enough to continue rehearsing the arguments of Marx
and Engels. There are new facts of crime, deviance, victimization, and social control to be discovered and, newly financed,
the radical criminologist intends to discover them. Thus, the
British Crime Surveys of 1982 and 1984 were held to be insufficiently attentive to the victimization of women and ethnic
minorities, and the Islington Crime Survey was one answer. It

[72] T. Jones, B. Maclean, and J. Young, *The Islington Crime Survey*, 2–3.
[73] J. Lea and J. Young, *What is to be Done about Law and Order?*, 262.

has disclosed the enormous weight of suffering which crime inflicts on people, especially older black women, living in the inner city. (For example, 30.7 per cent of the older Black women interviewed lived in households that had been burgled during the previous year; and 49.2 per cent of Black women between 25 and 44 had been assaulted.) In turn, crime and crime control have become identified as pressing problems for the critical criminologist. They are no longer to be dismissed as insubstantial distractions or mystifications. Crime has been redefined as painful and the police as necessary. The second task has been to rewrite radical criminology without radical censorship. The left realists seem less eager to discredit others whose politics they do not share, and they are correspondingly catholic in their range of sources and arguments. They are also less fearful of left-wing taboos. For example, *What is to be Done About Law and Order?* discusses the manner in which crime takes place *within* the working class. It also recognized the heavy participation of young British Blacks in crime, a recognition which encouraged other radicals to accuse its authors of racism. And having identified the significance of Black crime, the book could proceed to an informed, vivid, and telling analysis of the interplay between police, victims and young, marginalized Blacks in areas of high unemployment.

The argument runs that effective policing is reactive, not proactive, dependent on the willing co-operation of witnesses and victims. Yet there are particular forms of crime in the inner city that inhibit a reactive stance. Street crime, for instance, is not easy to detect, being anonymous and difficult to report. As unemployment and political marginality increase the alienation of certain groups in the inner city, so their co-operativeness recedes and the police receive less and less information that is tendered voluntarily. The police response has been 'aggressive patrol', 'saturation policing' and the harassment of young Blacks, strategies which increase marginality and animate a spiral of confrontation. Crime is thereby amplified and co-operation declines further.

Left realism is a new beginning to radical criminology and it displays a marked openness to evidence and criticism. Like the older radical criminology before it, it has a political agenda but, unlike the older criminology, it has few political anathemas. In its evolution, it is likely to become more and more a practical administrative criminology of the left, taking the problems of victimization seriously but giving a radical inflection to their solution, awarding prominence to special victims and seeking to control the police response to their needs.[74]

[74] See, for example, D. Downes and T. Ward, *Democratic Policing.*

11

Feminist Criminology

The 1980s have so far seen little that is original in theorizing about deviant behaviour. Theoretical energies are either focused elsewhere, as for example in the fresh analytical work being undertaken in the realm of social control, inspired by and engaged with the legacy of Foucault;[1] or inform the detailed empirical investigations of the social processes at work in policing, courts, and the criminal justice system in general, funding for which has been increased over the past decade, whilst that for graduate research, a prime source of theoretical innovation, has been curtailed. It is easy to discern the seeds of future crisis in this staunching of fresh talent. In the main, however, this lull in theoretical innovation is an opportunity for normal science: the plethora of theories outlined above have in general far outpaced the capacity of criminologists to explore their potential in all but the most selective fashion. Indeed, from the late 1970s to date the most notable development in theorizing about deviance has been the emergence of what has been termed 'feminist criminology', a diverse body of work united by the critical view that the understanding of the criminality of women, and the role of gender in theories of deviance in general, have been ill served both by traditional and new criminologies.

Despite earlier statements in both Britain and the USA which anticipated much of the force of the feminist critique,[2] the emergence of feminist criminology is generally assigned to the publication of Carol Smart's *Women, Crime and Criminology* in 1977.[3] Though not without its critics among female

[1] See in particular D. Garland and P. Young (eds.), *The Power to Punish*; S. Cohen, *Visions of Social Control*; D. Garland, *Punishment and Welfare*.

[2] F. Heidensohn, 'The Deviance of Women: A Critique and an Enquiry'; M. Chesney-Lind, 'The Judicial Enforcement of the Female Sex Role'; D. Klein, 'The Etiology of Female Crime: A Review of the Literature'.

[3] L. Gelsthorpe and A. Morris, 'Feminism and Criminology in Britain', p. 221.

criminologists,[4] and received sceptically by some male sociologists of deviance,[5] the work of those to the fore in feminist criminology has tended to reaffirm rather than challenge Smart's fundamental analysis. It is worth looking in some detail at her critique of the field as a template for feminist criminology in the past decade.

The basis for Smart's critique is that, not only is there a paucity of material on female criminality, but also what does exist:

shares an entirely uncritical attitude towards sexual stereotypes of women and girls. From Lombroso and Ferrero (1895) to Cowie, Cowie and Slater (1968) and from W. I. Thomas (1923) to Konopka (1966) the same attitudes and presuppositions reappeared, confirming the biologically determined inferior status of women not only in conventional society but also in the 'world' of crime and delinquency. [Despite rare exceptions], the majority of these studies refer to women in terms of their biological impulses and hormonal balance or in terms of their domesticity, maternal instinct and passivity.[6]

The neglect of female criminality by the predominantly male criminological profession had several undesirable consequences. First, the 'arrested development' of the subject as regards female offenders left it ossified at the positivist stage of development. Women offenders alone are subject to a form of intellectual atavism aping the Lombrosian theory of crime: theorizing female deviance is a throwback to the earliest stage of criminological evolution. Second, policies and attitudes towards female criminality mirrored such determinisms. 'In advanced industrial societies, there tends to be an a priori assumption that women are irrational, compulsive, and slightly neurotic. Criminological theories have reflected this predominant paradigm.'[7] Adolescent girls face much higher risks of institutionalization than boys for non-criminal forms of sexual 'deviance'. Such regimes as the 'new' Holloway prison confirmed the biological determinist view, with therapy but no vocational training for women prisoners. The

[4] See, for example, A. Campbell, *Girl Delinquents*, ch. 7.
[5] P. Rock, review of C. Smart, 'Women, Crime and Criminology'.
[6] C. Smart, op. cit., xiii–xiv.
[7] Ibid. 111.

'sick' role-model 'is a consequence of the failure of criminological theorists to explicate or treat as topics for analysis the understandings which they share with those engaged in formulating penal policy.'[8] Third, unreconstructed notions about women's 'nature' have lent undue prominence to 'sexual deviance' as the focus of inquiry appropriate to the study of female criminality. 'Double standards' become institutionalized across the board in theory, research, law, treatment, and control. Thus, prostitution is more studied than rape, as an example of female pathology—despite the male clientele—while rape, when it is studied at all, leans heavily towards the imputation of victim precipitation,[9] or on the need to protect the accused against false conviction. Though Smart overlooks his work, Heidensohn has pointed out (1985)[10] that even so relatively sophisticated a theorist as Albert Cohen assumed that 'female delinquency is relatively specialized. It consists overwhelmingly of sexual delinquency or of involvement in situations that are likely to "spill over" into overt sexuality.'[11] To paraphrase Gouldner, patriarchally inclined criminologists have portrayed the female deviant as 'woman on her back, rather than woman fighting back'.

In their concern to expose the defects of both classical and contemporary studies of female criminality, feminist criminologists have been energized as much by the belief that the task has been unduly neglected by their male colleagues and predecessors, as by the view that such work has exerted a malign effect on policy and control. Since the work of Matza,[12] zapping the positivists has become almost a spectator sport in the sociology of deviance, as indeed in sociology in general, encouraging forms of intellectual laziness[13] which have invited counter-attack by more sophisticated defenders of positivism.[14] By contrast, the perceived resilience of the Lombrosian underground in the realm of female deviance and control has provoked every sign of close and attentive reading of key sources by feminist criminologists such as Smart and Heidensohn. Tedious as it

---

[8] Ibid. 45.   [9] M. Amir, *Patterns in Forcible Rape*.
[10] See F. Heidensohn, *Women and Crime*.
[11] A. K. Cohen, *Delinquent Boys*, p. 144.
[12] D. Matza, *Delinquency and Drift*.
[13] N. Walker, *Behaviour and Misbehaviour: Explanations and Non-explanations*.
[14] P. S. Cohen, 'Is Positivism Dead?'.

may be to the jaded palate, the defects of criminological positivism have to be exposed once again, though this time with a female rather than a male subject as the target for concern. The work of Lombroso and Ferrero is not,[15] in their view, an antique intellectual curio, but a living body of thought, setting an agenda that is still operative: the subordination of women to the view that female crime is biological destiny, a view long since dispelled in the case of men.

The durability of the Lombrosian legacy in relation to female criminality is not simply due to its neglect as a topic, but inheres in the long-standing prescriptions about the female role and the 'essence' of the nature of women. Lombroso and Ferrero thus accounted for their finding fewer signs of degeneration among female, by comparison with male, offenders by resorting to the view that 'as all women are relatively "primitive", the criminals amongst them would not be highly visible and would be less degenerate than their male counterparts'.[16] Citing their belief that the greater conservatism of women must be sought 'in the immobility of the ovule compared with the zoosperm', Smart links their justification for the view that 'the born female criminal was perceived to have all the criminal qualities of the male plus all the worst characteristics of women, namely cunning, spite and deceitfulness'[17] with the confusions between sex and gender, and the attribution of masculine traits to female offenders, later to recur in the work of Pollak and others. The work of Cyril Burt[18] escapes her net, but he tended to this view, referring to posturing as 'masculine hobbledehoys'[19] as typical of female delinquents. The early theorists indeed gave more coverage to female delinquency than those writing after World War II: pictures of 'Girl Aged $18\frac{11}{12}$' are included as well as those of such oddly immortalized boy delinquents as 'B.I. $(15\frac{7}{12})$'.[20] The combination of the 'worst of both sexes' led to attributions of a third abnormality in this conception of the born female criminal: the lack of maternal instinct. In this respect, Lombroso and Ferrero reproduced in scientistic form the set of common-sense beliefs about female

---

[15] C. Lombroso and W. Ferrero, *The Female Offender*.
[16] C. Smart, op. cit. 32.   [17] Ibid. 33.
[18] C. Burt, *The Young Delinquent*.
[19] Ibid. 217.   [20] Ibid. 214 and frontis.

criminality which is exemplified in the apparently greater popular detestation of Myra Hindley, the accomplice of Ian Brady in the notorious 'Moors Murders' of several children. The majority of female offenders are not, however, so depicted: Lombroso and Ferrero viewed them as inferior criminals to the male, inadequate and more easily caught. In this respect, Pollak[21] was later to take the opposite view, whilst sharing their tendency to essentialize both female nature and female criminality.

The work of Pollak so perfectly encapsulates every feminist heresy that it might be said that, if it did not exist, it would have been necessary to invent it. Pollak's main empirical contention is that rates of female crime are much the same as those of male crime, but appear far lower because of under-reporting, lower detection, and greater leniency in prosecution and sentencing. None of these assertions is particularly outrageous, and some self-report studies can be found to lend some credence to at least the basis of the first assertion, that the disparity between 'real' and official rates of crime is quite marked for first offences,[22] and reduces the sex differential in general to two to one rather than several to one in respect of boys and girls. However, it was the manner of exposition and the nature of the theories he advanced that strained the credulity of successive generations of criminologists, though Heidensohn points out that some orthodox texts dealt quite respectfully with Pollak. First, Pollak sought evidence of greater female criminality, mainly in domestic and employment spheres, using highly problematic sources, and ignoring the potential for 'masked' male criminality in these selfsame contexts. Secondly, he imputed to women the time-worn catalogue of vices, such as cunning, deviousness, and deceit, as a way of accounting for the putative 'concealment' of their crimes. Thirdly, although giving cultural factors some weight, he located the ultimate source of legendary female deceitfulness in the woman's capacity to simulate sexual arousal. 'Thus rather than considering the implications of the sexual politics which produce a situation in which many women endure intercourse when they are neither aroused nor acquiescent, Pollak takes the existence

---

[21] O. Pollak, *The Criminality of Women*.
[22] M. Gold, *Delinquent Behaviour in an American City*.

of a passive engagement in sexual activity as a basis of assumptions about women's ambiguous attitude towards honesty and deceit.'[23] Fourthly, credence is lent to the 'chivalry' hypothesis, the claim that police and courts deal leniently with women offenders, being both self-deceiving and deceived about the essentially passive nature of women—a myth nurtured to justify women's inferior social status. 'However, in spite of an apparent recognition of the darker side of chivalry and the possibility of scapegoating the "fallen" woman, Pollak neglects to incorporate these elements into his study.'[24] While Lombroso and Ferrero were at least working in sympathy with the grain of their time—a period that also saw the rise of eugenics and the widespread acceptance of social Darwinism[25]—Pollak's study bore no resemblance to the then burgeoning sociological theories of crime and delinquency. As Sutherland and Cressey pointed out in a dismissive reference to Pollak's work,[26] the latter had made an earlier foray into the realm of hidden criminality among the aged.

A more formidable figure in the pantheon of un-feminist criminologists is that of W. I. Thomas, author of such key interactionist insights as: 'What men define as real is real in its consequences'. Applying that dictum to his study of female delinquency, *The Unadjusted Girl*,[27] feminist criminologists have found it to be depressingly accurate. For what Thomas defined as real was that the 'source of female criminality, which he believed to be mainly sexual, was the breakdown of the traditional restraints on women who formerly would not have thought of working outside the home or marrying outside the ethnic or community group . . . Because they have been most repressed, therefore, Thomas argued that women are more likely to become "maladjusted" when social sanctions are removed.'[28] On this basis, Thomas favoured the earliest possible intervention by welfare agencies into the lives of 'pre-delinquent' girls, and resistance to further moves away from

[23] C. Smart, op. cit. 84.

[24] O. Pollak, op. cit. 50.

[25] R. Hofstadter, *Social Darwinism in American Thought*; D. J. Kevles, *In the Name of Eugenics: Genetics and the Uses of Human Heredity*.

[26] E. Sutherland and D. Cressey, *Principles of Criminology*, 110, 112.

[27] W. I. Thomas, *The Unadjusted Girl*.

[28] C Smart, op. cit. 41–2.

existing social relations. The more enduring legacy of his work is to be found in the impetus it gave to the focus on treating individual maladjustment so characteristic of social work agencies, and the shying-away from any analysis of the structurally wrought constraints on improvements in women's social and economic situation. More damningly, Thomas is seen as the most authoritative link in the chain of criminologists lending their voice to the resistance to female emancipation, on the grounds that it would inevitably entail an increase in female deviance. This issue was later to become explicit in the work of Adler.[29]

Contemporary studies of female criminality are divided into those that carry on the classical tradition of Lombroso and Ferrero, Thomas and Pollak, with no fundamental change to the terms of reference they set; and work in the field of role theory which takes the social differentiation of gender roles as the point of departure for analysis, thus breaking with the biological and psychological determinism of the classical tradition. Smart sees marked continuity between the Lombrosian tradition and the study by Cowie, Cowie, and Slater[30] which takes an institutionalized sample of girls as representative of delinquents; which takes sex roles to be constitutionally predetermined; and which reduces social and cultural factors to 'channels' for abnormal biological states. Chromosomes rather than culture are seen as the root of the problem. The work of Thomas is influential in the study by Konopka,[31] with its emphasis on liberal treatment strategies as the most appropriate response to female delinquency: although sympathetic to the problems posed by poverty and unequal opportunities for women, these are viewed as secondary to personal maladjustment. Both fail to distinguish the biological variable of sex from the socially constructed and culturally fluid character of gender.

It was this crucial distinction that opened fresh possibilities within criminology, as well as sociology in general. From the late 1960s, presaged by such pioneering works as Hannah Gavron's *The Captive Wife*,[32] a veritable flood of sociological

[29] F. Adler, *Sisters in Crime*.
[30] J. Cowie, V. Cowie, and E. Slater, *Delinquency in Girls*.
[31] G. Kcnopka, *The Adolescent Girl in Conflict*.
[32] H. Gavron, *The Captive Wife*.

work, which had its philosophical, historical, and aesthetic counterpart, challenged taken-for-granted axioms about the nature, status, and role of women in contemporary society, and sought with varying success to mount a feminist critique and alternative mode of study to covertly male chauvinist orthodoxy. Though characteristically lagging a decade behind, early work in this vein in criminology mapped out an agenda for the analysis of female criminality in terms of 'such factors as differential socialisation, differential illegitimate opportunity structures and differential social reaction'.[33] Although focusing on such neglected topics as the extent to which the greater conformity of women may be attributable to quite distinct methods of socialization and supervision during childhood, and the generally subordinate character of their participation in crime as reflecting their role and status in the social structure in general, Smart argues that work until the mid-1970s still lacked the capacity to 'situate the discussion of sex roles within a structural explanation of the social origins of those roles'.[34] Nor did it address the motivation of those women who did engage in crime. She concluded by arguing that the time for a feminist criminology was ripe, but no precise shape could be given to its character. There was the clear risk of ghettoization on the one hand, tokenism on the other. Recognizing that a 'critique alone cannot constitute a new theoretical approach',[35] further research was needed before the goal of a 'women's perspective' could be achieved, on such questions as typical patterns of offending, the 'leniency' hypothesis, the treatment of female deviants and the role of gender in the framing and execution of laws.

In a paper on feminism and criminology in Britain, Gelsthorpe and Morris[36] take stock of what has been achieved in the decade following the publication of Smart's critique. Though much has been accomplished to redress the balance, and undo the neglect of gender in the study of crime, deviance, and control, they assert that 'a feminist criminology cannot exist.' As in sociology in general, 'just as we had to talk of

---

[33] F. Heidensohn, op. cit.; D. Hoffman-Bustamente, 'The Nature of Female Criminality'; K. Rosenhan, 'Female Deviance and the Female Sex Role'.
[34] C. Smart, op. cit. 89.   [35] Ibid. 183.
[36] L. Gelsthorpe and A. Morris, op. cit.

"feminisms", we have to talk of feminist criminologies, or, better still, feminist perspectives within criminology'.[37] Shared concerns are the opposition to positivism, stereotypical images of women, the use of methodologies sympathetic to such concerns, and the analytical centrality of gender and the subordination of women. In both sociology and criminology, however, the active pursuit of such concerns is far from transforming the subject, and the study of female criminality and its control, as well as the issue of gender in more general theories, faces constant problems of marginalization, incorporation, and tokenism.

Gelsthorpe and Morris, following Heidensohn,[38] regard existing theories as deformed by the almost unrelieved focus on the criminality of males and the invisibility or, at best, marginality of women and girls to the field. Nor can the situation be remedied by 'inserting' women into theories already formed on so patriarchal a basis: 'These critiques demonstrated that theories of criminality developed from and validated on men had limited relevance for explaining women's crime.'[39] On this view, this book should be titled 'Understanding Male Deviance', and has indeed been criticized by Heidensohn for neglecting gender in the assessment of the validity of the various theories.[40] They acknowledge, in criticism of a purely gender-based view, that criminological theories have neglected other variables: crimes of the powerful, ethnicity, and other 'blind spots'. Secondly, emptying such theories of sexism does not render them valid. Thirdly, 'masculinity' has been subject to stereotyping. Fourthly, variables mediating the significance of gender, such as class and race, tend to be ignored by feminist criminologists. Fifthly, sources of sexism tend to be analysed one-dimensionally, emanating from some global notion of men, or from the capitalist mode of production. The study of victimization constitutes the sole area in which gender has transformed research,[41] though even here the focus is on women's fear of crime, rather than their subordination to male domination as the source of that fear.[42]

---

[37] Ibid. 225.   [38] F. Heidensohn, op. cit.

[39] L. Gelsthorpe and A. Morris, op. cit. 226.

[40] F. Heidensohn, 'Women and Crime: Questions for Criminology'.

[41] R. Matthews and J. Young (eds.), *Confronting Crime*; T. Jones, B. Maclean, and J. Young, *The Islington Crime Survey*.

[*See p. 282 for n. 42*]

The substantive achievements of the past decade may, however, be more impressive than this self-appraisal from a feminist perspective might allow. Three substantive areas where
significant work has been accomplished are (1) the 'female
emancipation leads to crime' debate; (2) the invalidation of the
'leniency' hypothesis; and (3) the emergence from within
control theory of a gender-based theory of both male and
female delinquency. Nor does this begin to exhaust the
diversity of work in other respects. The contribution of women
to the subject has expanded momentously over the last ten
years or so, as has the contribution of writing on women, irrespective of its feminist credentials. Notably, Campbell has
explored the extent and character of female delinquency, and
found no support for Albert Cohen's view that it is predominantly sexual. Rather, it is manifest across the range of offences,
though with much lower prevalence than is the case for males
in all but a few offences, such as shoplifting, where gender-role
characteristics suggest greater exposure to 'consumer fetishism'.[43] Nor are girls so resistant to ganging as has often been
assumed; but within the gang, they can be seen to play roles
reflective of the subordinate and supportive female role in the
wider society.[44] Fighting among girls is far more prevalent than
is conventionally assumed, but lacks the group character of
much male violence.[45] Carlen has shown the diversity of ways
into delinquency, and their motivational complexity, for a
small number of 'criminal women'.[46] Welsh[47] documents how
the 'manufacture of excitement' is as real a motive for girls'
delinquency as for boys, though girls were subject to exclusion
from more serious forays by the male group. The capacity of
adolescent girls to practise more serious offences, such as
burglary, is demonstrated by Player.[48] An accumulation of
studies is now beginning to provide the makings of a basis for
the depiction of female crime and delinquency that forbid its
reduction to sexual role-frustration. Even so, the paucity of

---

[42] E. Stanko, 'Typical Violence, Normal Precaution: Men, Women, and Inter-
personal Violence in England, Wales, Scotland and the USA'.

[43] A. Campbell, *Girl Delinquents*.   [44] A. Campbell, *The Girls in the Gang*.

[45] A. Campbell, 'Self-report of Fighting by Females'.

[46] P. Carlen, *Criminal Women*.

[47] S. Welsh, 'The Manufacture of Excitement in Police–Juvenile Encounters'.

[48] E. Player, 'Women and Crime in the City'.

ethnographic evidence about female deviance remains marked. We really know very little about how girls grow up and what their involvement with gangs and subcultures might be.[49]

Female Emancipation and Crime

That females commit markedly fewer crimes than males, of a generally less serious character, and are less likely to persist after a first conviction, has been acknowledged by criminologists (with the single exception of Pollak) for most of the past century. Recent work has suggested that women have a lower threshold of shame and guilt than men, and are more prone to 'deviance disavowal' as a result.[50] Barbara Wootton wrote in short that 'if men behaved like women, the courts would be idle and the prisons empty'.[51] Two sets of theories have addressed this difference quite explicitly. Subcultural theories have assumed that females pursue less criminogenic and more attainable goals than men, namely marriage and family life, and are therefore insulated from the social sources of delinquency, the main exception being the strain to sexual deviance. Control theories specify with some precision the far more intensive and extensive informal social controls that are brought to bear on girls rather than boys, which constitute powerful inhibitors against criminality. In so far as female emancipation operates to weaken or alter either or both sets of conditions, to that extent, it can be argued, females will converge with males in their exposure to criminogenic influences. The assertion that such a consequence has already flowed from the activities of the Women's Liberation movement, in all its forms, or that such a consequence will necessarily occur in the future should emancipation be actualized more tangibly than is currently the case, is strongly contested by feminist criminologists. In the context of the crude ideological battles that have been fought around the issue of the 'maternal deprivation' of delinquent children by working mothers,[52] it is

[49] A. McRobbie and J. Garber, 'Girls and Subcultures'.
[50] R. Morris, 'Female Delinquency and Relational Problems' and 'Attitudes Towards Delinquency by Delinquents, Non-delinquents and their Friends'.
[51] B. Wootton, *Social Science and Social Pathology*.
[52] P. Morgan, *Child Care: Sense and Fable*; M. Rutter, *Maternal Deprivation Reassessed*.

not surprising that such a proposition should be fiercely challenged. For the 'female emancipation leads to more female crime' thesis offers a new guise for the same old double standard: the Angel in the House must not—for the sake of the social order—be allowed to 'fall'.

The thesis that the fall from grace has already begun, and that both the extent and character of female crime have converged quite significantly with those of males, has been argued by Adler[53] and Simon.[54,55] In the most rigorous review of the available evidence, Box concludes that when trends in crime are properly related to social and economic indicators of liberation, on the one hand, and economic marginalization, on the other, it is the latter which best accounts for the modest convergence in property crime rates between the sexes; and no change in rates of violent crimes is evident on that basis between 1951 and 1979. The 'new violent' female offender is a myth.[56] Even the convergence in convictions for property crime can be seen as the effect of changes in arrest and prosecution practice resulting from perceived changes in the criminality of women: though, on that basis, one would have expected as great, or greater, a rise in female rates of violent crime. Also, if it is indeed the economic marginalization of women over the past three decades which best accounts for property crime convergence, then female emancipation in its most basic form has not occurred at all—a view which most feminist sociologists hold. In that respect, the debate remains open. It should be emphasized, however, that the 'emancipation causes more female crime' view assumes that structured inequalities are held constant, when the preconditions for its attainment make such an assumption improbable.

Leniency and Control

The view that women and girls are treated more leniently, for reasons of 'chivalry' or self-deception, so commonsensically proposed by Pollak but quite widely shared, has been rebutted

[53] F. Adler, op. cit.
[54] R. Simon, *Women and Crime*.
[55] F. Adler and R. Simon (eds.), *The Criminology of Deviant Women*.
[56] S. Box, *Power, Crime, and Mystification*, ch. 5; F. Heidensohn, op. cit.

and in significant respects even reversed by a number of studies over the past ten years. In the most authoritative study of sentencing, Farrington and Morris[57] found that the lighter sentences passed on women offenders in a Cambridge court were accounted for by the nature of their offences and their previous convictions. Similar findings explained the greater proportion of females cautioned by the police.[58] In a review of the evidence, Heidensohn[59] finds much support for the view that women are doubly punished when their rule-breaking is compounded by perceived role-breaking. Carlen's interviews with Scottish sheriffs[60] elicited views consonant with a dual morality that justifies imprisonment more readily for women offenders who have 'failed' as mothers. The Cambridge study found that divorced or separated women, or those from 'deviant' family backgrounds, were more likely to receive severe sentences. This holds open the possibility that women who conform to the conventional female role do benefit from judicial discretion, for which some support exists in American research:[61] Eaton[62] has found, however, that family and employment factors of mitigation are deployed similarly for males and females alike. But it is in the realms of 'protective' custody for non-criminal behaviour that dual morality looms largest: girls are far more likely than boys to be 'taken into care' for a range of misconduct which may include truancy as well as sexual waywardness.[63] Leniency is also more apparent in cases of domestic violence for men who victimize their female partners, where non-prosecution is the norm;[64] and in cases of corporate or white-collar crime, which women are rarely given the occupational opportunities to commit, but where non-prosecution tends to be the norm. In these major respects, women—by comparison with men—are 'under-protected and

    [57] D. Farrington and A. Morris, 'Sex, Sentencing and Reconvictions'.
    [58] C. Fisher and R. Mawby, 'Juvenile Delinquency and Police Discretion in an Inner City Area'; S. Landau and G. Nathan, 'Juveniles and the Police'.
    [59] F. Heidensohn, op. cit., chs. 4 and 5.   [60] P. Carlen, *Women's Imprisonment*.
    [61] I. Nagel, 'Sex Differences in the Processing of Criminal Defendants'.
    [62] M. Eaton, 'Mitigating Circumstances: Familiar Rhetoric'; 'Documenting the Defendant: Placing Women in Social Inquiry Report'; *Justice for Women?*
    [63] M. Casburn, *Girls Will be Girls*.
    [64] R. Dobash and R. Dobash, *Violence Against Wives: A Case Against Patriarchy*; 'The Nature and Antecedents of Violent Events'; S. Edwards, *Female Sexuality and the Law*; 'Police Attitudes and Dispositions in Domestic Disputes: the London Study'.

over-controlled'.[65] Prostitution is perhaps the single most notorious instance of 'double standards', with a long history of vilification by statute and stereotype. 'Common prostitutes' are 'fallen' women: men, whether prostitutes or clients, escape both forms of censure.[66] Moreover, despite the strong economic incentives for women to become prostitutes in the context of job discrimination, motivation is usually ascribed to psychogenic causes.

Gender, Crime, and Social Control

In two notable studies, Hagan, Simpson, and Gillis[67] have directly addressed the relations between gender, crime, and social control, using a synthesis of control and conflict theories of deviance. Their first study, based on data gathered in 1976 from a mixed-sex sample of several hundred Toronto high school adolescents, tested and explored the theory that the self-reported rates of delinquency both within and between males and females would be linked to differentials in socialization and informal social control. 'There is a sexually stratified inverse relationship between structurally differentiated processes of social control such that women are more frequently the instruments and objects of informal social controls'.[68] Segregative formal control is seen as emerging with industrialization, with the site for informal social control increasingly confined to the private realm of the home, from which men are increasingly absent, and to which women became increasingly confined. Men therefore became increasingly subject to formal social control, from which women were relatively insulated. The exclusion of women from the 'rat race' and their lower crime rate are jointly rooted in family-based patterns of informal social control. It was stressed that informal social control is not synonymous with less, but probably more, control; and that exposure to formal and informal controls are inversely related. Also, even 'career' women tend to inherit the responsibility for the care

[65] D. Downes and T. Ward, *Democratic Policing*, 17.

[66] M. Sumner, *Prostitution and Images of Women*.

[67] J. Hagan, J. Simpson, and A. Gillis, 'The Sexual Stratification of Social Control'; 'The Class Structure of Gender and Delinquency: Toward a Power-Control Theory of Common Delinquent Behaviour'.

[68] 'The Sexual Stratification of Social Control', 25.

and control of children, so that inter-generationally transmitted gender roles flow from the earliest experiences.

The data bore out the hypotheses that subjecting girls to a dense array of informal social controls, primarily mediated maternally, would ensure greater compliance; while young males are freed to pursue more active forms of risk-taking, with the consequence that they are more at risk of encountering the world of formal control. Males more than females defined risk-taking positively; defined delinquency more positively; and engaged in delinquency more frequently and seriously. The control variables also produced the predicted relationships within gender groups. On this basis, Hagan, Simpson, and Gillis conclude that, accurate as Dennis Wrong's critique of functionalist sociology may be with regard to men, women *are* in effect over-socialized.

A key omission in the study was the interaction between sexual and social stratification, which is rectified in their second study,[69] carried out in 1979 on a similar sample in Toronto. Drawing more fully on a neo-Marxian class analysis than is usually the case, they differentiate four groups in the stratification order: employers, managers, and employed and unemployed workers. The power variable was therefore entered into the frame as well as control variables. Class was found to be unrelated to the common forms of delinquency measured, with the predicted exception that the children of employers were reportedly the most delinquent, being highest on power and least fettered by both formal and informal controls. Introducing gender revealed a decrease in the relationship between gender and common forms of delinquency with each step down the class structure.[70] In sum, as Bonger asserted over half a century ago (1916), differences in the way of life between the sexes are at their height in the upper reaches of society,[71] at their minimum in the lower working class. Among children of parents excluded from the labour market, delinquency

---

[69] J. Hagan, A. Gillis, and J. Simpson, 'The Class Structure of Gender and Delinquency . . .'.   [70] Ibid. 1151.

[71] Well caught in Flaubert's parody: '*Young gentleman*: Always sowing wild oats; he is expected to do so. Astonishment when he doesn't. *Young lady*: Utter these words with diffidence. All young ladies are pale, frail, and always pure. Prohibit, for their good, every kind of reading, all visits to museums, theatres, and especially to the monkey house at the zoo.' (J. Barzun (tr.), *Flaubert's Dictionary of Accepted Ideas*, 84.)

approached unity by gender, once parental controls are taken into account. It is stressed that the most serious forms of delinquency are not adequately covered by the research design, based on Hirschi's self-report questionnaire:[72] but such forms of delinquency are so uncommon that adequate sampling across all social groups would be scarcely feasible with current resources.

However impressive the analysis, and suggestive the data may be, we remain somewhat sceptical about too great a reliance on the self-report technique, applied to in-school populations, and lacking detailed specification of community type. Reiss and Rhodes established almost thirty years ago that community type was a key variable in delinquency rates:[73] working-class delinquency rates tended to increase with the degree of class homogeneity. What such work should stimulate is a redressing of the balance in respects other than gender alone, and by methods other than self-reported delinquency alone: in particular, the filling of the gap in ethnographies of 'employer class' crime and delinquency.

Criticism

Many feminist criminologists have gone much further than theorizing and deploring the neglect of female criminality, and defining priorities to remedy past omissions. They have made of the issue a criterion for the validity or invalidity of criminological theory. Thus Box and Harris put the case that 'any causal explanation of crime which does not include gender-related factors cannot be valid.'[74] Gelsthorpe and Morris[75] argue that 'Theories are weak if they do not apply to half of the potential criminal population; women, after all, experience the same deprivations, family structures, and so on that men do. Theories of crime should be able to take account of both men's and women's behaviour and to highlight those factors which operate differently on men and women.' And Heidensohn has stated: 'Criminology is poorer in all its forms (because it has)

---

[72] T. Hirschi, *Causes of Delinquency*, ch. 9.

[73] A. Reiss and A. Rhodes, 'The Distribution of Juvenile Delinquency in the Social and Class Structure'.

[74] F. Heidensohn, op. cit. 3.

[75] L. Gelsthorpe and A. Morris, 'Feminism and Criminology in Britain', 231.

not yet fully accepted and integrated the importance of gender, or its interaction with such factors as race and class.'[76]

Central as its role should be in the sociology of deviance, we do not regard the significance of gender in quite such stark terms. The impulses behind theorizing are diverse, but ultimately irrelevant to the criteria that govern the evaluation of its validity. It so happens that criminological theory has been crime-led, and that the subjects around whom theorizing has been formed have been predominantly white, urban, lower-class, and usually adolescent males in advanced industrial capitalist societies. We do not share the view (advanced by Smart) that the focus was chosen primarily because of govern-mental or State concern: it seemed to successive generations of sociologists—particularly in the post-war context of increasing affluence—that commonsensical and psychogenic explana-tions were most deficient in explaining the extent and character of delinquency amongst this sector of the population. In the process, the criminality and/or greater conformity of every other group became marginalized or bracketed away: not only females, but ethnic minorities, the middle-aged and elderly, rural communities, the middle and upper classes, corpora-tions, and both State socialist and developing countries were neglected as subjects. It is a massive catalogue of default, but it is not to be explained by patriarchy or an obeisance to State control. It may well be that the crime-led character of crimino-logy was profoundly mistaken, based on a misconception of what constituted crime (a revaluation begun systematically only with the emergence of labelling theory in the early 1960s); and that the questions posed were too inattentive to the under-lying problem of order. But that was the task consigned to mainstream sociological theory, though the Gluecks and control theorists took it as their point of entry into the field. The possibilities opened up by these approaches have already enlarged the scope of the study of female criminality in par-ticular and the significance of gender for deviance and control more generally.

The theories whose character we have sought to convey have, in our view, more to offer in the pursuit of the concerns of feminist criminologists than they have been prepared to

[76] F. Heidensohn, 'Women and Crime: Questions for Criminology', 27.

allow.[77] Matza's concept of 'drift' is a priori as applicable to female as to male subjects. The concepts of 'labelling', 'career', 'stigma' and the like should be as fruitful for the understanding of female deviance as that of males. In terms of substantive theories, Albert Cohen did not preclude girls from subcultural formations: though he may have erred in assuming too readily that his formulations of cause and effect did not apply at all to females, and that sexual deviancy exhausted their repertoire. The 'manufacture of excitement' is as germane to an understanding of female as of male delinquency.[78] The differentials in crime rates by age and sex remain central to theorizing delinquency, but existing theories as to why that should be so have not been supplanted by our greater awareness of the oppression of women: that has tended to reinforce their premises. Much theory is a moveable feast. A number of the older, apparently male-centred theories, have a good deal of utility in explaining female crime. Elaine Player, for example, found anomie theory the most satisfactory framework for explaining female burglary and robbery.[79] Literary convention has played a part in suggesting otherwise. For instance, although Matza uses the masculine pronoun throughout, his archetypal deviants in *Becoming Deviant* were all women. This raises the question of whether feminist criminologists are right in asserting that criminology has so markedly ignored women. Nor is the overt neglect of female criminality and the significance of gender quite as marked as the critiques insist. Heidensohn[80] and Morris[81] in Britain, and Mann[82] in the USA, have written texts which omit to mention Paul Cressy's *The Taxi-Dance Hall* and Reckless's *Vice in Chicago*. Pauline Morris's *Prisoners and their Families* somehow escapes attention in what is defined as uncharted territory. Willis's alleged attachment to the glamour of machismo, a general shortcoming of male sociologists according to Heidensohn, was accompanied by an unrivalled ability to situate the sexism and racism of his subjects.[83] Such persistent defects mar an otherwise powerful case.

It is claimed that the neglect of the positivist remainder in

[77] Cf. E. Leonard, *Women, Crime and Society*.   [78] S. Welsh, op. cit.
[79] E. Player, op. cit.   [80] F. Heidensohn, *Women and Crime*.
[81] A. Morris, *Women, Crime and Criminal Justice*.
[82] C. Mann, *Female Crime and Delinquency*.
[83] P. Willis, *Learning to Labour*.

the field of female criminality has had untoward consequences in the treatment of female offenders. This may be so, but the proposition is as yet almost wholly unsupported by evidence: and male offenders are not totally exempt from positivist measures. The jump is made from turn-of-the-century Lombrosianism to the 'new' Holloway prison for women: but the mediating links are not supplied. It is possible that studies such as that by Pailthorpe[84] pioneered the view that psychological approaches were peculiarly appropriate for female offenders. Drawing on the work of Burt and Healy in particular, rather than Lombroso, she studied 100 women prisoners and 100 women in 'preventive and rescue' homes, using a battery of contemporary psychological tests, and finding abundant signs of maladjustment and psychopathy. Her recommendations for the establishment of non-penal hospitals and 'small laboratories' for the treatment of women *at their first conviction* may have been the germ of the eventual compromise that is Holloway: a 'psychotherapeutic' prison for women. Detailed archival work would be needed to establish whether or not the organizational memory existed some forty years and a major war later to retrieve the model, and by what links. It remains more likely that commonsensical linkages between the smallness of the number of female offenders and mental illness proved decisive: but whether or not a determined campaign by criminologists to dispel that link would have proved decisive remains dubious, given the lack of impact made by criminology on public and penal policy in Britain in other respects.

Despite these criticisms, feminist criminology, broadly defined as women's perspectives within criminology,[85] has (despite their self-deprecation about their achievement) significantly reoriented the field. All paradigms are anomalies transformed into novel focus. For feminist criminology, the absence of gender, long acknowledged as regrettable in criminology, but easily lived with, has inspired a fresh insight that theories of male criminality do not fit too readily the 'facts' of female criminality. The sociology of deviance can only benefit from addressing more creatively the question of why the oppression of women has not led to rates of crime as high as those of males.

[84] G. Pailthorpe, *Studies in the Psychology of Delinquency*.
[85] L. Gelsthorpe and A. Morris, op. cit. 225.

All new paradigms transform the banal into fresh focus: radical criminology retrieved, but then threw away, the failure to address crimes of the powerful; labelling theorists built on the truism that 'deviant behaviour is that which is so labelled'; control theorists that the real question may be 'Why don't we all deviate?'; subcultural theorists sought motives and meaning in that which was considered 'mindless'; functionalists perceived the sources of conformity in deviance; and the Chicagoans saw that deviant traditions were inescapably social, and not products of individual pathology. Feminist criminology may not be a new paradigm in this sense: but it has undeniably revitalized the exploration of existing perspectives.

Deviance Theories and Social Policy

Introduction

In general, sociologists lavish the bulk of their time and energy on teaching and research whose formal objectives are the greater understanding of the social world and the attempt to explain social phenomena with some degree of scientific rigour. Many, though by no means all, would claim some ultimate justification for their activities in the realm of the public good. It is somewhat paradoxical, therefore, that so few of their resources are devoted to political activity in general, and social policy-making in particular. Their attention to this aspect of their work is usually cursory, often altogether absent. It is accordingly important to enquire why so little has been accomplished.

The answers lie chiefly in the direction of role-definition, translatability, and salience. The first implies a division of labour in which sociological teaching and research take priority. The rigorously academic may simply cancel out the pursuit of competing priorities such as politics and policy-making. These activities have their own practitioners in other departments or in other institutions. It is up to them to utilize such materials as sociologists may furnish. In some ways, the distinction is simply that between 'pure' and 'applied' science. In other respects, issues in role-definition are far more complicated. Sociologists may actively resist the agenda-setting that a concern for 'social problems' implies. 'Sociological problems' do not necessarily coincide with 'social problems' in any but the crudest respects. To force the former into a mould formed by the latter would be as absurd as to yoke astronomy to the tasks of space exploration programmes. Translatability refers to the differences between the 'systems of relevance'[1] of sociology and social policy. The

---

[1] M. Phillipson, *Sociological Aspects*, ch. 6, contains an interesting discussion of this theme.

sociologists' mode of discourse with its employment of what Schutz termed 'second-order constructs', is in principle quite distinct from the mode of discourse of policy-makers, which is framed in terms of 'first-order constructs' embedded in the 'natural attitude' of everyday life. However, sociological theories differ greatly in their receptivity to the constructs of everyday life, and the problems of translating theories largely constructed in commonsensical terms into social policy terms are not in principle acute, whatever the practical and political obstacles to their effective implementation may be. In the case of theories which address, for instance, the social functions of crime, or the phenomenological analysis of the meanings of particular forms of deviance, the implications for social policy may be either non-existent or ineffable. Doing something about 'anomie' is far more problematic than tackling vandalism by technical means. In this chapter, we shall attempt to assess the relations between theories of deviance and their implications for politics and policy-making with these considerations in mind.

All theories of deviance have implications for policy. The linkages between theory, policy, and practice are, however, immensely variable and as yet little understood. The extent to which theories are 'taken up' in practice depends only in part on the energy and commitment of the theorist, the degree of empirical support for the theory, or the ease with which the theory can be translated into policy terms. The salience of a theory for policy-makers may have as much to do with the scope of the proposals for action, the resources required, the extent to which significant interests are engaged as parties or adversaries, and the likely ratio of costs to benefits. Even these factors are likely to be secondary to the correspondence between the theory and the policy-makers' timetables and rhetoric.

What is evident, however, is the contingent nature of the relationship between theory, research, and policy, and it would not do to presume that the sociology of deviance has fixed implications for politics. On the contrary, the influence of ideas will change from State to State, administration to administration, government department to government department, and from one division or branch of a department to another. Very often, what concerns the politician and policy official is not the academic solidity of a theory but its political relevance. For instance, the recent Canadian Federal Government Justice for Victims of Crime Initiative was addressed quite explicitly at the needs of the elderly and female victims of crime.[2] Those victims were established by Government priorities, not by research, but a victims initiative could not have neglected them in the context of the special configuration of Canadian politics in the early 1980s. It would have been naïve to imagine that an initiative could have been grounded simply in the findings of victimological research.

What is also evident is that the language and emphases of policy documents are not constructed as if they were parts of an academic discourse. They are not shaped by questions of methodology, evidence, and intellectual pedigree. On the contrary, their nuances flow from concerns about constituencies and the practicalities of implementation. To be sure, there *will* sometimes be consultation with relevant experts (although how relevant expertise is established is itself a contingent matter). From time to time, theory and research will have the effect of discouraging officials from supporting recommendations that experts consider to be naïve, discredited, or impracticable. (None the less, politicians are not always unprepared to develop policies that are sociologically unreasonable: they heed other kinds of reason as well.) More generally, theory and research will tend to be a rhetorical resource to cite when needed: it is always useful to show that proposals are well anchored. And, in that process of formulating proposals, the role of theory and theorist is frequently transformed into that of a competent authority which may be relied upon *because* it is competent. Questions of demonstration and method are typically the private business of the expert. Policy-makers do not wish continually to scrutinize the academic qualifications of their experts or the logic of their arguments. They take them on trust. In turn, theory may well creep anonymously into politics. Advice will not be tendered or examined because it is a rational extension of phenomenology or control theory. It will enter as the accredited good sense of criminologists and researchers whose job it is to brief officials and politicians. Accordingly, it is frequently

[2] See P. Rock, *A View From the Shadows*. Most of the following argument is based on the implications of that case study of Canadian policy-making.

difficult to discover the precise intellectual provenance of proposals, and it is even more difficult to keep track of them as they
assume the clothing of political argument. After all, it would
look a little absurd to defend a political proposal before one's
Cabinet colleagues on the grounds that it is an instance of
sound ethnomethodology.

A third feature of the connection between theory and social
policy is that it is pervasive, piecemeal, and incremental. New
theories are rarely catapulted like tracts or manifestos into
political settings to be accepted or rejected in their entirety.
They 'trickle' in from many sources. Literate policy-makers
and researchers will have encountered Durkheim or Marx at
university when they were young. They will meet criminal-
logists at dinner parties. They will read research reports and
newspapers. They will gossip at conferences. In all this continuous talk, questions will be asked, ideas synthesized, and
opinions formed. Quite often, officials will forget quite who was
the author and what was the origin of a particular idea. It is
never easy to fix when it was that a theory began to influence
action or action a theory. Indeed, it would be naïve to attempt
to address the problem.

One other property of that contingent relationship is the
changing influence of ideas. As political and practical circumstances fluctuate, so will there be a responsive shift in the bearing of theory and research. Circumstances will colour theory,
and theory circumstances. Let us illustrate this, again turning
to the development of the Canadian Federal Justice for Victims
of Crime Initiative. One critical turning-point in the evolution
of policies for victims in Canada was the decision, taken in the
mid-1970s, to explore the possibility of a national survey of
Canadian victims. A principal object of that decision was to
improve what is called the criminal justice data base, to learn
more about the 'dark figure of crime'. But the decision was
taken in the context of concern about the prospective abolition
of capital punishment, and there were good political and
budgetary reasons to represent it as one of a package of
measures intended to evaluate the effectiveness of programmes
established to prevent violent crime. Because there are inevitable problems about capturing very small subsamples of
victims of violence and sexual assault, victim surveys are almost

always large and expensive and they require unusually thorough planning. In turn, as proposals were drafted to survey such a vast country as Canada, it became apparent that there were major methodological problems which had first to be mastered, and work on the survey was presented as an exercise in research methodology. Canadian research staff consequently undertook quite extensive consultations about the conduct of victim surveys and, in so doing, they became acquainted with the political pre-occupations of the American administrators of the National Crime Surveys, preoccupations which turned on measuring the pain of victimization and the provision of assistance. Their new acquaintance was to be one factor encouraging the growth of a domestic Canadian interest in the provision of services to victims. The planning of the Canadian victim survey was then itself bent towards an assessment of the impact of crime. When it was finally executed, the survey was presented as an exercise designed to support the relief of victims. The survey was thus defined by a succession of practical and political concerns which it also helped to shape. There was a dialectical and evolving interchange between research and politics which makes it impossible to point to simple, unilateral effects.

Many sociologists of deviance are quite mindful of the problematic character of the association between academic ideas and political action, and there have been a number of accounts of how it can shift over time. Scull, for example, argued that the case for 'decarceration' (or the emptying of prisons and asylums) changed little between its first exposition in the mid-nineteenth and its redeployment in the mid-twentieth centuries. He argued that the reasons for its initial rejection and its later acceptance have to be explained in terms of its relevance to changes in the political economy of capitalism. Economies undergoing a 'fiscal crisis' could no longer afford an ever-growing control apparatus: there had to be retrenchment. To be sure, Scull's case has been challenged, perhaps most notably by Cohen,[3] but it does point to the importance of the political and economic frameworks of penological debate.[4]

[3] S. Cohen, *Visions of Social Control*.

[4] Cf. Banting's use of the term 'salience' in his *Poverty, Politics and Policy: Britain in the 1960s*, 10 f. For the broader social policy field, see Bulmer (ed.), 'Social Policy Research' and his 'Social Science and Social Policy', and 'The Uses of Social Research'.

Other sociologists have pointed to the manner in which long-established theories can come into their own when the times are propitious; for instance, anomie theory had been formulated for twenty years before its transposition by Cloward and Ohlin into 'opportunity structure theory', and the rapid development of the Mobilization for Youth project. Short has commented that this example:

illustrates a principle of great importance for the relation of sociological theory to social policy: that sociological theory is typically crescive, developing by slow and often uncertain increments suggested by either an empirical discovery or a conceptual modification. One implication is that whose who would leap to specific concrete social engineering proposals on the basis of new developments in sociological theory are likely to find themselves on shaky ground. There is a scarcity of both social policy-oriented theory and replicated studies demonstrating valid and reliable knowledge.[5]

The issues of role-definition, translatability, and salience combine to make it a rare occurrence for a theory of deviance to be the progenitor of action programmes or social policy changes. It is more common to find competing social policies being justified by their adherents in terms of the support they may derive from theory and research. The theories we have discussed offer distinctive explanations for deviance, and it is logically to be inferred that they offer distinctive recipes for appropriate responses to deviance in political, policy, and practical terms. The search for such correspondences reveals the strengths and weaknesses of the theories anew: for they are subjected to the constraint that they specify with some precision just what should (or should not) be changed before there can be a significant improvement in the social response to deviance. In certain respects, the implementation of social projects or policies based upon a theory can provide more exacting opportunities to test that theory more searchingly. The difficulties involved in such evaluation, and the generally negative results that have been obtained in the few instances where it has been attempted at all rigorously, will be alluded to as we deal with each perspective in turn.

[5] J. Short, jun., 'The Natural History of an Applied Theory: Differential Opportunity and Mobilization for Youth'.

The *Chicago 'School' of Sociology* produced one major project based on the characteristic theoretical assumptions of several of its leading members. The Chicago Area Project was inaugurated by Clifford Shaw and Henry McKay in 1934, and has survived in modified form to the present. The Chicagoans' definition of the role of the sociologist was quite compatible with so direct an involvement in practical intervention. Burgess and Thrasher were similarly concerned to develop responses which embodied their insights into the group nature of delinquency. Thrasher, for example, wrote:

We need a new penology which shall be penetrating in its insights into the subjective aspect of the boy's life, and which shall be much broader in scope than institutional care and the present system of probation and parole . . . He must not be treated as if he existed in a social vacuum, but . . . as a member of all the various groups to which he belongs—not merely to the gang alone, but the family, the neighbourhood, the school, the church, the occupational group, and so on.[6]

The theory of 'social disorganization' seemed readily translatable into terms of social practice. If the causes of delinquency were to be found in the attenuation of social controls born of 'social disorganization', then the most effective responses should be the fostering of such potential for social organization as did exist in the areas most affected. Since the approach stressed the inherent capacity of communities to mobilize their own social control resources, the main burden of the projects should be to enhance the capacity of local residents to take the initiative in promoting links with 'disaffiliated' youth and in seeking indigenous sources for the promotion of their welfare. Shaw and McKay were keen to avoid the ossification of social work that they claimed to be so grave a handicap to the effectiveness and credibility of the settlement houses. They argued that problems had arisen from the recruitment of outside professionals who lacked substantial interests in the areas in which they worked. They wished to promote links between local leaders and local youths in terms that were primarily personal and social rather than clinical and individualistic. They improvised a broad range of community-based programmes, the

[6] F. Thrasher, *The Gang*, 499–500.

most imaginative of which was the use of ex-offenders to act as youth workers with gangs. Their aim was to redirect rather than repress or break up the gang. At times, their enthusiasm for such redirection seemed naïve. For example, a certain innocence characterized Thrasher's advocacy of the Scout movement and the YMCA as suitable outlets for the ganging process. But the reformist zeal of such policies received support in their time, and lent a salience to strategies which still clings to their modern counterparts. The strategies of redirection, detached youth work with 'unreached', 'disaffiliated', 'un-attached', or 'unclubbable' youth (the labels changing with time and place), and the co-optation of indigenous workers, remained in whole or in part basic to the work of the New York City Youth Board in the post-war period,[7] as well as influencing the programmes of Mobilization for Youth and other youth-related programmes in the American 'War on Poverty' in the 1960s. Such strategies tended to be regarded in Britain as 'experimental' well into the post-war period.[8]

The problems of assessing the work of the Chicago Area Project have been shared by all delinquency prevention programmes.

At the bottom the difficulty rests on the fact that such programmes ... cannot by their very nature constitute more than a subsidiary element in changing the fundamental and sweeping forces which create the problems of groups and of persons or which shape human personality. Declines in rates of delinquency—the only conclusive way to evaluate delinquency prevention—may reflect influences unconnected with those of organized programs and are difficult to define and measure.[9]

Kobrin's own assessment therefore rests on 'logical and analytic grounds', which somewhat weakens the force of his conclusion that 'in all probability these achievements (of the CAP) have reduced delinquency in the program areas, as any substantial improvement in the social climate of an area must'.[10]

---

[7] See, for example, New York City Youth Board, *Reaching the Fighting Gang*.

[8] See, for example, M. Morse, *The Unattached*; and G. Goetschius and M. Tash, *Working with Unattached Youth*. The use of ex-offenders as social workers has recently resurfaced as 'new careers': see D. Briggs, *Dealing with Deviants*; and C. Covington, 'The Hammersmith Teenage Project'.

[9] S. Kobrin, 'The Chicago Area Project', 323.   [10] Ibid. 330.

The circularity of this conclusion reflects the circularity of the parent theory: if delinquency is both symptom and consequence of 'social disorganization', then social programmes to reduce such disorganization must have reduced delinquency.

Finestone challenges Kobrin's view by taking as a basis for evaluation the sheer variety of the projects generated by the CAP. He addresses the problem of assessing the variable strength or weakness of the projects as organizations by adopting certain indicators of their performance. *Inter alia*, their degree of success in fund-raising, and their degree of autonomy from State-appointed staff workers, are taken as indicators of project success. On these purely organizational terms, the most successful projects correlated inversely with the seriousness of the delinquency problem in the areas. 'The Chicago Area Project has not provided a method of coping with the problem of delinquency in its most serous form in the areas of the city with the highest rates.'[11] Finestone's own assessment is limited by the absence of time-series data which alone would warrant so strong a conclusion. However, it does much to confirm the severe limitations of so exclusive an emphasis on community controls and activities alone. Such an emphasis precludes any attempt to deal with the social and economic processes, such as the relatively unchecked expansion of industrial and commercial land-use in the inner city, which arguably erode and 'disorganize' the community from without, and which can only be tackled by more comprehensive social and economic policies.[12] Such criticisms have force rather than weight, since we have yet to establish that more fundamental changes would actually promote the reduction of crime and delinquency, or that we have the understanding to implement such changes intelligently.

Functionalist theories would seem to offer the basis for policies that are at least comprehensive in their scope. After all, the analytical aim of functionalism is nothing short of the 'total interconnectedness' of social institutions. However, as Gouldner notes,

[11] H. Finestone, *Victims of Change: Juvenile Delinquents in American Society*, 144. A similar conclusion was reached by J. Mays in his analysis of an allied, smaller-scale Liverpool project in *On the Threshold of Delinquency*.

[12] See J. Snodgrass, 'Clifford R. Shaw and Henry D. McKay', and also P. Townsend, 'Area Deprivation Policies'.

one of Functionalism's basic methodological precepts is that there are no 'causes'. Functionalism thinks of systems as mutually interacting variables rather than in terms of cause and effect. Functionalism's elementary domain assumption has always come down to this: everything influences everything else. But Functionalism has had no theory about the weighting to be assigned to different variables in the system. It has had no theory about which variables are more, and which are less important in determining the state of the system as a whole.[13]

Above all, the functionalists sought to discern hidden order in apparent disharmony, to suggest that 'when problems arise in a group, there spontaneously emerge *natural* "defense" or adaptive mechanisms that serve to restore order and equilibrium.'[14] As a result, translating functionalism into policy options was a contradiction in terms. If what appear to be problems are—at the level of 'second-order constructs'—retranscribed as solutions, then State intervention is only likely, if anything, to make matters worse. From Spencer through Durkheim to Parsons's early and middle phases, functionalists argued that the power of the State was to be kept at a minimum to allow deep evolutionary processes to hold sway. Since the State could only acquire power from interventionist policies, such policies were best avoided. 'Hands off' would be the major functionalist recommendation.

In Gouldner's view, the seeming irrelevance of functionalism to social policy (and of social policy to functionalism) began to change as the Welfare State in America began to assume growing importance, both as an instrument of conflict-resolution and resource-allocation in the American economy, and as a major source of finance for social science research. In this changing context, Gouldner somewhat cynically argues, functionalists could not maintain their attitude of simon-pure detachment from political and policy issues. Even Parsons began to adjust his scheme to take account of 'input deficits' suffered by certain socially deprived groups.[15] And in the cases of Smelser and Moore, leading functionalists undertook an attempted convergence with Marxism in the rush to accommodate social change and policy relevance to their theoretical

---

[13] A. Gouldner, *The Coming Crisis*, 346–7.
[14] Ibid. 346.   [15] Ibid. 358.

work. In the process, however, the tensions between the parent theory and its new-found applications in the policy realm became all too apparent. Functionalism lost credibility, and the 1960s witnessed the pursuit of alternative sociologies, in particular symbolic interactionism, phenomenology, and Marxism.

Ironically, Gouldner ignores the one major respect in which functionalism indirectly led to the development of one theoretical model of great relevance to the realm of policy. *Anomie theory*, in the version formulated by Merton, did indeed share with functionalism a certain opaqueness in relation to policy. It also shared a problem of translating its 'second-order constructs'—culture, deviant 'adaptations'—into the accomplishment of social organization and meaning in everyday life. But its central tenet, that the consequences for high rates of deviance of the disjunction between goals and means would be grave, *was* a causal statement of considerable scope. The strain towards deviance induced by the gap between goals and means should in principle be reducible by the narrowing of that gap. Merton did not spell out this clear, implicit directive towards more egalitarian policies in other than parenthetical terms. It did, however, provide a basis for Cloward and Ohlin to define anomie theory afresh as opportunity structure theory some twenty years later. The crucial modification was their linkage of the emergence of delinquent *subcultures* to the experience of the closure of both legitimate and illegitimate opportunities in adolescence.[16] This change provided a rationale for the Mobilization for Youth project, whose main purpose was cast in terms of opportunity *expansion*. In its turn, MFY became a major influence on the American 'War on Poverty' that dominated US domestic policy in the 1960s.

The immediate origins of MFY lay in the theoretical synthesis offered by Cloward and Ohlin in *Delinquency and Opportunity*. But its salience was partly due to their original undertaking of that task at the request of a settlement house in the Lower East Side, the Henry Street Settlement. As sociologists, they evidently embarked on the process of theorizing with the requirements of policy initiatives in mind. To some

---

[16] J. Short, jun., 'The Natural History of an Applied Theory', 199–200, discusses this issue.

extent, the shape of their formulation accounts for the ready translatability of the theory into the language of social intervention. Its coincidence with the demand for initiatives from the new reforming administration of the Kennedys lent it a salience few projects have possessed before or since in either Britain or the US. The 'new Frontier' was underfoot. 'In summary, it is our belief that most delinquent behaviour is engendered because opportunities for conformity are limited. Delinquency therefore represents *not* a lack of motivation to conform but quite the opposite: the desire to meet social expectations itself becomes the source of delinquency if the possibility of doing so is limited or non-existent.'[17] Clearly aware that translating these tenets into practice would be far from easy, they also stated that 'an appropriate program of action is not necessarily self-evident once a theory of causation has been evolved; it cannot simply be assumed that once we know what the trouble is, we will have little difficulty remedying it.'[18] The difficulties that MFY came to encounter were not foreshadowed in the planning document, mainly because the theory dealt only very indirectly with the issue of power and vested interest with which the project came to engage. The core of these problems may be presented as lying in the inconsistency of tackling at the local community level inequalities that were theorized as rooted in the wider social structure. 'In both their employment and their education programmes, the projects were cramped by their inability to supersede the limits of local action, and tackle the national problems that underlay their frustrations.'[19]

It was a major irony that theory based on a comprehensive analysis of the links between delinquency and social structure should have been translated into a project which intervened at the community level. Yet the realities of American politics ruled out more sweeping reforms, and community action programmes could be justified in terms of their efficiency as 'demonstration projects'. 'Demonstration', however, hinged on the effectiveness of research monitoring the results of the projects, and on this count the project evidently could not cope

[17] Mobilization for Youth, *A Proposal for the Prevention and Control of Delinquency by the Expansion of Opportunities*, 44–5.

[18] Ibid. viii–ix.

[19] P. Marris and M. Rein, *Dilemmas of Social Reform: Poverty and Community Action in the United States*, 124.

with the sheer complexity of the evaluation involved. MFY launched enriched educational programmes, job training schemes, vocational guidance, even on occasion actual job provision from the resources of the project itself, and embraced diverse forms of community protest. As the decade wore on, however, changes of direction multiplied, and the job of monitoring the results, already flawed by the absence of a comparative basis, tended to become routinized into administrative book-keeping.[20] Moreover, the politics of the project proved contentious almost from the outset. As Cloward and Piven stated in retrospect: 'The Great Society programs were promulgated by federal leaders in order to deal with the problems created by a new and unstable electoral constituency—namely, blacks—and to deal with this new constituency not simply by responding to its expressed interests, but by shaping and directing its political future.'[21] This view of Great Society politics corresponds with Gouldner's assertion that some sociological backing is actively sought by governments to help legitimate their commitment to limited social reforms. The State must actively promote some reforms, or the massive subventions required for its support are vulnerable to retraction; but the reforms must not be too radical, or the State risks conflict with dominant (capitalist) interests. 'The upper apparatus of the Welfare State, then, needs social research that will "unmask" its competitors; it needs a kind of limitedly "critical" research.'[22] As the history of MFY shows, however, it is difficult to keep the 'critical' component of such research within bounds.

The potential for more radical action was explored early in the life of the MFY, and as a result that project drew the fire of local authorities and media. 'Community protest', never more than a minor aspect of MFY, took the form of embracing causes relevant to the aims of the project, while 'expanding opportunities' came to be defined as entailing 'decreasing the sense of powerlessness' among poor people.[23] Organizing a voter registration drive, aiding a local contingent of the March

[20] See the discussion ibid. 122–3 and *passim*.
[21] F. Piven and R. Cloward, *Regulating the Poor*, 279.
[22] A. Gouldner, *The Coming Crisis*, 350.
[23] G. Brager, 1964, quoted in P. Marris and M. Rein, *Dilemmas of Social Reform*, 77.

on Washington, encouraging rent strikes, and supporting a local group of Puerto Rican mothers in their campaign to oust a local school principal led to the pillorying of MFY by the New York *Daily News*. The project was accused of employing Communist sympathizers, of financial irregularities, and of inspiring riots in Harlem! The charges, none of which was substantiated on investigation, are evidence of the severe limits within which such projects are politically constrained.

The ultimate constraint upon MFY, the 'War on Poverty', and allied projects in Britain, was the impossibility of meeting the commitment to expand opportunities with the means available. Even for such generously funded projects as MFY, the limitations on creating all but the most temporary jobs were severe. Hence, the project came to focus increasingly on elaborate job-training schemes, and placement programmes in relation to existing jobs. Some of these schemes, such as simulated work situation training, were genuinely imaginative attempts to align job preparation with the kinds of jobs available and the lack of sophistication of the recruits: but there was little to offer trainees at the end of the process. Marris and Rein note the difficulties of establishing with any precision just what impact the projects made, but conclude: 'While the projects could claim many individual successes, and may well have increased somewhat the range of opportunities, they did so at great cost, and without benefit to perhaps two-thirds of those who sought their help.'[24] What remains even more problematic is whether or not these activities made any impact on delinquency in the area. No definitive assessment has emerged, but one study reports that most lower Eastside gangs 'ignored MFY and at times were openly hostile to the organization through vandalism'.[25] In one central respect, however, the project's principal assumption does seem borne out by experience. 'As soon as the projects offered an opportunity that seemed genuine, they encouraged more response than they could handle ... The children of the slums responded to the projects, because they recognized the sincerity of the intentions; they became discouraged only as it became clear that the promise could not be fulfilled. Disillusionment is not apathy, and to confuse them only complacently

[24] P. Marris and M. Rein, *Dilemmas of Social Reform*, 77.
[25] J. Short, jun., 'The Natural History of an Applied Theory', 199 n.

displaces the responsibility for failure.'[26] In the end, the aims of the project could only be achieved within 'a framework of national redistribution of resources, which deliberately redressed the balance of opportunities between rich and poor communities'.[27]

The experiences of the 'War on Poverty' were not unique to the United States. In Britain between 1968 and 1978, miniscule versions of similar projects were created by the Community Development Projects programme. The CDP programme represented a break with tradition in one respect, since British policy had tended to be shaped by the ideal of effecting social change through national reforms of fiscal, employment, and educational systems. The convergence with American practice was due in part to economic constraints reducing the scope for such reforms, at least within the political terms of the 1960s.[28] Despite some interchange between American and British policy-makers, in which the Americans took pains to spell out the deficiencies of the community-level approach, the Government continued to back the projects.[29] It was presumably assumed that the explicit linkage between the British local projects and central Government would ensure greater co-operation and enhanced effectiveness. But, in the event, despite occasional successes, the projects foundered on much the same rock as the US programmes: a chronic shortage of resources to meet well-documented needs utterly beyond the reach of the community itself. In some cases, project members arrived at much the same analysis as Marris and Rein: the need for national policy to reallocate resources from rich to poor. It must by now be clear that perhaps the major appeal of such projects for governments is that by their adoption the thorny political issues involved in such re-allocation can be, for a time, finessed. The price to be paid is that, with each successive failure, the limits of social-democratic reformism are cruelly exposed. It is in the wake of such failures that *radical theorists* have argued that capitalism is now so crisis-ridden that reformism has become untenable,

[26] P. Marris and M. Rein, *Dilemmas of Social Reform*, 124–5.

[27] Ibid. 126.

[28] The policy background is well analysed in Marris and Rein's preface.

[29] Home Office (UK), *Experiments in Social Policy and their Explanation*. For a fuller account, see M. Loney, *Community Against Government*.

and revolutionary praxis offers the only hope of attaining socialist ends.

Marxist theorists have never in principle had to face problems of role-definition that have so naggingly permeated sociology. 'Philosophers have long sought to understand the world: the point, however, is to change it.' The epitaph on Marx's tomb rams home the need for theory and practice to be related to each other in an urgent dialectic. Praxis represents their ideal unity, theoretically informed practice feeding back into practically informed theory, in a dynamic and self-critical process. Salience depends heavily, however, on the interpretations that are drawn from praxis. Until recently, the sheer force of the underlying theory had a truncating effect on revolutionary practice in Western academic Marxism. The more orthodox interpretations seemed to offer every reason *not* to act until the right conjuncture of revolutionary possibilities had materialized. Moreover, activism in sectors of society not directly connected with production seemed irrelevant. Least relevant of all were the realms of deviance and control. Crime and delinquency were in general defined as the inevitable by-products of the state of the lumpenproletariat under capitalism: little could be done about these phenomena until capitalism had been eliminated. Only with the redefinition of the potential of deviant groups for revolutionary struggle could criminologists engage at all in more salient activity. It was the achievement of the 'new' criminologists to discern in the upsurge of political consciousness among certain deviant and minority groupings the basis for a different strategy to traditional class action. Claimants' Unions, 'Gay Lib', 'Women's Lib', Preservation of the Rights of Prisoners, and Welfare Rights Movements, among others, suggested novel possibilities for the politicization of deviance. Participation in the various protest movements affords possibilities for their alignment to class conflicts, the promotion of alliances between them, and the internationalizing of joint experience and expertise.

Beyond the point of immediate struggle, however, the guidelines for action are thin. Suggestions for the control of policing and the administration of justice to be taken over by working-class communities have made little progress in addressing issues of representativeness, responsibility, and safeguards.[30] The problems of translating radical theory into practice remain formidable, not simply because the obstacles to such practice are in themselves so strong, but also because the theories do not offer criteria for discriminating between the myriad possibilities for action that exist.

There are two major exceptions which are instructive in their provision of polar answers to a radical dilemma. On the one hand, there is the accommodation proposed by radicals who are so impressed by the need to take working-class crime seriously that they are reluctant either to remove themselves from political engagement or to exacerbate what is an already doleful condition. The beginnings of a programme of pragmatic reform have been drafted by the radical criminologists who launched a revolution within radical criminology itself. We have described their 'left realism' as the new, typically local authority-based administrative criminology of the left. The realists are concerned with the working-class experience of crime and, in some respects, their solutions are not so very different from the more liberal proposals of Home Office officials in Britain or their counterparts in Canada, Australia, and New Zealand. Little concrete advice has yet materialized, but there is an interest in propounding remedies for the suffering experienced by poor, vulnerable, and ill-serviced working-class communities in urban areas. There is a demand for more responsive and efficient policing and, in particular, for policing that is directed at priorities which the working class themselves would choose, for policing which eschews aggressive patrol tactics, and for policing that is directed by a more intelligent system of targetting. There is a cautious welcome for neighbourhood watch programmes: 'left realists' are wary about the displacement of crime from middle-class to working-class areas and there is an apprehension that working-class communities are too disorganized to support such programmes themselves. There is limited support for a 'multi-agency' approach to crime, orchestrating the activities of shelters for battered women, social services, local authority crime prevention and target-hardening programmes, and the police. There is a recommendation that prison should be used

[30] See J. Young, 'Working Class Criminology', and 'Left Idealism, Reformism and Beyond', and for a discussion of the issues raised, S. Cohen, 'Guilt, Justice and Tolerance: Some Old Concepts for a New Criminology'.

much more sparingly, to be replaced by schemes that integrate rather than further 'marginalize' the already alienated. All these proposals display a marked affinity with those of experts from other theoretical positions, and there are the makings of a new professional consensus which possesses considerable authority.

The other major exception remains the work of Thomas Mathiesen in the field of penal reform, and it embraces none of the pragmatism of the left realists.[31] Instead, Mathiesen veers towards an uncompromising policy of resistance to co-optation. His work addresses the perennial dilemma for radicals of whether to pursue short-term reforms or long-term revolutionary aims. To pursue either exclusively entails severe costs. Reformism is held to risk strengthening the system, so undermining more radical change; and its advocates tend to become 'incorporated' into the system by endless compromise and the acceptance of system terms for the evaluation of reforms. To opt for purely revolutionary ends, however, means isolation from the system, assignment to an 'irresponsible revolutionary' role, and the loss of credibility in relations with the subordinate groups most affected: in this case, prisoners. Mathiesen proposes a means for resolving this dilemma which would enable radicals to pursue reforms in the short run which would not compromise their long-term revolutionary aims, and which would protect them from incorporation. It is crucial, he argues, to differentiate reforms which are 'system-strengthening' from those which are 'system-weakening'. The latter can be supported, and the former resisted, as a means to long-term aims. An example of the former is the 'medicalization' of deviance, superficially a progressive measure (rehabilitation), but fundamentally one which individualizes the causes of deviance, and therefore defuses its political aspects. It also dehumanizes deviant subjects by reducing their problems to those of a sickness from which, with appropriate treatment, the State will enable them to recover. Examples of 'system-weakening' reforms would be any concessions wrung from the State which would give greater autonomy to deviants in their relations with the system, which by definition weaken State power. Prisoners' rights to certain standards of work, educa-

[31] T. Mathiesen, *The Politics of Abolition*.

tion, and freedom from censorship, and, *inter alia*, to legal procedures in a prison context, are in this sense system-weakening. Principally, however, the main strategy to be employed is abolitionist. The abolition of repressive laws, and of coercive institutions, represents the most frontal attack on State power. The Norwegian prison reform movement in which Mathiesen plays a leading role could claim a major influence in the abolition of the vagrancy laws, and in the cancellation of a detention centre building programme planned for young offenders. As a corollary, Mathiesen argues that the ultimate trap for reformers is the insistence by authorities that 'alternatives' be specified in the advocacy of reforms, and of targets for abolition. It is necessary to avoid the specification of alternatives, he proposes, and instead to pursue a strategy which he terms the 'Unfinished': an open-ended commitment for future initiatives to be derived from praxis which otherwise would be ruled out as 'impractical'.

Mathiesen's strategy clearly has great appeal, particularly in the seemingly intractable field of penal reform, and it has its counterparts in other areas of social work. 'Client refusal' has evolved as a strategy whereby radical social workers aim to diminish what they define as collusion with State power. The general principle is to refuse

to condone the labels which are officially attached to deviants . . . At its most innocuous, client refusal consists simply of blocking the unjust suction of individuals into so-called therapeutic situations where they lose control and responsibility. Thus in the early 1970s, many groups of social workers refused to receive children into care simply because their parents were homeless . . . Taylor rightly goes further by arguing that client refusal, which in isolation could be seen as another form of rationing, should include an attempt to enlist the client as a political ally.[32]

Presumably, there are many non-radical social workers who could support the first, if not the second of these proposals, just as, in Britain, many reformist groups allied to mount campaigns for the abolition of capital punishment and the 'control

[32] M. Simpkin, *Trapped Within Welfare: Surviving Social Work*, 155. The reference is to I. Taylor, 'Client Refusal'. See also P. Corrigan and P. Leonard, *Social Work Practice under Capitalism*.

units' in certain prisons.[33] The aim of abolitionist practice is, however, to provide the basis for a more systematic assault on the power of the State than *ad hoc* reformist pragmatism allows. In principle, Mathiesen's model can be extended to cover social action in general, not only in the penal field. Its adequacy must therefore be assessed in terms firstly of its capacity to resolve the 'reform' vs. 'revolution' dilemma; and secondly of its potential for the achievement of a society based on 'socialist diversity'.

Even within the penal field, an examination of particular cases shows the immense complexity of interpretation involved in assessing the potential of reforms for system strength or weakness. The view that the 'medicalization' of deviance is automatically system-strengthening seems questionable in the case of drug dependence, where the right to treatment within the health service is one which many States are reluctant to concede.[34] Moreover, the concern with system-strengthening hardly seems the main point, which is whether or not 'medicalization' works for the deviant. The main grounds for opposing it ought to be its appropriateness, rather than its implications for the 'system'. Another problem is the extent to which 'treatment' ideologies may favour greater autonomy rather than the reverse. For example, the Barlinnie Special Unit was initiated along broad therapeutic lines but evolved in the direction of the prisoners gaining important concessions in terms of autonomy and joint decision-making, a practical exemplification in many respects of the 'Unfinished', but one that would arguably have been wrecked at the outset by an insistence on abolitionism, a refusal to specify alternatives, or a marked hostility to broad therapeutic aims.[35] It may be the case that the granting of certain rights to prisoners lessens the hold of the State in a repressive sense over certain aspects of their lives. Yet it does not take much sophistication (far less than Mathiesen displays

[33] 'Control Units' were established in two English prisons in the 1970s to control troublesome prisoners by techniques that amounted to sensory deprivation. Their closure followed adverse publicity stemming from the family of one of the prisoners subjected to this form of punishment, which led to a widespread campaign for their abolition. For a discussion, see M. Fitzgerald and J. Sim, *British Prisons*.

[34] See E. Schur, *Narcotic Addiction in Britain and America*.

[35] Sadly, no research has been carried out on the experience of the Unit, which was set up in 1972. The only source of detailed information remains the inside accounts by J. Boyle, *A Sense of Freedom*, and *The Pains of Confinement*..

in other respects) to see such a policy as system-strengthening. The 'State' gains in legitimacy from such enlightened procedures. Indeed, the burden of much Marxist 'critical' theory is to 'unmask' the reality of State power behind the façade of 'repressive tolerance' created by the progressive extension of citizenship rights to formerly dispossessed groups within capitalist societies over the past two centuries. In the United States and in Britain, quite significant reductions have occurred in the relative use of prison and mental hospitals.[36] In neither case have discernible system-weakening effects occurred, though the impact on certain families and communities may have been burdensome. In sum, the rationale for praxis offered by Mathiesen seems appropriate only in a very limited number of cases, where the State adopts purely repressive measures. Most reforms, however, have both positive and negative aspects in relation to State power. In the great majority of cases, we would suggest, the dilemma is not so much resolved as reconstituted in different, and ultimately ambiguous, terms by the abolitionist strategy.

Moreover, this complication of the issue is bought at the price of an over-simplified view of the nature of the 'State', capitalism, and class society. The problem of whether one might not actually *wish* to strengthen the system in certain respects, on the grounds that the 'not too bad' society is better than any revolutionary alternatives so far accomplished, is not even addressed. An unfalsifiable postulate of functional unity between the three phenomena runs through Mathiesen's analysis, much as it does through the work of more structuralist Marxists. 'His position provides for only one role for the state under the capitalist mode of production: it is basically repressive. In his quasi-functionalist analysis, everything from publishing (including the publishers of his book?) to the family (even those of 'revolutionary intellectuals'?) are part of the State's repressive apparatus.'[37] Pahl's reference is to Poulantzas, but although Mathiesen is more selective in his analysis of State power, much the same could be said of his class analysis. Prisons are seen as the quintessential mode of

---

[36] A. Scull, *Decarceration*.

[37] R. Pahl, 'Stratification: The Relation Between States and Urban and Regional Development', 9. The reference is to N. Poulantzas, *Classes in Contemporary Capitalism*.

repression under capitalism and, as the crisis in capitalism deepens, so will its resort to the penalization of working-class offenders. Such an analysis makes little sense of the immense variations in imprisonment that obtain between different capitalist societies, nor does it address the problem of the persistence and even extension of penal powers in State socialist societies. 'Of course if anyone wishes to argue that all capitalist societies are stratified in the same way and all industrial societies are capitalist, then there is nothing more to say.'[38] The point at issue is the insistence that all attempts at reform are doomed to 'correctionalism' save those that align with strategies to eliminate capitalism. This entails a drastic foreshortening of perspectives on deviance and control to 'a single-cause theory of conflict (class antagonism)'.[39]

It is possible to give a variety of readings to Mathiesen's concept of the 'Unfinished'. It is indeed absurd to expect reformers (let alone revolutionaries) to provide in advance of any actualization of their ideas the proverbial blueprint for their eventual shape. Such a constraint would rule out even the mildest reform, since it would be logically impossible to argue that no unintended adjustments to the change would occur. At the other extreme, however, the mirror-image of the above constraint is the insistence that alternatives should never be theorized at all. Quite how it would be possible to square this position with anything resembling democratic debate remains a mystery. The philosophical grounds for this strategy of accomplishing socialism reside in the dialectical method, which postulates the emergence of socialism from the final transcendence of the negation (the dictatorship of the proletariat) of the capitalist thesis. By definition, true socialism is not only unknowable in advance of its actualization: it is theoretically virtuous to avoid the very attempt to specify the central properties which would constitute a truly socialist society. The stubborn tendency of the realities of power, stratification, uneven development, and the division of labour to persist in already actualized State socialist societies need not be addressed.[40] This makes of praxis something that looks disturb-

[38] R. Pahl, 'Stratification', 9.
[39] E. Gellner, 'A Social Contract in Search of an Idiom', 141.
[40] See also R. Pahl, ' "Collective Consumption" and the State in Capitalist and State

ingly like blind faith, and leaves the revolutionaries *carte blanche*: yet the historical precedents for revolution (which we are asked to regard as irrelevant) provide no warrant for the abdication of distrust about its likely aftermath.

Symbolic interactionism as a source of policy remained largely untapped until the 1960s. Interactionists had never preoccupied themselves with the policy implications of their work. It is possible to read the work of Goffman, for example, without finding any systematic policy inferences. What came to be termed *labelling theory* was more precisely foreshadowed in the work of Tannenbaum (1938) and Lemert (1951), neither of whom was typical of interactionism.[41] Only with the publication of Becker's *Outsiders* in 1963 were these separate strands fused, and implications for policy quickly spelt out. Becker's own definition of the sociologists' role, whatever its limitations, made it clear at least that their sympathies should lie with the underdog, and no great difficulty was envisaged in bringing theory to bear upon the task of improving their lot. Translating labelling theory into practice consisted of variations on the theme of 'delabelling': decriminalization, destigmatization, and decarceration.[42] The salience of such themes grew as the costs of institutional care and custody increased sharply in the 1960s, though the trend towards the reduction of inmate populations had begun in the 1950s, in the case of the mentally ill. The salience of labelling theory was enhanced by the fact that attacks on institutionalization came from other quarters.[43]

The fact that these proposals found a ready audience did not mean that they were easy to formulate in practice. 'Decriminalization' has been linked by Schur in particular to 'crimes without victims', such as drug use, gambling, homosexuality, and abortion. The criminal sanction is applied to such forms of deviance more extensively in the United States than in Britain, but since in both societies the great majority of offences are crimes *with* victims, the scope for applying this principle much

Socialist Societies'; F. Parkin, *Marxism*; D. Downes, 'Praxis Makes Perfect' and 'Abolition: Possibilities and Pitfalls'.

[41] F. Tannenbaum, *Crime and the Community*; E. Lemert, *Social Pathology*.

[42] The most prolific translator of labelling theory into policy recommendations has been Edwin Schur. See in particular *Crimes Without Victims*, and *Radical Non-Intervention*.

[43] See, for example, P. Townsend, *The Last Refuge*; T. and P. Morris, *Pentonville*.

further soon runs into difficulties. Only Schur has argued that a policy of 'radical non-intervention' should be adopted towards delinquency. His slogan 'leave the kids alone wherever possible' begs the question of how to interpret the bounds of possibility. 'Status offenders', those whose offences would not be law-violations if committed by an adult, are the primary candidates for this policy. In the United States between 1965 and 1974, 'half of all juveniles arrested for a status offence were placed in secure detention for periods ranging from several days to several months. One-third of all juveniles in correctional institutions (training schools, group homes, half-way houses) were committed as adjudicated status offenders.'[44] Such 'offenders' should ideally be dealt with, if at all, within the community rather than in institutions, but Schur is vague about how its members should respond to runaways, truants, underage drinkers, and 'ungovernables'. 'Non-intervention can become a euphemism for benign neglect, which in turn is another euphemism for simply doing nothing.'[45] De-labelling does not dispense with the problems the labels addressed, however maladroitly. In California, re-labelling was accomplished by several devices after a bill was passed in 1976–7 ending secure detention for status offences. Arrests for status offences dropped by 50 per cent, but more offenders were re-labelled delinquent or neglected in order to achieve secure detention, or were held to require mental health commitments.[46]

'Destigmatization' turned out to be fraught with similar problems. Schemes to 'divert' the young offender from the stigmatizing processes of the juvenile court have 'now become a national fad: non-serious offenders are diverted to hundreds of agencies in lieu of being sent to court. Meanwhile, those who end up in court are being processed by prosecutors, sworn witnesses, and defense attorneys as well as by judges and probation officers. The benevolent assumption that the juvenile court should be society's super-parent has been discredited and is being discarded.'[47] Paradoxically, diversion has

---

[44] S. Kobrin *et al.*, 'Offense Patterns of Status Offenders', 233, n. 1.

[45] S. Cohen, review of E. Schur, *Crimes Without Victims*.

[46] K. Teilmann and M. Klein, 'Juvenile Justice Legislation: A Framework for Evaluation', 42–3.

[47] L. Empey, 'Revolution and Counter-revolution: Current Trends in Juvenile Justice'.

not reduced the number being sent to court, nor has it evidently reduced stigmas or the exposure of children to bureaucratic processing.[48] It has created a supplementary rather than an alternative means of disposal for juvenile offenders. Those who are 'diverted' to specialized agencies are the younger, less serious offenders whom the police used to caution and release. Evidence on the more recent British projects along these lines is scanty, but one study discerns the same tendency for a prestigious demonstration project to re-define its target population from the relatively serious to the less serious offenders, and to those 'at risk' of delinquency.[49] 'Re-stigmatization' and its extension to hitherto unaffected groups are predictable consequences of re-routing strategies. Indeed, Cohen has delineated a new vision of the carceral society in which the State, pretending to withdraw from formal social control, actually intrudes ever more invasively into the lives of its subject population. There is a dialectic at work, he argues, in which new classifications and remedies are propounded for the control of deviant groups, the exceptions and the failures present problems of management, and new institutions are formed to regulate them. In a series of 'iatrogenic feedback loops', social control is pushed ever further outwards.[50]

'Decarceration' is perhaps the strongest and best attested policy that labelling theorists have stressed in the past two decades. A combination of supportive theory, empirical evidence on high recidivism rates, and the soaring costs of institutional control has swayed governments in a sympathetic direction. However, the dangers of offending the judiciary, and alarming 'public opinion', meant that indirect means were usually chosen to reduce the prison population. Such methods tended to backfire or make only negligible impact; parole, suspended sentences, and diversion tended either to encourage 'compensatory' sentencing or widen the population at risk. A confusion of aims led to policy compromises that in some respects proved counter-productive. Only in the Netherlands did the trend towards shorter sentences prove sustainable in

---

[48] Ibid. 172.
[49] C. Covington, 'The Hammersmith Teenage Project'.
[50] S. Cohen, *Visions of Social Control*.

the face of rising crime rates.[51] In one case, however, a more radical decarceration was accomplished. In 1972, all juvenile reformatories in Massachusetts were closed down overnight. A number of community care alternatives have since then been adopted with varying success. The authors of the change in policy claim that, while mistakes have been made, 'there was no indication of an increase in crime by juveniles who knew they would not be incarcerated in a training school if they engaged in crime and were caught'.[52] Moreover, 'since 1972, the State of Massachusetts has not had more than 60 to 85 youngsters in a locked setting on any given day—that for a population of 7 million.'[53] It is claimed that Ohlin's investigation of the reforms showed that recidivism rates are roughly the same in the community-based programmes as in the State training schools, and that 'certain programs and combinations of programs work very well indeed'. Group-home programmes turned out badly, but specialized foster-care programmes 'do very well'.[54]

Less optimism is evident in Scull's evaluation of decarceration and community care policies.[55] Scull managed to offend both liberals and radicals with his argument that capitalist societies are actively encouraging decarceration (instead of the reverse), but for narrow budgetary reasons, and with generally distressing results. He is particularly scathing about the data on Massachusetts, which he lambastes as so sloppy as to be useless for policy evaluation purposes. Not even crime and recidivism figures are presented in such a way as to make before and after comparison feasible; costs are selectively given only for the period after the change; and no attempt is made to assess how well families coped with the responsibility for young offenders when alternatives are not available. No attempt is made in the later report by Bakal and Polsky to meet these criticisms. Scull's main argument is that the rhetoric of community care and decarceration masks a trend in which the State sloughs off responsibility for the 'mad' and the 'bad' on to cut-price private agencies whose standards of provision are ineffectively monitored. Moreover, in many cases, the real costs are regressively

[51] D. Downes, *Contrasts in Tolerance*.
[52] J. Miller, 'Systems of Control and the Serious Youth Offender', 144.
[53] Ibid. 142.   [54] Ibid. 143.   [55] A Scull, *Decarceration*.

heaped on to the deviants' own families and on those communities least able to mobilize to screen the deviants out. Hence, they gravitate downwards to form 'deviant ghettoes' in the already deprived inner-city slums. Scull's own evidence on this issue is a little inadequate, but several rigorous studies are cited in support of this argument. Rates of mortality and morbidity deteriorated among groups of psycho-geriatric patients released for various forms of 'community care' by comparison with hospitalized groups; and families of schizophrenics struggled to cope with negligible aid from 'the community'.[56] Scull's evidence is selective and does not meet the counter-criticism that adequate community care might resolve such problems, and may not be needed for large numbers of less seriously handicapped institutionalized people than psycho-geriatric patients. It is all too clear, however, that, as Titmuss warned two decades ago, community care can too easily slide into no care at all.[57] The major alternative, which is to improve institutions, is conveniently buried, largely on the grounds of cost.

The premiss that major savings are made by such policies is, however, considerably dented by Lerman's reanalysis of data produced by the California Youth Authority on their Probation Subsidy Scheme and Community Training Program in the 1960s, programmes which proved influential in leading other States to adopt similar measures.[58] The costs of the CTP group exceeded those of the matched group of young prisoners, largely owing to a change in the project's design which offered intensive services to the former group for far longer than originally planned. The larger claim of the CTP project was, however, to have achieved a much lower rate of recommittals by comparison with the young prisoner group. Yet when actual offences, as distinct from parole violations, were considered, recidivism was markedly higher among the CTP group, whose lower rate of recommittals is attributed by Lerman to greater organizational tolerance of parole violations. The Probation Subsidy Scheme made larger claims for cost-cutting which, on

[56] Ibid. 99–103, 141 ff., esp. 156, n. 46.
[57] R. Titmuss, *Commitment to Welfare*, ch. 9: 'Community Care: Fact or Fiction?'
[58] P. Lerman, *Community Treatment and Social Control: A Critical Analysis of Juvenile Correctional Policy*, esp. 58–69 and ch. 8.

reanalysis, are convincingly shown to stem from faulty methods of computing hypothetical savings. Lerman's study testifies to the formidable complexities involved in monitoring such projects, not least the dangers of confounding that arise from members' stake in organizational survival. The public availability of the fiscal, behavioural, and research data was crucial to this reappraisal, and the Californian correctional authorities have clearly set an exemplary standard in this respect. That no other projects have been the subject of so searching a scrutiny should make for a certain wariness in assessing their claims.

Too great a wariness also carries dangers. All too often, the period of time allotted to evaluation is very brief, usually only three years after the start of a project, and it is impossible to make an intelligent assessment of its effects. There has also been an indefensible and irrational tendency to dismiss a whole line of theoretical reasoning after the purported failure of a single demonstration project or experiment. In most other areas of enquiry, the consequence of negative or inconclusive findings would be to modify the original programme in order to change the outcome. Unusually hard criteria are applied quite precipitately in social reform experiments. It is not surprising that there have been difficulties in demonstrating any 'pay-off' from liberal reforms. Apparent failure, coupled with the longer-standing disillusionment with rehabilitative policies,[59] have helped encourage a revival of more conservative penal policies. The 'incapacitation' argument of James Q. Wilson is only the most extreme of a wide range of demands for a new traditionalism: the demand for a return to retributivism of the 'just deserts' model offered by the *Struggle for Justice* group,[60] and the desire to return to the strict legality of *due process* in the juvenile justice field, all chime with the tenets of control theories. Yet *control theories* are not necessarily reducible to the demand for control of a more traditional kind. As Heidensohn has pointed out, the extraordinary success with which females are socialized into conformity logically suggests—if we are serious about crime control—the feminization of male role-playing, and a greater emphasis on informal rather

[59] R. Martinson, 'What Works? Questions and Answers about Penal Reform', 22–54.
[60] American Friends Service Committee, *Struggle for Justice*; A. von Hirsch, *Doing Justice*.

than formal social controls. Instead of which, we currently sentence young male offenders to regimes which are in effect designed to promote macho hardness. Nor are the theories necessarily opposed to redistributive policies. 'Stake in conformity' and 'culture of poverty' theories basically imply much the same set of policies as strain theories: a better deal in terms of jobs, housing, and education for those relatively deprived of such bonds with the social order. The major differences between the two kinds of theories concern the causal priorities of the appropriate means to this end. Strain theories stress the need to expand opportunities, and take motivation for granted. Control theories see motivation as weak or absent, and argue that tackling the 'cultural deprivation' of the poor and most discriminated-against minority groups is a precondition for betterment.

A key example in the American 'War on Poverty' was *Operation Headstart*, a project for children in their pre-school year who were considered to be in need of an intensive preparation for education. Early results were encouraging, but after a few years in the school system, the 'head start' gained seemed to have been lost. The brief exposure to an enriched educational experience was assumed to evaporate as more persistent inequalities reasserted their hold. 'Head Start did not seem to promote any lasting improvement in children's school performance despite its popularity.'[61] Much the same assumptions and conclusions applied to the British experiments in 'positive discrimination', the designation of Educational Priority Areas which were allocated extra funding for a variety of teaching aids and strategies. However, a recent analysis of the *long-term* effects of the more rigorously designed Head-start programmes is more encouraging.[62] School 'failure' (as defined by indicators such as placement in remedial classes, retention in grade, and dropping out of school) was markedly higher for control group children (44 per cent) than for project children (25 per cent).

To use avoidance of remedial classes and 'grade failures' as measures of effectiveness is to focus on the minimal aspirations of a school's work. On the other hand . . . they are measures of actual educational

[61] P. Marris and M. Rein, *Dilemmas of Social Reform*, 330.
[62] A. Halsey, 'Education Can Compensate', 172–3.

experience, rather than abstractions like measured intelligence . . . For a government determined to relieve the handicaps of those who come from poor families, a pre-school programme discriminating in their favour seems to be one of the crucial weapons.[63]

Salience is reaffirmed though it has yet to be shown that making a discernible impact on the 'culture' of poverty—in so far as that can be inferred from such data—leads to a reduction in poverty itself, either for the target group, or among the poor in general by the permeation of different attitudes.

The 'situational' type of control theory has the most obvious salience for policy. Again, implications for policy do not necessarily coincide with traditionalist calls for more policing and harsher sentencing, measures which are vulnerable on the empirical grounds that they produce no more success in controlling crime than community policing and milder sentencing.[64] The controls that are successful tend to be preventive rather than punitive. There is obvious scope for a wide array of situational and technical controls to be experimented with along carefully monitored and relatively economical lines. In a few cases, such as the reduction in motor-cycle thefts consequent on the compulsion to wear crash helmets, whole classes of crime can be dramatically diminished.[65] In others, notably the inferences drawn from the 'defensible space' hypothesis, and the installation of non-toxic gas, initially promising causal links now seem more modest or largely spurious.[66] Overall, the main criticism remains that excessive reliance on such policies may lead to a 'double displacement' effect: that crime takes a more regressive form in relation to the more vulnerable groups in the population, and that attention is deflected from more complicated 'dispositional' variables of a social and economic character. What does remain in this area are important initiatives on the rehabilitation of disorganized or vulnerable communities. The physical remodelling of estates advocated by Alice Coleman, or the decentralization of management, maintenance, and lettings practised by the

[63] A. Halsey, 'Education Can Compensate', 173.

[64] M. Zander, 'What is the Evidence on Law and Order?', 591–94.

[65] R. Clarke, 'Situational Crime Prevention', 141.

[66] See, for example, R. Mawby, 'Kiosk Vandalism', 30–46; R. Clarke and P. Mayhew (eds.), *Designing Out Crime*; and P. Sainsbury, *Suicide Trends in Europe*.

Priority Estates Projects and the National Association for the Care and Resettlement of Offenders, may both do something towards the restoration of informal social control. The initiatives have yet to be properly evaluated but the mere presence of concerned people, visible consultation with affected agencies, the expenditure of money, and a new responsiveness to residents' problems may be enough to bring about some change. At the very least, local leaders may arise and acquire influence in the process of consultation, and their new influence may inject organization into what had once been disordered. Let us examine one family of initiatives in a little detail.

The Priorities Estates Project was developed by the Department of the Environment, not the Home Office, and it was not intended explicitly to reduce crime. Rather, it was supposed to reverse the decline of problem estates and to ensure that empty, unwanted property was once again occupied. None the less, it seems to have had quite real consequences for deviance. Tricia Zipfel, one of its consultants, has claimed that there is evidence of burglary rates decreasing on all but one of the Project's estates. The most conspicuous change was observed on the Broadwater Farm Estate in north London: between 1982 and 1984, the burglary rate dropped by 62 per cent.[67] On what Zipfel described as a 'nightmare estate', 'burglaries have virtually been eliminated . . . and the crime rate generally has plummeted.'[68]

The Priority Estates Project explains such changes as an indirect consequence of delegating services, management, and lettings. An elaborate process of negotiation with tenants, local authority departments, police, and local agencies invariably accompanies major intervention, and the result is that a great deal of practical control is returned to people living and working on a housing estate. One major example is the introduction of a devolved system of lettings which allows local people to obtain tenancies on hard-to-let estates without undue fuss. It allows networks of friends, acquaintances, and families to enter once-fragmented communities. More, these new tenants often

[67] T. Zipfel, 'Broadwater Farm Estate, Haringey: Background and Information Relating to the Riot on Sunday, 6th October 1985', unpublished.
[68] T. Zipfel, 'Hard Work Transforms a Nightmare Estate'.

want to live on the estates. Their coming reduces the numbers of vacant and squatted properties that damage 'local morale' and are 'a public announcement of trouble'. It helps to construct and restore community, and it serves to 'strengthen local ties'.[69] It installs tenants who are prepared to act as the willing, unpaid, and unofficial custodians of space that was formerly unprotected: 'housing would be guarded free of charge by the new occupants'.[70] It imports those who no longer resent living on a 'problem' estate, reversing processes that alienate residents from councils. It increases the homogeneity of a community. And it removes squatters and others who have been defined as a source of mischief. Similarly, the decentralization of maintenance work seems to improve the quality and rate of repairs, transforming the physical appearance and symbolic character of an estate. Such a decrease in visible public damage can eventually become self-propelling, reducing the number of cues that invite vandalism. Resident caretakers can act as peripatetic guardians of property and channels of information about deviance.

Again, the devolution of practical control may be accompanied by a remodelling of the physical environment. When boundaries are installed, there may be a decline in the amount of confused, impersonal public space and an increase in the area of private, defended space.[71] Consultation with the police and other agencies can demystify relations which were once wary or distant, enabling groups to reassess one another, respond sympathetically, and then collaborate: 'a commonly reported situation is one where, as a result of beat policing allied to better management of the estate, the tenants are more willing to report damage or challenge hooliganism.'[72] Above all, the very business of implicating tenants in plans and programmes can soften relations between suspicious neighbours and imbue them with a novel sense of organization, purpose, and effectiveness. It gives an opportunity to reassert control.

To be sure, there is some anxiety about the displacement effect of such policies, but there does seem to be an absolute

---

[69] Department of the Environment, *Local Housing Management*.

[70] A. Power, 'How to rescue council housing'.

[71] Department of the Environment, *Reducing Vandalism on Public Housing Estates*.

[72] M. Burbidge, 'British Public Housing and Crime—A Review'.

decline in the volume of victimization. Crime does not always travel when initiatives are introduced. Some simply stops.

Finally, *phenomenological* approaches favour a more austere set of relations between sociology and social policy than those that are sought by most sociologists. In some respects they adhere to the methodological principles of Weber. Weber had argued that whilst sociologists' own values are inevitably implicated in their choice of subject-matter and definition of a problem ('value relevance'), once they proceed with their investigations their methods and analytical procedures should be as objective as possible ('value freedom'). Moreover, the claims of scientific integrity preclude the use of sociological or scientific work for partisan or political ends in which, as citizens, they are quite properly engaged. Schutz's phenomenology proposed a more radical version of the separation of 'scientific' and 'natural' roles, in which the choice of problem for sociologists should properly be derived from sociological, and not lay or political, definitions of the problems at hand.

Sociological typifications of action and meaning, Schutz's 'second order constructs', by definition are removed from the common-sense, practical activities of members of society; these typifications are a product of certain kinds of reflection by sociologists on the common-sense world. This would suggest that the main relationship between sociological reflection about the world and practical activity in the world lies . . . in sociology's ability to clarify these practical activities . . . The contribution of sociology, then, . . . is that it can help the members of a society pose their own dilemmas more acutely and clearly.[73]

Worthwhile as this aim is, it disregards the potential of sociological work, for whatever reason, to enter into public and political discourse as a resource and 'stock of knowledge' in its own right. It becomes extremely difficult, if not impossible, under such circumstances for sociologists to claim that they are disseminating knowledge solely as citizens and not in any way as scientists. The distinction between the two roles is, however, an important one, and clearly holds implications for scientists in general, not sociologists alone.

[73] M. Phillipson, *Sociological Aspects*, 168–9, and ch. 6, 'Criminology, Sociology, Crime and Social Policy'.

Conclusions

If one theme has emerged, it is that, like facts, though for different reasons, theories do not speak for themselves. Sociologists have not, on the whole, taken very seriously Kant's assertion that 'nothing is so practical as a good theory'. There is usually no simple or automatic set of policy prescriptions to be drawn from theories. A variety of interpretations are possible, and ideally the theorist should attempt to clarify their character. Translating theories into practice entails further, complex, and difficult stages in which the implications for action (or inaction) may be specified, proposals for monitoring and evaluation made, and likely side-effects anticipated. A theory of social problems should be complemented by a theory of policy process. Otherwise, the casting of a theory into the world is naïve. The obstacles to these aspirations are great, both intellectually and practically, so that no great mystery surrounds the relative infrequency with which they are even attempted. Two obvious recommendations seem appropriate: one, that the monitoring and evaluation aspects of policy implementation be given far more emphasis than is currently the norm; and two, that the time-scales on which most projects operate, which seem in general disproportionately short (the average seems to be three years) be lengthened. The costs of such recommendations mean that the situation is unlikely to change, though such costs may be minimal compared with the losses incurred by the premature abandonment or non-monitoring of expensive projects. Monitoring is a consequential process in its own right, and it is too often crude and over-simple, dominated by the search for limited effects in a short time period. Models to follow seem to us to be Lerman's study of the Californian diversion projects, and Scott's exploratory work on the agencies for the blind in the United States. In Britain, as yet, in the field of deviance and control, we have little to place beside these examples of rigorous and appreciative monitoring.

13
Conclusion

Our conclusion will be brief, a simple recital of earlier arguments. We trust that we have given support to our earlier observation that the sociology of deviance is not a unified enterprise which has progressed to a neat conclusion. On the contrary, the sociology of deviance has failed to be cumulative. It is an extended train of partially examined and partially exhausted ideas. The result has not been an indiscriminate heaping-up of thoughts and claims, however. Some specific propositions *have* been discredited during the advance of criminology; for instance, it is no longer possible to trace a close and simple association between crime and poverty,[1] nor can it be maintained that criminals are always very different from those who are not called criminals.[2] Indeed, sociologists and criminologists have been chiefly effective in discrediting the work of their predecessors and contemporaries. Theirs have been destructive rather than constructive achievements.[3] As McDonald argued of penology and the study of social control, 'there is now a whole literature showing that rehabilitation programmes do not rehabilitate and prevention programmes do not prevent.'[4] But the underlying ideas which support specific criminological hypotheses have been more difficult to dispatch. Functionalism, phenomenology, interactionism, and radical criminology have resisted decisive refutation. They display a great resilience despite prolonged attack.

That resilience stems in large measure from the sheer diversity of the sociological population. Sociologists do not always share common problems, procedures, and perspectives. It is not at all difficult to dismiss another's criticisms as peripheral,

[1] See B. Wootton, *Social Science and Social Pathology*; H. Mannheim, *Social Aspects of Crime Between the Wars*.
[2] See C. Goring, *The English Convict: A Statistical Study*.
[3] See T. Hirschi, 'Procedural Rules and the Study of Deviant Behavior'.
[4] L. McDonald, *The Sociology of Law and Order*, 15.

ill-conceived, or misinformed. Thus, the radical criminologist's complaint that functionalism, control theory, interactionism, and phenomenology neglect the real world would be met with the retort that radical criminologists know nothing of the real world themselves, Indeed, one criminologist moved on to state that the entire concern about the relationship between a description and its objects is jejune, a curious distraction which should not divert scholarly minds.[5] Debates and agendas have occasionally been transformed in consequence. Theoretical schemes being relatively elusive and well-defended, there has been a propensity for some to attack on grounds which are more accessible. A few criminologists have levelled assaults at the alleged political, social, and ethical implications of an idea or thinker, it being suggested that the revelation of undesirable politics is tantamount to the provision of disproof. They hold that unpleasant thoughts cannot be consonant with the real world: such alternative viewpoints are presented as agents of unreason and mystification. Thus Platt believed that he was asking an important question when he enquired: 'What was and is the political practice of theorists like Sutherland, Cressey, Lemert, Turk, and others in terms of their support of struggles against oppression? This is not simply [a] rhetorical or "practical [question"]. Rather [it goes] to the root of explaining how ruling-class ideologies are formed and sustained and why it is important to undermine the hegemony of liberal theory.'[6]

It does not do to introduce criminological metaphysics by claiming that one group's reality is really real and all else is falsehood in this way. None of the theories we have discussed is so insubstantial that it can be dismissed in such a peremptory manner. On the contrary, each deserves a sympathetic examination. It is only after an intellectual system has been taken seriously that its possibilities can be assessed, one's own ideas can be revised, and the limitations of admired schemes can be appreciated. It is useful to remove oneself from familiar perspectives for a while. The constraints of thought tend to become newly visible when inspected from without, and the span of criminological theories may be read

[5] See P. Carlen, review of D. Downes and P. Rock (eds.), *Deviant Interpretations*, 837.
[6] A. Platt, review of *The New Criminology*, 598.

as an array of vantage-points which offer opportunities to see the world.

However, it is difficult, uneconomic, and probably foolish to remain attached to a great mass of conflicting ideas. The law of parsimony would have one discriminate and choose. After all, eclecticism is not intrinsically meritorious—the application of unrelated ideas often leads merely to a disorganized muddle. More praiseworthy is an informed, pragmatic, and intelligent selection from the range of available interpretations. Many criminologists and sociologists of deviance adapt explanations at will, blending their own and others' thoughts to advance the resolution of specific problems. Formal inconsistencies and conflicts seem frequently to disappear in practical research. Indeed, the classifications and schools which we have imposed on criminology are more than a little artificial. Sociologists of deviance, and research sociologists in particular, do not always adhere passionately to one set of doctrines alone. The very conception of a theory as a solitary, bounded, and consistent network of propositions is an artefact of the textbook, lecture, and seminar. It often does not reflect accurately the doings and assumptions of research. Neither does it reflect the infinite number of compromises, syntheses, and innovations which working sociologists produce in their writings. Although there are some who urge orthodoxy and conformity on their fellows, many criminologists are catholic enough in their use of ideas. The student would do well to imitate the practices rather than the admonitions of sociology—practices which usually give evidence of a wide acquaintance with various positions, and reconcile and marry explanations which are theoretically at war with one another. Talk about theory actually heightens and amplifies difference. Practical speculation may ignore it. As Becker remarked, many theoretical 'criticisms are those a certain kind of philosopher might make of almost any working scientist (e.g. . . . physics has gone right along in the face of contradictions that turn philosophers pale.)'[7] The activity of research seems to redefine the significance of classroom arguments, producing new criteria and new priorities.

The creation and application of theoretical compounds cannot always be intelligently planned in advance of research.

[7] Personal communication.

They are responses to particular problems, evolved to cope with particular stages of work, and mirroring the special needs of a person or situation. They are often provisional and pragmatic, representing tentative solutions to emerging questions. After all, research is supposed to be a process of discovery which cannot anticipate its conclusions.

In this sense, the sociology of deviance has a fugue-like or dialectical relationship with its own theory. That theory may be given an articulate and independent form which has little bearing upon its actual employment in research and detailed explanation. It represents a kind of analytic ideal which is unattainable, and its manufacture is a process apart from the concrete work of the criminologist. It is only when explanation is reconstructed for publication that the logical requirements of theorizing appear again. Indeed, novice criminologists are liable to be seriously disturbed about their inability to tease solid theory out of the social world. They are almost never warned that research is faltering, confusing, and unenlightening at first. They have believed what Cohen and Taylor call the 'chronological lie', a lie which methodically misrepresents the research calendar, giving one to imagine that enquiry flowed out of a neatly framed theory, asked its questions, and returned to ponder and amend the theory that fathered it.

We have attended to the more formal stages of criminological speculation ourselves. This book is not a description of methodology and research technique but a survey of the theory that supposedly buttresses the sociology of deviance. In our view, it is as well to know that theory in its simplest and most uncontaminated guise. The fullest implications and consequences of its arguments may then be recognized, and discarded alternatives and criticisms may be understood. Any consistent analysis entails a sacrificing of competing opportunities: only rarely should an explanation be received as 'obvious', 'natural', or 'inevitable'. It is generally one of a number of rivals which are grounded in the contending metaphysical schemes that we have outlined.

We have depicted the sociology of deviance as a series of exploratory expeditions which are launched by theory and return to a version of theory in the end. The interdependence between a relatively formal reasoning and the situated reasoning of research is exemplary and precarious. People do not always phrase their thinking in lucid models. Neither do they invariably change their ideas as they acquire practical experience. They are subject to strains which would keep theorizing and research apart. This very book might be regarded as an instance of just such a strain, since it discusses theory in a disembodied manner.

Sociology is most typically a topic in books and classrooms, talked about rather than practised. Those who study are led to consider theory and research as discrete, possibly antagonistic, pursuits. Specialist writing and a division of intellectual labour foster that separation. Theorists have arisen who would create systematic, formal, and comprehensive explanations of society. Theirs is the search for deep unities and underlying principles which elucidate basic problems. Thus propelled, they are prone to look upon detailed, low-scale empirical work without great interest: it takes the theorist away from central issues and tends to dwarf the scope of analysis; it is time-consuming and unbecoming.

They then define the minute empirical examination of deviant phenomena as a brake or distraction which should not detain the thorough theorist for very long. Deviance is certainly not thought to illuminate all the strategic problems of theory. It might, for example, represent an interesting demonstration of the workings of deep rules, but it is not as absorbing as those rules themselves, and there are many other instances. The result has been that any who profess to be concerned with global explanation tend not to be committed criminologists. Phenomenologists, for instance, have been urged to turn away from crime to more interesting matters.[8] Aaron Cicourel, Peter Berger, Mary Douglas, and the like would not describe themselves as criminologists. Similarly, some Marxists have tried to persuade their colleagues to abandon radical criminology:[9]

Criminology and crime are not central disciplines for radicalism—indeed . . . a concern with criminology will fade as a radical analysis is achieved . . . the idea of a radical criminology is not possible in *principle.* . . . Marxism as a form of theoretical system specifies its own

---

[8] See M. Phillipson, 'Thinking Out of Deviance'.
[9] See P. Hirst, 'Marx and Engels on Law, Crime and Morality'.

objects of analysis and . . . these objects are not crime or law, but the mode of production and the form of social formations in general. . . . Marxism, by the analysis of the relationship between and within social formations includes and subsumes (logically and empirically) the analysis of crime and law in these more general concerns.[10]

Our supposition is that the sociology of deviance will continue as it has begun. It will be a compound of two strands. The one strand has been deposited by those who have visited criminology briefly for rather particular purposes. Functionalists, phenomenologists, Marxists, and others have discussed deviance from time to time as they investigate wider theoretical and empirical problems. They have left their mark each time they have done so, enlarging perspectives and changing questions, but they have not established enduring schools committed to their theoretical stance. Such commitment would be under an excessive strain. Arrayed like geological strata, there may be found a succession of intellectual episodes which have had a discernible beginning and end. Their ending came as their authors moved back to other problems. Deep and systematic theorizing promotes empirical homelessness. But the outcome has been a series of intellectual seams which sociologists of deviance can explore for decades to come.

The other strand has been contributed by sociologists who seem to award a rather inferior position to theorizing as an end. They are able to remain attached to one area, being relatively unprepared to follow the logic of their thought to strange terrain. Following Herbert Blumer, they might describe theory as a reservoir of sensitizing conceptions which are insubstantial and inadequate in themselves. Sensitizing conceptions point sociologists to an area but they do not tell them what they will find when they get there. Interactionists are especially likely to retain their intellectual adherence to criminology. It has proved to be a most hospitable discipline for those concerned with the social anthropology of everyday life. Symbolic interactionism and allied work will probably form one pivot of a future sociology of deviance.

In Britain, a second pivot will be provided by those who have an occupational commitment to the study of crime and control.

[10] Z. Bankowski *et al.*, 'Radical Criminology or Radical Criminologist?'.

People whom Jock Young has described as 'administrative criminologists' are one major example. The research staff of the Home Office Research and Planning Unit have recently made a significant contribution to thinking about crime, opening up a whole array of intellectual possibilities. From them have come many neat little empirical investigations of surveillance and the workings of informal social control. Under Ron Clarke, especially, there was a flowering of interesting work that could not but be focused on crime.

And a third pivot is currently under construction by those radical and Marxist criminologists who seem to have decided that the social, political, and analytic problems of crime are more demanding than the theoretical problems of Marxist scholarship. Young, Pearson, Kinsey, and Lea have dedicated themselves to a new kind of empirical criminology which throws more scholastic issues out of focus. They are attaining a substantial presence.

What is particularly interesting, too, is that there are signs of a weakening in the combativeness of the sociology of deviance: the three groups have renewed their ability to listen to one another. Their interaction in the future promises a new kind of synthetic sociology which will busy itself with ethnographic and complementary studies of crime, deviance, dispute settlement, and control in community settings.

Bibliography

ADLER, F., *Sisters in Crime*, New York, 1975.
—— and SIMON, R. (eds.), *The Criminology of Deviant Women*, Boston, 1979.
AKERS, R., 'Problems in the Sociology of Deviance', *Social Forces*, 46.4 (1968).
ALIHAN, M., *Social Ecology*, New York, 1938.
AMERICAN FRIENDS SERVICE COMMITTEE, *Struggle for Justice: A Report on Crime and Punishment in America*, New York, 1971.
AMIR, M., *Patterns in Forcible Rape*, Chicago, 1971.
ANDERSON, N., *The Hobo*, Chicago, 1923.
ANON., 'The Life Histories of W. I. Thomas and Robert E. Park', *American Journal of Sociology*, 79 (1973).
ARMSTRONG, G. and WILSON, M., 'City Politics and Deviancy Amplification', in Taylor, I. and Taylor, L. (eds.), *Politics and Deviance*, Harmondsworth, 1973.
ARON, R., 'Max Weber and Power Politics', in Stammer, O. (ed.), *Max Weber and Sociology Today*, Oxford, 1971.
ASBURY, H., *The Gangs of New York*, New York, 1928.
ATKINSON, M., *Discovering Suicide*, London, 1979.
—— 'Societal Reactions to Suicide', in Cohen, S. (ed.), *Images of Deviance*, Harmondsworth, 1971.
—— and DREW, P., *Order in Court*, London, 1979.
BAKAL, Y. and POLSKY, H. (eds.), *Reforming Corrections for Juvenile Offenders*, Lexington, Mass., 1979.
BALDWIN, J. and BOTTOMS, A., *The Urban Criminal*, London, 1976.
BALDWIN, J. and McCONVILLE, M., *Negotiated Justice*, London, 1977.
BALL, D., 'An Abortion Clinic Ethnography', *Social Problems*, 14 (1967).
BANKOWSKI, Z., MUNGHAM, G., and YOUNG, P., 'Radical Criminology or Radical Criminologist?', *Contemporary Crises*, 1.1 (1977).
BANTING, K., *Poverty, Politics and Policy*, London, 1979.
BARZUN, J. (tr.), *Flaubert's Dictionary of Accepted Ideas*, London, 1954.
BENNETT, T. and WRIGHT, R., *Burglars on Burglary*, Aldershot, 1984.
BENNETT, W. and FELDMAN, M., *Reconstructing Reality in the Courtroom*, New Brunswick, 1981.
BEAMES, T., *The Rookeries of London*, London, 1850.
BECKER, H. (ed.), *Culture and Civility in San Francisco*, Chicago, 1971.

BECKER, H. (ed.), Labelling Theory Reconsidered', in Rock, P. and McIntosh, M. (eds.), *Deviance and Social Control*, London, 1974.
—— 'Marihuana Use and Social Control', in *Outsiders*, New York, 1963.
—— *Outsiders*, New York, 1963.
—— 'The Culture of a Deviant Group', *American Journal of Sociology*, 51 (1961).
'The Life History and the Scientific Mosaic', in *Sociological Work*, London, 1971.
—— 'The Self and Adult Socialization', in Norbeck, E. *et al.* (eds.), *The Study of Personality*, New York, 1968.
—— and HOROWITZ, I., 'The Culture of Civility', in Becker, H. (ed.), *Culture and Civility in San Francisco*, Chicago, 1971.
BECKER, J., *Hitler's Children*, London, 1978.
BELL, D., *The End of Ideology*, New York, 1960.
BELSON, W., *Juvenile Theft*, London, 1975.
BERGER, P., *The Social Reality of Religion*, Harmondsworth, 1973.
—— and LUCKMANN, T., *The Social Construction of Reality*, London, 1967.
BERSANI, C. (ed.), *Crime and Delinquency*, New York, 1970.
BITTNER, E., 'Radicalism and the Organization of Radical Movements', *American Sociological Review*, 28.6 (1963).
—— 'The Police on Skid Row', *American Sociological Review*, 32.5 (1967).
—— *The Functions of the Police in Modern Society*, Rockville, 1970.
BLAU, P., *Exchange and Power in Social Life*, New York, 1964.
BLUMER, H., 'Suggestions for the Study of Mass Media Effects', in *Symbolic Interactionism*, Englewood Cliffs, NJ, 1969.
—— 'What is Wrong with Social Theory?', in *Symbolic Interactionism*, Englewood Cliffs, NJ, 1969.
BONGER, W., *Criminality and Economic Conditions*, Boston, Mass., 1916.
BORDUA, D. (ed.), *The Police; Six Sociological Essays*, New York, 1967.
BOTTOMLEY, K. and PEASE, K., *Crime and Punishment*, London, 1986.
BOTTOMS, A., review of *Defensible Space*, *British Journal of Criminology*, 14 (1974).
—— MAWBY, R., and WALKER, M., 'A Localised Crime Survey in Contrasting Areas of a City', *British Journal of Criminology*, 27 (1987).
BOX, S., *Deviance, Reality and Society*, London, 1971.
—— *Power, Crime and Mystification*, London, 1983.
BOYLE, J., *A Sense of Freedom*, London, 1977.
—— *The Pains of Confinement: Prison Diaries*, Edinburgh, 1984.
BRAITHWAITE, J., *Inequality, Crime and Public Policy*, London, 1979.
BRAKE, M., *The Sociology of Youth Culture and Youth Subcultures*, London, 1980.

BRAUDE, L., ' "Park and Burgess": An Appreciation', *American Journal of Sociology*, 77 (1970).

BRIAR, S. and PILIAVIN, I., 'Delinquency, Situational Inducements, and Commitment to Conformity', *Social Problems*, 13 (1965).

BRIGGS, D., *Dealing with Deviants*, London, 1975.

BRODY, S. and TARLING, R., *Taking Offenders out of Circulation*, Home Office Research Study No. 64, London, 1980.

BULMER, M., *The Chicago School*, Chicago, 1985.

—— (ed.), *Social Policy Research*, London, 1978.

BURBIDGE, M., 'British Public Housing and Crime—A Review', in R. Clarke and T. Hope (eds.), *Coping with Crime*, Boston, 1984.

BURKE, K., *A Grammar of Motives*, New York, 1945.

BURT, C., *The Young Delinquent*, London, 1924 (1944, 4th rev. edn.).

CAIN, M., *Society and the Policeman's Role*, London, 1974.

CAMERON, M., *The Booster and the Snitch*, New York, 1964.

CAMPBELL, A., *Girl Delinquents*, Oxford, 1981.

—— *The Girls in the Gang: A Report from New York City*, Oxford, 1984.

—— 'Self-report of Fighting by Females', *British Journal of Criminology*, 26 (1986).

CAREY, J., 'Problems of Access and Risk in Observing Drug Scenes', in Douglas, J. (ed.), *Research on Deviance*, New York, 1972.

—— *Sociology and Public Affairs: The Chicago School*, Beverly Hills, 1975.

CARLEN, P., *Magistrates' Justice*, London, 1976.

—— review of D. Downes and P. Rock (eds.), *Deviant Interpretations*, *Sociological Review*, 27.4 (1979).

—— *Women's Imprisonment*, London, 1983.

—— (ed.), *Criminal Women*, Cambridge, 1985.

CASBURN, M., *Girls Will be Girls*, London, 1979.

CAVAN, S., *Liquor License*, Chicago, 1966.

CENTRE OF CRIMINOLOGY, University of Toronto, *Handbook and Annual Report, 1976*, Toronto, 1976.

CHAMBLISS, W., *Box Man*, New York, 1972.

—— *On the Take: From Petty Crooks to Presidents*, Bloomington, Ind., 1978.

—— 'The State and Criminal Law', in Chambliss, W. and Mankoff, M. (eds.), *Whose Law, What Order?*, New York, 1976.

CHESNEY-LIND, M., 'The Judicial Enforcement of the Female Sex Role', *Issues in Criminology*, 8 (1973).

CHEVALIER, L., *Labouring Classes and Dangerous Classes*, London, 1973.

CICOUREL, A., 'Interpretative Procedures and Normative Rules in the

338Bibliography

Negotiation of Status and Role', in *Cognitive Sociology*, Harmondsworth, 1973.

CICOUREL, A., *Method and Measurement in Sociology*, New York, 1964.
—— *The Social Organization of Juvenile Justice*, New York, 1968.
—— and KITSUSE, J., *The Educational Decision-Makers*, Indianapolis, 1963.

CLARKE, R., 'Situational Crime Prevention: Theory and Practice', *British Journal of Criminology*, 20 (1980).
—— and CORNISH, D., *Crime Control in Britain*, Albany, 1983.
—— and HOPE, T. (eds.), *Coping with Crime*, Boston, 1984.
—— and MAYHEW, P. (eds.), *Designing Out Crime*, London, 1980.
—— —— 'The British Gas Story and its Criminological Implications', in *Crime and Justice: An Annual Review of Research*, Vol. 10, M. Tonry and N. Morris (eds.), Chicago, University of Chicago Press, 1988.
—— —— 'Crime as Opportunity: A Note on Domestic Gas in Britain and the Netherlands', forthcoming.

CLEAVER, E., *Soul on Ice*, New York, 1968.

CLEMMER, D., *The Prison Community*, New York, 1940.

CLINARD, M. (ed.), *Anomie and Deviant Behavior: A Discussion and Critique*, New York, 1964.
—— *Cities with Little Crime: The Case of Switzerland*, Cambridge, 1978.

CLOWARD, R. and OHLIN, L., *Delinquency and Opportunity*, New York, 1960.

COCHRANE, R., 'Crime and Personality: Theory and Evidence', *Bulletin of the British Psychological Society*, 27 (1974).

COHEN, A., *Delinquent Boys: The Culture of the Gang*, Glencoe, Ill., 1955.
—— *Deviance and Control*, Englewood Cliffs, NJ, 1966.
—— *The Elasticity of Evil*, Oxford, 1974.
—— 'The Sociology of the Deviant Act: Anomie Theory and Beyond', *American Sociological Review*, 30 (1965).
—— and SHORT, J., 'Juvenile Delinquency', in Merton, R. and Nisbet, R. (eds.), *Contemporary Social Problems*, New York, 1961.

COHEN, P., 'Working Class Youth Cultures in East London', *Working Papers in Cultural Studies* (Birmingham University), 2 (1972), and in Clarke, J. et al. (eds.), *Resistance Through Ritual*, London, 1976.
—— and ROBINS, D., *Knuckle Sandwich: Growing up in the Working Class City*, Harmondsworth, 1978.

COHEN, P. S., 'Is Positivism Dead?', *Sociological Review*, 28 (New Series) (1980).
—— *Modern Social Theory*, London, 1968.

COHEN, S., 'Criminology and the Sociology of Deviance in Britain', in Rock, P. and McIntosh, M. (eds.), *Deviance and Social Control*, London, 1974.

—— 'Directions for Research on Adolescent Group Violence and Vandalism', *British Journal of Criminology*, 11 (1971).

—— *Folk Devils and Moral Panics* (2nd edn., rev.), Oxford, 1980.

—— 'Guilt, Justice and Tolerance: Some Old Concepts for a New Criminology', in Downes, D. and Rock, P. (eds.), *Deviant Interpretations*, Oxford, 1979.

—— (ed.), *Images of Deviance*, Harmondsworth, 1971.

—— review of Schur, E., *Crimes Without Victims, New Society*, 21 Nov. 1974.

—— *Visions of Social Control*, Cambridge, 1985.

—— and TAYLOR, L., *Prison Secrets*, London, 1976.

—— *Psychological Survival*, Harmondsworth, 1972.

—— and YOUNG, J. (eds.), *The Manufacture of News*, London, 1973.

COLEMAN, A., *Utopia on Trial*, London, 1985.

COLQUHOUN, P., *A Treatise on the Police of the Metropolis*, London, 1806.

CONANT, R. and LEVIN, M. (eds.), *Problems in Research on Community Violence*, New York, 1969.

CONNOR, W., *Deviance in Soviet Society*, New York, 1972.

CORNISH, D. and CLARKE, R., *The Reasoning Criminal*, New York, 1986.

CORRIGAN, P, *Schooling the Smash Street Kids*, London, 1979.

—— and LEONARD, P., *Social Work Practice Under Capitalism*, London, 1978.

COSER, L., *The Functions of Social Conflict*, London, 1956.

COVINGTON, C., 'The Hammersmith Teenage Project: social policy and practice in an experimental community-based delinquency project 1975–78', Ph.D. thesis, University of London (LSE), 1980.

COWIE, J., COWIE, V., and SLATER, E., *Delinquency in Girls*, London, 1968.

COX, B. *et al.*, *The Fall of Scotland Yard*, Harmondsworth, 1977.

CRESSEY, D., *Other People's Money*, Glencoe, Ill., 1953.

—— 'Role Theory, Differential Association and Compulsive Crimes', in Rose, A. (ed.), *Human Behavior and Social Processes*, New York, 1962.

CRESSEY, P., *The Taxi-Dance Hall*, Chicago, 1932.

DAMER, S., 'Wine Alley: The Sociology of a Dreadful Enclosure', *Sociological Review*, 22 (1974).

DAVIE, M, 'The Pattern of Urban Growth', in Murdock, G. (ed.), *Studies in the Science of Society*, New Haven, Conn., 1937.

DAVIS, D., *Homicide in American Fiction*, Ithaca, NY, 1968.
DAVIS, F., 'Deviance Disavowal', in Becker, H. (ed.), *The Other Side*, New York, 1964.
—— 'The Cab-Driver and his Fare', *American Journal of Sociology*, 64 (1959).
DAVIS, K., 'Illegitimacy and the Social Structure', *American Journal of Sociology*, 44 (1939).
—— 'Prostitution', in Merton, R. and Nisbet, R. (eds.), *Contemporary Social Problems*, New York, 1961.
—— 'The Myth of Functional Analysis as a Special Method in Sociology and Anthropology', *American Sociological Review*, 24 (1959). Reprinted in Demerath, N., and Peterson, R. (eds.), *System, Change and Conflict*, New York (1967).
—— 'The Sociology of Prostitution', *American Sociological Review*, 2 (1937).
DAVIS, M., 'That's Interesting! Towards a Phenomenology of Sociology and a Sociology of Phenomenology', *Philosophy of the Social Sciences*, 1 (1971).
DAVIS, M., *Smut*, 1983.
DAVIS, N., *Sociological Constructions of Deviance*, Dubuque, Ia., 1975.
DEBRO, J., 'Dialogue with Howard S. Becker', *Issues in Criminology*, 5.2 (1970).
DEFOE, D., *The True and Genuine Account of the Life and Actions of the Late Jonathan Wild*, London, 1725.
DENTLER, R. and ERIKSON, K., 'The Functions of Deviance in Groups', *Social Problems*, 7 (1959).
DENZIN, N., 'Crime and the American Liquor Industry', in Denzin, N. (ed.), *Studies in Symbolic Interaction*, I, Greenwich, Conn., 1978.
DEPARTMENT OF THE ENVIRONMENT, *Reducing Vandalism on Public Housing Estates*, London, 1981.
DEPARTMENT OF THE ENVIRONMENT, *Local Housing Management: A Priority Estates Project Survey*, London, 1980.
DEWEY, J., 'Perception and Organic Action', *The Journal of Philosophy, Psychology and Scientific Methods*, 11.24 (1912).
—— 'Realism without Monism or Dualism—II', *The Journal of Philosophy*, 19.13 (1922).
—— 'The Reflex Arc Concept in Social Psychology', *American Journal of Sociology*, 2 (1896).
DITTON, J., *Controlology*, London, 1979.
—— *Part-Time Crime*, London, 1977.
DOBASH, R. and DOBASH, R., *Violence Against Wives: A Case Against Patriarchy*, London, 1979.

—— —— 'The Nature and Antecedents of Violent Events', *British Journal of Criminology*, 24 (1984).

DOLLARD, J., *Caste and Class in a Southern Town*, New Haven, Conn., 1937.

DOUGLAS, J., *American Social Order: Social Rules in a Pluralistic Society*, New York, 1971.

—— 'Deviance and Order in a Pluralistic Society', in McKinney, J. and Tiryakian, E. (eds.), *Theoretical Sociology*, New York, 1970.

—— (ed.), *Deviance and Respectability*, New York, 1970.

—— (ed.), *Research on Deviance*, New York, 1972.

—— 'The Experience of the Absurd and the Problem of Social Order', in Scott, R. and Douglas, J. (eds.), *Theoretical Perspectives on Deviance*, New York, 1972.

—— *The Social Meanings of Suicide*, Princeton, NJ, 1967.

—— 'The Sociological Analysis of Social Meanings of Suicide', in Giddens, A. (ed.), *The Sociology of Suicide*, London, 1971.

—— (ed.), *Understanding Everyday Life*, London, 1971.

—— *et al.*, *The Nude Beach*, Beverly Hills, 1977.

DOUGLAS, M., *Implicit Meanings*, London, 1975.

—— *Natural Symbols*, London, 1970.

—— *Purity and Danger*, London, 1966.

—— (ed.), *Rules and Meanings*, Harmondsworth, 1973.

—— *How Institutions Think*, Syracuse, 1986.

DOWNES, D., 'Abolition: Possibilities and Pitfalls', in Bottoms, A. (ed.), *The Crisis in the British Penal System*, Edinburgh, 1980.

—— *Contrasts in Tolerance: Post-war Penal Policy in the Netherlands and England and Wales*, Oxford, 1988.

—— *The Delinquent Solution: A Study in Subcultural Theory*, London, 1966.

—— 'Praxis Makes Perfect', in Downes, D. and Rock, P. (eds.), *Deviant Interpretations*, Oxford, 1979.

—— and ROCK, P. (eds.), *Deviant Interpretations: Problems in Criminological Theory*, Oxford, 1979.

—— and WARD, T., *Democratic Policing*, London, 1986.

DRAKE, S. and CAYTON, H., *Black Metropolis*, New York, 1945.

DURKHEIM, É., *Suicide*, London, 1952 (originally published 1897).

—— *The Division of Labor in Society*, New York, 1964 (originally published 1893).

—— *The Rules of Sociological Method*, New York, 1964 (originally published 1895).

DUSTER, T., *The Legislation of Morality*, New York, 1970.

EATON, M., 'Mitigating Circumstances: Familiar Rhetoric', *International Journal of Sociological Law*, 11 (1983).

EATON, M., 'Documenting the Defendant: Placing Women in Social Inquiry Report', in Brophy, J. and Smart, C. (eds.), *Women in Law*, London, 1985.

EATON, M., *Justice for Women?*, Milton Keynes, 1986.

EDELMAN, M., *Politics as Symbolic Action*, Chicago, 1971.

EDGERTON, R., 'Pokot Intersexuality: An East African Example of the Resolution of Sexual Incongruity', *American Anthropologist*, 66 (1964).

EDWARDS, S., *Female Sexuality and the Law*, Oxford, 1981.

—— 'Police Attitudes and Dispositions in Domestic Disputes: the London Study', *Police Journal* (1986).

EINSTADTER, W., 'The Social Organization of Armed Robbery', *Social Problems*, 17.1 (1969).

ELLIOTT, D. and VOSS, H., *Delinquency and Dropouts*, Lexington, Mass., 1974.

EMERSON, R., *Judging Delinquents*, Chicago, 1969.

EMPEY, L., 'Revolution and Counter-Revolution: Current Trends in Juvenile Justice', in Shichor, D. and Kelly, D. (eds.), *Critical Issues in Juvenile Delinquency*, Lexington, Mass., 1980.

ERICSON, R., *Criminal Reactions*, Farnborough, Hants, 1975.

ERIKSON, K., *In the Wake of the Flood*, London, 1979.

—— 'Notes on the Sociology of Deviance', in Becker, H. (ed.), *The Other Side*, New York, 1964.

—— *Wayward Puritans*, New York, 1966.

—— 'Disguised Observation in Sociology', *Social Problems*, 1967.

EYSENCK, H., *Crime and Personality*, London, 1961 (3rd edn., rev., London, 1977).

—— 'Crime and Personality Reconsidered', *Bulletin of the British Psychological Society*, 27 (1974).

FARBERMAN, H., 'A Criminogenic Market Structure: The Automobile Industry', *The Sociological Quarterly*, 16 (1975).

—— 'Symposium on Symbolic Interaction—An Introduction', *The Sociological Quarterly*, 16 (1975).

FARBEROW, N. (ed.), *Taboo Topics*, New York, 1963.

FARIS, R., *Chicago Sociology, 1920–1932*, San Francisco, 1967.

FARIS, R. and DUNHAM, H., *Mental Disorders in Urban Areas: An Ecological Study of Schizophrenia and Other Psychoses*, Chicago, 1939.

FARRINGTON, D. and MORRIS, A., 'Sex, Sentencing and Reconvictions', *British Journal of Criminology*, 23 (1983).

FIELDING, N, *The National Front*, London, 1980.

FINESTONE, H., *Victims of Change: Juvenile Delinquents in American Society*, Westport, Conn., 1976.

FISHER, C. and MAWBY, R., 'Juvenile Delinquency and Police

Discretion in an Inner City Area', *British Journal of Criminology*, 22 (1982).

FISHMAN, M., *Manufacturing the News*, New York, 1980.

FITZGERALD, M., *Prisoners in Revolt*, London, 1977.

—— and SIM, J., *British Prisons*, Oxford, 1979.

FLETCHER, R., 'Evolutionary and Developmental Sociology', in Rex, J. (ed.), *Approaches to Sociology*, London, 1974.

FOUCAULT, M., *Discipline and Punish: The Birth of the Prison*, London, 1977.

—— *I, Pierre Rivière*, New York, 1975.

—— *Madness and Civilization*, London, 1967.

—— *The Birth of the Clinic*, New York, 1975.

FREIDSON, E., *Profession of Medicine*, New York, 1970.

FUCHS, V., *Who Shall Live? Health Economics and Social Choice*, New York, 1974.

GANS, H., *The Urban Villagers*, New York, 1962.

GARFINKEL, H., *Studies in Ethnomethodology*, Englewood Cliffs, NJ, 1967.

GARLAND, D., *Punishment and Welfare*, Aldershot, 1985.

—— and YOUNG, P. (eds.), *The Power to Punish*, London, 1983.

GAVRON, H., *The Captive Wife*, London, 1966.

GELLNER, E., 'A Social Contract in Search of an Idiom: The Demise of the Danegeld State?', *Political Quarterly*, 46 (1975).

—— 'Concepts and Society', in Wilson, B. (ed.), *Rationality*, Oxford, 1968.

—— 'Ethnomethodology: The Re-Enchantment Industry or The Californian Way of Subjectivity', *Philosophy of the Social Sciences*, 5 (1975).

—— *Legitimation of Belief*, Cambridge, 1974.

GELSTHORPE, L. and MORRIS, A., 'Feminism and Criminology in Britain', *British Journal of Criminology*, 28 (1988).

GENDERS, E. and PLAYER, E., 'Women's Imprisonment: The Effects of Youth Custody', *British Journal of Criminology*, 26 (1986).

GIBBS, J., 'Conceptions of Deviant Behavior: The Old and the New', *Pacific Sociological Review*, 8.1 (1966).

GIDDENS, A., *Émile Durkheim: Selected Writings*, Cambridge, 1972.

—— *The Class Structure of the Advanced Societies*, London, 1973.

—— (ed.), *The Sociology of Suicide*, London, 1971.

GILL, O., *Luke Street: Housing Policy, Conflict and the Creation of the Delinquent Area*, London, 1977.

GLUECK, S. and E., *Unravelling Juvenile Delinquency*, Cambridge, Mass., 1950.

—— —— *Five Hundred Delinquent Women*, New York, 1934.

GOETSCHIUS, G. and TASH, M., *Working with Unattached Youth*, London, 1967.

GOFFMAN, E., *Asylums*, Harmondsworth, 1968.

—— *Frame Analysis*, Cambridge, Mass., 1974.

—— *Stigma*, Englewood Cliffs, NJ, 1963.

—— 'The Moral Career of the Mental Patient', *Psychiatry*, 22.2 (1959).

—— 'Where the Action Is', in *Interaction Ritual*, London, 1972.

GOLD, M., *Delinquent Behavior in an American City*, Belmont, Calif., 1970.

GORDON, C., *The Old Bailey and Newgate*, London, 1902.

GORING, C., *The English Convict: A Statistical Study*, London, 1913.

GOULDNER, A., 'Anti-Minotaur: The Myth of a Value-Free Sociology', *Social Problems*, 10 (1962).

—— *The Coming Crisis of Western Sociology*, New York and London, 1970.

—— 'The Sociologist as Partisan', *American Sociologist* (1968). Reprinted in Gouldner, A., *For Sociology: Renewal and Critique in Sociology Today*, London, 1973.

GOVE, W. (ed.), *The Labelling of Deviance*, London, 1975.

GRIFFITH, J., *The Politics of the Judiciary*, London, 1977.

GRIFFITHS, A., *The Chronicles of Newgate*, London, 1884.

GURR, T. *et al.*, *The Politics of Crime and Conflict*, Beverly Hills, 1977.

GUSFIELD, J., 'Moral Passage', *Social Problems*, 15.2 (1968).

HABERMAS, J., *Legitimation Crisis*, London, 1975.

HAGAN, J., *The Disreputable Pleasures*, Toronto, 1977.

—— and LEON, J., 'Rediscovering Delinquency: Social History, Political Ideology and the Rule of Law', *American Sociological Review*, 42 (1977).

—— SIMPSON, J., and GILLIS, A., 'The Sexual Stratification of Social Control', *British Journal of Sociology*, 30 (1979).

—— GILLIS, A., and SIMPSON, J., 'The Class Structure of Gender and Delinquency: Toward a Power-control Theory of Common Delinquent Behaviour', *American Journal of Sociology*, 90 (1985).

HALL, S., *Drifting into a Law and Order Society*, London, 1980.

—— *et al.*, *Policing the Crisis*, London, 1978.

—— *et al.* (eds.), *Resistance through Rituals*, London, 1976.

HALLORAN, J. *et al.*, *Demonstrations and Communications*, Harmondsworth, 1970.

HALSEY, A., 'Education Can Compensate', *New Society*, 24 Jan. 1980.

HAMMOND, P. (ed.), *Sociologists at Work*, New York, 1964.

HARGREAVES, D., *Social Relations in a Secondary School*, London, 1967.

HARRIS, A., 'Sex and Theories of Deviance', *American Sociological Review*, 42 (1977).

HAWKINS, K., *Environment and Enforcement*, Oxford, 1984.

HAWTHORNE, G., *Enlightenment and Despair*, Cambridge, 1977.

HAY, D. *et al.* (eds.), *Albion's Fatal Tree: Crime and Society in Eighteenth-century England*, London, 1975.

HAYWARD, A. (ed.), *Lives of the Most Remarkable Criminals*, London, 1927.

HEATH, A., *Rational Choice and Social Exchanges*, Cambridge, 1976.

HEBDIGE, R., *Subculture: The Meaning of Style*, London, 1979.

HEIDENSOHN, F., 'The Deviance of Women: A Critique and an Enquiry', *British Journal of Sociology*, 19 (1968).

—— *Women and Crime*, London, 1985.

—— 'Women and Crime: Questions for Criminology', in Carlen, P. and Worrall, A. (eds.), *Gender, Crime and Justice*, Milton Keynes, 1987.

HENRY, J., *Culture Against Man*, London, 1963.

HENRY, S., *The Hidden Economy*, London, 1978.

—— and MARS, G., 'Crime at Work', *Sociology*, 12.2 (1978).

HEYL, B., *The Madam as Entrepreneur*, New Brunswick, NJ, 1979.

HILL, R. and CRITTENDEN, K., *Proceedings of the Purdue Symposium on Ethnomethodology*, West Lafayette, Ind., 1968.

HILLIER, B., 'City of Alice's Dreams', *Architecture Journal*, 39, 9 July 1986.

HINDELANG, M., 'The Social versus Solitary Nature of Delinquent Involvements', *British Journal of Criminology*, 11 (1971).

HINDESS, B., *The Use of Official Statistics in Sociology: A Critique of Positivism and Ethnomethodology*, London, 1973.

HIRSCHI, T., 'Procedural Rules and the Study of Deviant Behavior', *Social Problems*, 21.2 (1973).

—— *Causes of Delinquency*, Berkeley, Calif., 1969.

HIRST, P., 'Marx and Engels on Law, Crime and Morality', in Taylor, I. *et al.* (eds.), *Critical Criminology*, London, 1975.

HOARE, Q. and NOWELL SMITH, G. (eds.), *Selections from the Prison Notebooks of Antonio Gramsci*, London, 1971.

HOBBES, T., *Leviathan*, Oxford, 1957.

HOBSBAWM, E., *Bandits*, Harmondsworth, 1969.

—— *Primitive Rebels*, Manchester, 1959.

HOFFMAN-BUSTAMENTE, D., 'The Nature of Female Criminality', *Issues in Criminology*, 8 (1973).

HOFSTADTER, R., *Social Darwinism in American Thought*, New York, 1959.

HOLDAWAY, S., *Inside the British Police*, London, 1983.

HOMANS, G., 'Bringing Men Back In', *American Sociological Review*, 29 (1964).

—— 'Social Behaviour as Exchange', *American Journal of Sociology*, 64 (1958).

—— *The Human Group*, London, 1951.

HOME OFFICE STATISTICAL BULLETIN 7/85, 'Criminal Careers of those Born in 1953, 1958 and 1963', London, 1985.

HOME OFFICE (UK), *Experiments in Social Policy and their Explanation* (Report of an Anglo–American Conference held at Ditchley Park, Oxfordshire, 29–31 Oct. 1969), Community Development Project, 1970, mimeograph.

HOOD, R., *Sentencing in Magistrates' Courts*, London, 1962.

—— and SPARKS, R., *Key Issues in Criminology*, London, 1970.

HOOKER, E., 'Male Homosexuality', in Farberow, N. (ed.), *Taboo Topics*, New York, 1963.

HOPE, T., *Burglary in Schools*, London, 1982.

HOROWITZ, I., 'The Politics of Drugs', in Rock, P. (ed.), *Drugs and Politics*, New Brunswick, NJ, 1977.

—— and LIEBOWITZ, M., 'Social Deviance and Political Marginality', *Social Problems*, 15.3 (1968).

HORTON, J., 'The Dehumanisation of Alienation and Anomie', *British Journal of Sociology*, 15 (1964).

HOUGH, M. and MAYHEW, P., *The British Crime Survey*, London, 1983.

—— —— *Taking Account of Crime*, London, 1985.

HUBER, J., 'Symbolic Interaction as a Pragmatic Perspective: The Bias of Emergent Theory', *American Sociological Review*, 38.2 (1973).

HUGHES, E., 'Robert E. Park', in *The Sociological Eye*, Chicago, 1971.

—— *The Growth of an Institution: The Chicago Real Estate Board*, Chicago, 1931.

—— 'Good People and Dirty Work', in *The Sociological Eye*, Chicago, 1971.

HUMPHREYS, L., *Out of the Closets*, Englewood Cliffs, NJ, 1972.

—— *Tearoom Trade*, Chicago, 1970.

IANNI, F., *A Family Business*, London, 1972.

IGNATIEFF, M., *A Just Measure of Pain*, London, 1979.

IRWIN, J., *The Felon*, Englewood Cliffs, NJ, 1970.

JACOBS, J., *The Death and Life of Great American Cities*, Harmondsworth, 1965.

JAMES, W., *A Pluralistic Universe*, New York, 1920.

—— *Pragmatism*, New York, 1949.

JOHNSON, E., 'The Function of the Central Business District in the Metropolitan Community', in *Third Year Course in the Study of Contemporary Society*, Chicago, 1942.

JONES, T., MACLEAN, B., and YOUNG, J., *The Islington Crime Survey*, Aldershot, 1986.

JUDGES, A., *The Elizabethan Underworld*, London, 1930.

KEVLES, D. J., *In the Name of Eugenics: Genetics and the Uses of Human Heredity*, New York, 1985.

KINCHELOE, S., 'The Behavior Sequence of a Dying Church', *Religious Education* (1929).

KITSUSE, J., 'Societal Reaction to Deviant Behavior', in Rubington, E. and Weinberg, M. (eds.), *Deviance: The Interactionist Perspective*, New York, 1968.

—— and CICOUREL, A., 'A Note on the Uses of Official Statistics', *Social Problems*, 11.2 (1963).

KLAPP, O., *Collective Search for Identity*, New York, 1969.

KLEIN, D., 'The Etiology of Female Crime: A Review of the Literature', *Issues in Criminology*, 8 (1973).

KLOCKARS, C., 'The Contemporary Crises of Marxist Criminology', *Criminology: An Interdisciplinary Journal*, 16.4 (1979).

—— *The Professional Fence*, London, 1975.

KOBRIN, S., 'The Chicago Area Project', in Johnston, N. *et al.* (eds.), *The Sociology of Punishment and Correction*, New York, 1962.

—— *et al.*, 'Offense Patterns of Status Offenders', in Shichor, D. and Kelly, D. (eds.), *Critical Issues in Juvenile Delinquency*, Lexington, Mass., 1980.

KONOPKA, G., *The Adolescent Girl in Conflict*, Englewood Cliffs, 1966.

KORN, R. and McCORKLE, L., 'Social Roles', in Bersani, C. (ed.), *Crime and Delinquency*, New York, 1970.

KORNHAUSER, R., *Social Sources of Delinquency: An Appraisal of Analytic Models*, Chicago, 1978.

KUHN, T., *The Structure of Scientific Revolutions*, Chicago, 1961.

LAMBERT, J., *Crime, Police and Race Relations*, London, 1970.

LANDAU, S. and NATHAN, G., 'Juveniles and the Police', *British Journal of Criminology*, 23 (1983).

LANDER, B., *Towards an Understanding of Juvenile Delinquency*, New York, 1954.

LANDESCO, J., *Organized Crime in Chicago*, Chicago, 1968.

LAYCOCK, G., *Reducing Burglary*, London, 1984.

LEA, J. and YOUNG, J., *What is to be Done about Law and Order?*, London, 1984.

LEE, N., *The Search for an Abortionist*, Chicago, 1969.

LEMERT, E., 'An Isolation and Closure Theory of Naive Check Forgery', in *Human Deviance, Social Problems, and Social Control*, Englewood Cliffs, 1967.

—— *Social Action and Legal Change*, Chicago, 1970.

LEMERT, E., *Social Pathology*, New York, 1951.
—— 'Social Structure, Social Control and Deviation', in Clinard, M. (ed.), *Anomie and Deviant Behavior*, New York, 1964.
LENIN, V., *Materialism and Empirio-Criticism*, London, 1908.
LEONARD, E., *Women, Crime and Society*, London, 1982.
LERMAN, P., *Community Treatment and Social Control: A Critical Analysis of Juvenile Correctional Policy*, Chicago, 1975.
LEWIS, O., *Five Families: Mexican Case Studies in the Culture of Poverty*, New York, 1959.
—— *La Vida: A Puerto Rican Family in the Culture of Poverty*, London, 1967.
—— *The Children of Sanchez*, New York, 1961.
LEZNOFF, M. and WESTLEY, W., 'The Homosexual Community', *Social Problems*, 3.4 (1956).
LIEBOW, E., *Tally's Corner: Negro Street-corner Men in Washington*, London, 1967.
LINDESMITH, A., *Opiate Addiction*, Bloomington, Ind., 1947.
—— and GAGNON, J., 'Anomie and Drug Addiction', in Clinard, M. (ed.), *Anomie and Deviant Behavior*, New York, 1964.
—— and LEVIN, Y., 'English Economy and Criminology of the Past Century', *Journal of Criminal Law, Criminology and Police Science*, 27.6 (1937).
LIPPMANN, W., *Public Opinion*, New York, 1965.
LOCKWOOD, D., 'Some Remarks on "The Social System"', *British Journal of Sociology*, 7 (1956).
LOMBROSO, C. and FERRERO, W., *The Female Offender*, London, 1895.
LONEY, M., *Community Against Government: The British Community Development Project, 1968–1978*, London, 1983..
LOPOTA, H., 'The Function of Voluntary Associations', in Burgess, E. and Bogue, D. (eds.), *Contributions to Urban Sociology*, Chicago, 1964.
LUKES, S., 'Alienation and Anomie', in Laslett, P. and Runciman, W. (eds.), *Philosophy, Politics and Society*, Oxford, 1967.
—— *Émile Durkheim: His Life and Work*, London, 1973.
LUKES, S. and SCULL, A., *Durkheim and the Law*, Oxford, 1983.
LURIE, A, *Imaginary Friends*, London, 1967.
McBARNET, D., 'Pre-trial Procedures and Construction of Conviction', in Carlen, P. (ed.), *The Sociology of Law*, Sociological Review Monographs, Keele, 1976.
McCAGHY, C., 'Drinking and Deviance Disavowal', *Social Problems*, 16.1 (1968).
McDONALD, L., *The Sociology of Law and Order*, London, 1976.

McHugh, P., 'A Common-Sense Perception of Deviance', in Dreitzel, H. (ed.), *Recent Sociology: No. 2*, New York, 1970.

McIntosh, M., *The Organization of Crime*, London, 1974.

Mack, J., '"Professional Crime" and Criminal Organization', *International Journal of Criminology and Penology*, 6.4 (1978).

McMullan, J. L., 'Aspects of professional crime and criminal organization in sixteenth and seventeenth century London: a sociological analysis', Ph.D. thesis, University of London (LSE), 1980.

McRobbie, A. and Garber, J., 'Girls and Subcultures', in Hall and Jefferson (eds.), 1976.

McVicar, J., *McVicar by Himself*, London, 1974.

Malinowski, B., *A Scientific Theory of Culture*, London, 1944.

—— *Crime and Custom in Savage Society*, London, 1926.

Mandeville, B., *The Fable of the Bees*, London, 1714.

Mann, C., *Female Crime and Delinquency*, Alabama, 1984.

Mannheim, H., *Social Aspects of Crime Between the Wars*, London, 1940.

Mannheim, K., 'On the Interpretation of "Weltanschauung"', in *Essays on the Sociology of Knowledge*, London, 1952.

Manning, P., 'Deviance and Dogma', *British Journal of Criminology*, 15 (1975).

—— *Police Work*, Cambridge, Mass., 1977.

—— *The Narc's Game*, Cambridge, Mass., 1980.

Marcuse, H., *One-Dimensional Man*, London, 1964.

Marris, P. and Rein, M., *Dilemmas of Social Reform: Poverty and Community Action in the United States*, Harmondsworth, 1974.

Marsh, P., Rosser, E., and Harré, R., *The Rules of Disorder*, London, 1978.

Marshall, T., *Sociology at the Crossroads*, London, 1964.

Martins, H., 'Time and Theory in Sociology', in Rex, J. (ed.), *Approaches to Sociology*, London, 1974.

Martinson, R., 'What Works? Questions and Answers about Penal Reform', *Public Interest*, 35 (1974).

Marx, G., 'The New Police Undercover Work', *Urban Life*, 8.4 (1980).

Mathiesen, T., *The Politics of Abolition*, London, 1974.

Matthews, R. and Young, J. (eds.), *Confronting Crime*, London, 1986.

Matza, D., *Becoming Deviant*, Englewood Cliffs, NJ, 1969.

—— *Delinquency and Drift*, New York, 1964.

—— 'Subterranean Traditions of Youth', *Annals of the American Academy of Political and Social Science*, 338 (1961).

MATZA, D. and SYKES, G., 'Delinquency and Subterranean Values', *American Sociological Review*, 26 (1961).

MAURER, D., *Whiz Mob: A Correlation of the Technical Argot of Pickpockets with their Behaviour Pattern*, New Haven, Conn., 1964.

MAWBY, R., 'Crime and Law: Enforcement in Different Residential Areas of the City of Sheffield', Ph.D. thesis, University of Sheffield, 1979.

—— 'Kiosk Vandalism', *British Journal of Criminology*, 17 (1977).

—— (ed.), *Policing the City*, Brookfield, Vermont, 1979.

MAXFIELD, M., *Fear of Crime in England and Wales*, London, 1984.

MAYHEW, H., *London Labour and the London Poor*, London, 1862.

MAYHEW, P. *et al.*, *Crime as Opportunity*, Home Office Research Study No. 34, London, 1976.

MAYS, J., *Crime and the Social Structure*, London, 1964.

—— *Growing Up in the City*, Liverpool, 1954.

—— *On the Threshold of Delinquency*, Liverpool, 1959.

MEAD, G., 'The Philosophy of John Dewey', *International Journal of Ethics*, 46.1 (1935).

—— *The Philosophy of the Act*, Chicago, 1938.

—— 'The Psychology of Punitive Justice', *American Journal of Sociology*, 23 (1918).

MELLY, G., *Revolt into Style*, London, 1972.

MELTZER, B. *et al.*, *Symbolic Interactionism*, London, 1975.

MERTON, R., 'Social Structure and Anomie', *American Sociological Review*, 3 (1938). Revised and enlarged in successive editions of his *Social Theory and Social Structure*.

—— *Social Theory and Social Structure*, New York, 1949 and 1957.

—— and NISBET, R. (eds.), *Contemporary Social Problems*, New York, 1961.

MILLER, D., *George Herbert Mead*, Austin, Texas, 1973.

MILLER, J., 'Systems of Control and the Serious Youth Offender', in Bakal, Y. and Polsky, H. (eds.), *Reforming Corrections for Juvenile Offenders*, Lexington, Mass., 1979.

MILLER, W., *Cops and Bobbies*, Chicago, 1973.

MILLER, W. B., 'Lower Class Culture as a Generating Milieu of Gang Delinquency', *Journal of Social Issues*, 14 (1958).

—— *et al.*, 'Aggression in a Boys' Street-Corner Group', *Psychiatry*, 24 (1961).

MILLS, C., 'Situated Actions and Vocabularies of Motive', *American Sociological Review*, 5.4 (1940).

—— *Sociology and Pragmatism*, New York, 1964.

—— *The Power Élite*, New York, 1956.

—— *The Sociological Imagination*, New York, 1959.

MIZRUCHI, F., *Success and Opportunity: A Study of Anomie*, New York, 1964.

MOBILIZATION FOR YOUTH, *A Proposal for the Prevention of Delinquency by the Expansion of Opportunities*, New York, 1960.

MORGAN, P., *Child Care: Sense and Fable*, London, 1975.

—— *Delinquent Fantasies*, London, 1978.

MORRIS, A., *Women, Crime and Criminal Justice*, Oxford, 1987.

MORRIS, N. and HAWKINS, G., *The Honest Politician's Guide to Crime Control*, Chicago, 1970.

MORRIS, P., *Prisoners and their Families*, London, 1965.

MORRIS, R., 'Female Delinquency and Relational Problems', *Social Forces*, 43 (1964).

—— 'Attitudes Towards Delinquency by Delinquents, Non-delinquents and Their Friends', *British Journal of Criminology*, 5 (1965).

MORRIS, T., *The Criminal Area*, London, 1957.

—— and P., *Pentonville*, London, 1963.

MORSE, M., *The Unattached*, Harmondsworth, 1965.

MURDOCK, G. and McCRON, R., 'Youth and Class: The Career of a Confusion', in Mungham, G. and Pearson, G. (eds.), *Working Class Youth Cultures*, London, 1976.

NAFFIN, N., 'The Masculinity–femininity Hypothesis: a Consideration of Gender-based Personality Theories of Female Crime', *British Journal of Criminology*, 25 (1985).

NAGEL, I., 'Sex Differences in the Processing of Criminal Defendants', in Weisberg, D. (ed.), *Women and the Law*, New York, 1980.

NETTLER, G., 'Antisocial Sentiment and Criminality', *American Sociological Review*, 24 (1959).

—— *Explaining Crime*, New York, 1978.

NEWMAN, O., *Defensible Space: People and Design in the Violent City*, London, 1972.

NEWSON, J. and E., *Seven Years Old in the Home Environment*, London, 1976.

NEW YORK CITY YOUTH BOARD, *Reaching the Fighting Gang*, New York, 1960.

NOURSE, T, *Campania Foelix*, London, 1700.

NYE, F. and SHORT, J., 'Scaling Delinquent Behavior', *American Sociological Review*, 22 (1957).

O'MALLEY, P., 'War and Suicide', *British Journal of Criminology*, 15 (1975).

PAHL, R., '"Collective Consumption" and the State in Capitalist and

State Socialist Societies', in Scase, R. (ed.), *Industrial Society: Class, Cleavage and Control*, London, 1977.

PAHL, R., 'Stratification: The Relation Between States and Urban and Regional Development', *International Journal of Urban and Regional Research*, 1.1 (1977).

—— *Whose City?*, London, 1970.

PAILTHORPE, G., *Studies in the Psychology of Delinquency*, London (HMSO), 1932.

PALMER, J., 'Thrillers: The Deviant Behind the Consensus', in Taylor, I. and Taylor, L. (eds.), *Politics and Deviance*, Harmondsworth, 1973.

PARK, R., 'Community Organization and Juvenile Delinquency', in Park, R. and Burgess, E. (eds.), *The City*, Chicago, 1925.

—— 'The City as a Social Laboratory', in Smith, T. and White, L. (eds.), *Chicago: An Experiment in Social Science Research*, Chicago, 1929.

—— 'The City: Suggestions for the Investigation of Human Behavior in the City Environment', *American Journal of Sociology*, 20 (1915). Reprinted in Park, R. and Burgess, E. (eds.), *The City*, Chicago, 1925.

—— *The Crowd and the Public*, Chicago, 1921.

—— *The Immigrant Press and its Control*, New York, 1922.

—— and BURGESS, E. (eds.), *The City*, Chicago, 1925.

PARKER, H., *The View From the Boys*, Newton Abbot, 1974.

PARKER, T. and ALLERTON, R., *The Courage of His Convictions*, London, 1964.

PARKIN, F., *Marxism and Class Theory: A Bourgeois Critique*, London, 1979.

PARSONS, T., *The Social System*, New York, 1951.

PATRICK, J., *A Glasgow Gang Observed*, London, 1973.

PEARCE, F., *Crimes of the Powerful*, London, 1976.

PEARSON, G., '"Paki-Bashing" in a North East Lancashire Cotton Town: A Case Study and its History', in Mungham, G. and Pearson, G. (eds.), *Working Class Youth Culture*, London, 1976.

—— *The Deviant Imagination*, London, 1975.

—— *Hooligan: A History of Respectable Fears*, London, 1983.

PHILLIPSON, M., *Sociological Aspects of Crime and Delinquency*, London, 1971.

—— 'Thinking Out of Deviance', unpublished paper, 1974.

—— and ROCHE, M., 'Phenomenology, Sociology and the Study of Deviance', in Rock, P. and McIntosh, M. (eds.), *Deviance and Social Control*, London, 1974.

PIKE, L., *A History of Crime in England*, London, 1876.

PILIAVIN, I. and BRIAR, S., 'Police Encounters with Juveniles', *American Journal of Sociology*, 70 (1964).

PIVEN, F. and CLOWARD, R., *Regulating the Poor*, New York, 1971.

PLATT, A., review of *The New Criminology, Sociological Quarterly*, 14 (1973).

—— '"Street Crime"—A View From the Left'. *Crime and Social Justice*, 9 (1978).

—— *The Child Savers: The Invention of Delinquency*, Chicago, 1969 and 1975.

PLAYER, E., 'Women and Crime in the City', in Downes, D. (ed.), *Crime and the City; Essays in Honour of John Mays*, London, forthcoming.

PLUMMER, K., 'Misunderstanding Labelling Perspectives', in Downes, D. and Rock, P. (eds.), *Deviant Interpretations*, Oxford, 1979.

—— *Sexual Stigma: An Interactionist Account*, London, 1975.

POLLAK, O., *The Criminality of Women*, New York, 1950.

POLSKY, N., *Hustlers, Beats and Others*, Chicago, 1967.

POPPER, K., *Conjectures and Refutations*, London, 1963.

PORTERFIELD, A., *Youth in Trouble*, Fort Worth, Texas, 1946.

POULANTZAS, N., *Classes in Contemporary Capitalism*, London, 1975.

PRATT, M., *Mugging as a Social Problem*, London, 1981.

PRESIDENT'S COMMISSION ON LAW ENFORCEMENT AND ADMINISTRATION OF JUSTICE, *Crime and Its Impact: An Assessment*, Washington, DC, 1967.

PROBYN, W., *Angel Face*, London, 1977.

PRYCE, K., *Endless Pressure: A Study of West Indian Life-Styles in Bristol*, Harmondsworth, 1979.

PUNCH, M., *Policing the Inner City*, Lndon, 1979.

—— 'Officers and Men: Occupational Culture, Inter-rank Antagonism and the Investigation of Corruption', unpublished paper, 1980.

QUETELET, A., *Essai de Physique Sociale*, Brussels, 1869.

QUINNEY, R., 'Crime Control in Capitalist Society', in Taylor, I., Watton, P., and Young, J. (eds.), *Critical Criminology*, London, 1975.

—— *The Social Reality of Crime*, Boston, Mass., 1970.

RAINS, P., *Becoming an Unwed Mother*, Chicago, 1971.

RAINWATER, L., *Behind Ghetto Walls*, Chicago, 1970.

RAUSHENBUSH, W., *Robert Park: Biography of a Sociologist*, Durham, NC, 1979.

RAW, C., HODGSON, G., and PAGE, B., *Do You Sincerely Want to be Rich? Bernard Cornfield and IOS: An International Swindle*, London, 1971.

RAWSTHORNE, T., 'The Objectives and Content of Policy-Oriented Research', *Home Office Research Unit Research Bulletin*, 6 (1978).

RECKLESS, W., *Vice in Chicago*, Chicago, 1933.

—— *The Crime Problem*, New York, 1967.

—— 'The Distribution of Commercialized Vice in the City', in Burgess, E. (ed.), *The Urban Community*, Chicago, 1926.

—— DINITZ, S., and MURRAY, E., 'Self-Concept as an Insulator against Delinquency', *American Sociological Review*, 21 (1956).

—— —— —— 'The Good Boy in a High Delinquency Area', *Journal of Criminal Law, Criminology and Police Science*, 48.1 (1957).

REISS, A., 'Inappropriate Theories and Inadequate Methods as Policy Plagues: Self-Reported Delinquency and the Law', in Demerath, N. *et al.*, *Social Policy and Sociology*, New York, 1975.

—— 'The Social Integration of Queers and Peers', *Social Problems*, 9 (1961).

—— and RHODES, A., 'The Distribution of Juvenile Delinquency in the Social Class Structure', *American Sociological Review*, 26 (1961).

—— and TONRY, M. (eds.), *Communities and Crime*, Chicago, 1986.

Review Symposium, *British Journal of Criminology*, 24 (1984).

REX, J., *Discovering Sociology*, London, 1973.

—— *Key Problems of Sociological Theory*, London, 1961.

—— and MOORE, R., *Race, Community and Conflict*, London, 1967.

REYNOLDS, F., *The Problem Housing Estate*, Hants, 1986.

ROBINS, D, *We Hate Humans*, London, 1984.

ROCK, P., *Deviant Behaviour*, London, 1973.

—— (ed.), *Drugs and Politics*, New Brunswick, NJ, 1977.

—— Review of Smart, C., 'Women, Crime and Criminology', *British Journal of Criminology*, 17 (1977).

—— 'Has Deviance a Future?', in Blalock, H. (ed.), *Sociological Theory and Research*, New York, 1981.

—— *Making People Pay*, London, 1973.

—— *The Making of Symbolic Interactionism*, London, 1979.

—— *A View From the Shadows*, Oxford, 1986.

—— and COHEN, S., 'The Teddy Boy', in Bogdanor, V. and Skidelsky, R. (eds.), *The Age of Affluence*, London, 1970.

—— and McINTOSH, M. (eds.), *Deviance and Social Control*, London, 1974.

ROSE, A. (ed.), *Human Behavior and Social Processes*, New York, 1962.

ROSENHAN, D., 'On Being Sane in Insane Places', *Science*, No. 179 (1973).

ROSENHAN, K., 'Female Deviance and the Female Sex Role', *British Journal of Sociology*, 26 (1973).

ROTH, J. and EDDY, E., *Rehabilitation for the Unwanted*, New York, 1967.

RUBINGTON, E. and WEINBERG, M. (eds.), *Deviance*, New York, 1968.

RUBINSTEIN, J., *City Police*, New York, 1973.

RUDÉ, G., *The Crowd in History*, New York, 1964.

RUNCIMAN, W., *Relative Deprivation and Social Justice*, London, 1966.

RUSCHE, G. and KIRCHHEIMER, O., *Punishment and Social Structure*, New York, 1939.

RUTTER, M., *Maternal Deprivation Reassessed*, Harmondsworth, 1981 (2nd edn.).

SACKS, H., 'Notes on Police Assessment of Moral Character', in Sudnow, D. (ed.), *Studies in Social Interaction*, New York, 1972.

SAINSBURY, P., 'The Epidemiology of Suicide', in A. Roy (ed.), *Suicide*, Baltimore, Williams and Wilkins, 1986.

—— *Suicide Trends in Europe: An International Epidemiological Study*, forthcoming.

SAMUEL, R. (ed.), *Ruskin College, History Workshop Pamphlets*, Oxford, 1970– .

SCHEFF, T., *Being Mentally Ill*, London, 1966.

—— (ed.), *Mental Illness and Social Processes*, New York, 1967.

—— 'Negotiating Reality: Notes on Power in the Assessment of Responsibility', *Social Problems*, 16.1 (1968).

SCHUR, E., *Crimes Without Victims: Deviant Behaviour and Public Policy*, Englewood Cliffs, NJ, 1965.

—— *Narcotic Addiction in Britain and America*, London, 1963.

—— *Radical Non-Intervention: Rethinking the Delinquency Problem*, Englewood Cliffs, NJ, 1973.

SCHUTZ, A., 'Common-Sense and Scientific Interpretation of Human Action', in *Collected Papers*, I, The Hague, 1964.

—— 'The Social World and the Theory of Social Action', in *Collected Papers*, II, The Hague, 1964.

—— *The Structures of the Life-World*, London, 1974.

SCOTT, M. and LYMAN, S., 'Accounts, Deviance and Social Order', in Douglas, J. (ed.), *Deviance and Respectability*, New York, 1970.

SCOTT, R., 'A Proposed Framework for Analyzing Deviance as a Property of Social Order', in Scott, R. and Douglas, J. (eds.), *Theoretical Perspectives on Deviance*, New York, 1972.

—— *The Making of Blind Men*, New York, 1969.

—— *Why Sociology Does Not Apply*, New York, 1979.

—— and DOUGLAS, J. (eds.), *Theoretical Perspectives on Deviance*, New York, 1972.

SCULL, A., *Decarceration: Community Treatment and the Deviant—A Radical View*, Englewood Cliffs, NJ, 1977.

SCULL, A., 'Mad-Doctors and Magistrates', *Archives of European Sociology*, 15 (1976).

SELLIN, T., *Culture Conflict and Crime*, New York, 1938. Selected in M. Wolfgang *et al.* (eds.), *The Sociology of Crime and Delinquency*, New York, 1962, pp. 226–9.

—— 'The Significance of Records of Crime', in Wolfgang, M. *et al.* (eds.), *The Sociology of Crime and Delinquency*, New York, 1962.

SHARROCK, W., 'Ethnomethodology and British Sociology: Some Problems of Incorporation', unpublished paper, delivered to the British Sociological Association Conference, Lancaster University, 1980.

SHAW, C., *The Jackroller*, Chicago, 1930.

—— *The Natural History of a Delinquent Career*, Chicago, 1931.

—— and McKAY, H., *Juvenile Delinquency and Urban Areas*, Chicago, 1942.

—— —— 'Male Juvenile Delinquency and Group Behavior', in Short, J. (ed.), *The Social Fabric of the Metropolis*, Chicago, 1971.

SHIBUTANI, T., *The Derelicts of Company K*, Berkeley, Calif., 1978.

SHILS, E., *The Present State of American Sociology*, Glencoe, Ill., 1948.

—— 'Tradition, Ecology and Institution in the History of Sociology', *Daedalus*, 9 (1970).

SHOHAM, S., *The Mark of Cain*, Jerusalem, 1970.

SHORT, J., 'The Natural History of an Applied Theory: Differential Opportunity and Mobilization for Youth', in Demerath, N. *et al.* (eds.), *Social Policy and Sociology*, New York, 1975.

—— (ed.), *The Social Fabric of the Metropolis: Contributions of the Chicago School of Urban Sociology*, Chicago, 1971.

—— and STRODTBECK, F., *Group Process and Gang Delinquency*, Chicago, 1967.

SIMMEL, G., *Conflict and the Web of Group Affiliations*, New York, 1955.

SIMON, R., *Women and Crime*, Lexington, 1975.

SIMPKIN, M., *Trapped Within Welfare: Surviving Social Work*, London, 1979.

SKLAIR, L., 'The Fate of the "Functional Requisites" in Parsonian Sociology', *British Journal of Sociology*, 21 (1970).

SKOLNICK, J., *Justice without Trial*, New York, 1966.

SMALL, A., 'Fifty Years of Sociology in the United States', *American Journal of Sociology*, 21 (1916).

SMART, C., *Women, Crime and Criminology*, London, 1977.

SMIGEL, E. and ROSS, H., *Crimes Against Bureaucracy*, New York, 1970.

SMITH, D. and GRAY, J., *Police and People in London*, London, 1983.

SMITH, S., *Crime, Space and Society*, London, 1987.

—— and RAZZELL, P., *The Pools Winners*, London, 1975.

SNODGRASS, J., 'Clifford R. Shaw and Henry D. McKay: Chicago Criminologists', *British Journal of Criminology*, 16.1 (1976).

SOLOMON, P., *Soviet Criminologists and Criminal Policy*, London, 1978.

SPARKS, R. *et al.*, *Surveying Victims*, Chichester, 1977.

SPIEGEL, J., 'Problems of Access to Target Populations', in Conant, R. and Levin, M. (eds.), *Problems in Research on Community Violence*, New York, 1969.

STANKO, E., 'Typical Violence, Normal Precaution: Men, Women, and Interpersonal Violence in England, Wales, Scotland and the USA', in Hanmer, J. and Maynard, M. (eds.), *Women, Violence and Social Control*, London, 1987.

STEPHENS, J., *Loners, Losers and Lovers*, Seattle, 1976.

STINCHCOMBE, A., *Constructing Social Theories*, New York, 1968.

—— 'Institutions of Privacy in the Determination of Police Administrative Practice', *American Journal of Sociology*, 69 (1963).

—— *Rebellion in a High School*, Chicago, 1964.

SUDNOW, D., 'Normal Crimes: Sociological Features of the Penal Code', *Social Problems*, 12 (1965).

SUMNER, C., 'Ideology and Deviance', Ph.D. thesis, University of Sheffield, 1976.

—— 'Marxism and Deviancy Theory', in Wiles, P. (ed.), *The Sociology of Crime and Delinquency in Britain*, Vol. 2. *The New Criminologies*, 1976.

—— 'Race, Crime and Hegemony: A Review Essay', *Contemporary Crises*, 5 (1981).

SUMNER, M., *Prostitution and Images of Women*, unpubl. M.Sc. thesis, University of Wales.

SUNDHOLM, C. 'The Pornographic Arcade', *Urban Life and Culture*, 2.1 (1974).

SUTHERLAND, E., *Principles of Criminology*, Chicago, 1924. Extensively revised as Sutherland, E. and Cressey, D., *Criminology*, New York, 1979.

—— *The Professional Thief*, Chicago, 1956.

—— *White Collar Crime*, New York, 1949.

—— and CRESSEY, D., *Principles of Criminology*, Chicago and New York, 1955 (5th edn.).

SUTTLES, G., *The Social Construction of Communities*, Chicago, 1972.

—— *The Social Order of the Slum*, Chicago, 1968.

SYKES, G, *The Society of Captives*, Princeton, NJ, 1958.

—— and MATZA, D., 'Techniques of Neutralization', *American Sociological Review*, 22 (1957).

SZASZ, T., *The Manufacture of Madness*, New York, 1970.

TANNENBAUM, F., *Crime and the Community*, New York, 1938.

TANNER, D., *The Lesbian Couple*, Lexington, Mass., 1978.
TAYLOR, I., 'Client Refusal', *Case Conference*, 7 (1972).
—— and TAYLOR, L. (eds.), *Politics and Deviance*, Harmondsworth, 1973.
—— WALTON, P., and YOUNG, J. (eds.), *Critical Criminology*, London, 1975.
—— —— —— *The New Criminology*, London, 1973.
TAYLOR, L., *Deviance and Society*, London, 1971.
—— 'The Significance and Interpretation of Replies to Motivational Questions', *Sociology*, 6.1 (1972).
TAYLOR, R. and GOTTFREDSON, S., 'Environmental Design, Crime, and Prevention: An Examination of Community Dynamics', in A. Reiss and M. Tonry (eds.), *Communities and Crime*.
TEILMANN, K. and KLEIN, M., 'Juvenile Justice Legislation: A Framework for Evaluation', in Shichor, D. and Kelly, D. (eds.), *Critical Issues in Juvenile Delinquency*, Lexington, Mass., 1980.
THOMAS, W. I., *The Unadjusted Girl*, Boston, 1923.
—— and ZNANIECKI, F., *The Polish Peasant in Europe and America*, New York, 1927.
THOMPSON, E., 'The Moral Economy of the English Crowd in the Eighteenth Century', *Past and Present*, 50 (1971).
—— *Whigs and Hunters: The Origin of the Black Act*, London, 1975.
THOMPSON, H., *Hell's Angels*, New York, 1966.
THRASHER, F, *The Gang: A Study of 1,313 Gangs in Chicago*, Chicago, 1927.
TITMUSS, R., *Commitment to Welfare*, London, 1968.
TOBY, J., 'An Evaluation of Early Identification and Intensive Treatment Programs for Pre-Delinquents', *Social Problems*, 13 (1965).
—— 'Social Disorganization and Stake in Conformity: Complementary Factors in the Predatory Behaviour of Hoodlums', *Journal of Criminal Law, Criminology and Police Science*, 48 (1957).
TOWNSEND, P., 'Area Deprivation Policies', *New Statesman*, 6 Aug. 1976.
—— *The Last Refuge*, London, 1963.
TRASLER, G., *The Explanation of Criminality*, London, 1962.
TUNSTALL, J., *Media Sociology*, London, 1970.
TURK, A., *Criminality and the Legal Order*, Chicago, 1969.
TURNBULL, C., *The Mountain People*, London, 1973.
TURNER, R., 'Role-Taking: Process versus Conformity', in Rose, A. (ed.), *Human Behavior and Social Processes*, New York, 1962.

TYLER, G., 'The Great Electrical Conspiracy', in Wolfgang, M. *et al.* (eds.), *The Sociology of Crime and Delinquency*, New York, 1962.

VALENTINE, C., *Culture and Poverty*, Chicago, 1968.

VON HIRSCH, A. (ed.), *Doing Justice*, New York, 1976.

WADDINGTON, P., 'Mugging as a Moral Panic', *British Journal of Sociology*, 37 (1986).

WALKER, N., *Behaviour and Misbehaviour: Explanations and Non-explanations*, Oxford, 1977.

WALLERSTEIN, J. and WYLE, C., 'Our Law-Abiding Law-Breakers', *Federal Probation*, 25 (1947).

WALSH, D., *Break-Ins*, London, 1980.

—— *Heavy Business*, London, 1985.

WARD, D. and KASSEBAUM, G., *Women's Prison*, London, 1966.

WEIS, J., 'Dialogue with Matza', *Issues in Criminology*, 6.1 (1971).

WELSH, S., 'The Manufacture of Excitement in Police–Juvenile Encounters', *British Journal of Criminology*, 21 (1981).

WERTHMAN, C. and PILIAVIN, I., 'Gang Members and the Police', in Bordau, D. (ed.), *The Police: Six Sociological Essays*, New York, 1967.

WEST, D., *Present Conduct and Future Delinquency*, London, 1969.

—— and FARRINGTON, D., *The Delinquent Way of Life*, London, 1977.

—— —— *Who Becomes Delinquent?*, London, 1973.

WESTERGAARD, J., 'The Withering Away of Class: A Contemporary Myth', in Anderson, P. and Blackburn, R. (eds.), *Towards Socialism*, London, 1965.

WESTLEY, W., 'Violence and the Police', *American Journal of Sociology*, 59 (1953).

WHYTE, W., *Street Corner Society*, Chicago, 1965.

WILKINS, L., *Social Deviance*, London, 1964.

WILLIS, P., *Learning to Labour: How Working Class Kids Get Working Class Jobs*, Farnborough, Hants, 1977.

—— *Profane Culture*, London, 1978.

WILMOTT, P., *Adolescent Boys in East London*, London, 1966.

WILSON, H., 'Parental Supervision: A Neglected Aspect of Delinquency', *British Journal of Criminology*, 20 (1980).

—— and HERBERT, G., *Parents and Children in the Inner City*, London, 1978.

WILSON, J., *Thinking About Crime*, New York, 1975.

—— *Varieties of Police Behavior*, Cambridge, Mass., 1968.

WIRTH, L., 'Culture Conflict and Misconduct', in *On Cities and Social Life*, Chicago, 1964.

—— 'Human Ecology', in *On Cities and Social Life*, Chicago, 1964.

WIRTH, L., 'Ideological Aspects of Social Disorganization', in *On Cities and Social Life*, Chicago, 1964.

—— *The Ghetto*, Chicago, 1928.

WOLFE, T., *Radical Chic and Mau-Mauing the Flak-Catchers*, London, 1971.

WOLFGANG, M. and FERRACUTTI, F., *The Subculture of Violence*, London, 1964.

—— *et al.*, *Evaluating Criminology*, New York, 1978.

—— *et al.* (eds.), *The Sociology of Crime and Delinquency*, New York, 1962.

WOOTTON, B., *Social Science and Social Pathology*, London, 1959.

WRONG, D., 'The Oversocialized Conception of Man in Modern Sociology', *American Sociological Review*, 26 (1961).

YARROW, M. *et al.*, 'The Psychological Meaning of Mental Illness in the Family', in Rubington, E. and Weinberg, M. (eds.), *Deviance*, New York, 1968.

YOUNG, J., 'Left Idealism, Reformism and Beyond', in Fine, R. *et al.* (eds.), *Capitalism and the Rule of Law*, London, 1979.

—— 'Mass Media, Drugs and Deviance', in Rock, P. and McIntosh, M. (eds.), *Deviance and Social Control*, London, 1974.

—— *The Drugtakers*, London, 1971.

—— 'The Role of the Police as Amplifiers of Deviancy', in Cohen, S. (ed.), *Images of Deviance*, Harmondsworth, 1971.

—— 'Working Class Criminology', in Taylor, I., Walton, P., and Young, J. (eds.), *Critical Criminology*, London, 1975.

YOUNG, P., *The Pilgrims of Russian Town*, Chicago, 1932.

ZANDER, M., 'What is the Evidence on Law and Order?', *New Society*, 3 Dec. 1979.

ZIPFEL, T., 'Broadwater Farm Estate, Haringey: Background and Information Relating to the Riot on Sunday, 6th October 1985', unpublished.

—— 'Hard Work Transforms a Nightmare Estate', *Peptalk*, 2 (1985).

ZORBAUGH, H., *The Gold Coast and the Slum*, Chicago, 1929.

Index

Philosophy

—————

Editor

PROFESSOR H. J. PATON

MA, FBA, D.LITT, LL.D

Emeritus Professor of Moral Philosophy
in the University of Oxford

AN INTRODUCTION
TO ETHICS

J. D. Mabbott
President of St John's College, Oxford

HUTCHINSON UNIVERSITY LIBRARY
LONDON

HUTCHINSON & CO (Publishers) LTD
3 Fitzroy Square, London W1

London Melbourne Sydney Auckland
Wellington Johannesburg Cape Town
and agencies throughout the world

First published 1966
Reprinted 1967, 1969, and 1974

Printed in Great Britain by The Anchor Press Ltd
and bound by Wm. Brendon & Son Ltd
both of Tiptree, Essex
ISBN 0 09 078850 8 (cased)
0 09 078851 6 (paper)

ACKNOWLEDGMENT

The author is grateful to the Bodley Head Ltd for permission to quote from *Beasts and Superbeasts* by Saki.

CONTENTS

PREFACE

This book is intended as an Introduction in a double sense. It is written not only for readers who have not previously encountered moral philosophy but specifically for those who have read no philosophy at all and who wish to start philosophy with ethics.

There are strong arguments against such a start. The language and ideas of morals present great difficulties; the delimitations of the subject, especially from philosophical psychology, are not easy to determine. Logically it would seem better to start with the analysis of more straightforward factual propositions, together with some study of logic. In my experience, able students starting a full-scale honours course find this latter approach entirely satisfactory. Like the puppies in Plato, they enjoy tearing to bits the ideas thrown to them. But there are many who find this approach barren, negative, destructive, and unsatisfying. They include mature students, amateurs who have no continuous instruction to help them, and undergraduates who are not naturally attracted by or equipped for abstract speculation or a purely linguistic approach. Many of them have also got the idea that philosophers should concern themselves with problems which would seem genuine problems even to a non-philosopher. The problems which arise or are put before them in the alternative approach through logic and scientific analysis often seem to them to be artificial creations. The philosopher, says Wittgenstein, shows the fly how to get out of the fly-bottle, but they suspect that the philosopher has put the fly into the bottle to begin with.

Between the two world wars political philosophy provided a useful way into philosophy for the non-logician. There were real differences between the political parties; there were international conflicts which appeared to raise the deepest issues of conscience and principle; few young people were politically indifferent; rights and liberties, sovereignty and nationalism, loyalty and world revolution were common talk in café and bar. All this has gone. The main problems now seem to be those of personal and human relationships. Apart from CND, there is political apathy and a feeling of political helplessness in the face of vast and insoluble problems. So moral philosophy is now the discipline which can start from the things that matter to ordinary people.

But I have found recent books on moral philosophy (such as those of P. H. Nowell-Smith, R. M. Hare, and B. Mayo) too difficult for a complete philosophical novice, though admirable for those who have previously broken into philosophy by some other door and come to ethics late in their philosophical education.

For the beginner, Mill's *Utilitarianism*, Moore's *Ethics*, and Rashdall's *Theory of Good and Evil* (all genuine antiques) have the necessary simplicity and have previously had to serve my pupils as introductions.

This aim explains some features of the present work which would otherwise seem odd: the start from the hackneyed hedonist position, the traversing of the dead debates of the thirties, and the postponement, to the end, of any recognition of the recent revolution in ethics. This procedure seems justified, because the recent revolution was in fact a reaction against what had gone before, and is both less intelligible and less plausible if stated in isolation as itself a starting point.

References have been sparingly given in the text, but brief bibliographies are attached to each chapter.

I

INTRODUCTION

It often happens in philosophy, as in other subjects, that it is difficult to say in advance what an enquiry is about. Here only a few preliminary indications will be given before plunging into the subject itself.

We shall be concerned, then, with the meanings of certain *words*: 'good', 'bad', 'ought', 'right', 'duty', 'praise', and 'blame'. It might be said that we shall deal with these characteristics of human conduct, but this would itself be to accept a certain theory of morals. Hence the definition with reference to words is, at this stage, safer. It might be thought that, so far, we have said what is obvious. 'Good', 'bad', 'right,' etc., are obviously moral terms. But are they? They can all be used in non-moral senses. This car *ought* to go faster. Is it the *right* petrol? Or would a *good* brand be X? Should we *blame* the carburetter? And even in connection with human actions there are non-moral uses. He is a good bat, plays the right stroke, covers up when he ought; we praise his stance, blame only his caution. How are we to eliminate these non-moral uses? Again only a provisional answer is possible to a question which is still much debated.

We would start by eliminating those uses which are common to human and non-human contexts, leaving only the uses which are specifically human. For example, 'Tulloh ought to be coming round the last bend soon' is exactly parallel to 'the 4.15 ought to be coming round the last bend soon'. But there is no railway parallel to 'Jones ought to be kind to his children'. But, it might be said, all this is unnecessary. 'Moral' is a quite ordinary word which anyone can use and understand. We know that 'good' cannot be used in a moral sense of petrol or trains or cricketers. So Jones may be a good cricketer and a bad man. But it is not so easy. Good parent and bad man? Good teacher and bad man? So problems remain. But here, as often, the best initial answer to a question 'what is X?' is to demonstrate X, whether X is shrugging or skating or scalloping. I propose, therefore, to work through one or two traditional moral problems and the traditional theories about them. And I start with the most hackneyed and well-worn theory of all.

2

PLEASURE UTILITARIANISM

The key words in morals are 'good', 'right', and 'ought'. What does the pleasure Utilitarian say about them? On good, he distinguishes between what is good as a means to an end and what is good as an end. Petrol, a knife, a short cut are good if they are effective for their purposes. But is there anything that is good for its own sake? There must be, otherwise there would be no reason to choose any means. A knife is used to cut a twig, a twig to make a broom, a broom to clear leaves, cleared leaves to encourage plants, plants for their flowers, flowers for their scent—and do we stop there? For the Utilitarian (or specifically the *hedonistic* Utilitarian) only one thing is good in itself, good for its own sake—pleasure. And only one thing is bad in itself—pain. Everything else called 'good' is good because it increases pleasure or diminishes pain.

I meet a friend walking and ask him what he is up to. I may get three quite different kinds of answer. First, he may say 'I am going to the bank to get some money' or, second, 'I am taking exercise for my health' or, third, 'I like walking'. It is to be noted that in the first answer the means-and-end analysis is appropriate. Walking is a means to reaching the bank and reaching the bank a means to getting money. The stages succeed each other. But walking is not a *means* to exercise; walking is a kind of exercise, as a box-body is a kind of motor-car. And in the third case walking seems not to be a means at all. The three answers seem to suggest three different ends: having money, having health, and walking itself. But the hedonist pushes the analysis further (and obviously in the first answer it must be pushed further). 'Why do you want the money?' 'To buy a TV.' 'Why?' 'Because I get pleasure from looking at TV.' And again, 'Why do you want to keep fit?' 'To avoid disease.' 'Why?' 'Because disease is painful.' And finally: 'You say you like walking. You mean walking gives you pleasure.' And so in all other cases. This is obviously a very plausible theory, and one often maintained by people who have never heard of moral philosophy.

What then is the Utilitarian account of 'right' and 'ought' as terms to be applied to human actions? On any particular occasion the right act—the act a person ought to do—is the act which will produce the greatest possible amount of pleasure and the greatest diminution of pain. This too is a very plausible view, and it also is frequently maintained or implied by ordinary people innocent of philosophical sophistication. To spread happiness, to diminish suffering—what more need we ask of anyone? It is the fact that these theories are so popular and so natural which justifies their selection as the first to be examined here.

First criticism

This line of attack is aimed at the account of 'good'. The suggestion was that, whatever a man does or pursues, his one aim is pleasure and removal of pain. But many men would deny this. They would claim that ends other than pleasure are desired for their own sake. The miser pursues money, the thirsty man drink; the child cries for the moon; the parent pursues his child's welfare, the scientist truth, the martyr the triumph of his Church. Of course, it is *possible* to say on each case that it is his own pleasure that is the goal. 'He must get a kick out of it.' 'He wouldn't do it unless he thought it would please him.' But is it true? His whole heart is often set on his special goal: he does not calculate how much pleasure it will give him.

Bishop Butler was the first British philosopher to emphasise this. 'All particular appetites and passions are towards *external things themselves*, distinct from the pleasure arising from them; . . . there could not be this pleasure were it not for the prior suitableness between the object and the passion.'[1] Pleasure comes when I get what I want. The pleasure could not occur unless I wanted the object. A man who gets what he does not want gets no pleasure. Butler would maintain that pleasure is *always* a by-product of the achievement of some goal other than pleasure. He goes too far here, because it is possible to do something purely for the pleasure it gives. Eating sweets, choosing a menu, are examples of this. Nevertheless Butler is surely right in general. Most men most of the time pursue different specific objects without a thought of the pleasure which (no doubt) will come if they attain their objects.

The hedonistic analysis is plausible because of the regularity with which pleasure accompanies the achievement of any object. And similarly pain accompanies unsatisfied desire. But, though it is easy to confuse a welcome result with an end, it is not necessary to do so.

Second criticism

The hedonistic analysis of 'good' turned out to be an explanation of *all* human action. But how then can it explain specifically moral or right actions? Bentham's great work begins: 'Nature has placed mankind under the governance of two

1. *Sermon XI* (*British Moralists*, ed. Selby-Bigge, vol. I, para. 229)

sovereign masters, *pain* and *pleasure*. It is for them alone to point out what we ought to do as well as to determine what we shall do. On the one hand the standard of right and wrong on the other the chain of causes and effects, are fastened to their throne.'[1] But it would seem to follow that every man always does what he ought to do. There is one solution of this difficulty and it is the one to which much of the rest of Bentham's work points. The act a man does is always the act in which *he thinks* at the time will bring him the greatest pleasure. The right act, the act he ought to do, is the one which *really will* bring him the greatest pleasure. It is, of course, true that 'ought' and 'right' can be so used. 'You ought not to eat lobster. You forget it doesn't agree with you.' But, on this analysis, virtue is enlightened selfishness and sin merely mis-calculation of one's own private interest. This does not begin to look like a moral theory; nor this usage of 'right' and 'ought' a moral usage. And one fatal result would follow from it. On this view no one could do something wrong, knowing or believing it to be wrong. For this would mean knowingly to reject one's greatest pleasure which (on the theory we are examining) is psychologically impossible.

Third criticism

This turns on the question 'whose pleasure?' What is it that makes an act right? That it leads to the greatest amount of pleasure *for me* or *for all those affected by it*? Bentham and Mill constantly confuse this issue and repeatedly give both answers. In Bentham's definition of utility the weakness is obvious. 'The principle of utility judges any action to be right by the tendency it appears to have to augment or diminish the happiness of the party whose interest is in question . . . if that party be the community the happiness of the community; if a particular

1. *An Introduction to the Principles of Morals and Legislation* (opening sentences)

individual, then the happiness of that individual.'[1] But this will not do. Bentham must choose. Only the general happiness would seem a possible basis for a moral theory; and this might have served as an alternative solution to the paradox in Bentham that pleasure and pain determine not only what we ought to do but what we shall do. My own pleasure and pain determine what I shall do; but the greatest happiness of the greatest number determines what I ought to do. Both of these propositions (as we have seen) are plausible. But unfortunately they are incompatible with each other. Utilitarianism owes its perennial attractiveness to the belief that it is possible to ride these divergent steeds side by side. But if I necessarily do pursue only my own pleasure it is impossible for me to pursue the general happiness and so impossible for me to do what I ought to do.

The solution proposed both by Mill and by Bentham for this difficulty is the use of sanctions. I am necessarily selfish so why should I bother about the feelings of others? Bentham replies: 'If you do not, the law will catch up with you and you will not like that' (political sanction), or 'If you do not you will be shunned and boycotted and you will not like that' (popular sanction) or 'God will punish you hereafter' (religious sanction). Mill adds: 'You will not beat your children because you have parental feelings and you will be unhappy if they suffer; or you have sympathetic tendencies and other people's happiness will make you happy' (internal sanctions). But there are two difficulties about such solutions. First the sanctions are not certain. 'Crime doesn't pay' only for the criminal who is caught. The NSPCC is kept well occupied by parents who can be quite happy when their children suffer and even because they suffer. And secondly the sanctions again reduce morality to enlightened selfishness, which is not moral at all.

1. *British Moralists* I, paras. 359, 360

Fourth criticism

This criticism applies whether one adopts private pleasure or the general happiness as one's criterion. The great claim of Bentham and Mill (as of all other Utilitarians) is that their theory provides a single objective standard of right and wrong. Bentham uses the word 'calculate' and the criticism now relevant is aimed against the notion of a calculus of pleasure. Most people would agree that a pleasure (or pain) may vary in quantity. A drink gives more pleasure when one is thirsty and some kinds of drink give more pleasure than others. But, for calculation, this is not enough. How much more pleasure? Twice as much? Or thirty per cent more? This is bad enough; but there are greater difficulties still. Bentham says, rightly, that there are various factors to take into account in estimating pleasures; intensity, duration, fecundity (i.e. productivity of further pleasures), purity (i.e. freedom from pain). But now how are we to measure one of these against another? How long has a mild pleasure to last if it is to balance an intense but brief pleasure? It is obvious that these questions are unanswerable. And there is a final difficulty of the same kind. 'Mankind is under the dominion of *two* sovereign masters—pleasure and pain.' But how are *they* to be compared? There would have to be some third entity, common to both and applicable as a standard. It seems clear that the Utilitarians thought of the pleasure-pain scale as if it was a single scale with pleasure as plus and pain as minus, like a temperature scale. But this is clearly a mistake. On a temperature scale—if it is to allow measurement—what we call hot and cold must both be degrees of heat and the position of the scale zero is arbitrary (it differs in Centigrade and Fahrenheit) while the true zero is the unattainable absence of all heat at the lower end of the scale. But the zero in pleasure-pain is freedom from both, as in unconsciousness. So here too calculation is impossible.

Fifth criticism

A final problem for the Utilitarian is our use of 'good' and 'bad' in describing motives and intentions. We might agree with him that a man did the *right* thing in leaving money in his will to help on medical research, resulting in the decrease of human suffering. But if he did this from the motive of spite and with the intention that his children should not get his money, we should say this motive or intention was bad. The logical line for a Utilitarian to take is that taken by Bentham. We call motives bad when in most cases they lead to bad results, though not in this; and we call the intention bad because the result aimed at is bad. But these answers seem unconvincing.

REFERENCES

J. Bentham in *British Moralists*, ed. Selby-Bigge
J. S. Mill, *On Utilitarianism*

Criticism of the theory that pleasure alone is desired:
H. Sidgwick, *Methods of Ethics*, i, pp. 31–40

Criticism of measurement of pleasure:
Sidgwick, ibid., i, pp. 109–35

General criticism of pleasure utilitarianism:
G. E. Moore, *Principia Ethica*, ch. iii

3

IDEAL UTILITARIANISM

Among the difficulties of pleasure Utilitarianism were the following:

(a) men value ends other than pleasure;

(b) are we to pursue our own good or the general good?

(c) what value can be attached to motives and intentions?

All three are met by the type of Utilitarianism we shall now consider, the 'Ideal Utilitarianism' of G. E. Moore.

(a) *Ends other than pleasure*

Moore holds that aesthetic enjoyment and personal affection are good in themselves. This is clear to him, first because either of them by itself without any other accompanying or resultant good would be considered by all as worth having or bringing about, and second because the addition of either to any state of affairs would make the total worthwhileness of that state of affairs greater. And, in connection with the latter point, Moore notes that the word 'addition' may be misleading. Pleasure, for example, as such by itself, has little value, but pleasure associated with aesthetic experience greatly enhances the total value of the state of affairs. Knowledge by itself has little value but the knowledge associated with personal affection ('human understanding') greatly enhances the total value. This is Moore's principle of 'organic unities' by which the value of a whole depends on the relationships of the parts and is different from the values these parts would have if they were separately estimated and simply added.

(b) *Private or general good*

Moore is clear that the good results which make actions right must include the results for people in general and not for the agent only. With characteristic accuracy he insists that all that counts is the total quantity of good. The Utilitarian principle 'greatest good of the greatest number' may be self-contradictory. For it may be possible to produce a greater good in total by restricting it to a smaller number of people. Or again Utilitarians speak of the general happiness or the good of the community. But who are included in 'general' or in 'the community'? Again it is obvious that the only logical answer is to reject any limitations (to a particular nation or society), but yet not to say 'all mankind' when some of mankind will be wholly unaffected. The accurate formula would be 'the greatest total good for all those affected by the action in question'.

(c) *The value of motives and intentions*

Moore maintains that an act can be judged *right* or *wrong* without any reference to motives or intentions. But, besides passing judgment on the act as right or wrong, one can reach quite a different judgment on the agent as morally praiseworthy or blameworthy. To this second judgment motives and intentions are relevant. Moore is right in drawing attention to this dual nature of moral judgment, a duality frequently emphasised but also frequently overlooked. 'The surgeon did the wrong thing but you couldn't blame him as he couldn't have known the patient had this allergy.' For confusions one need only look at judgments on great political decisions such as the Munich Agreement. It is clearly possible to hold that it

was right to make the agreement, because if we had fought in
1938 we should have fought without the Commonwealth, and
without the Hurricanes and Spitfires which won the 'Battle of
Britain'; but that Chamberlain deserves no praise for it,
because these were not his intentions and motives. Or, vice
versa, it may be said that it was the wrong decision because if
we had fought in 1938 we should have had Russia and a
strong Czech army and frontier to help us, but that Chamberlain was to be praised for the decision because his motive was
an overwhelming desire for peace.

Now clearly these developments by G. E. Moore are an
immense advance on pleasure Utilitarianism both in clarifying
it and in turning it into a defensible moral theory.

Criticism of Moore's theory

Moore himself noticed that the main alternative moral theory
to his own was the theory that acts are right when they
exemplify certain moral rules (such as the Ten Commandments). Against this view he urged that every moral rule has
exceptions and these exceptions occur precisely when keeping
the rule would do harm or breaking it would do good. Such
moral rules, he thought, are adopted and followed because
their implementation usually produces good results and thus a
man can save time by not having to think out the results of
every action.

Moore did not notice that there are other kinds of exception
to moral rules, which arise when two rules conflict. I am told
something in confidence and then asked a question which I
can answer truthfully only by breaking the confidence. But
these exceptions would reinforce the case against binding and
absolute rules. In fact since *any* two moral rules may conflict
it is possible to hold a theory of absolute rules only if you
have only *one* absolute rule. Some pacifists come near this
position. Their absolute rule prohibits taking human life (or

using violence) and any other rule or moral obligation which conflicts with this is overridden by it. As against a theory of absolute rules, then, Moore's arguments are effective.

But there is a version of the 'Rules' theory which avoids these difficulties. It is that defended by H. A. Prichard and Sir David Ross. A theory of absolute rules has to maintain that a rule must be kept no matter what the consequences. '*Fiat justitia, ruat caelum.*' Prichard and Ross agreed that if the consequences of keeping a rule were *sufficiently* bad or of breaking it *sufficiently* good it should be broken. And they held that a rule was binding only if no other rule was involved and if two rules conflicted the more stringent rule should prevail. They observed that the reference to consequences was equivalent to adding rules requiring the production of good and the diminution of bad results. They were thus not anti-Utilitarian —their moral system included a Utilitarian element. They were left with two problems. (a) How are rules themselves to be justified? (b) How is a decision to be made when rules conflict? They answered the first question by saying that justification was unnecessary. It is just self-evident that promises ought to be kept and the truth to be told, as mathematical truths are self-evident. This and other answers to this first question are considered in this next chapter. In answer to the second question Ross says that cases of conflict are to be settled by each individual's judgment of the relative stringency of the claims upon him. No principle for such decisions is available. For if there were such a principle it would be the one absolute duty, which is just what the Utilitarians thought their principle was.

This case against Utilitarianism then has to depend on showing that keeping a promise and telling a truth are right not because of their consequences, not because of the good they will do. Here the critics appeal directly to the ordinary man's moral experience. If I owe my tailor ten pounds and I have ten

pounds it will not do to say 'How can I do most good with
this money?' or to consider that it will do more good if I
give it to Famine Relief than to my creditor. If anyone does
not *see* this there is no way of proving it to him. I can try to
clarify the situation by saying: 'But it's really your tailor's
money. Charity is not a virtue when you give away other
people's money.' But Robin Hood and socialist governments
think it is. It is obvious that, so far, Ross and Prichard do
express ordinary moral standards better than the Utilitarian.
The normal Utilitarian explanation of examples such as the
debt example is to appeal to the indirect consequences of
breaking promises or not paying debts. These actions do not
merely deprive people of goods; they deprive them of
expected goods; they cause disappointment as well as loss.

To meet this, examples may be cited in which no disappointment arises. I promise A to do something for B who does
not know about my promise, and is therefore not disap-
pointed if I break it. But A knows, and my failure will shake
his confidence in promises. Not to pay a debt deprives a
creditor but also weakens the credit system. To meet this
sort of case, Ross devises an example in which *no one* will
know the promise has been broken. 'If we suppose two men
dying together alone, do we think that the duty of one to
fulfil before he dies a promise he had made to the other would
be extinguished by the fact that neither act would have any
effect on the general confidence?'[1]

The reaction of many readers to such an example is to say
that 'desert-island morality' cannot be quoted in evidence.
Professor Nowell-Smith says, for example: 'I confess to being
quite unable to decide *now* what I should say if a desert-
island situation arose. Moral language is used against a background in which it is almost always true that a breach of
trust will, either directly or in the more roundabout ways

1. *The Right and the Good*, p. 39

which Utilitarians suggest, do more harm than good; and if this background is expressly removed my ordinary moral language breaks down.'[1]

I admit that when I first read Ross my reaction was similar to this and other critics must have urged a similar misgiving. For Ross, in his later book *Foundations of Ethics*, produces obviously real-life examples to illustrate the same point. I too kept an eye open on my own experience and within a few years I had come across half a dozen such cases. The essential point in all these cases is that no one should know the rule has been broken and so there can be no effect on the general confidence, etc. I have quoted some of these cases elsewhere,[2] so one example will suffice here. A former pupil of mine told me he had become secretary to a very rich man. He asked his employer what should be done with begging letters and was told: 'Put them in the waste-paper basket. We have no time to verify them all, and you know the list of my charities, which I have thought out with care.' The employer had a habit of stuffing a roll of bank-notes into the pocket of any suit he was wearing and his secretary was constantly extracting these bundles from suits being sent for cleaning. He handed them to his employer who always put them in his pocket uncounted. One morning, having nothing to do, my friend looked through the begging letters before destroying them. One was a winner—fully authenticated and making a good case for an immediate need of £10. My friend had just fished a bundle of fifty-seven pound notes out of a pair of tennis trousers. I said, 'Well, did you send the £10?' 'No!' 'Why not?' 'It wasn't my money.' Now this is clearly not a Utilitarian reason. And the secretary had every reason to believe that no one would know that he had broken his

1. *Ethics*, p. 241
2. Cf. 'Punishment', *Mind* XLVIII (1939), p. 156; 'Moral Rules', *Proceedings of the British Academy* XXXIX (1953), p. 103

employer's instructions. And so general trust and confidence would have been entirely unimpaired.

There is a last ditch for the Utilitarian, and in his second book Ross foresees it.[1] One person does know that the undertaking has been broken and that is the man who has broken it. What about the effect on him, on his character? There are two effects which may be alleged. It may make him a morally worse man; and, if virtue is an end of intrinsic value, then the act is wrong as damaging that value. Or it may make him more likely to break other promises in future and while *this* broken promise has no direct bad consequences, they will.

Both these arguments, however, fail. A man's character can be damaged only by doing what he believes to be wrong. A Utilitarian must therefore have other reasons than this for believing it wrong to break a trust. The argument is circular. The other line is no better. To break a promise in order to do good will indeed weaken a man's habit of keeping promises. But no one, except a rigid Kantian, thinks that all promises are to be kept no matter what—and if he does he is no Utilitarian. As a parallel let us take the rule, sometimes given to beginners at whist or bridge: 'Third player plays high.' Thus, suppose I hold the King of spades and the first two players have played low spade cards I should play my King. (One reason being that if the whereabouts of the Ace are unknown the odds are two to one against the fourth player holding it.) But now suppose the first player plays the two of spades and the second player the Ace what do I do? What would we think of my bridge tutor if he said: 'You should play your King because the general rule is a good rule—third player plays high—and if you do not play your King you will weaken your habit of playing high at third player, and *in other cases* you will be liable to lose tricks.' Surely the answer is that the rule is a good rough guide but one to be scrapped when its appli-

1. *Foundations of Ethics*, p. 104

cation would be obviously useless. It would be a bad thing to get into a *rigid* habit of playing high as third player. If this is to be a habit it must be a flexible habit capable of being broken on suitable occasions. So too for a Utilitarian moral rules are rough guides to good results—to be broken when better results will accrue; and the case in question is precisely one of those.

So I conclude, with Ross, that the Utilitarian cannot explain our conviction that it is frequently right to pay a debt or keep a promise when we could do more good by using the money for some other purpose or by breaking the promise.

Ross sums up his attack on Utilitarianism by saying that it 'fails to do justice to the highly personal character of duty. If the only duty is to produce the maximum of good, the question who is to have the good—whether it is myself, or my benefactor, or a person to whom I have made a promise to confer that good on him, or a mere fellow man to whom I stand in no such special relation—should make no difference to my having a duty to produce that good. But we are all in fact sure that it makes a vast difference.'[1]

This reference to the 'personal character' of duty and to 'special relationships' seems to me, however, to conceal the fact that these exceptions to the Utilitarian position are of two very different types and involve rejecting two quite different corollaries of the Utilitarian position. And, as ordinary people sometimes confuse these two, it is worth distinguishing them. It is sometimes my duty to do something for someone because of what is rightly called a 'special personal relationship'—for example, my parents, my colleagues, my pupils. This offends against the inevitable corollary of the Utilitarian principle that, provided the good is produced, it does not matter who has it —or, as Bentham put it, everybody is to count for one and nobody for more than one. But it is also sometimes my duty

1. *The Right and the Good*, p. 22

to do something because of some past occurrence; promise-keeping and debt-paying are the obvious cases here. The corollary of Utilitarianism against which these cases are fatal is that the past can never affect the rightness of a present action. Only the future counts because acts are made right by their results. Of course such duties involve other people (creditor and promisee) but their special point seems to me to be lost if they are described as depending on special personal relationships. I have no 'special personal relationship' to Messrs Dodson and Fogg to whom I owe money. Indeed I do not know who they are. They may have been 'taken over' years ago.

To see how ordinary people are sometimes misled here, two examples will suffice. One sometimes hears that a man's duty to his parents rests on what they have done for him—here a personal bond is confused with a debt. But it is clear that this is not the whole truth. No doubt when my parents have done a lot for me, I owe them a double duty as parents and as bene-factors. But if gratitude were the whole story then what would happen to the duty of parents to children? It would rest on a lively expectation of favours to come. Similarly if it is asked why I should cherish my wife, I am sometimes told that this is because of my marriage vows. Here again a duty to a person depending on a special relationship is confused with a duty (that of promise-keeping) depending on the past. It is clear that this answer too is no good because, if the vows were the reason, then husbands married by ceremonies which include no vows would have no duties to their wives. No doubt I (having made my vows) have a double duty, both to my wife and to my word.

REFERENCES

On Ideal Utilitarianism:
G. E. Moore, *Principia Ethica* especially chs. v, vi; *Ethics* especially ch. v
W. D. Ross, *The Right and the Good*, chs. i, ii

H. A. Prichard, 'Does Moral Philosophy Rest on a Mistake?' in *Mind* (1912), reprinted in *Moral Obligation*

On 'desert island' examples:
    J. Narveson in *Analysis* (January 1963)

4

MORAL RULES

(1) *Self-evidence*

We have seen how the criticism of Ross and Prichard against Ideal Utilitarianism is based on the acceptance of certain moral rules and how their theory avoids the difficulties of a Kantian commitment to absolute rules. It is natural to ask how such moral rules can be justified. The view maintained by Ross and Prichard was that such rules are self-evidently valid. In some cases this self-evidence is achieved by the words used. 'Debts ought to be paid' raises the question of the meaning of the word 'debt'. If it means 'moneys owed' then, of course, the money ought to be paid. In the authorised version of the English Bible (1611) the ten commandments in Exodus xx include 'Thou shalt not kill'. Now here there is nothing in the word 'kill' to make this tautologically self-evident, like 'moneys owed ought to be paid'. And, of course, the difficulty arose that the Old Testament is full of killings of which God is held to show no disapproval. So in the Revised Version (1885) the commandment reads: 'Thou shall do no murder.' But now what does 'murder' mean? Does it not mean those killings which are reprehensible, which ought not to be committed? It might be replied that murder can be defined as killings which are not intentional, not carried out under legal warrant, not in pursuance of a military duty, etc. But it is surely true that, alongside all this, 'murder' has a morally condemnatory sense and therefore the Revised Version commandment is a tautology.

It is clear, however, that some rules are not tautologies— 'Tell the truth', 'Honour thy father and mother'—and the problem of validating these still remains. The difficulty for Ross is that not everyone recognises the moral rules he does. Ross meets this by saying that such people have not reached a sufficient degree of maturity. 'Three threes are nine' is self-evidently true, even though its truth is not evident to a savage who cannot count beyond five. While this answer will explain why some men do not see the truth of moral propositions which are self-evident to Ross, it does not explain why other men have rules of which Ross would disapprove. The variation in moral rules from people to people and man to man seems to rule out a self-evidence theory.

In his later work Ross meets this by distinguishing between basic rules and dependent or derivative rules, which result from applying a basic rule to special circumstances. Ross holds that apparent differences rest on agreement on basic rules. The difference arises either from the special circumstances in which the basic rule is applied or from different factual beliefs entertained by the people in question. Thus the duty of a Briton to help the police to arrest a murderer and the duty of a Sicilian to kill a member of the murderer's family are basically the same duty of requiting murder or deterring murderers applied to different sets of circumstances, those with and without an effective central legal authority. The early fathers of the Church explained the polygamy of the Jewish patriarchs by the fact that the Jews had a small population and were surrounded by hostile peoples who constantly took toll of their adult males in war. It was essential that the birth-rate should be maintained.

B

There are equally obvious examples of cases where duties which seem to us very odd are explicable by the *factual* beliefs of the people concerned. The tribesman from northern Siberia when he kills a woman who steps across his shadow shares with us the basic (and self-evident) moral belief that deleterious influences should not be allowed to damage the souls of men, along with the mistaken beliefs that a woman is an inferior creature and that his shadow is part of his personality. Other tribesmen who kill and eat their parents show both the features noted above. They agree with us that we should be kind to our parents. But, as they are nomadic tribes who have to rely on fleetness of foot to escape enemies, animal or human, the kindest thing is to kill them. As for eating them, they agree with us that we should honour our parents and try to acquire their virtues. They combine this with the dietary belief that men come to resemble what they eat.

But it is not possible to reduce all differences in moral rules to variations on agreed themes. The conscientious objector and his opponents are not agreed on fundamentals nor are those who think that suicide and divorce are sometimes right and those who hold they are always wrong.

(2) *Empirical generalisations*

Those who for these reasons or others reject the self-evidence of moral rules are liable to go to the opposite extreme and hold that moral rules are empirical generalisations resting on particular moral judgments, which are ultimate. A number of particular actions are recognised, each independently from the others, as being right. It is then noticed that all of them have some other similarity in addition to their rightness and it is then inferred with a certain degree of probability that rightness and this other characteristic will accompany each other always or in the next observed case. This was the view of

Adam Smith. 'General maxims of morality are formed, like all other general maxims, from experience and induction. We observe in a great variety of particular cases what pleases or displeases our moral faculties, what these approve or disapprove of, and by induction from this experience we establish the general rules.'[1] This theory is echoed, though without Adam Smith's clarity, by other moralists right down to the present day. C. L. Stevenson, for example, holds that the attachment of a moral adjective each as 'right' to a *kind* of action is merely the result of 'habit and rough generalisation'. It is due to 'the psychological economy that comes from ordering of attitudes in some sort of classification'.[2]

Thus in order to establish that acts having a certain characteristic X are right it is necessary first to recognise that they are right independently of their possessing this character X, and then to observe that they also have the character X, and only then to conclude that rightness and the character X are connected. These recognitions must be independent. For, if the agent approved of giving a book to Jones *because* he had borrowed it or disapproved of sticking a pin into Smith *because* it would cause pain, the connection between right and the return of borrowed articles or between wrong and causing pain would not have been an inductive generalisation empirically established. It is this feature, concealed in most statements of it, which inclines me to hold that it is indubitably false.

The existentialists would seem to come near this view with their insistence that actual choices determine our valuations and not vice versa. But their examples show that the valuations come first. In an example given by Sartre a young man is torn between the claims of his mother who, deserted by her husband and bereft of her other son, lives only in him, and the call of

1. *The Theory of Moral Sentiments*, 1st ed., p. 502 (*British Moralists*, ed. Selby-Bigge, vol. i, para. 344)
2. *Ethics and Language*, p. 95

the Free French movement in England which would mean leaving his mother. But the anguish of the choice is due to the fact that these claims precede it. It is true as Sartre rightly stresses that there is no third principle available to guide the choice between these two. Therefore, in a sense, it is not clear *what* value he places on devotion to his mother until he has made the choice, not clear even to him. But this throws no doubt on the concept of moral rules, as Ross interprets them, as claims on the individual. Another way in which it can be seen that the basic moral judgments cannot be concerned with particular acts is to ask what the description of a particular act would be. Helping at that car smash in the High Street last Tuesday, or paying that £5 to Brown. But the full description would include the number of the car, the clothes I was wearing: the writing of a cheque and enclosing it in an envelope and . . . and . . . Of course you will say all this is irrelevant. But how is it to be decided what is irrelevant? One remembers the cricketer who

> Bowled twenty-one wides in an over,
> Which had never been done
> By a clergyman's son
> On a Tuesday, in August, at Dover.

Relevant features of a particular situation are precisely those which, being general, fall under some rule or other.

It may be suggested that Utilitarianism holds that moral rules are empirical generalisations. We discover that several actions are alike in that each produces the maximum good possible in the circumstances. We find they also resemble each other in being the keeping of promises or the telling of the truth. We conclude that promise-keeping or truth-telling will be likely in most cases or the next case to produce good and therefore to be right. But this is not a pure case of the theory, for the empirical generalisation has to be supplemented by two other general statements before it is relevant to moral conduct at all. First the statement that certain *kinds of result* are good and second that an action is right if it produces more good than any possible alternative action. Neither of these is an empirical generalisation. It follows too that the empirical generalisation is itself not a moral generalisation but an ordinarily factual generalisation asserting that certain kinds of actions have been found generally to conduce to pleasure or whatever other result the first supplementary principle holds to be good.

(3) *Utilitarian precepts*

We may now consider on its merits the Utilitarian view analysed above. We have seen that, on this view, it would follow that where an action exemplifies a moral rule but would have less good consequences than an action breaking the rule a Utilitarian would seem compelled to say the rule should be broken. We have also seen how Utilitarian attempts to evade this conclusion break down. G. E. Moore when faced with this type of case reaches a very odd result. He admits that we believe it right to keep a rule in cases where we believe more good would be done by breaking it. He holds the first belief is justified but only because the second is likely to be mistaken.

For if it is certain that in a large majority of cases the observance of a certain rule is useful, it follows that there is a large probability that it would be wrong to break the rule in any particular case; and the uncertainty of our knowledge both of effects and of their value, in particular cases, is so great, that it seems doubtful whether the individual's judgment that the effects will probably be good can ever be set against the general probability that that kind of action is wrong. Added to this general ignorance is the fact that, if the question arises at all, our judgment will generally be biased by the fact that we strongly desire one of the results which we hope to attain by breaking the rule. It seems, then, with regard to any rule which is *generally* useful, we may assert that it ought *always* to be observed, not on the ground that in *every* particular case it will be useful, but on the ground that in *any* particular case the probability of its being so is greater than that of our being likely to decide rightly that we have before us an instance of its disutility.[1]

Now this is a very queer theory indeed for a Utilitarian to have to adopt. Moral agents are now subject to rules of Kantian rigidity, rules with no exceptions. In the hackneyed example I must tell the murderer which way his victim went because truth-telling generally has good consequences. I must never break a date to help at an accident even if I am a doctor because promise-keeping generally has good consequences. Moreover the supporting arguments used by Moore are odd. The crucial cases for morals arise over 'conflicts of duty', and, in these, desire is not normally strongly engaged on one side. I have no violent desire to help Dr Barnardo's Homes rather than my tailor.

We return to the difficulty mentioned earlier that different people have different rules. Other men have felt about *hara-kiri*, about duelling, and about vendettas just as we feel about debts and promises. We feel it wrong to ask what good it will do to pay the debt. So they would feel it wrong to ask what good will result from my committing ceremonial suicide or calling out my traducer or killing a brother of my brother's murderer. There is no question of doing good; it is a plain duty; honour not utility is at stake.

Faced by this difficulty some may sit back contented with a subjectivist or relativist view, as they would with differences of judgment of beauty. They would say that it is just a matter of individual taste and needs no explanation, any more than differences over oysters or caviare.

1. *Principia Ethica*, p. 162 (italics original)

Others will urge a causal explanation. We approve of debt-paying and the Sicilians of vendettas because we and they have been brought up so to approve. Rules are accepted because society has indoctrinated men. Get a child young enough and you can give it moral scruples about anything whatever. This, however, cannot be the whole truth. If it were, it would be impossible for a man ever to question the rules of his society and therefore impossible for its rules ever to change (unless the man came like the Prince Consort, bringing into a society the rules of some other society in which he had been brought up, or one society was forcibly absorbed into another as Latvia and Estonia were during the last war, with consequent changes in their moral codes).

It is clear, however, that moral rules can be criticised and sometimes changed by the members of a society whose rules they are. So they should be capable also of being defended. How can this be done? I think by using Kant's test, but by giving it a Utilitarian twist which he tried to avoid. To find whether a rule is justified, Kant asks 'what if it were universalised?' In some cases universalisation—what would it be like if everybody did this?—produces a self-contradiction and then we know the act is wrong for no rule is possible. A lie is a false statement made when it will deceive a hearer. A fairy story is not a lie because it will not deceive the hearer, for he is not expecting the truth. But if everyone said what was false, no one would expect the truth and so no one could be deceived. Hence 'universal lying' is a self-contradiction. Stealing is *appropriating* the private *property* of another. But, if everyone took what was in other people's keeping, there would be no private property and 'appropriation' would be impossible. So 'universal stealing' is a self-contradiction.

In other cases, however, Kant has to admit that he cannot will the action to be universal not because of self-contradiction but because we would not welcome the results. There would be no self-contradiction if all men agreed to let their talents atrophy; but, says Kant, I cannot will this universally because I cannot will that my own talent should be allowed to lie unused.

Kant has been accused of Utilitarianism in using these arguments as if he had said that the world would be a worse place if all men lied or stole or refused to cultivate their talents. This is not so. But the self-contradiction argument leaves a gap. Why should the institution of communicative language or private property be accepted at all? Why should we not use language (as the Irish are sometimes said to do) to please or amuse rather than to inform? There is no logical impossibility about a lotus-eating society in which no one develops his talents. How would it be, then, to add the Utilitarian criterion? A rule is acceptable if a society in which it was observed would live a better life than one in which no rule, in this field, or some other rule were accepted. This solution seems first to have been suggested by Francis Hutcheson. 'The way of deciding about any disputed *practice* is to enquire whether this conduct or the contrary will most effectively promote the public good. The morality is immediately adjusted when the natural tendency or influence of the action upon the universal natural good of mankind is agreed upon.' And compare his remark on passive obedience: 'The point disputed among men of sense was whether *universal* submission would probably be attended with greater evils than temporary insurrections where privilege were invaded.'[1]

I wish to emphasise the difference between accepting the Utilitarian validation of a rule and accepting the Utilitarian justification of a particular action. As this is crucial and often missed or obscured, it has to be made clear. Even G. E.

---

1. *An Inquiry concerning the Original of our Ideas of Virtue or Moral Good,* sect. ii, para. iii, *British Moralists* (ed. Selby-Bigge, vol. i, para. 112) (my italics)

Moore—usually so meticulous—obscures it when he says, 'Apart from the immediate evils which murder generally produces, the fact that if it were a common practice the feeling of insecurity thus caused would absorb much time which might be spent to better purpose is perhaps conclusive against it.' What is not clear here is whether Moore is judging a particular murder to be wrong, on the grounds that, *if* murder were general, the results would be bad. This is indeed the theory under review in the present section. I judge a particular act to be right though its consequences may be less good than those of some alternative act open to me. It is right because it exemplifies a certain rule. But I judge the rule to be right because *if* it were generally observed the consequences would be good. This is often how what we call 'acting on principle' is in fact defended. Two hundred years ago I might have refused to challenge to a duel a man who had pushed me off the pavement. Yet I am the better swordsman and he a man of whom the world would be well rid. Asked for my reasons for refusing I should not appeal to the consequences of the particular duel (for they would be good). Nor should I cite the consequences of my refusal on the general system of duelling. This is the 'indirect' argument examined earlier (p. 26). For I should still claim I was right to refuse even if I was regarded as a crank or a coward and the system remained unshaken or even fortified by my refusal. I should say that duelling is a bad system. Its adoption makes all injuries equivalent and all a matter of life and death. This clearly could not be a reason against fighting any particular duel.

It is interesting, as an example of the variations in persuasive language, to see how this same point about the system can be described in opposite ways. Hegel speaks of 'the barbarity of the formal code of honour, which found in every injury an unpardonable insult'. Burke refers to 'that sensibility of principle, that chastity of honour, which felt a stain like a wound'. Moreover the duelling system considered as a reaction against wrongs and injuries has absurd consequences. It makes punishment depend on aim or swordsmanship, not on guilt, so that a bully who is good with his weapons would be able (and would be encouraged by the system) to go about insulting people and counting on his skill to get him out of trouble. This argument too cannot be used in my particular case, when I refuse to fight though I am the better swordsman and the bully would not escape punishment.

What can be said against this validation of moral rules by their consequences? It has been objected[1] that nobody who keeps a promise or pays a debt does so for such recondite reasons. It is of course true that, in life as in games, many rules are obeyed by people who have no idea why the rule holds. And 'why' here demands not history but justification. Most of our beliefs in all fields including ordinary matters of fact are held with no reflection on their justification. But this does not mean that there can be no evidence for them. Moral life like all ordinary life is too short for everyone to be constantly considering or obtaining or demanding adequate evidence for all his beliefs. But when a belief is challenged one may ask what would be the right kind of evidence and have some idea where to look for it.

Second, it has been objected[2] that a man has a duty to pay his debts even if he regards the system whose rule this is as inferior in its consequences to other possible systems such as barter or loans only on security. Hence the rightness of his payment cannot be derived from the superior good produced by the system. There are two answers to this. First there is the duty of supporting the existing system even if it is inferior because of the good done by such support in maintaining trust and confidence. Second, the man himself accepted the system when

1. I. Gallie, 'Oxford Moralists', *Philosophy* (1932)
2. N. G. H. Robinson, *The Claim of Morality*, p. 277

he incurred the debt. People who disapprove of credit systems should not incur debts. A parallel case is that of a judge who enforces a law whose general results he deems to be bad, because of the good done by law enforcement in general, and because he accepted this set-up when he took up his appointment. He could resign.

It may be objected that I have now myself reduced moral rules to empirical generalisations—the view I rejected earlier. For if an action is justified by reference to a rule and the rule is justified by the fact that its general observance would have good results how else could this be determined? Must it not rest on the inspection of repeated applications of the rule compared with the results of observed applications of other rules or no rules in the field in question?

Here the parellel with rules of a game may help. Some of the rules of a game may be called 'constitutive'. They determine what kind of a game it is to be: that each bridge player should have thirteen cards; that the association footballer should not handle the ball. It might be said that there is no question of justifying a rule of this kind. If you don't like the rules, don't play this game. Changing the rules would simply result in a different kind of game, such as we owe to Mr W. W. Ellis who in 1823 'with a fine disregard for the rules of football as played in his time first took the ball in his arms and ran with it'. But it could well be argued that the new game is a better game, as it has been by Mr Ellis's sectaries; and as most would agree that bridge is a better game than whist and contract than auction bridge. So even these rules can be justified by their consequences. Then there are other rules which can be altered without changing the whole character of the game like the revoke rule in bridge or the offside rule in football. These may be called 'regulative' rules. But few of these rules, whether 'constitutive' or 'regulative', could plausibly be called empirical generalisations. They are not justified by observing, prior to the formation of the rule, a number of games and discovering that those in which a certain practice was followed were better than those in which it was not and then laying down the practice as a rule. (This is not to deny that such experiments are possible, and there have been some recent cases in Rugby football.) But it does not require repeated experiments to establish that the reduction of services in tennis from two to one would diminish the present advantage of the server and hence the premium placed on height and strength. No repeated observations are needed to show that a check on bodyline bowling would improve the spirit of cricket or that the change from auction to contract would reduce the element of luck in bridge. As in games, so in life. No repeated observations are required to establish that loans on security will be given more readily than credit without it, or that the duelling system encourages the bully who is a good swordsman or shot. It is indeed one reason for some current suspicion of sociology as an empirical science that it goes to much trouble to establish by empirical methods conclusions which are obvious without them, such as that the children of divorced parents tend to be emotionally disturbed, that two juries faced with the same evidence may reach different conclusions, or that a visible luxury, such as a car or a television apparatus, will become a 'status symbol' and will be bought by some people who cannot afford it and by others who seldom use it.

Moral rules vary in the degree to which they are constitutive or merely regulative. There are some rules without which no civilised society could survive and few values could be achieved. The rules against killing and promise-breaking are of this kind (and this may be the reason why they have been supposed to be self-evident). Then there are other rules essential to a particular institution or a particular kind of society such as the rule against theft. Its abolition would involve a complete change—for example to a communist society. Or the abolition of the rules making parents responsible for their children would mean a change to a Platonic Republic in which children were taken from their parents at birth and brought up in government crèches and nurseries. These other societies too would have their own constitutive rules in place of those against theft and parental neglect; the communist state a rule against sabotage and the Platonic Republic a rule that children should not know who their parents are. Then there are regulative rules which are alternative to others within a given system and alterable without destroying society altogether or changing it to a completely different set-up. The age at which children cease to be the responsibility of their parents may be altered or a property system may rest on entailed inheritance or free testamentary disposal. But in regard to all these alternative institutions, or rules within institutions, it is always possible and legitimate (and sometimes necessary) to ask which are the best rules and this means asking what consequences follow or would follow from their observation or imposition.

A further complication in considering a rule as an empirical generalisation based on observing the good consequences of a series of similiar particular actions arises when the rule is one of a number or rules essential *together* for the working of an institution so that the rule cannot be said *alone* to have good results, since any alteration in it would involve altering other rules. If we defend the opening of all professions to women, we shall find (as Plato did) that we shall have to alter our views about the duties of mothers to their children. If we defend equal pay we may find ourselves forced to defend family allowances.

In estimating the effects of having a certain rule there is a further consideration which again makes 'empirical general-isation' seem an inadequate description. This description would require that the rule be kept in a large number of cases and from each case taken by itself (or from each of a majority of all cases) good results be seen to follow. But normally the good results of a rule do not follow seriatim on the several observances of it. They follow from *awareness* that the rule has been adopted. A rule is laid down that thefts will be punished. The best results are achieved not when a series of people are punished for theft, but when no one is punished at all, when the threat succeeds. The good produced by a rule that loans will be repaid is produced by the *belief* that they will be repaid; for the good in question is the availability of resources in time of need. Actual punishments or repayments come in primarily as applications of the rule and not as sources of good (though they may incidentally achieve some good too).

This point may be seen in another way. If the good produced by a rule were produced by the individual actions of keeping it, one would expect the good to vary, at least roughly, with the number of observances and the harm done by breaking it to vary with the number of breakages. But this is not the case. A few failures to repay or to punish may produce no harm at all. People feel no less secure because a few more thieves escape justice. They find it no less easy to get credit when the few bad debts which any tradesman expects rise from one to two per cent. But as the breakages rise there are two successive danger points, one when confidence is shaken and another when the system breaks. When the first point is reached people who have previously paid no special attention to the rising tide of failures to pay or to punish suddenly take special precautions, looking up customers in the local directory before giving them credit or double-locking their doors and taking their valuables to the bank. Then, if the failures mount further, a new crisis comes when the system collapses altogether; tradesmen stop giving credit to anybody or citizens arm themselves and organise posses of vigilantes. Banks know these two danger points. Ordinarily there is no problem; deposits balance withdrawals. Then as confidence weakens and saving ceases owing to a threat of inflation withdrawals may rise. And, at a certain point, measures may have to be taken to counter this—restricted credit or a rise in the bank rate. But if withdrawals still increase there may come a new crisis of confidence, a run on the bank and a collapse of the system.

These successive crises of confidence may indeed be largely independent of the number of breakages of the rule. Confidence and the loss of it are infectious. A whole series of thefts at a railway terminus will not shake confidence because one victim rarely knows that there are others, while far fewer thefts in a single local area will make a substantial difference. A dozen murders widely distributed and unpublicised will shake confidence less than three given front-page treatment or restricted to one locality.

Another corollary of the importance of confidence is that a bad rule may produce good results simply because it is a rule and thus makes planning possible. So a bad rule may be better than none. A doctor may disapprove of black market transactions but if he can ensure regular supplies of a drug essential to his patients only on the black market this may be better than having no reliable source of supply. A business man may be able to plan his affairs better in a country where every official has his price and the prices are well known than in one where nobody knows whether a service will be rendered without a bribe, and he may take up his time insulting the honest or failing to bribe the venal.

This point about confidence explains why G. E. Moore maintained that a moral rule should be observed only if it is both generally useful *and generally practised*. 'In a society in which certain kinds of theft are the common rule the utility of abstinence from such thefts on the part of a single individual is exceedingly doubtful even though the common rule is a bad one.'[1] Moore admits that this position may be weakened by the possibility that the example given by breaking the bad rule may tend to break down the existing custom and so may have good results. But surely this consideration is *not* how most people would decide the question. It is surely obvious that anyone who is convinced that society would be better off without such thefts (and promiscuity and bootlegging provide similar examples) will have a duty to abstain from them even if they are the established custom and his example will do nothing to weaken the practice. I would therefore reject Moore's conclusion which he states as follows:

The question whether the general observance of a rule not generally observed would or would not be desirable cannot much affect the question how any individual ought to act; since on the one hand there is a large probability that he will not by any means be able to bring about its general observance, and on the other hand the fact that its general observance would be useful could, in any case, give him no reason to conclude that he himself ought to observe it in the absence of such general observance.[2]

This is entirely in line with Moore's own Utilitarian position by which actual results of individual actions are the test of right and wrong. But I have shown earlier how strong is Ross's argument that some acts are right independently of their actual consequences and I am now suggesting that, at least in some cases, the rule which such acts observe is to be justified by the consideration that if it were generally adopted the results would be good. People act on principle and when acts against their principles are suggested they say 'what would it be like if everyone did that?' I do not see that this argument is weakened in the case where everyone *does* do that—with the results predicted.

1. *Principia Ethica*, p. 164
2. Ibid., p. 161

There is I think one exception here. Where other principles are involved whose application involves following the bad rule I may have a duty to follow it even while I think it bad. I may think tipping is a bad practice and am inclined to refuse to tip (accepting the bad service which results as the price I pay for my principles). But when it is pointed out to me that the fact that the practice is general has resulted in the waiter being paid a minute wage or the car-park attendant no wage at all, I may revise my views.

There is a further argument against the explanation of moral rules as Utilitarian precepts. Problems are bound to arise concerning the *distribution* of good in any society, and these seem to be independent of the amount of good produced and therefore of Utilitarian considerations. And the principles involved for such distribution cannot therefore themselves be regarded as Utilitarian precepts. The simplest of all these principles is that of equality. When there is a budget surplus it might be naturally suggested that a general remission of taxation in equal shares would be fairest. But this might well produce less good results than a large distribution to the neediest group. And this raises another principle, 'To each according to his need'. But it is felt to be unfair to reward the idle (though not the incapacitated). So a third principle would distribute in accordance with work done. It may be possible (and Mill tried to achieve this) to show that principles of justice have in fact a Utilitarian basis—as, for example, that reward for work is needed as an incentive. But this is a very difficult and little worked field and it must be left here as one well worth further consideration.

REFERENCES

On rules as Utilitarian precepts:
H. W. B. Joseph, *Some Problems in Ethics*, ch. viii
J. Rawls, 'Two Concepts of Rules', *Philosophical Review* (1955)

J. Harrison, 'Utilitarianism, Universalisation and Our Duty to be Just', *Proceedings of the Aristotelian Society* (1952–3)

Criticism of this view:

J. J. C. Smart, 'Extreme and Restricted Utilitarianism', *Philosophical Quarterly* (1956)

On the problems of justice and distribution:

J. S. Mill, *Utilitarianism*, ch. 5

J. Rawls, 'Justice as Fairness', *Philosophical Review* (1958)

S. I. Benn and R. S. Peters, *Social Principles and the Democratic State*, chs. 5, 6

5

RIGHT, OUGHT, AND DUTY

Moore and Ross, as we have seen, differed greatly about what makes an act right. But they were completely agreed on one central issue. They both thought that, in any given circumstances, there is one act which is the right act for a man to do and this act is his duty and is what he ought to do. What makes it right are the existing circumstances; and the man's own beliefs and motives have nothing to do with it. As we saw, Moore held that motives will come into our judgment of whether an agent was praiseworthy or blameworthy, but not into the question whether he did his duty. There are various corollaries of this view.

(a) My duty does not depend on any belief of mine nor need I know that it is my duty in order to do it. This may be illustrated by two examples, one using Moore's account of what makes an act right and the other using Ross's. On Moore's view that act is right which, of all courses open to the agent, will produce the best results. Now suppose a surgeon diagnoses a disease for which he believes an operation essential but (unknown to him and unknowable to him) the patient has a blood condition which will make the operation fatal. The surgeon's duty here is *not* to operate. With Ross's account, if I am in funds and my parents are in need I ought to help them.

Now suppose they are in need but owing to war conditions we have been separated and I cannot know they are needy. Yet my duty is to help them.

(b) My duty does not depend on my motives. It does not matter, for Ross and Moore, *why* I do the right thing; so long as I do it, I shall have done my duty and done what I ought to do. So a man who pays his debts not because of any sense of obligation but because he fears legal proceedings has done his duty. A man who tells the truth in order to hurt his hearer's feelings (but who fails to hurt him) has done his duty. A man who leaves money to a good cause *solely* in order to spite his relatives has done what he ought.

(c) My doing of duty must be successful. It is no use merely trying. Again the surgeon is a good example. If there was anything he could have done which would have cured his patient, he fails in the duty and does what he ought not to do, if he does not do this curative action. And it is no defence that he tried to cure him or that he did his best.

An effective attack on this view was launched by H. A. Prichard. He maintained that my duty depends on my *beliefs* about the facts and not (as Moore and Ross thought) on the facts themselves. Two kinds of facts are relevant here, facts about the situation and facts about the consequences of actions. So if a surgeon believes a man has smallpox and if he believes that a heavy inoculation will help him it is his duty to inoculate (even if it turns out later that the man had cowpox or that an inoculation would make him worse). If he does this he has done what he ought to do. Prichard goes on to point out that, on the view he is attacking, there are no duties of insurance or precaution. The question whether I ought to stop at a blind cross roads depends on whether there is in fact any traffic coming. I have sometimes been a passenger in a car when the driver took a shocking risk—overtaking over the rise of a hill—and when I showed signs of anxiety he would say, when the danger was over, 'There, you see, it was all right.' For Ross and Moore it *was* all right since in fact there was no danger. But Prichard would say he ought not to have done it; his duty was to hold back until he could see the road was clear.

Prichard's second criticism is to attack the view that my duty is to succeed and not merely to try. Prichard points out that any change in the world which I bring about is the end of a chain of causes which begins with a motion of my body; and once I have performed this motion other causes may come in unexpectedly which will prevent the end result from occurring. Moreover, says Prichard, even the motion of my body is not wholly within my control. Just as I may carve my patient skilfully but peritonitis may set in and he dies; so I may *try* to carve my patient skilfully but fail. All that can be demanded of a man is that he should '*set himself*' to achieve what he *believes* is appropriate to the situation *as it appears to him*. If he does this he has done his duty and done what he ought.

Ross forestalls this second point by an example. Suppose I borrow a book and then pack and post it carefully, but it fails to reach its owner. I have set myself to do what I believe is appropriate. But, says Ross, when I hear it has not arrived, surely I must send him another copy and go on doing this until one does arrive. For one's duty is to return borrowed articles not merely to try to do so. Now I think most people would agree that, when they heard the first copy had not arrived, they would not wash their hands of the matter. But suppose they do what Ross would require. It is surely clear that they are not carrying out the original obligation until they succeed. For in the end the book which gets through is not the 'borrowed article' but a substitute (as would be clear if the borrowed book had the owner's notes or a presentation inscription in it). And the fact that we are not continuing to perform the *same* duty would also be obvious if our reaction, while not one of inaction, was not that of Ross. In such

circumstances I think I would go first to the Post Office and
see whether they would compensate the lender. If not, then I
doubt whether I would simply send him another copy of the
same book. I might ask him what he would like or send him a
'book token'. And this makes clear that when I packed and
posted the book I *had* done the duty appropriate for borrowed
articles. I had set myself to return it (nor, as Ross would say,
had I failed in *this* duty). Then when things went wrong I had
another different duty, a duty of compensation. This situation
is really quite common. A man does what he ought; then
things go wrong, and he has another new duty. If it is asked
why *he* should have the duty of compensation when the loss is
not his fault, the first answer is that he should *not* bear it, the
Post Office should. The second is that, if the Post Office will
not pay and he does not, then nobody will; and it is more
unfair that the lender should end up worse off than that the
borrower should. So if I press the claims of a man for a job
(in all honesty and sincerity) and he turns out a failure then
I have a particular duty to help if I can, not because I failed in
my duty (as Ross would say) but because, if I had not pressed
his case, he would not have been appointed. So Ross fails to
shake Prichard's case that our duty is not to succeed but to try.

Now how are we to decide between Ross and Prichard?
In his later book, *Foundations of Ethics*, Ross recognises the
strength of Prichard's case but it does not lead him to give up
his view of the meanings of 'ought' and 'duty'. He says that it
shows that 'ought' and 'duty' are used in two different ways—
an 'objective' way defined by success in the actual situation and
a 'subjective' way defined by beliefs and efforts. And Ross
seems to me clearly correct in this claim.

For objective uses of 'ought' and 'duty' we may quote 'He
tried his best to do his duty,' or 'He ought not to have operated
but he could not have known that,' where, for the subjective
view, to try one's best *is* to do one's duty and where his duty

was to operate *because* he could not have known that the operation would fail. For examples of the subjective view compare 'Captain Oates did his duty though his sacrifice was in vain'; 'The juryman did his duty in voting "guilty", though in fact later evidence showed the man was innocent.'

What are the alternatives to Ross's conclusion that 'ought' and 'duty' are used both in his way and in Prichard's, and that there is no more to be said? There are only two. One is to give up these ordinary (and ambiguous) words and coin technical terms and give them exact and unambiguous meanings—'deontic' and 'rectal'. The other is to *legislate* for the ordinary words—to say 'duty' and 'ought' are used ambiguously but they *should* be used in Prichard's way only (or in Ross's). Just as whales are sometimes called 'fish' but they should not be.

I started this book by saying that it is concerned to analyse the use of moral words and, if so, the solution in *Foundations of Ethics* would seem the proper one. If words are ambiguous, say so, clearly distinguishing the meanings. Take the word 'pupil'. It would be absurd to say that the word in English means both a student and a part of the eye, but that the latter is wrong and illegitimate.

I am not altogether satisfied by this. If I accept it, I want to add —yes, but the Prichard or subjective use of 'ought' and 'duty' is more accurate, less misleading and dangerous. The Ross or objective view leads to a number of paradoxes. These in fact are no more than striking reiterations of Prichard's criticisms.

First, on the objective view, I can do my duty and do what I ought from a bad motive and with immoral intent. I borrow a book, I fully intend never to return it, I leave it in the lender's room in a fit of absence of mind; I have done my duty, the lender has got his book back.

Second, if I do my duty it will often be by luck. In a review of Ford Madox Ford's *Autobiography* I came across this:

But nothing in the author's brilliant and high-spirited narrative
is more striking than his account of how he met in London a lady
who said he had changed the whole of her life and saved her from
total disaster. Ford said he had never seen her before. 'Yes you have,'
she said. 'Ten years ago you came with Willa Cather to visit me in
Bronx Park. I was just about to elope with a married man but you
stayed so long and talked so much that I missed my train.' Mr
Ford says elsewhere that he 'rather dislikes virtue' but he does not
say whether he chalks this up to himself as one of his good deeds.

So the inscription on a tombstone 'He always did his duty'
could mean 'He was a man who went through life doing what
the circumstances required but always either by accident or
under compulsion or from a bad motive.' It is all very well for
Moore to say that motives have nothing to do with 'right',
'ought', and 'duty' but much to do with moral praise or blame.
This is precisely the paradox. We find it very odd to say that
the statement that a man has done or failed to do his duty (or
done or not done what he ought to have done) has nothing
to do with praise or blame. (It is interesting that 'right' and
wrong' seem much less paradoxical, as we shall see later.)
So it is tempting to legislate and say that 'ought' and 'duty'
are *wrongly* used in Ross's objective sense, or at least to say
'duty' is used in both ways but with a warning about its
objective uses.
But, if so, why is the objective use current? There are several
reasons. First the subjective view is a comparatively recent and
highly civilised achievement. People used to be held to blame
for acts for which we now absolve them from responsibility—
heretics or lunatics for example. Our recognition in this
country that a conscientious objector should not be penalised
or victimised or treated as a coward came about only after the
First World War. This change seems to me to be an advance,
but the older view hangs on. Then again, in earlier times
still, unintended crimes and even inanimate objects were

punished, in the spirit in which children kick a table which has tripped them up.

A second reason why the objective view is current is that there is a sense of the word 'duty' or 'duties' which is certainly objective: 'sentry duty', 'duty lists', etc. The duties of an orderly officer or of a clerk of court are objective because they are laid down in official documents. They do not depend on my beliefs or anyone's beliefs or motives or efforts.

A third reason why the objective use is current is that if we use 'duty' and 'ought' subjectively we seem still to need *some* objective term. In order to see this let us follow Prichard's argument to its conclusion. His final formula is that I ought 'to set myself to do what I believe will bring about a certain state of affairs'. But this is not enough. The blackmailer or thief sets himself to bring about a certain state of affairs. What is the difference between him and the moral man? It must lie in the state of affairs. We have to distinguish what the good man sets himself to bring about from what the bad man does and for this we need a moral term at the end of our formula. The term 'right' would serve. A man does his duty (and is a moral man) if he sets himself to do what he believes to be right. The bad man sets himself to do what he believes to be wrong. Here 'right' and 'wrong' are used objectively, and this would be another reason for legislating about the use of 'duty' and 'ought'. For if 'right' is used objectively, 'duty' and 'ought' so used would simply be synonymous with it.

But there is a further element of subjectivity to be considered. Prichard had argued that my duty depends on my beliefs about facts. But, as E. F. Carritt pointed out, there are other beliefs which have to be taken into account—beliefs about moral principles and moral values. Sometimes this is not obvious, because moral agreement is taken for granted. A surgeon's duty depends on his factual beliefs; if he believes an operation will save his patient's life his duty is to operate. Another

surgeon who believed an operation would kill his patient
would have a duty not to operate. Their different duties
depend on their different factual beliefs. We take it for
granted that the moral principle involved—that life should be
saved—is one on which they are agreed. But this is not always
the case. One doctor may recommend a heavy dose of morphia
—the other says 'that will kill him'—the first replies 'Yes, I
know.' Here they agree on facts and disagree on moral
standards. One man may reject another's bellicose reaction
because he believes in the efficacy of passive resistance—here
the disagreement is factual; but he may reject it because he
believes violence is never justified—this is a moral conflict.
Carritt accepts all the subjectivity in Prichard but goes further.
On his view a man's duty is to set himself to do what his own
moral estimate of the supposed situation requires. ('Set himself'
and 'supposed' are Prichard's subjectivisms; 'moral estimate' is
Carritt's addition.) There is a special difficulty in connection
with moral beliefs. We might be inclined to agree that the
duty of a pacifist is to refuse to fight in any cause however
'just'. But there are extreme cases where we may feel less
certain. What about the fanatics: Nazis persecuting Jews,
inquisitors torturing heretics, communists brainwashing prisoners—all believing these activities are right and proper? Are
they to be regarded as doing their duty and earning moral
commendation? What is the difference between them and the
pacifist? I am inclined to think that there is no difference, and
that we must accept the paradox and award Hitler moral
approval. Why are we less inclined to do so than in the case
of the pacifist? It may be because we are not so absolutely
certain that the pacifist is wrong; it may also be because the
pacifist is overemphasising a value we accept—the evil of war
and the merits of peaceful and persuasive solutions; it may be
again because pacifists (Quakers for example) are in all other
ways people we admire. But it has to be remembered that

toleration of pacifists is a very recent phenomenon. In the First World War they were prosecuted and otherwise persecuted with very general popular support. So we may be in a transitional stage in this matter and tolerance of people we now consider fanatical may well come. It should also be remembered that moral praise is only one kind of valuation. One may disapprove of the fanatic in other ways, and one may even (without blaming him) have a duty to restrict him (as one would a lunatic) or destroy him (as one would a mad dog).

There is one final added element of subjectivity to be considered—the most doubtful and debated of all. That is motive. It may be said that a man might satisfy Carritt's formula and still not be said to do his duty. For example, I am an elector to a Chair of philosophy; it falls vacant and I have to give my vote. Have I done my duty? What moral principle do I believe relevant? I believe the best man should be elected. What relevant beliefs of fact did I entertain? I believed Jones was the best man. Did I set myself to get Jones elected? I did; I voted for him. So I did my duty. But suppose my motive was friendship for Jones or malice against his rival. Then I should have voted for Jones whether I believed him the best man or not. I said to myself: 'What a bit of luck that his record is the best too. No one can cast a stone at me.' (We recall how, on the objective theory, the doing of duty is often a matter of luck.) The result of refusing to include motive in the definition of duty is the same paradox as we noted before, the separation of praise and blame from concepts of 'duty' and 'ought'. For obviously I deserve no praise for voting for my friend or voting from dislike of his rival.

Ross and Prichard both provide arguments against including a reference to motive in the definition of duty. First, it is said, such inclusion results in a regress; for what is the motive whose presence would be required? Surely a sense of duty.

My duty will then be 'to set myself to do what I believe appropriate to the situation from a sense that it is my duty'. That is 'from a sense that I ought to set myself . . . from a sense of duty'. But the regress arises only if we identify, as Ross does, duty with right and hold an objective theory of duty. If, as suggested above, we distinguish 'duty' from 'right' and use 'right' objectively, our formula now becomes 'My duty is to set myself to do what I believe to be right because I believe it to be right.' The regress or circle vanishes.

The second argument against including motive in duty is that 'ought implies can' and that our motives are not within our control. 'Ought implies can' is a central and agreed principle among all the moralists whose views we are considering. There are great problems about its analysis, but for the moment we must leave them aside. What is being maintained is that when I say someone ought to do something this implies that he can do it. Now the objection is that I cannot have a motive at will. I can decide to get up or to help a friend. But I can't decide to be angry or hungry, to love or to hate. Yet these are typical motives. There are two answers to this argument; the first goes a long way to meet it; the second, I think, goes all the way. First our motives are not wholly independent of our will. Ross admits that we can *cultivate* a motive. But this is not enough because it is a long-term plan and the definition which includes motive would seem to require us to have the appropriate motive *now*. Ross would still deny that we can alter our immediate motives by immediate choices. But sometimes we can. When people are angry we tell them to count ten. This reduces their anger. But this is to alter an exisiting motive not to produce a new one. But I can produce anger by recalling an injury someone has done me. I can generate hunger by imagining Lucullan feasts, or love for Chloe by dwelling on her charms. But it may be said that these procedures are indirect and consequently may fail. I may find I can't be angry after all and no pictures of feasts can rouse my appetite. And after all there may not be techniques known to me for arousing any motive. So this is a very limited answer.

But it leads to the second answer which seems entirely satisfactory. The motive required is the sense of duty. Now what is the technique for having this motive? It is simply to consider the rights and wrongs of any situation. It makes sense to say 'I can't be angry with Jones this morning; I can't be angry with anyone; the sun is shining and I'm brimful of happiness' or 'I can't feel hunger this morning. I have tried every device but I can't.' But it would sound very odd if a man said 'I find I can't have a sense of duty this morning.' This is because he would be saying that he could not recognise anything as right or wrong, good or bad.

We may recall Saki's Clovis:

'My mother never bothered about bringing me up. She saw to it that I got whacked at decent intervals and was taught the difference between right and wrong; there is some difference, you know, but I've forgotten what it is.'

'Forgotten the difference between right and wrong!' exclaimed Mrs Eggelby.

'Well, you see, I took up natural history and a lot of other subjects at the same time and one can't remember everything, can one? I used to know the difference between the Sardinian dormouse and the ordinary kind, and whether the wryneck arrives at our shores earlier than the cuckoo, or the other way round and how long the walrus takes to grow to maturity. I daresay you knew all these things once, but you've forgotten them.'

'These things are not important,' said Mrs Eggleby, 'but . . .'

'The fact that we have both forgotten them proves that they *are* important,' said Clovis, 'you must have noticed that it is always the important things one forgets while the trivial unnecessary facts of life stick in one's memory.'[1]

1. *Beasts and Super-Beasts* (collected 1926 ed). p. 159

It may well be that he cannot see anything wrong in some particular action and therefore has no sense of duty about *it*. But (on the subjective theory we have so far accepted) he would not then believe it to be wrong and would have no duty to abstain from it.

There may indeed be exceptional situations in which a man is unable to see *any* distinctions between right and wrong. It may be that extremes of torture or exhaustion or starvation, or the use of certain drugs or of Russian methods of brain-washing or (as some claim) the brain operation of frontal lobotomy—one of these may make recognition of all or any moral distinctions impossible. Then a man can't have the motive of duty. But under these circumstances he can't have duties either. It makes no sense to say that he ought not to have betrayed his colleagues or confessed to sabotage or treachery. So the exception confirms the rule. Unless the motive can be present duty cannot be present either.

There is another way in which this conclusion can be reached. We started from the difficulty that I might set myself to do what I believe to be right from various motives. My motive in voting for Jones might be duty or friendship or malice towards Jones's rival. But this assumes that I can set myself to do the same action from different motives. But is this really so? An action is not just a bodily motion—an affixing of an ink X to a form—it is a psychological affair. What am I really setting myself to achieve? Surely in one case to get the best man elected (or Jones qua best man) in another to get my friend elected (or Jones qua my friend) and in the third to do down Robinson by voting for Jones. Suppose that I set myself to get Jones elected qua best man but that I knew in addition that Jones was a Freemason or a three-handicap golfer. Could my enemies say that I had set myself to get a Freemason or a golf-tiger elected? So when I set myself to get my friend elected knowing him to be the best man it is equally inappropriate to say that I set myself to get the best man elected. Any distinction between bodily movement and willed action, and any distinction between involuntary and voluntary action, has to include a reference to motive as a part of willed voluntary action. So what happened in this election case was not that I set myself to do the right thing from the wrong motive, but that I did not set myself to do the right thing at all. I set myself to do an act of favouritism or spite which by good fortune had the same external character and actual results as the act I would have done if I had set myself to get the best man elected.

To sum up, Moore and Ross said duty was objective. To know whether a man had done his duty or done what he ought, one need know only the facts about the situation and the actual consequences of his action. One need know nothing at all about his beliefs and motives. I have argued, following Prichard (on factual beliefs), Carritt (on moral beliefs), and my own nose (on motives), that in order to know whether a man has done his duty one must know:

(a) his beliefs about the situation (not the facts about it)
(b) his beliefs about the consequences of his action (not the actual consequences)
(c) his moral beliefs
(d) his motive
(e) what he set himself to do (not what he actually achieved).

REFERENCES

W. D. Ross, *The Right and the Good*, pp. 4–7, 31–2, 42–7; *Foundations of Ethics*, chs. vi, vii

H. A. Prichard, 'Duty and Ignorance of Fact', *Proceedings of the British Academy* (1932), reprinted in *Moral Obligation*

E. F. Carritt, *Ethical and Political Thinking*, ch. ii

For defences of the objective theory of duty:

H. Nystedt, 'The Problem of Duty and Knowledge', *Philosophy* (1951)

K. Baier, 'Doing my Duty', *Philosophy* (1951)

For the subjective side:

H. J. N. Horsburgh, 'Baier on Doing one's Duty', *Philosophy* (1952)

N. H. G. Robinson, 'The Moral Situation', *Philosophy* (1949)

On the relevance of motive to duty:

I. Gallie, 'Oxford Moralists', *Philosophy* (1932)

G. E. Hughes, 'Motive and Duty', *Mind* (1944)

H. D. Lewis, 'Moral Freedom in Recent Ethics', *Proceedings of the Aristotelian Society* (1946-7)

On motives and 'ought implies can':

J. Wheatley, *Analysis* (January 1962)

A. Savile, *Analysis* (March 1963)

J. Wheatley, *Analysis* (December 1963)

P. Taylor, *Analysis* (October 1964)

6

THE DUTY TO THINK

Throughout the last chapter it has been repeatedly urged, in favour of all the subjective criteria for 'duty' and 'ought', that only with these criteria can praise be associated with 'ought' and blame with 'ought not'. So a man is to be praised if he sets himself to do what he believes to be right because he believes it right. But there seem to be exceptions to this. We use 'well-meaning' as a term of blame and we say that the path to Hell is paved with good intentions. When do we do this? When a conscientious action leads to bad results. But not in all cases. We should not describe an eighteenth-century surgeon who operated without chloroform or a nineteenth-century physician who failed to prescribe penicillin as well-meaning. This is because they could not have known any better. We condemn the well-meaning man in cases when he could have found out the relevant facts or thought more effectively about them.

Here, however, we are blaming him not for a present dereliction of duty but for a past one, as the tenses of our verbs show. 'Why did you do that?' 'I thought it would help him.' 'But don't you know he can't bear that sort of help?' 'Yes, of course, but I didn't think of it.' 'Well, you *ought to have thought*.' But it follows that the man is still to be commended

for doing what he does *at the time*. For he can *then* do no
better. He is making the best of a bad job. A single-handed
village doctor takes a glass too much sherry at a party and then
is called out to an accident. It is no good saying his duty is to
drive his car as he would if he were sober; he can't. If he
drives it as carefully as he can (in his actual condition) he has
done his duty. He can do no more. He ought not to *have had*
the extra sherry. This case is clearly parallel to those in which
failure to think precedes by a long interval the time of action.
Suppose I am asked to read a paper in Scotland early in
October, and I do not stop to consider that this is the beginning
of the Oxford term and accept the invitation. When the time
comes I must make the best of a bad job, either cancel my
paper or absent myself from Oxford at a time when a great
many people want to see me. Whichever of these I do will be
the best of a bad job. I ought never to *have* accepted. No, but
October is here and I have a duty now; which will be very
different from the duty I would have had if I had not failed in
the duty of thinking.

People may find it very hard to commend the well-meaning
action at the time it is done. But if you ask them what else
they would have the agent do (in the circumstances in which
he has landed himself), they will see the reason for commending it. One of the difficulties they meet is that the duty of
thinking may be so close in time to the duty of action that it is
difficult to distinguish them.

An extreme case of this is raised by Professor Ryle's account
of intelligent action. He argues that in many cases (perhaps in
most, and certainly in the best cases) there are not two distin-
guishable processes, thinking and acting. A really intelligent
games player does not think first and act afterwards, nor does
an intelligent speaker. Intelligence is shown not by a prior
process of thinking but by the way the act is done—intelligently. And even when plans are laid by prior thinking, they

have still to be carried out intelligently. Now what happens to my solution of the 'well-meaning' problem? I think I must say that there is a duty not only to act but to act intelligently (thinking what you are doing). And the well-meaning man while he satisfies the other factors in duty fails to satisfy this one. There are parallels. I may have a duty to tell a man an unpleasant truth and this includes a duty to tell him it *tactfully*, and in this respect I may fail. Or I may have to announce a decision and to announce it *firmly* (so that there is no doubt about its finality) and in this respect I may fail. Perhaps we would not call a man who fails to perform a duty thinkingly 'well-meaning' or 'well-intentioned'; we should more likely call him 'casual' or 'careless' or 'slapdash'—but these would still be words of blame. Perhaps 'negligent' covers both cases. We tend to associate 'intention' with prior thinking (again mistakenly as Ryle would urge; much is intended which is not precognised).

The second difficulty about this explanation of 'well-meaning' is that the duty to think appears unlimited. Prichard says that, before action, I must 'consider as fully as I can' whether my action will be appropriate.[1] But at first sight this would seem to have obvious dangers:

> The native hue of resolution
> Is sicklied o'er with the pale cast of thought.
> And enterprises of great pitch and moment
> With this regard their currents turn awry
> And lose the name of action.

Hamlet's trouble was 'thinking too precisely on the event'. It might be said that Prichard meant by 'as fully as I can' 'as fully as the circumstances allow' and this would take care of the danger of missing the bus. But there are other cases where excessive thought would be condemned, where much thought

1. *Moral Obligation*, p. 27

is given to a trivial decision and Prichard could not cover this case. So now it is tempting to say that the amount of thinking I have a duty to do is limited by the time available and by the importance of the decision.

But once again the subjective factors return upon us. How can a man be sure how much time is available? I once saw a man go through the ice on a lake, and taking some risks I went over cracking ice for a ladder. If I had stopped to watch him I would have seen that he was sinking quite slowly into mud, so I had much more time available than I thought. But I acted on the belief that time was short. Or again can we always be sure what decisions are important? The decision which has most greatly affected my life seemed at the time quite trivial—whether to make a social call rather late at night on my pre-war professor. The call changed my whole career. So here too we must devote as much time as *we believe* to be available, or as much as the importance which *we attach* to the decision seems to require. So what began as a difficulty in the subjective theory of duty turns out to be another duty subjectively qualified.

It follows that the thinking may be unsuccessful and the results still unsatisfactory. In particular we can take account only of considerations which 'occur' to us; and, as 'occur' indicates, this is something over which we have no direct control. We may cultivate interests and acquire knowledge to help the right ideas to occur; and we can take counsel and advice so that ideas which may occur to other people may often be recognised at once as relevant to our problem.

There is however a final difficulty about the 'duty to think' as a solution of the use of 'well-meaning'. The 'duty to think' seems to be an *objective* duty. For it is no defence to say 'I did not believe I had to think, it never occurred to me to stop and think'. To fulfil the duty of thinking is *not* to set myself to do what I believe to be right. This difficulty can be partially met by pointing out that it is impossible to do any duty without *some* thought; so what is complained of is that I didn't think enough. But 'enough' brings us back to the questions raised earlier about the limits on the duty of thinking. Nevertheless it does seem that there is a genuine problem here.

REFERENCE

Ryle on acting intelligently:
 The Concept of Mind, ch. ii

7

VARIATIONS IN MORAL BELIEF

Up to this point our argument has followed the example set by Moore, Ross, Prichard, and Carritt in appealing, in support of any moral theory, to our actual use of moral words. How could you decide . . .? What would you say if . . .? Moore's argument that pleasure is not the only thing good in itself, good as an end; Ross's demonstration that production of the maximum good is not the sole duty of man; Prichard's subjective theory; Carritt's addition to it;—all these rest on such an appeal. But even if these arguments succeed all they show is that these theories fit the moral discourse of ourselves and of these philosophers. Some people do not agree with us and with them. Some would hold against Moore that knowledge is not good in itself, or that aesthetic enjoyment is good only for the pleasure it involves (and Puritans might reject even that). Others would hold against Ross that lying is not wrong as such; and, as we have seen, it is only recently that we have come to accept the Prichard-Carritt view of the conscientious objector. Most people in 1914 held that he did not do his duty. So the theories mirror the morals of mid-twentieth-century middle-class Britons. And a theory based on the use of moral terms in China or Peru might look very different. Views on morals differ and it is to be expected that the theories built on them will differ too.

In other fields, when beliefs differ we normally appeal to argument and evidence to help us to decide which view is correct. And indeed the final conclusion of Chapter 5 that a man's duty depends on his *moral* beliefs as well as on his factual beliefs implicitly recognised both the differences in moral beliefs and the consequence that when beliefs differ one must be mistaken. The same point was implied by our acceptance of 'right' as an objective term, though 'duty' remained subjective (p. 57). For how are we to decide what *is* right when beliefs differ?

As we have seen, most actual moral judgments are a fusion of factual and moral beliefs. 'I ought to pay Jones the money' rests on 'I borrowed the money and have not yet repaid it' (which is a factual belief) and 'debts should be repaid' (which is a moral belief). The factual beliefs can be verified or falsified by ordinary argument and evidence. But what about the moral beliefs? We have seen in Chapter 4 that some philosophers (Ross and Prichard) thought moral rules required no validation because they were self-evidently true, but that this line and the attempts to defend it are unconvincing. In that chapter it was argued that a moral rule is justified, if the consequences of its general acceptance would be good. This justification again breaks up into two elements, the factual element (what will the consequences be?) and the moral element (would these consequences be good?)

Now some ordinary men, and some philosophers too, would reject this Utilitarian derivation of moral rules. A pacifist would reject violence as a general method of solving problems, no matter how good the consequences were; and so too with certain churches in regard to divorce or birth-control. But even if this derivation is accepted we are still not able to provide a complete verification procedure for moral beliefs. For the question remains 'which results are good?' And, as we have seen, some have rejected the view that knowledge is good or that beauty is good or that pleasure is good. Moore's appeal here is to self-evidence and it is as inconclusive as that of Ross on moral rules. But here indeed there seems to be a deadlock. For what types of arguments could be involved?

When a statement is attacked we sometimes defend it by showing that it follows from some other statement deductively. Why is the hydrogen bomb a bad thing? Because anything involving the mass destruction of innocent people is bad. But this only pushes the question back. And clearly to prove in this way that anything was good in itself or good as an end would seem self-contradictory.

Induction or an appeal to facts would seem equally suspect. For the facts here are the moral judgments of men and we have seen that they differ and contradict each other.

In both cases the difficulty is one put very clearly by Hume.

In every system of morality, which I have hitherto met with I have always remark'd, that the author proceeds for some time in the ordinary way of reasoning, and establishes the being of a God or makes observations concerning human affairs; when of a sudden I am surpriz'd to find that, instead of the usual copulation of propositions, *is* and *is not*, I meet with no proposition that is not connected with an *ought* or an *ought not*. This change is imperceptible; but it is, however, of the last consequence. For as this *ought*, or *ought not*, expresses some new relation or affirmation, 'tis necessary that it shou'd be observ'd and explain'd; and at this same time that a reason should be given, for what seems altogether inconceivable, how this new relation can be a deduction from others which are entirely different from it.[1]

Conclusions containing the notion of ought (or ought not) cannot be derived from premises none of which contain such notions. Or, more generally, to include good and bad also, conclusions involving any moral terms cannot be based on

1. *Treatise of Human Nature*, book III, part I, section 1

premises none of which contain any moral terms. Thus it would seem that standard methods of argument *must* fail to validate or falsify moral judgments. This important principle has been called (by Professor Max Black) 'Hume's guillotine'.

There is, however, another kind of defence which might seem to escape Hume's guillotine. When a statement is attacked it is sometimes defended by showing that it is supported by a lot of other similar statements—this is sometimes called the 'coherence test' and is applied to the stories of witnesses in cases where external verification is not obtainable. But there are difficulties here too. First, the moral beliefs of a man are seldom coherent in this sense. Indeed as we have seen they often clash with each other. But, even if they were coherent, coherence cannot guarantee truth, though incoherence does indicate falsehood. A witness's coherent story may be completely false; or a barrister's coherent reconstuction of a crime may be completely false as based on the evidence of perjured or collusive witnesses. Some moral principles do cohere (as we shall see later) in such a way that altering one involves altering others and so that they together form what has been called a 'culture pattern'. But there may be rival culture patterns and how is one to be preferred to another? 'Coherence' cannot tell us that.

REFERENCES

Hume's guillotine

Attacked: P. Foot, *Proceedings of the Aristotelian Society* (1958–9)
J. R. Searle, *Philosophical Review* (1964)
M. Black, *Philosophical Review* (1964)
G. I. Mavrodes, *Analysis* (December 1964)

Defended: A. Flew, J. E. McLellan and B. Komisar, D. Phillips, all in *Analysis* (December 1964)

8

THE EMOTIVE THEORY

The subjective theory to which the argument of Chapter 5 led was a subjective theory of *duty* and was combined with an objective theory of *right*. The formula was 'I must set myself to do what I believe to be right'. It was pointed out that my belief that a particular action would be right is always the resultant of certain *factual* beliefs about the situation and the probable consequences of the action and of certain *moral* beliefs about what in general is right or good. In the previous chapter we have seen that there are difficulties about verifying moral beliefs when these differ. This difficulty has led philosophers to ask whether the moral element in an assertion of right or wrong is really a *belief* at all. For, if it were a belief, it would have to be true or false; and there seems no way of showing whether it is the one or the other. What makes a belief true or false must be the facts. For a moral belief, it must be the moral facts. But these moral facts are inaccessible. So let us deny there are any moral facts. I say that divorce is sometimes right; you say it is always wrong. I say that Jones's doctor ought to tell him the truth about his disease; you say he ought not. We find we cannot establish whose belief is true: that is, we cannot determine the moral facts about divorce or truth-telling. So there are no such facts. So what we called our 'beliefs' cannot be beliefs. What then are they?

What do the words 'divorce is wrong' express, if not a belief? Hobbes had a first shot at this. When a man says 'this is good' he means to state that he desires it.

Whatsoever is the object of any man's Appetite or Desire; that is it, which he for his part calleth *Good*: and the object of his Hate and Aversion, *Evill*; and of his Contempt, *Vile* and *Inconsiderable*. For these words of Good, Evill, and Contemptible are ever used with relation to the person that useth them: There being nothing simply and absolutely so; nor any common Rule of Good and Evill to be taken from the nature of the objects themselves.[1]

So when a man says 'truth is good' he is speaking not about truth but about himself and saying he desires truth. When he says 'Communism is bad' he is not describing or saying something about Communism, for Communism is not itself either bad or good. He is describing his own aversion to it. Now this theory, though very interesting as such an early specimen, will not do. It cannot explain the *moral* use of 'good' or 'right', because there is often a conflict between duty and desire; and then I am compelled to say 'It is not good but I want it'— (drugs, for example, or my rival's death). But for Hobbes this would mean 'I do not desire it but I do desire it.'

A theory which meets this difficulty was that of Hume, by which to say something is 'good' is to say that I approve of it, and 'bad' that I disapprove of it.

Take any action allowed to be vicious: wilful murder, for instance. Examine it in all lights and see if you can find that matter of fact or real existence which you call *vice*. In whichever way you take it, you find only certain passions, motives, volitions, and thoughts. There is no other matter of fact in the case. The vice entirely escapes you as long as you consider the object. You can

1. *Leviathan* (Everyman edition), ch. 6, p. 24

never find it till you turn your reflexion into your own breast and find a sentiment of disapprobation, which arises in you, towards this action. Here is a matter of fact. It lies in yourself, not in the object.[1]

So the formula with which this chapter opened must lose its implication of objective rightness by losing its reference to *moral beliefs*. It will now run 'My duty is to set myself to do what I believe will bring about *what I morally approve* in the situation as I believe it to be.' Here the factual beliefs (about the situation and the results of my action) are retained because they can be verified and the facts made known.

In this theory, good, bad, right and wrong function like 'nice' and 'nasty'. If I say 'beer is nice' this means I like it. If you say 'it is nasty' this means that you dislike it; and both these propositions are true. I like beer and you dislike it. 'Beer is nice' 'beer is nasty' seem to be about beer and seem to contradict each other. But they are about you and me and are quite compatible with each other. It would of course be a contradiction for *me* to say 'beer is nice' and 'beer is nasty' because this would mean that I both like and dislike it. In most cases the truth of a proposition is independent of the person of the speaker. If I say 'Queen Anne is dead' this is just as true if you say it. But in some sentences the truth depends on the speaker; for instance 'I am short-sighted' which is true if said by me and false if said by you. This is because the 'I' refers to the speaker. Now, on the Hume theory the truth of the statement 'beer is nice' depends on who says it, though it does not look as if it did because it has no reference to 'I' in the actual words. It is misleading in this respect. Similarly with 'Nero was a bad man' which seems to say something about Nero, as in 'Nero was a stout man'. But it

1. *Treatise on Human Nature* (ed. Selby-Bigge), book III, part I, section 1, pp. 468–9

does not; it tells us about the speaker, that he disapproves of Nero. It is to be noted on this theory that moral propositions are still propositions; they are still true and false; there are still moral facts, but they are propositions, truths, facts about the speakers who enunciate them.

A variant of this view has recently been put forward by, among others, Professor A. J. Ayer. For him moral judgments are not propositions at all; they are not true or false; they do not *describe* anything, not even the feelings of the speaker. They are more like exclamations; they *evince* or *show* approval and disapproval. Ayer's argument for this is that

we can reject the view that a man who asserts that a certain action is right or a certain thing is good is saying that he himself approves of it on the ground that a man who confessed that he sometimes approved of what was bad or wrong would not be contradicting himself.[1]

This argument seems unsatisfactory. If the terms 'bad', 'wrong' and 'approved' are all used *morally* then a man could not confess what Ayer suggests. He might morally approve of something which was legally wrong or bad for his purse or his health. Or he might non-morally approve (aesthetically or as an object of desire) of something which he would describe as morally bad or wrong. What he cannot do is to say 'I feel moral approval of this action or thing but it is morally wrong or morally bad.' And indeed Ayer himself a few pages later[2] makes this admission: 'If I say "Tolerance is a virtue" and someone answers "You don't approve of it" he would on the ordinary subjectivist theory be contradicting me.' I should say it is obvious on *any* theory that he could be contradicting me. It may also be that Ayer was misled by his word 'sometimes'. I can say 'Regulus did the right thing though I have

1. *Language, Truth and Logic* (2nd ed.), p. 104
2. Ibid., p. 109

sometimes morally disapproved of his action.' I can certainly say 'This is bad or wrong, though I used to approve of it morally when I was younger.' Or Ayer may mean (by 'sometimes') 'in some exceptional cases'. But if he approved of x in this exceptional case he could not hold that in this case it was wrong. A similar point on which the subjectivist theory must be clear is that the approval which a moral judgment describes is *present* approval though the verb in the sentence concerned is past or future. 'Nero was a bad man,' 'You will do right if you tell him the truth' must be analysed as 'I *now* disapprove of Nero's character though Nero is dead' and 'I *now* approve of your hypothetical future act of truth telling.'

Though Ayer's argument for rejecting the view that moral judgments describe the speaker's feelings may be mistaken, it is still possible that the view itself may be right. A man who says 'That *was* a shocking thing to do' does not seem to be giving a calm and dispassionate account of his own feelings. Indeed 'How shocking of you!' would often be an equivalent utterance. An exclamation is normally taken to be an expression of a feeling involuntarily forced from the utterer of it. A groan evinces pain as sweating evinces embarrassment or pallor evinces fear. The man who in *The Hunting of the Snark* shouted 'Hi' or some other loud cry was simply giving vent to his feelings. But some exclamations may be used to *communicate* my feelings. I am offered a glass of wine to taste and I say 'Lovely'. But this means that I can use an exclamation to deceive. I can say 'Lovely' when I taste ouzo because my host is a Greek and I do not want to offend him. I can say 'Ow' at my dentist's before he hurts me because I think he is getting very near the nerve. It is to be noted that not all exclamations can be so used. If I see a man dancing about I have no way of knowing whether he is rejoicing or furious, or his feet are hurting him or the bricks are hot. So he cannot deceive me. But exclamations which have a conventional attachment to certain feelings like 'Ow' and 'Boo' and 'Lovely' and 'Hurrah' can be used to communicate feelings and therefore to mislead. Ayer says that a moral judgment expresses feeling 'by a suitable convention'. But it thereby communicates the fact that I have the feeling. And this is not so far off from describing the feeling, as in Hume's theory. Indeed it would seem that the best line for a holder of the Emotive theory to take would be to say that moral judgments lie somewhere between pure descriptions and pure exclamations and have some of the characteristics of both.

The fullest working out of the Emotive theory of ethics is to be found in the writings of C. L. Stevenson. He makes a number of useful points, and one important addition to the theory as we have seen it in Hume and Ayer. He distinguishes conflicts of belief from conflicts of attitude. Many disagreements about what we ought to do or about what is good or right are not really moral disagreements at all. One doctor says 'We ought to operate', the other says 'No, we ought to try antibiotics.' They are in complete moral agreement (that the patient should be cured); they differ in belief about what will cure him. Sometimes such a quarrel may therefore be quickly settled. 'He did wrong to leave his wife and children and go off to Peru like that.' 'No he didn't.' 'What? Not wrong to desert his family and leave them unprovided for?' 'He didn't. They are going out to join him on the next boat.' 'Oh, I didn't know that.' Here from the beginning there was moral agreement between the disputants (wife-desertion is wrong); the question was one of fact and of conflicting beliefs about fact. This is Hume's distinction brought out clearly. The point Stevenson makes is that the vast majority of disagreements about what is right or my duty turn out on examination to be disagreements in belief and therefore in principle soluble by evidence. The moral is that, even if we accept Emotivism, it is wrong in ninety-nine cases out of a hundred to apply the theory *simply* in every case. When I say 'x is right' and you say 'x is wrong' it is almost always an error to say this just means that I approve of it and that you disapprove of it; and there is no more to be said, because morals are a matter of taste not argument. No doubt the first move is correct. When I say 'x is right' then I do approve of it. But we must ask 'why?'. I may be afraid of that creature in the field. There is no doubt that I *am* afraid of it. But why? Because I think it is a bull. Then I see it isn't. My fear vanishes. He disapproved of Jones's departure to Peru. Yes he did. But why? Because he thought it was desertion. When he found it was not, his disapproval vanished. For basically my fear is of bulls and his disapproval is of wife-desertion.

Having emphasised this good point, Stevenson then makes a further equally good point. I have suggested that it is normally easy to find out whether a disagreement is one of belief (factual) or one of attitude (moral) by asking 'why?'. But this is not always so easy—as in the case of the poet who did not love Dr Fell. An obvious recent example is Nuclear Disarmament. Some of the arguments are clearly the one or the other. 'If we give up the bomb other states will follow our example.' This is a purely factual prediction, for which there can be evidence, and for which there could in principle be verification. 'If giving up the bomb meant that our country would be overrun without resistance and annexed by the USSR, I don't care. I'd rather die or live under communist rule than be a party to the use of such a weapon.' This is a pure moral preference. There are no facts which could be brought against it (or to support it either). But apart from these extreme cases, the rest of the CND issue is certainly one in which the moral and the factual elements are hard to disentangle.

Stevenson goes on to point out that language itself frequently helps to blur the distinction between moral and factual elements. Many terms appear to be factual but are also morally loaded and they can therefore be used to deceive. 'We can't give him a vote; he's a nigger.' 'We can't give him the job; he's a Yid.' 'We can't trust him; he's a Red.' In each case a reason seems to be given for the actions in question. And the reason seems to state a fact; and to some extent it does. But it also expresses an attitude. In these cases the trick is obvious; no one could be misled, because words like 'nigger', 'Yid', and 'Red' stink. But it is not so easy. What is the non-stinking and purely factual alternative to each of these words, 'Negro', 'Jew', 'Communist'? But these too can function as condemnatory, by tone of voice, by emphasis, and by context. For a pleasant example we may recall A. E. Housman's obituary of Arthur Platt, which ends 'He was addicted to tobacco, he was indifferent to wine, and he would spend long afternoons watching the game of cricket.' Housman prefaces this with the sentence 'I must now enumerate his vices'. But, even without that, 'addicted' and 'indifferent' would give the clue; and, in that context, it would be obvious what Housman's own attitude to cricket was. Stevenson does not note the difficulty of finding non-loaded terms as equivalents. But, in order to see this, let anyone take a strong controversial letter to a newspaper and underline the loaded words. And then let him try to substitute 'aseptic' words for them, words which give the same information but without bias. I once attended an enquiry on a Road Plan. The counsel attacking the road said to the expert witness who had devised it: 'You will agree, I take it, that the object of this is to inject another thousand cars a day into St Giles' Street.' With an eye open for this kind of thing I noticed the word 'inject'. The expert witness could not deny this suggestion. To my great delight the Counsel defending the road arose at once to re-examine. 'You will agree, I am sure, that the traffic which blocks the High Street cannot be relieved unless a large number of cars are led into an alternative route.' 'Led'—'lead kindly light' and so on! Of course the expert had to answer 'yes' to this question too. I said to myself 'What is the aseptic alternative to "inject" and "lead"?' And I found there was none. This is not surprising, because language, like other social institutions, is commonly used to win friends and influence people; so it is to be expected that little of it (except scientific terminology—here perhaps 're-route'!) is aseptic and non-loaded.

The last point on which I think Stevenson makes an advance on Ayer is that he describes the state of mind concerned with moral approval as an 'attitude' rather than as an 'emotion'. There is an admission by Ayer which indeed takes us towards this change. In the second edition Preface to *Language, Truth and Logic* he says[1] that he failed in the first edition

to bring out the point that the common objects of moral approval and disapproval are not particular actions so much as classes of actions . . . if an action is labelled right or wrong or good or bad as the case may be it is because it is thought to be an action of a certain type.

But, in that case, the state of mind of the speaker is obviously better described as an 'attitude' than as an 'emotion' or 'feeling'. To say that he judges an action right or wrong because it belongs to a certain class is to say that he would tend to judge other actions belonging to that class right or wrong too, and this is a hypothetical proposition or a group of them. Ayer goes on to say—but in words which show he has not wholly mastered the change from 'feeling' to 'attitude'—

What seems to be an ethical judgment is very often a factual classification of an action as belonging to some class of actions by which a certain moral attitude on the part of the speaker is habitually aroused.

1. p. 21

But 'aroused' is ambiguous. It may merely mean that the recognition of the action as belonging to the class provides an occasion for the attitude to be *expressed* (and this is what 'habitually' suggests). But a general tendency cannot be said to be 'aroused' by the occasions for its expression. Squeezing a piece of rubber does not *arouse* its elasticity nor does the writing of this chapter *arouse* my capacity to write grammatical English. Of course 'arouse' might mean that the occasion actually altered my attitude. I am sorry for the Armenians; I have some tendency to pity them when I hear of their sufferings and to subscribe to Armenian Rehabilitation Funds. But when I hear Gladstone and, like his other hearers, I find my pity 'deeply aroused', this means that I tend to do things which, without Gladstone's oratory, I would *not* have tended to do. Tears flow; I send unusually large donations to the Fund; I demand war with Turkey.

Stevenson too is inconsistent about his term 'attitude'. It is true that he explicitly prefers it to 'emotion' and for the right reason. Response is to a range of emotions or rather 'an attitude (which is itself a complicated conjunction of dispositional properties)'.[1] To say I have an attitude to a situation is to say that I am reacting to a certain feature of this situation *and* that I should react similarly to any similar situation. Yet, when Stevenson speaks of moral rules, he traces these to 'psychological economy', to 'the convenience of generalisation'.[2] 'The hearer like the speaker will instinctively avail himself of the psychological economy that comes of ordering the objects of his attitudes in some rough sort of classification.' This suggests that reaction to particular cases could be independent of and prior to their classification. But in that case 'attitude' is not the right term. There are two possible alternatives: (a) I have feelings towards particular actions. These

1. *Ethics and Language*, p. 60
2. Ibid., p. 95

feelings are actually occurrent and not dispositional. I can then notice similarities between the events which arouse these feelings, and make rough classifications of them for convenience; or, without such explicit attention, I can form a habit of having such feelings. Or (b), I have an attitude to this particular action. This means that I approve of it in virtue of some general characteristic it has, and that I should approve of any other action which had this characteristic. But if so the rule 'actions of this kind are right' is not the result of generalisation, but is essential to and implicit in the particular occurrence of approval.

There is another reason for the use of 'attitude' rather than 'feeling'. If I have an attitude of approval towards something it will express itself not only in a class of moral *judgments* but in all sorts of other ways: in decisions, choices, advice, praise, blame, remorse. This also accounts for what would otherwise be an argument against the Emotive theory. It may be said that a historian can pass a moral judgment on a past action without any noticeable feelings, quite dispassionately. But this is because judgments of commendation or condemnation are just as adequate expressions of a moral attitude as are feelings. Anything which can be introspectively recognised as a feeling of approval occurs usually in extreme cases or where other expressions are blocked. For, in a sense, the other expressions are both more natural and the best evidence of this attitude. Actions speak louder than words. A man may never express his feelings about marriage or communism or slavery in moral judgments but you could discover what his attitude is in each case by observing his conduct.

There is one other amendment Stevenson makes to Ayer's type of theory; it is the one he himself regards as of the greatest importance; but, as we shall see, it is doubtful whether it is an improvement on the original theory. The reason for this amendment is a criticism regularly urged against the

Hume-Ayer theory (by G. E. Moore among others). Moore regards it as 'an absolutely fatal objection'.

If, when one man says 'This action is right' and another answers 'No, it is not right' each of them is always merely making an assertion about *his own* feelings, it plainly follows that there is never really any difference of opinion between them; the one of them is never really contradicting what the other is asserting.[1]

It would be like two people saying 'I like sugar', 'No, I don't like sugar', where the word 'No' is obviously absurd. As Moore says elsewhere:

If two persons think they differ in opinion on a moral question (and it certainly seems as if they sometimes *think* so) they are always on this view making a mistake, and a mistake so gross that it seems hardly possible that they should make it: a mistake as gross as that which would be involved in thinking that when you say 'I did not come from Cambridge today' you are denying what I say when I say 'I did'.[2]

Stevenson admits that the argument has great force and devises an addition to the Hume-Ayer theory to meet it. He maintains that a moral judgment has a double function. It describes the attitude of the speaker and it also attempts to impose this attitude on the hearer. This second feature, the 'persuasive' element, is Stevenson's answer to Moore. 'This is right' and 'this is not right' (so far as they both describe the attitudes of the two speakers) are mutually compatible and are both *true*. But what about persuasion? I was asked by a government department to describe the political affiliations and psychological balance of an ex-pupil. I asked two colleagues what they thought about my doing this. One said: 'It would be right' and the other said 'No, it would be quite wrong.'

1. *Ethics*, pp. 100–1
2. *Philosophical Studies*, pp. 333–4

Now on Stevenson's view both of them are trying to persuade *me* and the result is a conflict. The word 'No' becomes quite appropriate. Compare 'Shut the door,' '*No*, leave it open.' Not only is there conflict, but in a sense there is logical contradiction, because it is logically impossible for me to be persuaded by both of them.

Moreover this persuasive element explains why people go on conflicting about moral issues. When it is a matter of taste, we do not mind saying 'tastes differ' and leaving it at that. And indeed the results are sometimes satisfactory; 'Jack Sprat would eat no fat, his wife would eat no lean.' But since moral judgments are intended to be persuasive we cannot agree to differ, any more than rival missionaries can, when they both meet a possible convert. But there is still a fundamental difference between Moore and Stevenson and between this kind of conflict and the normal case of contradiction. When two ordinary statements contradict each other one must be true and the other false. 'Liverpool is bigger than Manchester'; 'No, it is not.' This conflict is resolved by population statistics. But when two 'persuasives' conflict, neither is logically superior to the other. The solution of the Liverpool/Manchester conflict is the prevalence of truth. The solution of a conflict of 'persuasives' is simply victory (and the victory of either side, no matter which).

Nevertheless Moore admitted in a later work that Stevenson's theory went a long way to meet his difficulty and that as a result he was uncertain whether his original view or Stevenson's was correct.[1]

It has also to be remembered that the conflict is solved by the victory of either side no matter which and also *no matter how*. The weakness of duelling as a way of settling problems of honour is that the best (most honourable) man need not win.

1. *The Philosophy of G. E. Moore*, pp. 535–54

Truth is merely the ideas which are felt in a certain way and are felt to dominate in a mind or set of minds . . . You may indeed ask psychologically, if you please, how they come to dominate, but however they have come to dominate, their truth is the same. If you and I disagree . . . and if you argue with me and persuade me that is one way of agreement. But if you prefer to knock me on the head, that, so far as truth goes, is the same thing, except that there is now truth not in two heads but in one. And as to there being any other truth *about* all this state of things, or in short any truth at all, except mere prevalence, the whole notion is ridiculous. And if you deny this you do but confirm it, since your denial (though of course true) must also be false since it is true only because in fact it has prevailed.[1]

Stevenson's insistence on the persuasive element in moral judgments certainly fits some instances of these very well. 'You ought to see it through' is such an example. And perhaps *any* moral judgment thought of as a communication between people can be represented as having this character. So far as moral judgments enter into history or biography they can be regarded as attempts by the author to persuade the reader to adopt the author's attitude to Nero or Nelson or Lloyd George.

But there seem to be equally clearly examples of moral judgment where the persuasive element is lacking. Stevenson admits this, when he says he has 'concentrated on the inter-personal use of moral terms and treated the personal use by implication only'.[2] What is this 'personal use'? It occurs when I make a moral judgment without communicating it to any-body. For example, I may say to myself: 'I ought to see this through', or I may write in my diary (carefully locked away from human eye): 'I treated Jones badly today' or 'Jones treated me badly today.'

1. F. H. Bradley, *Essays on Truth and Reality*, p. 112
2. *Ethics and Language*, p. 134

Now surely these *are* moral judgments, but how can Stevenson argue that they are persuasive as well as expressive? He tries to do this by treating them as *self-persuasions*.[1] I am trying to persuade myself. He asks ´How do we come to a decision? How do we resolve a moral conflict?' and replies: 'We imagine ourselves to be one of our own heroes; we picture ourselves in conflict with a doughty opponent whom we finally convince. We personify the opposition within our-selves. We call it the devil within us, the old Adam; we exhort it to surrender.'

Now what decision are we trying to reach, what conflict are we trying to resolve, in these cases? Not a conflict or a decision about what is right or wrong. We have already reached that decision; for, if we had not, we could not call the opposition the devil in us or the old Adam. The decision then is a decision what to *do* and the conflict is one between duty and desire (the devil, the old Adam). When I call up images of my heroes or picture myself wrestling with the dragon, I am trying to get myself to do what I have already decided that I ought to do.

But persuasion of *this* kind is irrelevant to Stevenson's analysis. His formula to explain 'x is good' is 'I approve of x; do thou likewise'. Do thou what? Do thou *approve*. And indeed only such an analysis can deal with judgments about third parties or the past. When I say to you 'de Gaulle is behaving badly'. I am trying to get you to *disapprove* of de Gaulle. I am not trying to get you (or de Gaulle) to *do* what you or he approve. When I say to you 'The Treaty of Versailles was unjust' I am getting you to disapprove of it and not trying to get you (or the treaty makers) to do what you or they approve. But when I say to myself or write in my diary 'Jones behaved badly' I am expressing disapproval of Jones and I cannot possibly be persuading myself to disapprove. For why

1. Ibid, pp. 147ff.

should I? Either I *do* disapprove already and persuasion is pointless, or I don't and persuasion is groundless. The cases of Couéism or genuine self-persuasion well described by Stevenson are cases in which I am trying to persuade myself to do what I already approve. There is a story that the undergraduates of an Oxford college during the 1914 War used to share their bathhouse with the Head of their college. And they used to hear him say, in his impressive deep voice: 'Come along now, Phelps. Be a man, Phelps. In you go, Phelps.' This was obviously self-persuasion. But the Provost was clearly not trying to persuade himself to *approve* of taking a cold bath. He already approved and was persuading himself to take it. So I conclude that Stevenson's amendment of the expressive theory to meet Moore's criticism, by the addition of a persuasive element, fails because, in some moral judgments, no such persuasive element occurs.

The truth is surely that moral judgments (like any other judgments) may be used to persuade, as well as to do their proper job. The judgment that the earth goes round the sun is properly and primarily a statement in astronomy about planetary movement. But it could be used as it was (unsuccessfully) by Galileo as an attempt to persuade his persecutors to change their beliefs. And so 'Eppur se muove' takes its place not only in astronomy where it properly belongs but also in social history. So also 'that's nice', said meditatively (and this is the proper use) by the gourmet as he savours his caviare, may also be used by Nurse to persuade Tommy to eat his porridge.

This use of the moral judgment for persuasive purposes is another justification of the substitution of 'attitude' for 'emotion' which was discussed earlier. It means that one of the activities which I shall (on appropriate occasions) pursue, if I have an attitude of disapproval of something, will be to try to persuade others to share this attitude.

There is a final difficulty about Emotive theories, also raised by the previous discussion. Any kind of language may be used for persuasion; and all such persuasions imply approval. How then is *moral* approval to be distinguished from other kinds? This is especially difficult if the theory is one of 'feeling' or 'emotion' and not of 'attitude'. For the only way in which *feelings themselves* can be distinguished from each other is by introspection or direct awareness. It is no use to say that the kinds of things towards which the feelings are directed provide the differentia, for the whole point of an emotive theory is to deny that there is anything specifically moral in the states of affairs which are approved or disapproved. Stevenson seems to be attempting to indicate such a differentiation between emotions when he says[1] that where 'good' means 'morally good' it 'refers not to *any* kind of favour the speaker has, but only the kind that is marked by a special seriousness or urgency'. But this is surely unsatisfactory. Aesthetic approval may be serious or urgent also. Stevenson goes on to adopt in effect the attitude analysis and to appeal to a variety of responses in which the attitude (or disposition) of disapproval may be actualised. The observer may be indignant or shocked and these are clearly different from mere displeasure. The agent may feel guilty or conscience-stricken and these are different from merely feeling annoyed with oneself. And there is a peculiarly heightened sense of security when what is approved prospers, which is not mere pleasure. 'These differences of response . . . help to distinguish the attitudes which are moral from those which are not.' But here again the appeal is ultimately to introspection. And it is difficult to see any connection between these different feelings.

It was agreed in the first chapter of this book that the distinction between moral and non-moral uses of the word 'good' is not an easy one. What is here suggested is that the

1. Op cit., p. 90

Emotive theory fails to cope with this difficulty satisfactorily. Indeed one of the theories Emotivism was meant to reject was intuitionism—the theory that we just directly apprehend that kindness is good or that cruelty is bad. But Emotivism is itself a kind of intuitionism. We just directly apprehend the difference between feeling moral approval and feeling aesthetic approval or between feeling shocked and feeling displeased.

REFERENCES

A. J. Ayer, *Language, Truth and Logic* (2nd ed.), chapter vi and Preface, pp. 20–2

C. L. Stevenson, articles in *Mind*, January 1937 and July 1938; *Ethics and Language; Facts and Values* (a collection of essays which includes the articles from *Mind* noted above)

9

SUBJECTIVISM AND OBJECTIVISM

Theories of the Emotive type examined in the previous chapter are examples of a subjective view of moral values. Subjectivism in the past has rested on the evidence of variation in moral judgment and the lack of any verification-procedure when moral views differ. This has naturally led to the conclusion that, when views differ, it makes no sense to ask which judgment is nearer the truth, and consequently to the conclusion that moral judgments do not express cognitive states such as knowledge, belief, opinion; for if they did it would make sense to ask about their truth and falsity.

The evidence of variation and non-verifiability has been supplemented in recent philosophy by other considerations making for subjectivism. It has been noted that an objectivist theory has to rest on a number of propositions of a type which modern logic rejects entirely. These propositions assert necessary connections between different characteristics of states of affairs in the world. They are called technically 'synthetic *a priori* propositions'. 'Synthetic' because the states of affairs are different from each other; for obviously one could assert a necessary connection between being a horse and being an animal if animality were part of the *analysis* of the term 'horse'. '*A priori*' because necessary in a strict sense. For scientists may be said to discover necessary connections—between microbes and diseases, between friction and heat. But these connections are not necessary in a strict sense as they rest on empirical evidence (are '*a posteriori*') and have only the degree of probability such evidence justifies.

Some examples of the way in which objectivist theories involve *a priori* synthetic judgments may now be given. Ross argues against the view that moral judgments merely express attitudes of approval. He says that we cannot decide whether or not to approve of something until we have a *reason* to do so; and the reason why we approve of an action is that we recognise in it the attribute of rightness. Now what sort of connection is this, between approving and recognising as right? It is surely a *necessary* connection, and *a priori*. For if it were of the scientific type it would require evidence and it would be possible to apprehend the one characteristic without the other. But what evidence could there be requiring us to connect approving with recognising as right? And it would be odd to say 'I recognise this act as right but I do not approve of it.'

Other examples can be elicited from such a theory as that of G. E. Moore. Moore holds that goodness—intrinsic goodness—is a simple characteristic which certain states of affairs possess. But which states of affairs? Those involving enjoyment of beauty or personal affection. Now the connection between aesthetic enjoyment and intrinsic goodness is, for Moore, a strictly necessary connection, which is just directly apprehended, which is independent of the actual existence of particular people, and which requires and can receive no demonstration. Here then is our first example from Moore of an *a priori* synthetic proposition. 'If any state of affairs includes aesthetic enjoyment that state of affairs is intrinsically good.' The second example which Moore exhibits is the proposition connecting obligation and goodness. 'Ought' and 'intrinsically good' are clearly for Moore different notions, though at one time he failed to notice this; and they are necessarily connected.

If the total amount of good brought into the world by my doing an action would be greater than that produced by any alternative action I could do instead, then it *necessarily follows* that I ought to do this action.

This is Moore's basic principle.

Yet another example of an *a priori* synthetic proposition central to moral philosophy is that already referred to in Chapter 5—'ought implies can'.

In all these cases two different characteristics of states of affairs are said to be necessarily connected. The philosophers who reject *a priori* synthetic propositions divide all propositions into two classes, those resting on empirical evidence and those whose truth rests on our use of language. The only propositions which assert necessary connections are 'analytic'. An example is a dictionary definition. 'Democracy is a form of government' tells us about how the *word* 'democracy' is used. It tells us nothing about the existing world. To discover whether there are any democracies would require observation. Now it is obvious that analytic propositions which do nothing more than *analyse* the meaning of a word do assert necessary connections. A black horse is necessarily black. A triangle is necessarily a plane figure. But there are problems here. A man may know what the word 'triangle' means and say correctly that it is a plane figure bounded by three straight lines. But how many *angles* has it? It is obvious that if a figure has three straight sides it has three angles; but these two characteristics are different yet necessarily connected. If this is thought to be too easy and obvious an example (for, after all, 'triangle' might be said, by its derivation, to include having three angles) another example may be given. What is a cube? It is a solid, all of whose sides are squares. How many sides? Gamblers might well think this also an obvious characteristic *included* in the notion of cube, for dice are a help. But how many edges? To say that *this* is *included* in the nature of 'cube' is unplausible. Hence some of those who reject synthetic *a priori* propositions define an analytic proposition as one asserting the inclusion of one characteristic in another *or the entailment of one character-istic by another*. But it now becomes unplausible to say that analysis deals with *linguistic* facts because entailment of one characteristic by another does not look like a linguistic fact. These are difficult logical problems and cannot be further pursued here. But they lead to a problem which is very relevant to the subject of this chapter.

Those who believe that there are no synthetic *a priori* propositions have to decide what the propositions of philosophy are. And they decide inevitably that they are all analytic. Philosophy tells us no new facts about the world. It tells us how certain words are used; it clarifies their usage and removes confusions and paradoxes into which their use might tempt us to fall. Now most of those who hold this view are sub-jectivists in moral philosophy; and it will be the object of the following argument to throw doubt on the compatibility of these two views—the 'analytic' view and subjectivism.

Let us return to the Emotivist theory as an example (for Professor Ayer combines the Emotivist view with the rejection of *a priori* synthetic propositions). This view maintains that, when Mr Churchill called Hitler 'that bad man', anyone who really understood the situation would realise that he was not attempting to describe Hitler but was expressing or describing a characteristic of his own mind. And when Dr Goebbels would reply that Hitler was not a bad man he too was saying nothing about Hitler but describing or revealing something about himself. And both descriptions were true. No matter what sort of a man Hitler was, Churchill and Goebbels were fully and equally justified in what they said. For what they meant to assert or express was something wholly independent of any moral facts about Hitler. For there are no moral facts.

Now can such a view of a moral judgment claim to be an *analysis* of it? The analysis of a statement presumably should tell us what we mean when we make it, or what we shall accept as being what we mean when we see the matter more clearly and any confusions are removed.

Now it seems to me that no normal user of an ethical sentence would accept a subjectivist formulation as an *analysis* of it. There is no question of his being muddled or confused. In fact, as I shall try to show, the boot is on the other leg. It is only confusion and muddle that enables a subjectivist theory to pose as an analysis of moral judgment. The more clearly you get anybody to see the meaning and implications of subjectivism, the more emphatically would he reject it as an account of what he meant to say. Imagine yourself trying to persuade Mr Churchill that when he said 'that bad man' he was not describing Hitler and in no way contradicting Dr Goebbels.

Why have subjectivist theories been accepted as analyses of ordinary language? One reason certainly is that language can be used for a great variety of purposes. 'The man's a fool' may be used to express fury with him as well as to state a fact. A judgment concerning spatial location may function as a command. Does this sound wild? 'There is the door' may be one command and 'here is your castor oil' another. The second reason why people have claimed that subjectivism gives an analysis of moral judgments is that they have confused here (as often elsewhere) the meaning of a statement with its truth or with the evidence for it or (as above) with the other purposes for which it may be used or (again above) with the psychological states for whose existence its utterance is evidence.

I may write a letter to *The Times* and say 'Seventeen murderers were hanged in 1947'. In its context this statement evinces a belief of mine; it also evinces an interest in capital punishment. Moreover being written to *The Times* it is intended to influence the attitudes of others. But the meaning of my sentence is wholly independent of these facts about my state of mind when I wrote it. It is true that we sometimes use the word 'mean' so as to include these wider implications. I say 'Jones is a bore'. You reply 'You mean you don't want him asked to lunch'. This is the same use as in 'smoke means fire'. But even here we should probably distinguish between what I mean and what *my words* mean. It would be odd to say that the *statement* 'Jones is a bore' *means* that we don't want him to lunch. Stevenson, it is true, limits the meaning of an ethical judgment to include only those psychological antecedents or consequences of it which would not have been associated with the words used without a process of conditioning.[1] Thus the frowns and praises by which we were originally persuaded to call something 'right' or 'good' are part of the meaning of 'right' or 'good' 'in the psychological sense of meaning which is here in question' provided that the frowns and praises were indispensable.[2] What is the meaning of 'King Charles I was executed'? Suppose I had been so bad at history that I could not be got to learn this fact without lines and beatings; then these indispensable conditioning stimuli would be part of the meaning of the statement. Its meaning would include my sufferings as well as the King's. In any case, the psychological associations of uttering a sentence cannot be discovered by 'clarification' of it and are not entailed by its terms. If this were so, logic and semantics would be engulfed by empirical psychology.

It is doubtful whether Stevenson can be classed as belonging

1. *Ethics and Language*, pp. 57, 61
2. Ibid., p. 69*n*

D

to the school which holds that the statements of moral philosophy are analytic. He admits that the ordinary man claims
objectivity for his moral judgments. But he asks:

When the confusions of belief and attitude are cleared away and
when psychological mechanisms which these confusions have
fostered were accordingly readjusted, would people then feel that
some more objective criterion is required?[1]

He is saying here that ordinary people do hold an objective
view, but that he believes that he could so re-adjust their
psychological mechanisms that they would become subjectivists. He is on the way to the view held by J. O. Wisdom that
the correct analysis of moral judgments is objectivist but that
psycho-analysis of those who assert them could substitute
subjectivist judgments for them, as it can cure people of a
belief that they are being persecuted.

A man says that there are fairies at the bottom of his garden.
You are entitled to say to him: 'Your only evidence—that
flickering blue light—is compatible with an escape of marsh-
gas for which there is other evidence about here.' He might
be shaken or even convinced. But you cannot now say to
him 'When you said there were fairies down your garden,
you *meant* there was marsh-gas down your garden'. Or,
moving to an argument which has been held to be philosophical, we may take the example of colours. The plain man
certainly clothes objects in their qualities. Like Berkeley he is
convinced that snow is white and fire hot. It is not too difficult
to convince him that the colours he sees are not 'in' or 'on' the
objects, but are 'in' his retina or his pineal gland or his sense-
data or his mind. But it will not do to say that when he said
'snow is white' he *meant* that light is falling on its surface and
all the radiations are being reflected from it to the retina where
...etc., etc. Or, to take Wisdom's case, a man may be cured of a

1. Ibid., p. 31

persecution complex by psycho-analysis and come to agree that he is not being persecuted. But it will not do to say that when he said (before treatment) that he was being persecuted he *meant* that he was not being persecuted. Similarly with morals. It is very easy (all too easy) to turn a beginner from being an objectivist to being a subjectivist (by such arguments as those from the variation of moral judgments and the impossibility of verifying them). But even the most stupid beginner is usually quite clear that he was not a subjectivist when he sat down in your armchair for treatment.

I conclude then that subjectivist theories of morals are not compatible with the analytic theories of philosophy with which they are so often associated. The most a subjectivist can say is that an objectivist attitude is 'built in' to our use of moral language. We believe in the objectivity of 'good' and 'right', as ordinary men believe in the objectivity of 'white' and 'hot'. But these beliefs are simply false. There is a standing tendency to error in the ordinary use of moral language as there is in the ordinary use of colour language. This error can be corrected by the traditional arguments for subjectivism urged long before the linguistic theory of philosophy was advanced, and cannot be corrected by linguistic considerations, all of which point in the opposite direction.

A further difficulty for subjectivism is this. Many subjectivists fail to go the whole way with their theory, and thus give reluctant and unintentional support to the objectivist tendencies which are so hard to eradicate. A preliminary example may be taken from the closely parallel field of aesthetic language. Here, too, ordinary people hold strongly to objectivist usage. They may think there are doubts about whether the paintings of Picasso and the music of Schoenberg are beautiful; but they regard this as a genuine question and not one to be removed entirely by saying that it is all a matter of individual feeling.

It is true of course that some men have much experience of

the variations of aesthetic judgment, and experience for themselves the impossibility of *proving* to anyone that a picture they love is really beautiful. And some of them do in fact become subjectivists as a result. They use aesthetic language quite differently. They do not contradict people who differ from them. Instead of saying 'That picture is a daub' they say 'That is not the kind of picture I fancy'; or they say 'Pope may please other people but he says nothing to me' or 'Schoenberg is not *my* kind of music'. But the subjectivist must be consistent. My example of a failure here is from Anatole France.

There can no more be objective criticism than there can be objective beauty; and anyone who thinks that he puts into his appreciation of art anything but himself is a dupe of the most fallacious sophistry. We must recognise that we speak only of ourselves when we have not the self-control to remain silent. The good critic is one who recounts the adventures of his own soul as it voyages among masterpieces.

In the last sentence the key words are 'good' and 'masterpieces'. To indicate the difficulty, I may quote a speech delivered in the legislature of Georgia by Mr Hal Wimberley.

There are only three books in the world worth reading: the Bible, the Hymnbook and the Almanac. Read the Bible; it teaches you what to do. Read the Hymnbook; it contains the finest poetry ever written. Read the Almanac; it teaches you to figure out what the weather is going to be. There is not another book which it is worth anyone's while to read and therefore I am opposed to all libraries.

Or again one of the gems in my collection of bad poetry is a slim blue volume which I forbear to name. The volume carried with it a flysheet of review notices. 'Contains good poetry and some very nice thoughts' (*Hertfordshire Mercury*);

'Excellent verses arranged with touching delicacy' (*Galloway News and Kircudbrightshire Advertiser*). Now, on the subjectivist view, it makes no sense to say my slim blue poet is a *bad* poet. Nor can the adventures of the soul of Anatole France claim any precedence over the still more astonishing adventures of the souls of Hal Wimberley and the *Hertfordshire Mercury*.

So also in ethics. Philosophers who deny all absolute values and say values are made in individual choices are found asserting absolute values themselves. The existentialists reject all rules and abstract propositions about duty or goodness. Each man makes his values as he makes his choices. Yet we find constant emphasis on the essential value of 'commitment' (Kierkegaard) or 'engagement' (Sartre). And the existentialists echo a very common 'subjectivist' view which one often hears among ordinary men. 'We differ on every issue but I respect his *integrity*.' (So we do *not* differ on *every* issue.) This universal and absolute value is common ground to the existentialists. 'Authenticity' (Kierkegaard and Heidegger), 'fidelity' (Marcel), 'sincerity' (Sartre) are other names for it. And the effect of many individual standards is 'tolerance', but that is itself not an individual but an absolute standard.

So too with British philosophers. One of the earliest upholders of an 'approval' Emotive theory of morals was Adam Smith. For example:

> To approve or disapprove of the opinions of others is acknowledged by anybody to mean no more than to observe their agreement or disagreement with our own.[1]

Yet he recognises the greater insight of some judges in morals as in aesthetics.

> It is the acute and delicate discernment of the man of taste, who distinguishes the minute, and scarce perceptible, differences of

1. *Theory of the Moral Sentiments* (1759), p. 24

beauty and deformity; it is the comprehensive accuracy of the experienced mathematician, who unravels, with ease, the most intricate and perplexed propositions; it is the great leader in science and taste, the man who directs and conducts our own sentiments, the extent and superior justness of whose talents astonish us with wonder and surprise, who excites our admiration and seems to deserve our applause.[1]

This is not subjectivist language nor compatible with the sentence previously quoted concerning approval.

There is a similar inconsistency in a recent presentation of the subjectivist theory by Professor W. H. F. Barnes.[2] Barnes says that I answer moral questions by consulting my own moral feelings. But suppose these change? It does not make sense to say they have *improved*, for that would suggest a standard beyond them. If Barnes says his moral sensibility has improved this simply means that he himself approves more of its later than of its earlier judgments. And if I say he has progressed I mean that I approve more of him now than then. (Compare the first quotation from Adam Smith above.) But Barnes talks of *refining* his moral attitudes[3] and of 'a moral sensibility *awakened to new facts*' and of '*undeveloped* moral sensibility'[4]. I find it difficult to see how these phrases can be compatible with complete ethical subjectivism.

So too Miss Margaret Macdonald, writing about 'Natural Rights', says that 'there are no true or false beliefs about values but only better or worse decisions and choices'.[5] Yet she also says 'a criminal cannot be cast out of humanity',[6] and 'It is in

1. Ibid, pp. 32–3
2. *Proceedings of the Aristotelian Society*, suppl. vol. XXII
3. Ibid., p. 24
4. Ibid., p. 27
5. *Proceedings of the Aristotelian Society* (1946–7), p. 250 (reprinted in Laslett, *Philosophy, Politics and Society*, p. 54)
6. Ibid., p. 246 (p. 51)

some sense true that no one ought to be ill-treated because he is a Jew or a Negro or not able to count above ten.'[1] Yet on her own view there is nothing true or false here. These sentences record only her own decisions. Hitler and the Ku Klux Klan decided contrariwise. Therefore it is equally (in some sense) true that Jews and Negroes should be victimised. And how can there be better and worse decisions? Is the statement 'Miss Macdonald's decision is better than Hitler's' a moral statement? If so, it simply records the decision of a third party or Miss Macdonald's reiteration of her own.

The subjectivist view also makes a great deal of our ordinary talk pointless or misleading. If I say of a man that his moral judgments are bigoted, perverted, or prejudiced, I can mean only that they differ from mine. When I say 'Jones has reformed during the year' I can only mean that I disapprove of him as he was last year and approve of him as he is now. I cannot mean that his moral standards have changed for the better. There can have been no moral change *in him*. Of course it may be said that, when we say of a man that he has reformed, we do not mean that his moral standards have changed, but that he has begun to live up to them, as he did not do last year. But this leads to the even more unpalatable conclusion that this change too is not a moral change *in Jones*. It is just that I approve of people who live up to their own moral standards. To say this is a moral merit *in them* is mistaken.

Moreover, if there is no truth in these matters any difference between me and one man in our moral estimates should matter as much or as little as any difference between me and any other man. But what I find is that some such differences shake me and some leave me unperturbed.

A disagrees with me. A is a man I respect. He lives up to his own highest standards. I hesitate to claim that I have as much right to my view as he to his. B disagrees with me. He

1. Ibid., p. 243 (p. 49)

is a man for whom I have no respect; he makes no effort to live up to his own standards. I don't mind his difference from me. C differs from me. C is a man of moral scruples. He has often noticed some subtle moral issue which I might have missed. He sees the relevance of related problems. My difference from him worries me. D differs from me. He has regularly shown himself a man of no discrimination at all. He sees no difference between different cases and no relation between similar ones. He would not steal the railway company's cutlery, but he thinks it quite all right to travel without a ticket. He defends free enterprise as a recognition of the value of the individual and treats his staff in a way that it would be polite to call feudal. My difference from him causes me no worry. E differs from me. E is a man of wide experience of men and affairs. He is of the world without being worldly. I hesitate to differ from him. F differs from me. He is a narrow man, shut off by upbringing and vocation from human contacts, with a nature obviously warped and embittered by these limitations. I have no hesitation about differing from him. G differs from me. He is a man of good practical judgment. His opinions about people and policies, whenever they can be checked, are highly reliable. He is alert, critical, and sensible in human relations. I wonder whether he is not perhaps to be relied on in moral matters too. H differs from me. His judgment on practical affairs is normally bad. He is silly and impractical in choice, credulous and superstitious in belief, hasty and rash in his judgments and predictions about people and policies. I naturally expect him to be an unreliable moral judge too.

What am I doing in making these contrasts? Just what I would do if I were on a jury in a case where there is no direct evidence and two witnesses disagree. I ask myself which witness seems the more trustworthy. Of course this is a risky procedure. Sometimes the most candid and best qualified witness is wrong and the most shifty and ignorant witness right. Nevertheless, in the absence of other decisive evidence, my procedure is rational. And it presupposes objectivity. For where there is no truth no one can be more trustworthy in judgment than anyone else. These contrasts are insignificant for, if 'good' and 'right' signify nothing but the approval of the speaker, there is nothing to choose between A and B, C and D, etc.

The parallel with aesthetic judgment may help us again here. Variations in judgments of beauty are even more striking and obvious than in judgments of right and wrong. They have led to subjectivist theories of beauty. We have seen in the examples of Anatole France how difficult it is to keep out all objectivist elements. Here too, as Anatole France suggests in his talk of 'the good critic', the same issue arises. While variations do occur we take more seriously the judgment of a man who has spent his life with pictures, whose 'attributions' are later verified, who can spot late additions, than those of someone who merely 'knows what he likes'.

In art we are equally tempted to use the language of Professor Barnes and talk of 'improving' or 'refining' one's 'sensibility'. In art too I do not see how one can talk like this without implying that the more refined sensibility is capable of better judgment. It might be said that one man may be more sensitive to pain than another but that this does not mean that there is one objective pain, which they are both assessing. It only means that one man feels pain more acutely than another (perhaps from a similar stimulus). But we do not mean this when we speak of aesthetic or moral sensibility. The difference is not here a quantitative one (though it may also be true that a good critic's enjoyment or distaste is in fact greater than that of the ordinary man).

The alternative to subjectivism both in aesthetics and in morals is to claim that men are endowed in varying degrees

with a capacity for aesthetic and moral appreciation and discrimination. It is a mistake perhaps to call this faculty a
rational faculty because of the difficulties of verification and
proof which we examined earlier. It is perhaps equally mistaken to react to the opposite extreme and call it a '*sense*'. We
have a word for this kind of faculty in other fields and it is the
word 'judgment'. Judgment is exercised in a wide variety of
ways. A manager may be appointing someone to a position of
responsibility; a selection committee may be interviewing
candidates for admission to a college, for a service commission, or for the treasurership of a charity; a juryman may be
estimating the reliability of two conflicting witnesses; a
farmer may be deciding whether to enlarge his holding; an
investor whether to move into equities at once. It may be said
that in all these cases there may be later evidence that the
judgment in question was sound. The departmental head goes
on to further successes, the selected candidate gets his first class
or a staff college job in due course, the farm prospers, the
investments double their yield. But in morals and aesthetics
there is never a pay-off like this. While this must be granted,
there are still sufficient similarities between the actual processes
of judgment in the verifiable and the unverifiable cases to
make the differences seem irrelevant or at least much less
relevant. In all cases an alert mind, an attention to relevant
detail, the holding together of a great variety of different
'indications', all these result in an 'impression' of reliability,
potentiality, integrity, propriety, 'rightness' in each field.
Everybody knows how fallible these processes are, how they
may be dismissed as 'hunches' or 'intuitions', and how resistant
they are to any formulable type of inference. Yet everyone
knows even better, who has worked on such matters, that
people do differ enormously in this capacity of judgment;
and that the 'hunch' based on a single meeting a year ago or
the 'impression' left by 'the look in his eye' is *different* from the

'judgment' resulting from long experience, from working alongside a man (or fighting alongside him), though there is in neither case anything that could count as 'strong evidence' or a case which would convince an impartial spectator.

So it seems to me that a Board of Directors may have two items on its agenda: (a) whether to retire its general manager or keep him on for two more years, (b) whether to dismiss its treasurer who has been detected in some questionable activities with its funds. I should expect these two decisions, the first an economic and the second a moral one, to be reached by discussions remarkably similar in their general pattern—the citation of relevant considerations (with some debate on whether they are relevant) the weighing against each other of pros and cons which can have no quantitative or measurable valuation, the attempt by each director to pull together these variegated threads into a decision, the tendency to be influenced, in the first decision by colleagues with long experience, in the second by colleagues of notable integrity; and a final verdict which will be felt to be justified at least partly by the care and attention spent on it.

So I conclude that, powerful and popular as the subjectivist theory now is, there are insuperable objections to it as an 'analysis' of ordinary language, and some considerations against it and in favour of an objectivist account of the values this language attempts to express.

REFERENCES

(a) Synthetic *a priori* propositions in morals:
   (i) Right and approved: W. D. Ross, *Foundations of Ethics*, p. 23
   (ii) Good and aesthetic experience: G. E. Moore, *Principia Ethica*, pp. 188–9
   (iii) Ought and good: G. E. Moore in Schilpp (ed.), *The Philosophy of G. E. Moore*, pp. 554–71

(b) The logic of *a priori* propositions:
Analytic but including entailment, which is linguistic: A. J. Ayer, *Language, Truth and Logic* (2nd ed.), pp. 16–18 (with references)
The cube and its edges: Langford in *The Philosophy of G. E. Moore*, p. 327; accepted by Moore, pp. 575–6, 599

(c) Subjectivism not an analysis of moral judgments:
J. O. Wisdom, *Proceedings of the Aristotelian Society* (1935–6)
C. D. Broad, *Proceedings of the Aristotelian Society* (1944–5)

10

FREEDOM OF CHOICE[1]

In an earlier argument we used the principle that 'ought implies can'. If a man is forced to do something he can neither be praised nor be blamed for doing it. 'I could not help it' is always a complete defence. But this raises the very difficult problem of free will. The problem has been carefully formulated by Henry Sidgwick. 'Is my voluntary action at any moment completely determined by (i) my character as it has been partly inherited partly formed by my own past actions and feelings, and (ii) my circumstances, or the external influences acting on me at the moment? Or not? Could the volition I am just about to originate be certainly calculated by anyone who knew my character at this moment and the forces acting upon me? Or is there a strictly incalculable element in it?'[2]

During the two past centuries, up to 1900, there had been a sharp opposition between science and free will. Science maintained a rigid determinism and a belief in universal

1. This chapter and the next incorporate material from an article on 'Freewill' for the *Encyclopaedia Britannica* and a contribution, on *Freewill and Punishment*, to *Contemporary British Philosophy* (*third series*), with the kind permission of the editors and publishers of these volumes
2. *Methods of Ethics*, p. 46

causation, which rejected free will as it rejected miracles. It is true that no scientist would defend the crude fatalistic view, that my action or my 'fate' is determined by forces wholly independent of me, so that it is bound to come to me no matter what I do to prevent it. This is the attitude of the soldier who says 'The bullet which is going to kill me has got my number on it, so it does not matter whether I take cover or stand up in full sight of the enemy'. This type of fatalism, sometimes called 'oriental', is wholly unscientific: for every scientist would insist that the behaviour of the object in which a change occurs must always be one of the factors contributing to the causation of the events which happen to it. So what the soldier does must make a difference.

But the prevalent scientific view was that all observable events are subject to scientific law and therefore completely determined and in principle completely predictable. It was inconceivable that the behaviour of a single species on a minor planet in one among countless solar systems should escape a type of determination which had been succesfully found to apply on the widest scale of stellar magnitude and to the smallest microscopic bodies. It was true that up to 1850 the successes of science had stopped short at inanimate matter. But from that time onward Darwin in biology, Marx in sociology, Pavlov and Freud in psychology were advancing causal explanation across the frontiers of life and mind.

In the last fifty years, however, the scientific atmosphere has greatly changed. 'Determinism' is no longer an acceptable scientific term. There is little talk in science of 'irresistible forces' or indeed of any 'forces' at all. To talk of magnetic *attraction* is unscientific for the force of attraction is completely unobservable. What can be verified, and therefore should be said, is that, in the vicinity of certain bodies, iron filings move in certain paths or arrange themselves in certain patterns. There is no 'compulsion' here. What is observed is regular conjunction and no more. And again in this regularity there is no observable *necessity*? Scientists no longer *explain why* events occur. They *describe how* they occur. Nevertheless, though the assertions of compulsion and necessity disappear, the claim to predict still remains. Yet it is also noteworthy that the predictions are not endowed with certainty but only with that degree of probability that the evidence justifies. Yet even this would still seem to threaten free will. For prediction with a very high degree of probability that a man will choose A seems to threaten his freedom to choose A or B.

There are, however, some special features of human experience which make even these milder claims of modern science of doubtful application to it. There are three features of scientific method which seem essential for any close approximation to accurate prediction. The first is measurement. There are always differences between the specimen whose behaviour is to be predicted and the specimens whose behaviour is evidence for the prediction: differences of mass, of chemical constitution, etc. These differences are accommodated by having laws with variables, to which quantitative values can be given from the measured features of the particular case brought under the law. In order to predict from the law of gravity how body X will behave in relation to body Y the distance between these bodies must be inserted as a determinate element in our calculations. Now the psychological phenomena from which human conduct would have to be predicted are not measurable though they may be quantitative in intensity. It makes sense to say that I am feeling more angry or suffering more pain than a minute ago. But it does not make sense to ask whether my pain has doubled or my anger gone up by nine per cent. The only way to try to measure psychological phenomena is to measure their physiological accompaniments. (For pain, twice as many tears or twice as many decibels in the groaning!) But to predict conduct wholly

e.g.
Suppose
I want to
know whether
something is
hot or cold —
I can measure
it with the monometer
or feel it with hand.
One gives a
number and the
other a feeling

from physiological data is to deny either the existence or the causal relevance of psychological states. The former denial (that involved in materialism or behaviourism) is now generally discredited. The latter, holding that psychological events are 'epiphenomena', accompanying but making no difference to physiological processes, is difficult to reconcile with evolutionary theory. For such 'epiphenomenal' states would be useless to the organisms which manifest them and would have been expected to atrophy rather than to increase in number and complexity as they have done.

If, then, psychological states are not quantitatively measurable, prediction is impossible. For example a psychologist may establish that a child who has been shut in a dark cupboard will subsequently tend to fear being shut in. But he cannot give any quantitative value to the fear and consequently cannot predict whether in any particular case a rival factor such as hunger will overcome it.

The other two features of scientific method which make it inapplicable in full rigour to human conduct are analysis and repetition. By 'analysis' is meant the power to deal with one feature of an object at a time and to regard some features as wholly irrelevant to the calculations required. For calculations of motion, mass and shape are relevant, chemical constitution is irrelevant. For spectroscopic behaviour, chemical constitution is relevant, mass and shape irrelevant. But, if no features of a substance could be thus regarded as irrelevant to the establishment of a law concerning its behaviour, then no such laws could be established. There are grounds for holding that such abstraction is impossible (or possible only in a very rough and ready fashion) in regard to human beings and their psychological characteristics. The features of a man's character are so interwoven that none of them would be what it is without the others and these features correspond to the forces or features of a scientific object which go to determine its behaviour. We tend to predict the actions of men by establishing that they have certain dispositions such as courage, wit, intelligence, etc. But a man's quick temper helps to determine his kind of courage; his wit gives his temper its peculiar edge; his intelligence lightens his wit; his sensitivity broadens his intelligence; his imagination extends his sensitivity, and so on. Even this language is misleading for it suggests that these features exist separately and *then* affect each other. But the truth is that to understand any one of them is to find it stamped with the man's individuality. The unity of the self makes any attempt to abstract or isolate psychological components impossible. Such dissection spells death. So, in writing testimonials or references, I find that, when I do not know a man well, such general words as 'impetuous', 'tolerant', 'vigorous' seem to describe him very well. But the better I know him the more utterly they fail to convey the person I know. Kierkegaard makes the same point: 'It is more difficult to describe one actor than to write a whole philosophy of art . . . The more one can depend on generalisations the easier it is, for the material is so vast that all the completely abstract observations, which anyone can learn by heart, seem to mean something. But the more concrete the observation the more difficult it is.'[1]

The third feature required for scientific prediction is repetition. By this is meant the assumption that any feature isolated within a single specimen can be expected to recur in other specimens with a difference which is either irrelevant or expressible in quantitative terms as values of the variables in the scientific law which governs the inference. But each human personality is unique. Study of pieces of sodium provides good evidence for the behaviour of the next piece of sodium. Study of the behaviour of Smith, Jones, and Robinson is poor evidence for the behaviour of Brown. This is recognised by those who have devoted themselves to any field of human

1. *Journals 1834–1854*, English trans., p. 147

experience. A few quotations out of a great many possible sources will illustrate this. They are all protesting against the attempt to bind human action by rules and formulae.

Martha Graham, a choreographer of genius, said 'There is a vitality, a force, an energy, a quickening that is translated through you into action; and because there is only one of you through all of time this expression is unique. If you block it, it will never exist through any other medium and will be lost'.[1] Benedetto Croce, the great critic, writing on the attempt to establish rules for the creation of beauty, refers to 'erroneous modes of criticism' which ask whether a work of art 'obeys the *laws* of epic tragedy, of historical painting or landscape . . . Artists have always disregarded these laws. Every true work of art has violated some established law and upset the ideas of the critics, who have thus been obliged to broaden the laws until finally even the broadened law has been proved too narrow, owing to the appearance of new works of art, naturally followed by new scandals, new upsettings—and new broadenings'.[2] T. E. Lawrence had studied the textbooks of strategy and the campaigns of Alexander, Caesar, and Napoleon. Lying out in the desert one night thinking about his campaign against the Turks he meditated on what he had learned.

In military theory I was tolerably read, my Oxford curiosity having taken me past Napoleon to Clausewitz and his school, to Caemmerer and Moltke and the recent Frenchmen . . . my interest had been abstract, concerned with the theory and philosophy of warfare.

Now, in the field, everything had become concrete, particularly the tiresome problem of Medina; and to distract myself I began to recall suitable maxims on the conduct of modern scientific war. But they would not fit and it worried me.

The algebraical element looked to me a pure science subject to

1. Speaking to Agnes de Mille. Cf. *Dance to the Piper*, p. 307
2. *Aesthetic*, English trans., p. 37

mathematical law, inhuman. It dealt with known variables, fixed conditions, space and time, inorganic things like hills and climates and railways, with mankind in type-masses too great for individual variety ... It was essentially formulable ... But a line of variability, Man, persisted like a leaven through its estimates making them irregular. . . . Nine tenths of tactics were certain enough to be teachable in schools, but the irrational tenth was like the kingfisher flashing across the pool and in it lay the test of generals. It could be ensued only by instinct (sharpened by thought practising the stroke) until at the crisis it came naturally, a reflex.[1]

Finally A. E. Housman the leading Latinist of our day writing about textual criticism, that is the amendment of the texts handed down to us, in cases where it seems they are 'corrupt' and their readings mistaken.

Textual criticism is not a brand of mathematics nor indeed an exact science at all. It deals with a matter not rigid and constant like lines and numbers, but fluid and variable; namely the frailties and aberrations of the human mind, and of its insubordinate servants the human fingers. It is therefore not susceptible of hard and fast rules. It would be much easier if it were; and that is why people try to pretend that it is, or at least behave as if they thought so. Of course you can have hard and fast rules if you like, but then you will have false rules and they will lead you wrong, because their simplicity renders them inapplicable to problems which are not simple but complicated by the play of personality.[2]

There is one special difficulty in regarding human conduct as completely determined and completely predictable. Human thought is part of human conduct and the moral or scientific or philosophical beliefs of any man would have to be regarded as predictable consequences of his causal situation. While this kind of explanation is often welcomed by any thinker as

1. *The Seven Pillars of Wisdom*, 1940, p. 193
2. *Proceedings of the Classical Association* (1916), p. 68 (reprinted in A. E. Housman, *Selected Prose*, p. 132)

accounting for the errors of his opponents, he would not like to accept it as applicable to the truth of his own view.

A Marxist will maintain that there are no objective standards of moral or political belief. All human conduct is determined by economic processes and ultimately by the class structure of society. A man may think he is making a choice and deciding on a course of action because it is right. This is an illusion. All his decisions are determined, and determined by class interest; what he calls his moral or political beliefs are those rules which enable the class to which he belongs to acquire or maintain domination in his society. For Marx, the Benthamite *laissez-faire* theory of economics has no rational validity. It simply reflects the interests of the bourgeois industrialists who dominate capitalist society. But if so Marxist economic determinism has no validity either. It also is an illusion on its own showing. It is the inevitable by-product of material forces, of local and temporary class interests, bound to be dialectically destroyed as history develops. Nineteenth-century working men necessarily had to believe it but there is no reason why anyone else should.

It may be objected that any attempt to shut off an area as impervious to scientific treatment is a counsel of despair. Failure has always attended such exclusions; science has swept in and conquered. The area of human conduct is, moreover, an insignificant one on a world scale. Why in this tiny field should laws fail and prediction falter? Perhaps the answer is that only in this tiny area (so far as we know) can such questions be asked. Knowledge of the universe is already so astonishing an exception to the general pattern that it would be even more surprising if other special features did not distinguish men's lives. It is a surrender to sheer size that makes us think the spiral nebulae a more impressive wonder than the minds of Newton and Einstein.

The main arguments here advanced, however, do not shut

off any area from scientific enquiry. Psychology, sociology, and economics all rightly cover human conduct. All that is said is that they will have a lower probability in their predictions than other studies and that their attempts to deal with individual cases will be liable to considerable margins of error. They will succeed so far as quantitative physiological behaviour provides clues to psychological processes, so far as elements in the self can be safely isolated from the rest, so far as men resemble each other in the characteristics relevant to the enquiry and differences do not affect the result. Shylock was right in his evidence, 'If you prick us, do we not bleed? if you tickle us, do we not laugh? if you poison us, do we not die?' But dubious in his conclusion, 'if you wrong us, shall we not revenge?' There is good reason to believe that in the parts of conduct which count most (parts other than pricking and tickling, blinks and knee-jerks) these conditions are largely unfulfilled. Nevertheless, for large-scale statistical purposes such as life insurance or advertising, scientific prediction may yield a result both informative and useful.

If we ask for positive evidence for free will some would answer that every man has direct experience of it. Just as he knows he is in pain, he knows as directly and certainly that he is making a free choice between, for example, going to the cinema and digging in his garden. This claim as it stands must be rejected, for it is difficult to see how anyone could be directly and immediately aware of the truth of the proposition that his decision has no determining cause. But it may certainly be said that most men *believe* this proposition and that this belief is ineradicable. It may be said that it does not follow that the belief is true and that its prevalence, even if it were false, might be explained by its biological utility. As Ross has said, a man is more likely to work for an examination and therefore to pass it if he believes it is uncertain whether he will pass or fail. If he thought either result was certain he might well slacken his efforts (as voters for safe seats or the defenders of forlorn hopes are apt to do). Yet we also saddle ourselves with burdens of guilt or remorse which are linked with our belief in freedom and responsibility, and these burdens would seem to hinder effective action, and to be useless illusions and therefore biologically puzzling, if they are in fact false.

perhaps they help cause us to behave better in the future.

The strongest evidence for free will is indeed the link with moral judgment. 'Ought implies can.' If I cannot help doing X, I cannot be blamed or praised for doing it. If I cannot do X, X cannot be my duty. Now some philosophers have attempted to maintain that this linkage between moral responsibility and free will is not defensible, and even that such responsibility requires a determinist view of human action. Suppose it were the case that, everything being the same including my own self, two alternative actions were possible (e.g. a brave or a cowardly one), then neither could be *my* action as issuing from my character. Choice would be equivalent to chance. If I were to give a reason why I acted in a certain way (that I love Bach's music, or that I was hungry, or that I felt I ought to help the victim of persecution) this could not be *the* reason: for, given that exact degree of admiration, hunger, or pity, I could still have acted otherwise. Mental life for the free will believer is a series of unconnected, inexplicable, unmotivated choices.

On the other hand, as is argued, for example, by F. H. Bradley, there is a kind of determinism which is morally acceptable. That is determinism of action by the self as a whole. If anyone predicts my action on the basis of statistical enquiry, I am properly indignant. If anyone says 'I know what you will do because I have calculated exactly the strength of the rival forces battling within you, your desire for praise, your ambition, your addiction to gambling; and the answer comes out as follows', I laugh at this claim. But suppose he says 'I know you well enough to know you could not have done that' or 'You are one of our most reliable members; I knew I could count on you', I accept and welcome this kind of prediction because it is based not on statistics nor on abstractions but on knowledge of *me* as a person.

It does seem true that this kind of prediction based on experience of a person as a person is the only kind that comes within sight of recognising human individuality and reconciling this recognition with the claims of moral responsibility. Yet it too has serious difficulties. It claims that prediction of action based on knowledge of character is both legitimate and acceptable to any self-respecting person. But it is *acceptable* only if the action predicted is a good one. Suppose someone says 'I knew you well enough to be sure you would not say anything; you are too afraid of unpopularity' or 'I was sure you would keep us all waiting'. In such cases the very word 'reliable' would seem like irony or a joke. In welcoming those other predictions I was confusing prediction with praise. It was the latter I really welcomed.

Moreover prediction from knowledge of a person has its own pitfalls as a rational process. It assumes relevantly similar situations and, more seriously, it implies that character cannot be changed by actions and that people cannot learn by experience, especially experience of their own mistakes. There can be no adequate evidence of what this *changing* self will do. Winston Churchill has described how the German ambassador to London was recalled to Berlin for not having foreseen what Lloyd George would say in his important Mansion House speech in 1911. Mr Churchill comments: 'How could he know what Mr Lloyd George was going to do? Within a few hours before his own colleagues did not know. Working with him in close association, I did not know. Until his mind was definitely made up he did not know himself.'[1]

Another argument for relating determinism to moral res-

1. *The World Crisis*, pp. 49–50

ponsibility is that of R. E. Hobart. The free will theory maintains that freedom of choice is necessary if we are to praise or blame anyone for his actions. On the contrary, argues Hobart, determinism is necessary. For we praise or blame a man for his actions; we praise the self whose act it is. We say 'that was a brave deed' or equally 'that was the deed of a brave man'. But here there is a link between the act and the man. If it were possible, given the brave self, for a brave or a cowardly act to be done, then the act cannot be attributed to the brave self but only to the free will. Hence there must be a necessary causal connection between the self and its acts, for praise or blame to be possible. The difficulty with this argument is that the connection between courage and the brave act, while necessary, is not causal. Courage is a *disposition* or tendency. Causes precede effects but the courage we attribute to the man is not a courage he had just before he acted. The courage was *manifested in* the act. We say that rubber stretches because it is elastic. But it is not because the rubber *was* elastic that it *now* stretches. To say rubber is elastic just means that if you pull it it will stretch; if you stamp on it it will flatten; if you twist it, it will be distorted. So of course there is a necessary connection between stretching and elasticity but not a causal one.

Another argument for determinism was originally put forward by Schlick and has recently been fully worked out by P. H. Nowell-Smith and F. Ebersole. It too works on the link between praise and blame on the one hand and moral responsibility on the other, the link which was previously supposed to require free will. The problem is to find a criterion for 'free' action. The answer on this theory is that those actions are 'free' which can be influenced by praise and blame (or by punishment). A schoolboy is not reproached or punished for stupidity because blame and punishment cannot make him less stupid. He is blamed or punished for laziness because a talking to or punishment may make him less idle.

To say that idleness is a moral failing and idle actions are actions a boy 'could help doing' is just to say that idleness is amenable to blame and punishment. 'If it is true that praise and blame are means employed to bring about good events and prevent bad ones, they are appropriate not to all good and bad events but only to those they can in fact bring about or prevent. Since a moral action is one that can fittingly be praised or blamed, it follows that a moral action is one which can be brought about or prevented by those means.' Thus a moral action is not an action without a determining cause but one which is or can be affected by praise and blame and punishment.

The first difficulty about this view concerns the effect of blame or punishment which it requires. As the quotation shows, it must *prevent* wrong action. Ebersole sticks to this strong line. 'We must be able to know that the condemnation will reform. It must fulfil its intention to prevent repetition of the wrong for which the person is punished.' But he has to admit the difficulty here: 'In the strong sense of "justification" which I have been using punishment is never justified. We are forced to take action on the best knowledge available; attempted reform more often than not does not come off.' But surely a justification which can never justify any actual punishment cannot be worth discussing. Nowell-Smith, however, sometimes moves to a less extreme view. 'Fear of punishment will *affect* the future behaviour of the thief . . . there will be a motive *tending to* make him refrain.' 'The point of blame is to strengthen some motives and weaken others.' Here then we shall hold that a man is responsible for an action if punishment would make it less likely that he will do it. But the criterion is now too mild to delimit responsibility. A kleptomaniac does not steal when a policeman or shop assistant is watching him and he takes ingenious steps to avoid detection. His behaviour is therefore affected by fear of punishment. The

this sounds like a dog ↑

reason for regarding him as irresponsible is not that this fear fails to affect him but that he shows other signs of motiveless irrationality. He steals one kind of article only—silk stockings or suspenders—and then proceeds to hoard them and not to resell.

The second main difficulty about this view is that the act which is affected by blame or punishment is never the act for which the blame or punishment is awarded, since the one always follows and the other necessarily precedes the award. This is not always clearly recognised. For example in the passage quoted above: 'Since a moral action is one that can fittingly be praised or blamed it follows that a moral action is one that can be brought about or prevented by these means.' But when the praise is given the action it is to bring about cannot yet have occurred. So this action cannot be the action which is being praised. Ebersole again takes the logical way out. The only relevance of the act for which (as we inaccurately say) man is punished is *evidential*. It shows us the sort of man we have to deal with and we can deal with him accordingly. 'Our justifiable concern is with the person as he has been made by the result of his wrong choice. Our concern with his former self is justifiable only because, without enquiring what he was like before, we do not have any way of knowing what he is like after the condemned action.' But surely previous commission of the wrong is not the only evidence we may have. We may sometimes know that a man was baulked in his attempt by external circumstances. The rope broke, the gun misfired. And in such a case Ebersole would have to say that the punishment was equally justified. His own extreme imaginary example confirms this admission. 'If we possessed a sensitive brain-wave machine which would predict whether a person would commit a crime and what sort of censure or punishment would prevent it, then we should have no need to be concerned with a person's past.' We shall be dealing with punishment in more detail in the next chapter; but it is surely obvious that it is impossible to blame or punish someone who has done no wrong.

We noted previously (p. 99) that the view of philosophy as linguistic analysis cannot be combined with subjectivism. Here again there is a conflict. Ebersole agrees that the account he gives of 'ought' and 'moral' and 'free' involves a complete break with ordinary usage. For usage is indeterminist and rejects blame or punishment when no wrong has been done. But a change of usage to determinism and a reform theory of blame and punishment would not be merely linguistic. It would not indicate a triumph of philosophers in persuading man to use language in a way more fitted to the unchanging facts. If language changed, it would be because the facts had changed; since the facts in question are men's actions and attitudes. If deterministic and reform language were adopted it would be because men no longer felt guilt and remorse for past sins but only regret for past mistakes. They would no longer blame but pity the wrong-doer. They would say 'to know all is to pardon all' and they would pardon all; or rather pardon like forgiveness would disappear. I do not pardon or forgive a stick for tripping me or a man for what he does sleep-walking or hypnotised.

So far we have been discussing theories which argue for a necessary connection between responsibility and determinism. We may now consider a type of theory which makes determination possible though without necessitating it. These theories arise from the possible meanings we might attach to the words 'I could have done otherwise'. First there are obviously cases where the possibilities of alternative action derive from one particular feature of the situation. I went to France last vacation. I could have gone to Chile, so far as time was concerned. But of course I could not go there as I hadn't the necessary money. Or I could have gone to Russia, so far as time and funds were concerned; but I could not get a visa. This type of solution, however, is no help in our present problem. It is not enough that in respect to some one or two conditions I could have done otherwise if it remains the case that in relation to some other feature of the situation I could not have done otherwise.

Another model is that adopted by G. E. Moore. The key here is to regard the phrase 'I could have done otherwise' as a concealed hypothetical. As a parallel to this analysis, take the following examples. 'Jones could easily have won the race. He left his sprint too late' which could reasonably be taken to mean 'Jones would have won the race if he had sprinted sooner'. Or 'Hitler could have won the war. His delay at Dunkirk saved the allies', which again would seem to mean 'Hitler would have won the war if he had continued his drive against Dunkirk'. In both cases it is to be noticed that there is in addition the implication that, *having* delayed his sprint, Jones could not have won the race and, *having* held up his attack, Hitler could not have won the war. The analysis of 'I could have done otherwise' adopted by G. E. Moore is 'I should have done otherwise if I had chosen'. This is clearly a possible meaning of the phrase. It is the sense in which we say 'He was quite free to accept the job but of course he didn't as he dislikes that kind of work'. This means there was nothing to stop him from taking the job except his own desires. But is this an adequate theory to justify praise and blame? It would now seem to depend on the further question which is naturally suggested by the formula 'I should have done otherwise if I had chosen', namely the question 'could I have chosen otherwise?' Moore says that there are two senses in which it may be said that 'I could have chosen otherwise'. First we apply the same analysis and then we have 'I should have chosen otherwise if I had chosen (sc. to choose otherwise)'. He points out that I can force myself to make a choice and sometimes to make a choice which I am reluctant to make, and if I did not make this effort I would choose otherwise. But we are now embarked on a regress. Could I have made the effort I did not make? This would mean 'Should I have made the effort if I had not chosen to do so?' Somewhere we seem driven to decide whether we are simply embarked on a causal series, and if so it is *never* the case that I could have done otherwise *conditions being the same*, but only that I should have done otherwise had they been different. The other sense in which Moore thinks that it can be said that 'I could have chosen otherwise' is that no one could possibly predict which I should choose. This too is a common meaning for 'could' where it is equivalent to 'may' or 'might' expressing ignorance. 'Jones could have been at the party but I didn't see him.' This too, however, is irrelevant to our problem. Whether or not someone knows what I am going to do, the real issue is one of fact not knowledge—the issue whether I could do otherwise in the same circumstances.

Another reason why Moore's analysis is unacceptable is the meaning he attaches to the word 'do'. Take an example. 'I told a lie. I should have told the truth if I had chosen.' Moore sometimes uses the word 'willed' instead of 'chosen'. 'I should have told the truth if I had so willed.' Now what about this distinction between choosing or willing to do something and doing it? In what circumstances could it be said that I chose or willed to do something and did not do it? Perhaps if I were tongue-tied or paralysed. But, as we have seen earlier (p. 53) the judgment of moral praise or blame is passed on what I choose or will and not on what I do (where these diverge). Thus my freedom to do what I will (while of course immensely important in many other respects) is not relevant to questions or moral praise or blame. What matters is my freedom to choose or will.

There are therefore difficulties about accepting any solution which relies on a hypothetical analysis of 'could have done otherwise'. C. D. Broad has put this case effectively. If it can be said that I ought to have acted otherwise, then another action must be *categorically substitutable* for the action I in fact did. Hypothetical substitutability is not enough. Broad finds it impossible to give a clear and satisfactory account of *how* an action can be categorically substitutable for another and concludes that it can never be the case that I ought to have acted otherwise. There are no moral obligations. The other alternative would be that moral obligations exist and that the corollary of categorical substitutability must simply be accepted, as a fact beyond explanation. This may be made more palatable by recalling that explanation would inevitably be in terms of scientific or analytic procedures to which, as I argued above, the self may be recalcitrant.

(Moore himself later agreed that he had been mistaken in thinking that hypothetical substitutability was adequate for moral obligation as a result of criticism by A. C. Garnett, and agreed that it was essential, if obligation is accepted, that a man could have chosen otherwise than he did.)

REFERENCES

The literature on Freewill is vast, and references are given below only to those views and lines of argument examined in the foregoing chapter

Self-determinism:
    F. H. Bradley, *Ethical Studies*, ch. i

Responsibility implying Determinism:
    R. E. Hobart, article in *Mind* XLIII (1934); P. H. Nowell-Smith, *Ethics*, chs. 19, 20, articles in *Mind* LVII (1948) and LXIII (1954); F. Ebersole, article in *Mind* LXI (1952)

Hypothetical and categorical substitutability:
    G. E. Moore, *Ethics*, ch. vi; A. C. Garnett in *The Philosophy of G. E. Moore*, pp. 179–99, accepted by Moore, ibid., pp. 623–4; C. D. Broad, *Determinism, Indeterminism and Libertarianism*, reprinted in *Ethics and the History of Philosophy*; C. L. Stevenson, article in *Mind* (January 1938) reprinted as ch. viii of his *Facts and Values*

I I

PUNISHMENT[1]

The problems of punishment are closely connected with those of free will discussed in the previous chapter. The main division between theories of punishment is that which separates the retributive theory from the rest. The retributive theory maintains that punishment is justified because of the wrong done by the person to be punished. The other theories justify punishment by the various consequences which it may produce. Punishment is thus a special case of the dispute between Utilitarians and their opponents which was examined in Chapter 3 of this book. It was there maintained that there are some duties (such as promise-keeping and debt-paying) which depend on previous events, whereas, for the Utilitarian, all duties depend on subsequent events (consequences) for their justification. Is punishment one of these?

The various Utilitarian theories of punishment can be divided into (a) preventive, (b) deterrent, (c) reformatory. When a murderer is hanged or imprisoned for life this *prevents* him from repeating his offence. When a thief is sent to prison this *deters* him and others from stealing again. When a prisoner

1. This chapter uses material from an article on Punishment in *Mind* XLVIII (1939) and a discussion note in *Philosophy* XXX (1955) with the permission of the editors of these periodicals

is visited by the chaplain or the psychiatrist or the probation officer and, as a result, decides to 'go straight' in future, this *reforms* him. The deterrent theory is sometimes limited to the effect on other people, but I think this is confusing, because it results in classifying the effect on the criminal as reform. But a criminal who abstains from repeating the offence solely from fear of the punishment is in no way reformed. If he thinks he can get away with it he will do it again. Another possible confusion requires to be cleared away in connection with these Utilitarian theories. A great deal of what is called 'Penal Reform' has nothing to do with the reformatory theory of punishment, and indeed has nothing directly to do with the theory of punishment at all, except in a negative way. The greatest prison reformers have not been concerned with punishment but with its accessories. A sentence of imprisonment need not and should not involve partial starvation, physical maltreatment, or disease. A book which has left a mark on prison administration—*Walls Have Mouths* by W. F. R. Macartney—is full of illustrations of this. His chapter on 'Food' is one, as also is his comment on Governor Clayton's administration.

To keep a man in prison for many years at considerable expense and then free him charged to the eyes with uncontrollable venom and hatred generated by the treatment he has received in gaol, does not appear to be sensible.

Clayton

endeavoured to send a man out of prison in a reasonable state of mind. 'Well, I've done my time. They were not too bad to me. Prison is prison and not a bed of roses. Still they didn't rub it in.'[1]

This reasonable state of mind is one in which a prisoner feels

1. p. 152

he has been punished but not *additionally* maltreated or insulted. We have no more right to keep a convict in a Dartmoor cell 'down which the water trickles night and day'[1] than we have to keep a child in such a place. If our sentimentalists cry 'coddling of prisoners' let them come into the open and incorporate whatever brutality and disease they require into the sentences they propose. Another prisoner, Jim Phelan, makes the point well.

One of the minor curiosities of jail life was that they quickly provided you with a hundred worries which left you no time or energy for worrying about your sentence, long or short . . . Rather as if you were thrown into a fire with spikes in it, and the spikes hurt you so badly you forgot about the fire. But then your punishment would *be* the spikes, not the fire. Why did they pretend it was only the fire when they knew very well about the spikes?[2]

It may be thought odd to go to criminals for arguments on punishment. But, after all, they are the people whom we are supposed (on these Utilitarian theories) to be reforming and deterring; and what they think of our doings is of primary significance. But they are not the only authorities who make the point. The greatest recent authority, Sir Alexander Paterson, says

The first duty of a prison as an institution of the State is to perform the function assigned to it by the law; and its administration must ensure that a sentence of imprisonment is a form of punishment. It must be clear at the outset, however, that it is the sentence of imprisonment which is the punishment and not the treatment accorded in prison. Men are sent to prison *as* a punishment and not *for* punishment. It is doubtful whether any of the amenities granted

1. Ibid., p. 258
2. *Lifer*, p. 40

E

in some modern prisons can in any way compensate for the punishment involved in deprivation of liberty.[1]

The last sentence is over-cautious. Let any 'amenity prison' offer release to its inmates and how many would stay to enjoy its amenities? But this in turn suggests that Paterson himself is not quite clear. A prison administration need not 'ensure that a sentence of imprisonment is a form of punishment'. All it need do is to ensure that its prisoners do not escape, and otherwise that they suffer no 'uncovenanted' maltreatment.

Having cleared away these possible confusions, we may now turn to punishment itself. The reform theory involves, in some cases, the confusion we noted earlier between punishment and its accessories. The visit of the prison chaplain (or the string quartette) are not *parts* of the punishment, nor is a criminal imprisoned in order that he may be so visited. The duty of reforming prisoners is a different duty from that of punishing them. A parallel is the case of tact and truth. If you have to tell someone an unpleasant truth you may do what you can to spare his feelings and soften the blow while still making sure that he understands your meaning. Here no one would say that your care of him before and after are *reasons* for telling him the truth. You do not tell him the truth in order to spare his feelings; but having to tell him the truth you try also to spare his feelings. So prison authorities may make it possible for a criminal to reform. They cannot ensure this, and, if they fail, the punishment would be no less justified.

Some moralists see this and exclude such 'extra' arrangements for reform from their theory of punishment. They say the punishment *itself* must reform. It should bring home to the criminal the error of his ways. It should teach him a salutory lesson. Now it is certainly a good thing if these results occur, and once again special efforts may be made, by the judge when he

1. *Paterson on Prisons*, p. 23

pronounces his sentence, for example, to try to achieve them. But once again if they meet with bravado or bitterness and fail, this does not show that the punishment has lost any of its justification. Reform, therefore, while it seems to be an admirable by-product of punishment, does not appear to constitute its justification.

We are thus left with prevention and deterrence on the one hand and retribution on the other. It is sometimes urged against the deterrence theory that it would justify stepping up punishments to a maximum. So long as *anyone* breaks a given law this shows the punishment was not enough. There are two objections to this conclusion. First, it is said that such severity would defeat its own object. When the penalty for sheep-stealing was death, juries refused to convict even those thieves caught in the act. This argument might be met by abolishing the jury system and leaving it to Judge Jeffreys to pass both verdict and sentence. And, in any case, the objection is itself a retributivist one, for the jury say that death is *too heavy* a sentence for sheep-stealing (and 'too heavy' does *not* mean 'unnecessary for deterrent reasons'). The other objection to maximum severity goes further to meet it. It is that if minor crimes are severely punished major crimes will be encouraged. If a man is to be hanged for sheep-stealing he will shoot his way out of trouble. Thus over-enthusiasm for deterring sheep-stealers encourages murder. But even this argument does not go the whole way. As long as there can be *some* more severe sentence for the possible added crime the lesser one can still be punished severely. So this remains a difficulty.

The retributive theory has very few defenders in these days. Philosophers have mostly rejected it and practical men have welcomed its decline in our penal arrangements. Yet some of the arguments against it are certainly answerable. Rashdall associates retributive punishment with vengeance and even calls it 'the vindictive theory'.[1] He argues that revenge is an

1. *The Theory of Good and Evil*, ch. ix

immoral attitude and that retribution is incompatible with
forgiveness which is the appropriate response to injury. Now
all this is confusion of terms. The only person who can feel
vengeful or vindictive where an injury is done is the injured
party. The name of the feeling of a third party on such an
occasion is 'indignation'. While vindictiveness is certainly an
unchristian and immoral attitude, though a very natural one,
moral indignation is surely entirely respectable. So far then as
punishment is not inflicted by the injured party it cannot
express vindictiveness, though it can express indignation. Similarly with forgiveness. The only person who can and therefore
ought to forgive is the injured person. If A damages B, it is
absurd for C to forgive A. The appropriate word here is
'condone'. Thus there is no inconsistency between forgiveness
and retributive punishment since these duties fall on different
shoulders. It is true that this conclusion is sometimes avoided
by maintaining that 'society' is the injured party and therefore
'society' is taking revenge on the criminal. But here, as elsewhere, the treatment of society as a moral agent leads to error
and confusion. Statements about the moral feelings and actions
of 'society' have to be analysed in terms of the feelings of
individuals and the actions of citizens and officials. And in the
present case 'society feels vindictive' has to be analysed as
'citizens feel indignant'.

Rashdall also describes retributive punishment as 'the
infliction of pain for pain's sake'[1] and as 'adding evil to evil'.
The first objection to this is that pain is not evil. If a man
has a toothache in bed, is there something evil in his bed?
Pain is in some sense bad, regrettable, to be removed if possible;
but the dentist is not a moral straightener. Then, secondly, pain
is no part of punishment. Only flogging, among all our
penalties, is the infliction of pain and it is on the way out. But,
says Rashdall, the pain may be mental or physical. Here again

1. Ibid., p. 286

surely is an abuse of language. Our standard punishments are not inflictions of suffering but deprivations: of life (capital punishment) of liberty (imprisonment) and of property (fines). It is true that no one *likes* to be deprived of any of these good things. But to represent these dislikes as pains or evils is a mistake. It is curious that Rashdall did not revise the text of his argument for he admits in a footnote that

Pain is an accident of retribution and I am not aware that I made it even an inseparable accident. If a criminal is shot, are we, if there is no pain, to say that there is no retribution?[1]

The Royal Commission on Capital Punishment defends hanging as the most painless method of execution.[2] If it be said that this does not diminish the mental agony of waiting for the execution, the answer is that the aim of the sentence is not the infliction of this agony. If it were, the duration would be specified and the suffering would be an essential part of the punishment. The Commission argue[3] that the delay is regrettable, but is to be defended as allowing time for an appeal or application for reprieve. And 'the preliminaries of the execution should be free from anything that unnecessarily sharpens the prisoner's apprehension'.[4] The world is a worse place the more evil there is in it, and the more unnecessary suffering there is in it. But it does not seem to me necessarily a worse place whenever men are deprived of something they would like to retain. And this is the essence of modern punishment.

A preliminary difficulty about the retributive theory is raised by the question 'What is the retribution for?' Most holders of the theory have answered this by saying 'for moral guilt', though some would restrict this to anti-social wrong-

1. Ibid., p. 287
2. *Report*, paras. 726–31
3. Ibid., para. 763
4. Ibid., para. 724

doing. My difficulty with this view is the question of status. It takes two to make a punishment, and for a moral or social offence I can find no punisher. I am therefore inclined to think that punishment is retribution for *crimes* not for *sin*. A criminal is a man who has broken the law. Many bad men are not criminals. An 'innocent man' is a man who has not broken the law, in connection with which he is being tried, though he may be a bad man and have broken other laws. We may be tempted to say when we hear of some brutal assault 'he ought to be punished' but I cannot see how there can be duties which are nobody's duties. If I see a man beating a horse in a country where there is no law against cruelty to animals, I cannot say 'I am now going to punish you'. He will reply rightly 'Who are you?' I may have a duty to try to stop him and one way may be to hit him or another may be to buy the horse. Neither the blow nor the price is a punishment. For moral offences, God alone has the status necessary to punish: and the theologians are far from agreement about whether this status is to be brought into action. There is of course much confusion about this. Many people think of all kinds of suffering as being visited on men 'for their sins'. In Dostoievsky's *Crime and Punishment* Raskolnikov found he was losing control of his thoughts after the murder and cried 'Can this be the punishment already beginning? Indeed, indeed, it is!' Here as usual in Dostoievsky the whole moral atmosphere is deeply theological. The police come in late and almost as an irrelevance.

It seems to me then that punishment is a corollary of lawbreaking. The crucial difficulty about the deterrence theory (and this applies to the reform theory too) is that it would justify the punishment of an innocent man—that is to say a man has not committed the crime for which he was punished —provided he was believed to be guilty by those likely to commit the crime in future (or, in the case of the reform theory, provided that his treatment in prison improved his character). A typical illustration is that of Oscar Slater. He was prosecuted, on very unsatisfactory evidence, for the murder of Mrs Gilchrist in 1908. Public opinion was violently against him and he was sentenced to death. If he had been executed, the deterrent effect on other would-be murderers would have been exactly the same as if he had been guilty. The Secretary for Scotland, however, against the advice of his legal advisors, reprieved Slater; and, after twenty years of agitation by legal experts, his conviction was 'set aside' and he was consoled by a grant of £6,000. Only one fact can justify a man's punishment and that is a *past* fact, that he has broken a law.

Macartney confirms this line. It is striking that he never uses the word 'injustice' to describe the brutality and provocation he experienced. In his view only two types of prisoner were *unjustly* imprisoned, those who were insane and not responsible for the acts for which they were punished,[1] and those who had not broken the law.[2] It is irrelevant that some of these latter were, like Steinie Morrison, dangerous and violent characters who, on utilitarian grounds, were well out of the way. That made their punishment no whit less unjust.[3] And, for a specific instance, he cites the sentences on the Dartmoor mutineers.

The Penal Servitude Act . . . lays down specific punishments for mutiny and incitement to mutiny, which include flogging . . . Yet on the occasion of the only big mutiny in an English prison, men are not dealt with by the Act specially passed to meet mutiny in prison . . . but under an Act expressly passed to curb and curtail the Chartists—a revolutionary movement.[4]

Here again the injustice lies in condemning men for breaking a law they did not break.

1. Macartney, *Walls Have Mouths*, pp. 165–6
2. Ibid., p. 298
3. Ibid., p. 301
4. Ibid., p. 255

Hegel argues that retributive punishment alone honours the criminal (in contrast with the view that deterrence and reform are the modern, progressive, reasonable theories). For it treats him as an adult rational being with a choice of conduct. Deterrence and reform treat him either as a means to frighten other people or as requiring remoulding by fear or treatment. Macartney is with Hegel here: 'To punish a man is to treat him as an equal. To be punished for an offence against rules is a sane man's right'.[1]

An attempt has been made by A. M. Quinton[2] to meet this demand, that nothing but law-breaking can justify punishment, by treating this as a logical or linguistic point. The *meaning* of 'punishment' includes a reference to previous crime. This means that it is *logically* impossible to punish the innocent. We *can* only punish the guilty. But this does not mean that we ought to punish them. The reasons for this are the utilitarian reasons of deterrence and reform.

Now it seems to me that Quinton is right on the linguistic or logical issue. The meaning of 'punishment' does include a reference to the past. But this does not exclude an ethical judgment on the procedure so described. 'Divorce', 'revenge', and 'forgiveness' all include in their meaning a reference to the past. But this does not prevent us from condemning revenge, commending forgiveness, and differing about the morality of divorce.

I maintain that the officer of a society whose rule has been broken not only *can* but ought to punish the offender. Quinton recognises that this is a possible account of one *kind* of legal system, a system in which *fixed* penalties are allocated for breaches of rules. I take it that he would apply this to those cases in actual systems for which fixed penalties are laid down. So an English judge not only can but has a duty to impose the

1. Ibid., p. 165
2. *Analysis*, vol. 14, p. 133

death sentence on a person found guilty of murder. I assume Quinton would not hold in this case that he *can* impose the death sentence but ought to impose whatever sentence will have the best consequences. Quinton points out that, in cases other than murder, the penalty laid down is a maximum and the judge has discretion within it. So here he should decide the actual sentence by considerations of utility. To which I would give two answers. First, the discretion is given by the law; so, even if it would take more than forty shillings to deter or fourteen days to reform, the judge has no right to impose sentences above these maxima. Secondly, I do not admit that the considerations which fix the penalty within the maximum are utilitarian. They normally concern not the effect on the criminal or others in the future, but the degree of guilt in the past, or responsibility in the past also. Negligence varies in degree; one man knew his brakes were faulty and did nothing about it, the other did not know, though he could and should have found out. Conspirators vary in responsibility; one is ring-leader, another his tool. The Report of the Royal Commission on Capital Punishment says

Offences of the same legal category differ greatly in gravity and turpitude and the courts make full use of the wide range of penalties they have power to impose.[1]

Moreover the vast majority of sentence-revisions by Courts of Appeal take the form 'The sentence of . . . appears to us too heavy (or inadequate) for the offence of . . .'.

The line adopted above takes the existence of laws for granted, and it is at this point that utilitarian considerations are relevant. They are considerations for legislators. Should there be laws, and what laws should they be? Should penalties be attached to them and if so what penalties, and should they be fixed or maxima? None of these choices is Hobson's choice;

1. *Report*, para. 20

and the majority of them are Utilitarian. The association of a penalty with a law is certainly deterrent. Legislators make a choice here. They do not choose to punish. They hope the threat will succeed and no punishments will be needed. Their laws would thus have the best results possible. Many men obey the law because they see its order is reasonable, some because they trust the authorities, some from inertia, some from fear. Over this whole field, and it will include the majority of the citizens, law achieves its ends without punishment. Punishment then is not a mere corollary of law. Another choice beside that of the legislators is needed; and that is the criminal's choice. He 'brings it on himself'. Here, as often, the sound commonsense of Dr Johnson outpaced the wits of many cleverer men. He said to Boswell:

To punish fraud when it is detected is the proper art of vindictive justice; but to prevent fraud and make punishment unnecessary is the great employment of legislative wisdom.

Note. The above extended discussion of punishment has been included because it illustrates a number of general points raised in previous chapters: the rejection of Utilitarianism, the distinction between justifying a particular act and justifying a rule, the justification of rules by their effects, the distinction between linguistic and moral issues, and the moral relevance of free choice.

REFERENCES

(apart from those given in the text of the chapter)

A. C. Ewing, *The Morality of Punishment*

G. W. F. Hegel, *Philosophy of Right* (tr. T. M. Knox), pp. 66–74

F. H. Bradley, *Ethical Studies*, ch. i

12

RIGHTS AND DUTIES

There is one sense of the word 'right' which we have not yet examined. Previously we considered its use to describe the action appropriate to the circumstances in which a moral agent finds himself. But there is, besides this mandatory or obligatory use, a *permissive* use. 'Will it be all right for me to go now?' 'Yes certainly, but stay if you like.' Connected with this use, but not identical with it, is the use when a man is said to have *a right* to something. Connected, because he need not exercise his rights. Just as it is all right to go but he may stay, so I have a right to free speech even if I remain silent. But the uses are not identical; for the assertion that I have rights seems to involve claims on other people, though just what these are will be a problem for later discussion. The purely permissive use of 'all right' seems to be basically negative. I shall not do wrong if I go (nor if I stay). There is no objection to my going. The objection need not be a moral one. An employee may be told that it is all right for him to go; his employer does not need him any longer tonight.

What is meant by having a right? Rights are both positive and negative. I have a right to free speech or to the practice of my religion; this means that I should be left free from inter-ference in these fields. Or I may say I have a right to a living wage or to medical treatment; this means that these things should be provided for me. It now seems clear in what sense rights are claims on other people. When I have a right, someone else, or other people, or the authorities have a duty to leave me alone or to provide the service I claim. Rights imply duties. Is the reverse the case? Take the following definition of a right:

A man has a right whenever other men ought not to prevent him doing what he wants or refuse him some service he asks for or needs.[1]

The word 'whenever' implies that if A has a duty to leave B alone or to provide him with some service, then B has a right to that permission or service. The relation between rights and duties is then one which works both ways. Now I find this doubtful. If I am asked by a colleague for the loan of a book which he needs and if I am not using it, I think I have a duty to lend it to him; but I do not think he has a right to it. If I have a seat in my car and I overtake a weary walker I think I ought to give him a lift; but I do not think he has a right to it.

Of course it is possible to avoid this difficulty by restricting the use of the word 'duty' so that it applies only to those obligations to which others have rights. One's duties could then be a minimal set of moral obligations, the discharge of which would still leave one free and indeed obliged to go on to a higher level of moral actions. We shall return to these two levels later.

But first there are some other points about rights to be cleared up. A distinction must be drawn between legal and moral rights. The actions in which the law protects me and the services and privileges the law awards me are my legal rights.

1. J. P. Plamenatz, *Proceedings of the Aristotelian Society*, suppl. vol. XXIV, p. 75

When I go to my solicitor and ask him what are my rights in a certain situation, legal rights are in question. But we require, in addition, the notion of moral rights. For women and slaves and negroes have all claimed rights (or had rights claimed for them) before they had corresponding legal rights.

This leads to the question how far rights depend on society and on social recognition. Legal rights obviously do so depend. But it seems impossible to say that moral rights depend on social recognition. Slaves and women had rights before these were socially recognised. A right need not even be recognised by the person who has it. The definition above, in saying a service must be 'asked for or needed', seems to fall into this error. Children have a right to education even though they do not know this and therefore cannot ask for it. Of course in one sense rights may be said to be social and to require recognition. If it is true that when a man has rights other people have duties, then in this sense rights involve social relations. And if anyone is to *assert* that a man has a right then at least the speaker has to recognise the right. But the 'social relations' could be limited to a couple of people; and it would seem reasonable to hold that slaves had rights even when no one asserted this and consequently no one recognised it.

We now return to the problem of distinguishing those moral obligations to whose performance other people have a right from those to which they have not; or (on the restricted view of duty) of distinguishing duties from other moral obligations. J. S. Mill draws the latter distinction but does not explain it very satisfactorily.

Duty is a thing that may be *exacted* from a person, as one exacts a debt . . . Justice implies something which it is not only right to do and wrong not to do, but which some individual person can claim from us as his moral right. No one has a moral right to our generosity or benevolence, because we are not morally bound to practise these virtues towards any given individual . . . If a moralist attempts to make out that mankind generally though not any given individual have a right to all the good we can do them, he at once by that thesis includes generosity and beneficence within the category of justice. He is obliged to say that our utmost exertions are *due* to our fellow creatures, thus assimilating them to a debt.[1]

Mill seems here to think that *duties* are always owed to specific individuals whereas generosity and beneficence are not. It is true that in some cases particular individuals have rights against me (my creditor, my employer). But the negative rights (not to be interfered with) are not claims on particular people but on people in general. Mill thus provides no criterion for distinguishing duties and justice from moral obligations which go beyond these. These higher level obligations were called by the medieval philosophers 'duties of supererogation'. But they too failed to provide a very convincing distinguishing feature for them. In St Thomas Aquinas, 'supererogatory' has two meanings: (a) when a certain act is not necessary to salvation, (b) when an act is necessary to salvation, but there is a choice between alternative methods of doing it. The second sense is clearly not relevant here. The first does not seem clear by itself. But if we ask what Aquinas meant by being deprived of salvation, it may be said that this is equivalent to holding that neglect of duties is punishable, but neglect of acts of supererogation is not. Mill comes close to this answer too.

We call any conduct wrong according as we think the person ought to be punished for it. And we say it would be right to do so and so *or* merely that it would be desirable or laudable according as we should wish to see the person whom it concerns compelled *or* only persuaded and exhorted to act in that manner.

It might be thought that this reference to punishment is too narrow (though we shall see grounds for accepting it later in

1. *Utilitarianism* (Everyman ed.), ch. v, pp. 45–7

this argument). If so it might suffice to say that people should be blamed for not doing duties but not for not doing supererogatory actions. We might be tempted to add, with an eye on symmetry, that people are not praised for doing duties but are praised for doing supererogatory actions. We do not praise judges for passing the sentence prescribed by law, nor debtors for paying their debts nor our friends for keeping their dates with us, nor the passerby for telling us truthfully the way to the station. All these are certainly duties, which it would be blameworthy *not* to perform. But the second point is certainly mistaken. We do sometimes praise men for doing one of these duties. It depends how difficult the duty is. When Regulus was sent by his Carthaginian captors to Rome to try to negotiate a peace he promised to return. The Romans pressed him hard not to go back but to lead them in continuing the war. His decision to return was surely praiseworthy. We should also be inclined to praise Sir Walter Scott's long struggle to repay his debts. And even the first half of the distinction is doubtful— that men are not to be blamed for not doing supererogatory duties. Men certainly feel an obligation to do supererogatory duties and blame themselves when they fail to do them. 'We have not done what we ought to have done.' If freedom from blame goes with failing in these duties then the Saints clearly would say that they had *no* supererogatory duties.

A different line to distinguish duties which involve rights from those which do not may now be considered. It is suggested in a remark by Tom Paine: 'Whatever is my right as a man is also the right of another and it becomes my duty to *guarantee* as well as to possess.'[1] These rights should be *guaranteed*. This means that my enjoyment of negative rights (free speech, religious freedom) should be *protected* from those who have a duty to respect them but do not do so. And that my enjoyment of positive rights should be *ensured by compulsion* if need be.

1. *The Rights of Man* (Everyman ed.), p. 98

We can amend the definition given at the beginning of this chapter (p. 140) to read: 'A man has a right whenever other people should be *stopped* from preventing him from doing something or *compelled* to provide him with some service.'

There is no reference here to the identity of the people who should prevent or compel. Tom Paine's view that *I* myself should guarantee to others the rights I claim for myself makes an impossible demand on the individual. The clue is given, however, in his first sentence. A right I have as a man is a right all men have. And, even if there are restricted classes of claimants, the claim concerns classes of people, not individuals. If a child has a right to education, all children have a right to education. If an able child has a right to university education, then all able children have this right. Now the only body which can *guarantee* rights to all men or all children or even all gifted children is an inclusive body with compulsory powers. The State comes nearest these requirements. But there are some rights which even the State cannot guarantee—for example the repayment of debts by foreigners. And, while there are some rights the State could guarantee, it may fail to do this through poverty or policy. Then what? The final resort would seem to be international action, where an international body would guarantee those rights which States cannot or will not guarantee. The work of the League of Nations against slavery and the Charter of Human Rights of the United Nations are both attempts to put pressure on States which do not guarantee the rights of men. Here we come back to Mill's view, that a wrong is something for which a person ought to be punished, and a right something he should be compelled to respect.

The only recent philosopher who has emphasised the difference between these two moralities, the morality of rights and claims and the morality of supererogation, is Bergson. The first morality he says is social, the second human.

Our duties are determined by our relations to particular individuals within the associations to which we belong. The obligations of this first morality are prescribed by rules and correlated with rights. We feel these obligations as a pressure and a constraint. The higher morality involves duties which, if owed to anyone, are owed to mankind. This morality comes before us not as a code of rules but through a living individual example. It is therefore frequently associated with religion. But this is not a necessary connection, for anyone may have a hero and try to live up to his example. The obligations here concerned do not affect us by external pressure and constraint but by attraction and magnetic appeal.

A good half of our morality comprises duties whose obligatory character is explained in the first analysis by the pressure of society on the individual; we accept it without too much trouble because these duties are regularly practised, because they are clear and definite, and because it is easy for us to grasp their fully visible part and descend thence to their roots and discover the social requirements from which they take their rise. But that the other half of morality is the translation of an emotion in which one yields not to a pressure but to an attraction many would hesitate to admit. The reason is that it is not possible in most cases to discover in the depths of one's own personality the original emotion. It has left behind it certain formulae in which are enshrined in the social conscience what was originally immanent in that emotion—a new conception of life or rather a new attitude towards it.[1]

Bergson describes this distinction as one between an *open* and a *closed* morality. He criticises convincingly the suggestion that the move from particular obligations within a closed society to obligations to human beings as such is simply a *widening* like that from family to tribe or tribe to nation. The widest service differs in kind and not in degree only from the service of family or fellow-countrymen. These services are exclusive

1. *Les Deux Sources de la Morale et de la Religion*, p. 46

and consequently combine naturally and easily with distrust and hostility towards outsiders. They are also 'natural' to man. The Christian love which includes loving one's enemies is not a natural feeling but something which can come only with a new vision.

Bergson also explains convincingly how it is that the frontier between the two moralities seems to shift and become blurred. The original inspiration of the saint or hero fades, leaving only his 'message'. This message in turn crystallises into new rules which look just like the old social duties of the closed society, and borrow from them an obligatory character.

We find ourselves before the ashes of a dead emotion and because the driving force of that emotion came from the fire within it, the formulae which survive it would be unable to arouse our wills if the more ancient rules which express the basic needs of social life did not communicate to them by infection some of their obligatory character. Then the two juxtaposed moralities seem to blend, the second derives an obligatory character from the first, the first a widened application from the second. But remove the ashes and you will find heat still below and the spark can be rekindled, the fire relit, and it will then spread from point to point.[1]

Thus justice is enlarged by charity and what was once thought to be charity comes more and more to seem simple justice. So we have to make the distinction, but it is continually being lost and won again. Hence there can be no criterion for distinguishing those obligations which are supererogatory from the rest. For with each age the frontier moves. Objects of charity—children, the old, the unemployed—become bearers of rights.

We may now return to the use of 'right' in such phrases as 'It is all right for you to go now'. This, we suggested, marks a choice as morally neutral. It would not be wrong for you to go

1. Loc. cit.

(or to stay). This in turn leads to the question of distinguishing moral from non-moral decisions and the area of moral conduct from that of non-moral conduct.

Many people, if asked how many moral decisions they made on a given day, or how long it is since they made a moral decision, might well answer 'very few' or 'a long time'. This is because it is natural to limit 'moral decision' to cases in which two alternatives are explicitly present to the mind— either two alternative moral courses or one moral and one immoral—and where there is a conscious and explicit moral judgment. This restriction is also influenced by the tendency to think that moral action must be preceded by moral judgment. This emphasis on moral judgment is mistaken. We seldom have to make such judgments; normally only when we are uncertain of what is right or where we have to educate or judge other people. But most of us spend little time in moral indecision and still less in preaching or writing testimonials. The primary job of a moral agent is moral action, and only in a few cases are moral actions themselves the making of judgments or require to be preceded by such judgments. (The error here is a particular case of the general error of thinking that intelligent action of any kind is action preceded by thinking. This error, with Professor Ryle's criticism of it, was noticed previously in Chapter 6.) We may grant that actions are moral if they are the execution of moral judgments or decisions and that the making of moral judgments is itself a type of moral action. But how are we to decide whether an action is moral when no explicit moral judgment or decision seems to precede or accompany it? Some of them certainly are but some certainly are not. Even if we might find it difficult to say of any field of action *as a whole* (e.g. hobbies or other leisure activities) that it was morally indifferent or neutral what we did or how we did it, we do believe that many particular choices we make are indifferent or neutral, for example whether I pay a debt by cheque or cash or tell a man the way by talking or pointing. If it is objected that these are trifling matters then it is possible to find decisions which make a considerable difference to my life and are yet not moral decisions: whether to give up skiing altogether, where to go on sabbatical leave, whether to lecture next term or the term after. The common answer here is that any of these decisions *may* be a moral decision. If my continued skiing involves leaving my wife at home, if I am not very fit and Yorkshire air will do me more good on my leave than Venice, if lectures on my subject are short next term—well then, of course, the case is altered. But if my wife would welcome my absence to get the house redecorated, or if I am fit and would find Venice no menace, or if lectures are in equally good supply both terms—then it does not make a particular choice moral to say that in different circumstances a similar choice would be a moral choice.

But it is not always so easy to be sure whether actions are moral when no conscious moral judgments or explicit moral decisions precede or accompany them. Take a morning's actions. I write letters from 9 to 10, I teach from 10 to 12, I attend a committee from 12 to 1. How much of all this is moral action and how much indubitably neutral? Some perhaps counts as moral. My 11 o'clock pupil is both stupid and obstinate and I hope I show what an impartial observer would consider to be patience and tolerance. I hurry to my committee so as not to keep the others waiting. But what of all the rest, the steady doing of the job (with the 10 o'clock pupils who are neither stupid nor obstinate), my contributions to the discussions of the committee? I should be astonished to be praised (or blamed) for taking up these rather than those points in my pupils' essays or for the points I made in the committee discussion.

To distinguish the moral actions from the others we should, at any rate, include the cases in which, if questioned, I should have formulated a moral judgment as, at least, part of the explanation of my action, as its motive or intention. I may never say to myself as I set out or go to the meeting 'I ought to hurry' or 'it would be wrong to keep them waiting'. But nevertheless if I had been stopped, in the street, by someone who said 'Why the hurry?' my answer, and an honest answer, would have been 'because I mustn't keep them waiting' and not 'because I am trying to get warm' or 'for exercise'. If either of the latter explanations had been the true one, I should have said my hurrying was non-moral and of no concern to moral philosophy. This of course is not always so easy. My explanation may not be honest, or I may not really know why I am hurrying or my motive may be mixed. (If it was a hot day, I should not be going so fast.) But there may be good evidence here all the same. There is my relief when I arrived at the meeting and found all the others there but the clock at 11.58, or the clock at 12.2 but two other members missing. As to mixed motives, I must ask myself 'Should I have hurried even if I had not been cold?' This may not be easy to answer though again there may be evidence that I hurried last time when it was warm, and that I continued to hurry this time even after I got warm. But even if decision is difficult in a particular case this does not matter if the principle is clear. If I do not know whether I can honestly say 'I hurried so as not to keep them waiting', then I cannot say whether my act was moral. Moral philosophy cannot decide whether particular acts are moral but only under what conditions an act would be moral.

Even the inclusion of actions which would be explained by a moral reason still leaves many, perhaps most, everyday actions as neutral. We still ask what we are to say about the steady doing of the job, the normal contributions to a committee's discussion, the weekend's leisure. The word 'steady' perhaps begs the question by suggesting the overcoming of

occasional reluctances or difficulties; for these occasions would
probably be consciously moral choices. 'Routine' would be
better, provided that it does not imply mere habitual repetition, which in many jobs (teaching or medicine) would impair
the performance. In most jobs, however, there are general
considerations which must be regarded as moral. There is
earning one's wage, and not letting down one's fellow-workers,
besides (in some fortunate cases) the worth-while character of
the job itself. How far are such motives operative in everyday
life? We all know cases where they are conspicuously absent,
cases where the placard 'Men at work' is an irony. But the
difficulty arises when people seem to be just jogging along, not
conspicuously slacking nor conspicuously stakhanovite. It
arises even more acutely when a man obviously enjoys his
work, like the artist painting a picture or the professional
cricketer knocking up a century. As before, we must say that
it may be impossible to tell whether any such activity has a
moral element in it. As with mixed motives, we may not
know whether the moral factor is there, nor if it is in what
strength. But again there may be some evidence. The word
'steady', for example, provides it. If the joy in the work flags,
if difficulties come, but yet the work goes on, this is evidence
that the moral factor was there all the time, though it needed
an obstacle to reveal it. In the distance the river may look still
and motionless, but where a rock sticks up the strength of the
current is revealed. There are also usually some parts of any
job which are not likely to be enjoyed. There are the administrative details of teaching and doctoring, the recognition of
the work of others (colleagues or subordinates), and if these are
well handled, the moral element is clear. So too with the
committee; the matter under discussion may be in itself
interesting or a man may just enjoy discussion. But it is still
possible to notice whether a man slumps back in the chair as
soon as the item which interests him is settled, how fair he is

to points made against him, how far he is prepared to revise his own view when the point against him is a good one, how far he raises difficulties just for the fun of discussing them, and so on. And so too again with leisure. Even though a man is doing just what he likes to do with his Saturday afternoon, there are still ways and ways of doing it which in most cases would give some clue as to whether he is wholly self-centred. There are not here, of course, as there are with the job (and perhaps the committee) the overall moral principles controlling the situation: value for money, the value of the work itself, the concern for colleagues and subordinates. Leisure is to that extent a moral holiday too. But there remain the claims of one's family, the general public, one's fellow-players—all of them very relevant, for example, to the Bank Holiday motorist.

So after all the field of morality is not so limited as at first seemed likely, though it must still be emphasised that there are wholly non-moral choices and wholly non-moral factors in choices with mixed motives.

13

CONCLUSION

There are two lines of criticism which might very properly be urged against the preceding chapters. First that the examples are very uninteresting and second that very different types of problem are not adequately distinguished.

The choice of examples has been an intentional policy. It would have been much more interesting to look for examples of heroic virtue, or of really difficult complexity, as the existentialists do. Keeping promises, paying debts, telling the truth—these are the small change of moral lives. The two difficulties about the more fascinating examples are these. First they require a great deal more space to set them out; and secondly they are liable to deflect attention from the point they are illustrating especially if (as would usually be the case) they are themselves debated issues. The middle of the road is not an exciting area and one meets few fascinating creatures there in comparison with the gutter and the ditch, but one gets along faster and with fewer distractions.

The confusion of types of problem is a more serious matter. There are first the most general and abstract questions; the distinction between means and ends; between factual and moral beliefs; between description and expression. Then there are questions like the issue between the Utilitarians and their opponents, between free will and determinism, between sub-jectivism and objectivism. The first range of questions could have been fully discussed without raising or deciding any of the second range. Then thirdly there are the questions about what *has* moral value or other value. This is the issue between the pleasure-Utilitarians and G. E. Moore. And finally there is the discussion of the rights and wrongs of some particular kind of action. In this book, the chapter on punishment might be held to fall under this head.

One reason why these distinctions have not been drawn earlier and then adopted as the basis of this book is that those who draw them tend to exclude some of these areas from moral philosophy altogether. I have not wished to do this because I am not convinced by these restrictionist policies. It is arguable that a moral philosopher should not discuss the rights and wrongs of particular moral issues; and there are people who have done this effectively who are not philosophers— Shaw and Ibsen on marriage and divorce for example. But otherwise I see no reason for excluding any of the areas dis-tinguished above. The reason for not separating them was that the theories I wished to discuss did not separate them. If they had been separated the problem of order of discussion would have been insuperable. To start with the most abstract section (what has been called meta-ethics) would have involved a very difficult argument and topics including hardly any specifically *moral* philosophy. To begin with the later sections would have raised questions from the abstract section without answering them. Hence I think the drawing and justifying of these distinctions is a task to be faced late in the day and not one to be done first as the basis for the rest of the argument.

INDEX